A Bastard's Refuge II
Rejected by Man, but Adopted by God

J. Godley-Ramos

GGG

A Gutter to Grace to Glory Communication

"An authentic rose gracefully conquers ugly thorns."

A Bastard's Refuge II
Rejected by Man, but Adopted by God

JGGodsbest@aol.com
ProphetessJ@Guttertogracetoglory.org

Cover by:
J. Godley-Ramos

Design and layout by:
J. Godley-Ramos

Published and sold in the United States by
Gutter to Grace to Glory Ministries Int. Inc.
P.O. Box 6377
Newark, New Jersey 07106

www.Guttertogracetoglory.org

Library of Congress Control Number: 2007906363
ISBN   978-0-6151-5836-5

All Scripture references are taken from the King James Version of The Bible unless otherwise specified. Words and capitalization are written <u>exactly</u> as they appear in The Holy Scripture.

❧About The Grammar❧

In no way is it the intention of this writer to *purposely* offend anyone. If you are of a different faith or have another point of view, that is your right, as you are certainly entitled to your own opinion. However, because I am a "Blood Brought Believer", through faith in The Lord Jesus Christ, I too must stand firmly upon my own convictions.

In so doing, throughout my book, you will notice several words and/or names that begin with upper case letters. Many appear that way although they are 'mid sentence' or 'mid paragraph.' You will also notice words and/or names that are normally subject to rules of capitalization, but alas, they will not be capitalized. My reasons for this are quite simple.

All references to **"God",** as well as anything that pertains to **Him** or to **His Kingdom,** shall have the first letter capitalized. The name **"satan",** or any other common name, that references him and/or his kingdom, shall not be capitalized or glorified, at any time, not for any reason, at all. To those of you who are sticklers for the English language and for its proper usage thereof, to you I apologize for the <u>grammatical</u> scheme of things <u>only.</u>

I am fully aware of satan's power, and while I do recognize him as being capable of reeking havoc and sowing much discord into peoples' lives, still he shall receive no glory. While I further realize that the beginning of every "common name" *should* be capitalized; yet the adversary's name shall not be esteemed.

Although The Bible declares him to be "the god of *this* world", because *he has* managed to blind the eyes of so many; however, he does not *now* possess, and neither shall he ever have total control and dominion over *ALL THINGS or ALL PEOPLE.* Therefore, not even through written form, will I exalt his name. I will not give it the same credence or degree of honor, authority, and power as Almighty God. I refuse to do so, even if it means being grammatically incorrect always.

❧ Table Of Contents ❧

Psalm 91   Part 1 the Journey Begins

Part 2 – Controversy just ahead. Stay focused & alert!

Warning: "Fire" will fall! Prepare for a "Holy Encounter."
Enter – if you dare!

✒Dedication✒

A Bastard's Refuge, has been written on behalf of the countless number of human beings, who have found themselves orphaned, rejected, or branded "illegitimate." It is for those of you who may be wondering where you fit, *in the service of The Lord* or even *in this world.* It is for every reject, ugly duckling, bewildered, lost or confused soul.

I write for each of you who the world has seen fit to treat with disdain and/or little to no regard. I write this book for people everywhere, who for whatever reason, will never have the courage nor the opportunity to write it for themselves; it is for them, and also for myself, that I dare to tell the painful story. A Bastard's Refuge offers much love to the "underdog", the "forgotten crew", "the little people" and to the "sheep" who have lost their way. "ABR" is particularly sympathetic towards those who have been wounded in the "earthly household" of The Living God. To every "blurb", every "human stain", and every displaced member of "society" and "church", this book is for you.

My heart goes out to all who have been tossed aside and thought of as unimportant, with their needs going constantly unmet. I write for each of you who have yearned for a father's blessing or a dad's loving embrace but instead, have received only pain. I dedicate this book to those of you who have been pushed aside, stepped on, shuffled to the back of line and in many cases, even left for dead – I love you, and it is for you that I write.

My heart is in agony for you who have been kicked out, given away and trampled upon. Without any concern as to the damage *they* were inflicting, your caretakers simply discarded you like a rotten piece of meat fit for the slop. Have you ever felt as though you were merely "tolerated" and not at all accepted or loved? I offer encouragement, to each of you who desired only to fit in, but were never given the opportunity to even look in. This work is dedicated to *anyone,* who has ever wrestled with self-hatred, with feelings of negativity regarding his or her identity and/or appearance or with tormenting feelings of insecurity.

I write for each of you who find yourselves engaged in an emotional thrashing, as you desperately attempt to revisit the beauty of your own tattered soul. You allowed yourself to become oblivious to your potential and to your own self-worth, as the barrage of negativity from others, seemed always to dim your sight.

In your local assemblies as the *"wolf clerics" ruled f*rom their lofty positions, *they* refused to even acknowledge your value. Never mind acknowledging *your value,* hell they refused to even see *you,* because *they* considered *you* to be beneath them. Be it known brothers and sisters, none of these people are higher than God; neither should their opinions matter to you more than His. It matters not what *"they"* have told you or what *"they"* think of you. You need only to, "Look unto to the hills from whence cometh your help."

Please know that your true help really does come only from The Lord (Psalm 121:1-2).

This book was God's precious gift to me, which I now share with you. It has been written with love, and comes directly from the heart of one rejected, wounded soul, to others of like kind. At the command of The Father, I have penned it especially for you. Finally, this work is for anyone who has come to the end of his or her rope, and who are now wondering, if whether or not, he or she is the only person, dwelling in the lonely land of misfit.

It is a terrible thing to desire a father, a family, friends, pastoral approval or perhaps, even a reason for living, only to come up empty-handed. You hurt to the core, as you come to terms with the painful reality of knowing, that you have been ostracized, overlooked and criticized for much of your life. I pour out myself, as I write from the soul, for people who feel as though, absolutely no one understands them and therefore, have no one in whom they can confide.

This work is for every little boy and for every little girl, who on a daily basis, is forced to eat lunch all alone in the school cafeteria. This they do, day after day, because nobody else wants them around. I write for every social misfit, outcast and lonely child, who are left daily with only shadows and imaginary friends with which to play. Their only companions are those they have conjured up in their hearts and in their minds.

This book is dedicated to and has been written for everyone whose only desire has been to receive genuine love, and acceptance, for who they are. It is for every person who has ever wished to fit in or be shown the same kindness that he or she has unselfishly lavished upon others. For those of you who find yourselves in an emotional whirlwind, I need you to know, that The Father dedicates this book especially to you. He urged me not to give up, but instead, **He insisted** that I see this work to completion. The Father would often remind me, that there are many to rescue.

"THERE ARE SO MANY OF <u>MY</u> BABIES TO ROUND UP," He'd say.

<u>You beloved are His "babies." You are His children, and He wants you to know, how very much He loves you.</u>

I pray that in some small way, this book will serve as a token of comfort to you, who although with sincere motives, have still found yourselves being misunderstood, misguided, misappropriated and altogether ignored. Your heart broke into a million pieces as you *accidentally* got wind of the party. With your face pressed firmly to the window's glass, peering in on the festivities, you discover that once more, *you alone* were the *only* person who did not receive an invitation. Once again, the gang *purposely* excluded you. Yeah, once more, you were branded 'a reject.'

To every high school boy and girl, who didn't get invited to the prom; (yes, that also includes you *adult child,* who STILL wrestle with the painful memory). For you, my heart breaks into pieces. Everyone thought you were ugly; nobody wanted to be seen with you, and you couldn't get a date, if your life depended on it. And so...you spent the most important and *the most exciting evening,* of your high school experience all alone. Those of you who *were asked* to go, your plight was no better, in fact, yours may have been worse. You see, for either you were the object of scorn (once at the prom), or you ended up losing your virginity as well as your dignity. You were passed around like a piece of cheap meat. Yes young lady, I know what you told me.

Your voice has also come across clearly young man. "At least you got to go", you both retort. Ahhhh, yes you did go, *but* at what price? It cost you so much; do you not yet realize the sacrifice? You paid with your self-worth, maybe your health or worse - even your life. In the back seat of a rented car, tell me, how was it? Was popularity, for *one evening,* worth a lifelong disease? And what of the [bastard] child, abandoned by its father, on the *same night, that it was conceived?* At least you got to go to prom night!

I write for you who have been the subject and object of ridicule and scorn at the *secret meetings* that *they* held without you. For you The Father's heart is breaking. I write for every child, both young and old alike, who practiced for days on end for the choir solo, the role in the school play, or even for the Easter speech. My goodness, you even brought the record and purchased the playbook; you studied extra hard. This you did because those in charge, **promised** you that this would be your time. You were finally going to get a chance – *they* said. You however found out on the day of rehearsal, that the part had also been promised to another.

When they called the other person to the microphone, your heart sank and your bottom lip quivered, as you made a gallant effort to brave it out. Battling to fight back the tears, you proved to be a warrior indeed.

They motioned for someone else, to take the very role, that had been promised to you. You were well prepared. In fact, you were much better than the other person; but *they* would not even give you a chance. *They* didn't even want to see or hear you; neither did they care anything about what you had to offer, as you were only the victim of someone's sick thoughts and cruel prank. You later found out that the only reason they promised you in the first place was to get you off their backs. Moreover, they encouraged you and built you up, on purpose, knowing that they were planning to let you down – real hard! They longed to see the hurt in your eyes and the disappointment on your face, as you realized that you would not be singing the solo after all.

The truth of the matter is they *never* intended on giving you the part to begin with. You my friend were the *only* person present who did not know. *They were all* in on the plot from the very beginning. The joke was on you, as *they each* witnessed your heartbreaking devastation. Everyone in the room had a great laugh at your expense, just the way they had planned it. I pray *this book* serves as a memorial, to all of the precious people, who carried out the ***irreversible decision,*** of ending their lives, simply because, they could stand it no longer. May "ABR" also serve as a deterrent for those who ARE ***RIGHT NOW*** *somewhere,* contemplating the very same decision.

I FOR ONE, CAN CERTAINLY UNDERSTAND ***HOW*** IT IS THAT A PERSON CAN BE, (OR FEEL AS THOUGH HE OR SHE HAS BEEN) "DIRVEN" TO A PLACE OF NO RETURN, OR FEEL AS IF, THERE IS "NO WAY OUT" (OF HIS OR HER TROUBLES), OR AS THOUGH HE OR SHE HAS NO REASON TO LIVE. THIS WORLD CAN BE BRUTAL; BUT KILLING ONE'S SELF, OR TAKING THE LIFE OF ANOTHER, IS ***NEVER*** THE ANSWER (NEITHER SHOULD IT [EVER] BE CONSIDERED). ***DON'T DO IT!***

In no way am I defending or condoning rash acts of violence; neither am I advocating suicide or any other form of tragic display. *Never* should these be viewed as coping mechanisms or as acceptable and/or easily accessible methods whereby we use for the purpose of escaping our pain. Nor do I deem these actions as appropriate avenues of revenge, to bestow upon those who have hurt or wronged us in some way. Inflicting violence upon others, (even if they deserve it) is not the answer!

I do however wish to acknowledge the thousands, perhaps even millions of people, young and old alike, who one day may have simply lost hope, and in poor judgment or out of sheer desperation and/or rage, carried out such acts of violence towards others and/or even towards themselves. I pray to God that we never forget Columbine High School. I hope that somehow we will remember every life that was tragically snuffed out by the horrific and senseless massacre. Let this work also be in remembrance of those who carried out the hideous crime, which ended in tragedy personified. I remind society, to please take the time to be concerned about *all* people with whom you make contact.

We have no way of knowing at any given time, if whether, a kind word or a sincere smile will be the precise antidote which will prevent a person from self-destruction.   Who knows how many lives have already been spared, simply because someone took the time, to show an act of kindness or common courtesy, to just one single hurting individual.

Likewise, condescending mannerisms and/or nasty comments could be just the thing to push a person over the edge. I have heard that people deemed the boys, who committed the Columbine murders, as strange, disconnected, and weird. In a word, they were seen and treated like 'outcasts.' The world, in which we live, is not always a pleasant place. People with their unkind, rude remarks and prideful behavior patterns, can literally drive a person to a place of no return. I wish those boys had known Jesus! He could have made such a difference in their lives and as a result, perhaps the lives of their victims would have been spared.

A Bastard's Refuge is dedicated to every person who has ever felt just like a boy named Cliff Evans, whose touching story I once read in a textbook entitled, "Looking Out Looking In", while enrolled in an "Interpersonal Communications" course. His only contribution to society would be that others would forever remember him as the boy who had been a 'sub-human.' He would be thought of as a 'zero.'

In the course of his young life span, we are told that Cliff had never played on a team, belonged to a club or held an office. His touching story lets the reader know that, "He had never been anybody at all." In the sight of those around him, his life had served absolutely no purpose whatsoever. Though he had been part of a community and had attended the local school [for years], still administrators could not find even 10 students, who had known him well enough, to attend his funeral as friends.

Written comments about him, in reports from his teachers, describe him as being, "uncooperative, a slow learner, dull, slow witted and as having a low IQ." In the 3rd grade, his IQ had been 106, when he suddenly died, while in the 9th grade, it had dropped to 83. *Something* had gone terribly wrong, but *nobody* had bothered to find out what – no one had ever taken the time to care. I suppose people had not thought of him as being worth their effort. Additional notes from his teachers, give the reader greater insight as to what may have happened, and when it was that things might have started to plummet.

We discover that Cliff's mother had remarried, and that his stepfather had never legally adopted him. Cliff also had five younger stepsisters and brothers with whom to contend, and he was the *only* child present, who was not a biological offspring of the patriarch in that home. Knowing this, I suppose, made him feel even more like an outsider. Cliff's biological father is never mentioned. The reader is not told whether or not he is deceased, or if perhaps, he and Cliff's mother had divorced.

Though his mother *loved* him, it was apparent that her new husband ruled with an iron hand. Cliff's mother seemed unable to stand up for herself, as well as for the fair treatment of her son. Reading his story, one can easily conclude that Cliff's stepfather had been anything but loving and kind. He seemed to be the mean and selfish type, you know, the kind of person who thinks only of 'self' and what he needs and wants. He had [probably] *never* treated Cliff like a son at all. The only thing that Cliff had to bequeath to this world was the long string of "D" grades left behind on his school records.

Why is it that people hardly ever make an effort to find out, "What happened?" How is it that a person who is happy and thriving, can suddenly plunge into the depths of despair without anyone noticing or without anyone caring? Oftentimes changes in someone's personality go completely uninvestigated until *something* happens. It is not uncommon for this sort of thing to rear its head, even in our houses of worship. Rarely are people even interested, as to *the reason(s) why* a fellow brother or sister, who hardly misses a service, or is *jubilant, whenever* he or she is a at service, *suddenly becomes withdrawn or missing altogether.* If by chance the individual *does* happen to show up, appearing sullen and depressed, people rarely make an inquiry. Those in charge hardly ever stop what they are doing long enough to lend an ear.

Such seemed to be the case with Cliff. His haunting family issues proved to be more than he could handle. It is my belief, that his heart had been deeply bruised; as a result he carried a heavy emotional burden, until he could take it no longer. One day, he buckled under its pressure and simply gave up.

As the school bus pulled over, Cliff simply stumbled off the bus, collapsed into a snow bank at the curb and died. Though doctors listed the cause of death as, "heart attack", I know that his *physical heart,* had not been the primary reason for his sudden early demise, but rather *life* had let Cliff down. *People* had let him down! Cliff gave up the ghost after having *silently suffered* from devastating emotional wounds. His mental bruising had given way to a sadness and tormenting anguish from which he could not quite recover.

There exists little to no doubt in the mind of *this writer,* or likely in the mind of *anyone* who reads his touching story, that Cliff Evans collapsed under the massive pressure of a weighty sadness and a gnawing grief. Suffering first, from the pain of coming to terms with, and then having to cope with, *knowing* that he was not wanted, neither was he cared for, nor was his presence ever acknowledged by *anyone at all.*

Besides his mother, he had no genuine nurturing relationships. But even the cohesive bond with mom, would seemingly come 'unglued' in the presence of his tyrannical stepfather. Everything accounted for, life had simply become too much to bear. Cliff suffered from the trappings of his home life as he struggled to adapt to all of the changes. These changes would include, the [now] absence of a father, who loved and had taken an interest in *him.* And so...no longer fitting into family, and neither into life, Cliff began to gradually fade - and now he was gone forever.

When the initial news of his death reached home, Cliff's stepfather wanted nothing more than to fill his stomach with more food. The fact that Cliff was dead did not faze him or move him in the least. The child had just fallen dead in a pile of snow, and dad could not have cared less. His mother, who was preparing breakfast, when the call came in, immediately pushed back the pan on the stove, and attempted to untie her apron, in order to rush to the remains of *her* son. Her husband snapped at her about how he just *had* to have his breakfast! He snorted something more about how, "Cliff had never said he was ailing." He further retorted, "There was nothing else that could be done." "If Cliff hadn't been so dumb, he'd have told us he didn't feel good." He never shed a single tear. It was painfully obvious that Cliff's stepfather had never loved him at all.

My heart pains for anyone who has ever felt like Cliff. He brought into the lies of the people, and it wasn't long before he also began to see himself as valueless. He started to see himself as nothing; because that's the way, other people had always treated him – like nothing! *In the eyes of those surrounding him, he had been nothing more than a big fat zero.*

Ladies and gentlemen, that is how a boy named Cliff Evans died!

As a child, I found myself always siding with the underdog, and now I know why. For even now, I have great compassion for the left out; and I seem always to route in favor of the 'have-nots.' For as long as I can remember, I have identified with fictional characters such as Rudolf The Red Nosed Reindeer and The Ugly Duckling. Like both these characters, I too know how it feels to be left out and/or to be made fun of because of a physical imperfection. Albeit a person does not necessarily have to display a [physical] defect in order to become the object of someone's ridicule or scorn. Society can be down right vicious in their cruelty. For no reason at all, there are people who simply choose to single out and to make fun of other individuals.

Many of *you* have been excluded from the [reindeer] games of life, and as a result, you have suffered much pain. My fellow rejects, (and I call you that most lovingly); you need to know that there is good news. While we my never fit on man's agenda and while man may never select us for anything at all, you need to know that someone does want you, and that someone cares. We have been carefully selected and personally handpicked by The Father. For years, we have begged for crumbs of acceptance from other people, but instead we have emerged empty, shattered, angry, frightened and emotionally starved to death.

Even though we were wounded, and nobody else wanted us, still we decided to try our hand at *true love* - just *once more.* We decided to get close to *Him*. I represent a generation of people, many of whom have been ignored and terribly mistreated. Families, jobs, churches and society have hurt them deeply; and as a result, at times they have even hurt themselves.

To this writer, it has become apparent that our only "firm refuge" exists under the wings of The Most High. *Only there should we ever expect to find unconditional safety, love and acceptance. He is the ONLY source of stability, for all others will surely fail us.* In Him, we discover the truth about *who we really are.* Under his protective wings is where we can cease from our struggle to fit in. It is there wherein we discover that we too are valuable and that we *can* be of use to The Lord. In His presence, we can be made whole, and can come alive. If we can but drown out the opinions of people, then surely, we would hear God.

As we are engulfed in His care, and are taking care of the things that He has assigned to our hands, He then is obliged to handle our business. As our Heavenly Father, our business becomes His obligation. If we lose ourselves in Him, God will show us Himself in ways that we have never seen before. He prepares us, blesses us and eventually He distributes us into a world that needs us. As we abide in Him, we will discover that which is to be our contribution to His Kingdom.

The assignment(s) for which we are responsible will become increasingly evident as we seek His face and stay under His protective care and watchful eye. While some assignments have been designed for the masses, others have been specifically formulated to reach a *single* individual only. But who knows though, if whether or not *you are the one* person, who has been given, the awesome task of reaching the next mighty Apostle, who will in turn go on to win many more souls for The Lord. Maybe God has raised someone else up for no other reason, than for the express purpose of reaching YOU!

We have no way of knowing exactly who or how many lives will be saved because of *our* testimony and through *our* godly acts of service. However, you and I beloved, *must show up. We cannot let them stop us!* God knows how to bring us to our rightful estate, so that with our minds in tact we can begin doing our very best work for Him. We can help heal the hurts of others who have been wounded. Each of us has a vital part to play, but again, *we must be present and accounted for.* We may not all be the same, but we are each very important to The Lord. Humans can always refuse to give us the time of day. They can also refuse to appoint us to a position with a fancy title. This writer for one is so glad that it does not take *a title* to be anointed by God.

While man may control many things, he certainly cannot now, nor will he ever be able to control the anointing; neither will God ever allow mere flesh to decide upon whom it is to be bestowed.

Brothers and sisters, fellow colleagues and ministers of The Gospel of our Lord and Saviour (or Savior) Jesus Christ, don't you dare leave this earth without finding out who you are in *Him*. Who or whatever The Lord says you are, can best be discovered as you spend time alone with Him. If He has a job for you, He anoints you for that task. You will discover just as I have, that your God given assignment(s) will fit you perfectly because He makes no mistakes. Even if you are afraid, you can still go forward, asking for faith and strength every step of the way as you do. As you are actively moving towards your destiny, you may find yourself trembling in fear. The good news is that, the same sound of The Master's voice that you heard calling your name in the first place, will be the same one that reminds you to, "Be not afraid."

<u>I must warn you though, do expect for the enemy to immediately attempt to steal that which The Lord has fitly spoken.</u> We always think that if God is for us, nobody will ever dare come against us. Beloved, this simply is not true. If God be for you, sometimes it means that nearly <u>everybody will come against you.</u> The forces of hell, the world and sadly to say, oftentimes, even the church will oppose you; this you can count on.

The key to <u>your victory</u> however, is in knowing <u>for yourself</u> that none of these forces can win. They cannot take you down as long as God holds you up! This question, when asked in Scripture, is done from an eternal perspective, with the answer already in view. "If God be for us, who can be against us?" In light of God's omniscience, we know that the enemy will never [totally] prevail against us, as our God knows exactly how to defeat our foe. Still we will be in for the fight of our lives if we <u>are truly</u> endeavoring to do the will of God.

The devil often launches his most brutal and vicious attack while The Word is still fresh. Long before you ever act upon it, you can count on him trying to discourage you – this is how he *steals* it. If he cannot shake your faith at *that* time, he will do the same as he did with Jesus; satan will simply wait for, "A more opportune time." Perhaps he will wait until you are at your weakest moment or until he sees that you are facing a major decision or challenge of some sort. Either way, he is not simply going to just give up and go away. *No <u>true</u> child of God will ever totally avoid doing battle with the enemy.*

I don't care what *they* preach. Sometimes a "Well done" from Jesus might just cost you everything; but you owe it to yourself and also to The Kingdom to do The Father's will. You owe it to Him to do your very best. Don't give up! But often *look* up! We have a cloud of witnesses surrounding us. I believe that The Lord allows them to peer over the banister of Heaven in order to encourage us.

Can't you hear them as they cheer? "You can do it!" "Come on, you can do it!" "Get up!" "Don't let the enemy deceive you, come on!" "Get up I say!" "Don't quit now because you've come too far." "Get back in the race; you're too close to the prize now." "Go for it." "Get up Apostle, Prophet, Evangelist, Preacher and Teacher!" "Get up lawyer, doctor, engineer, babysitter, and sanitation worker!" "Come on secretary you can make it!" "Let's go single parents; keep it moving!"

"We know it is not easy, but many who have gone on before have walked in your same shoes." "You *can* raise that child alone; – do it!" "Don't you dare throw that baby away; keep it!" It doesn't matter who you are or what you do for a living. It matters not if your ministry is in the forefront or behind the scenes. What matters is that you do not give up on yourself or on God. What matters is that you report for duty with a readiness and with a determination to accomplish His will. You particularly owe it to God; but you also owe it to yourself, as well as those who are depending on you.

Somebody's child may be waiting especially for you. Now, stop feeling sorry for yourselves. Find out who you are and what you have been put on this earth to accomplish. For goodness sake run *your* race. I commission you by The Authority of Almighty God, to go forward in peace –

"Looking unto Jesus, the author and the finisher of your faith."
(Hebrews 12:2)

"Remember, Jesus loves you; and Lord knows, I'm trying to."
From the depths of my heart,
Prophetess J.

<u>Near The Cross</u>

Jesus keep me near The Cross,
　　there's a precious fountain.

Free to all a healing stream,
flows from Calvary's mountain.

Near The Cross, Near The Cross,
　　be my glory ever.

Till my raptured soul shall find,
rest, beyond the river.

❧Acknowledgements❧
To Those Who Rejected Me

I'd like to publicly thank the people who never believed in me as well as those who wanted nothing to do with me. I acknowledge and thank each person who never wanted to be bothered with me. To you who hardly looked my way, but even when you did, you looked straight through me as though I were nothing at all - to you I say thanks. Honestly, I am indebted to you. I could have never made it this far without *your* input. Some of you made my life a living hell. I spent countless nights crying over the horrible things that you said and did to me. I've often pondered the many nice things that you *could have* said or done but instead, chose not to.

How can I ever forget those of you who would move away whenever I sat next to you? I shall always remember you (especially the choir members), who *always* insisted that I happened to be, **"Sitting in your seat", or "Standing in your spot." No matter where I sat or stood, you would always show up to claim that space as your own. Never did you ever fail to remind me that I just happen to be in "YOUR SPOT."** Some of you made me so agitated by your nasty wicked spirits, that I probably would have moved anyway. For whatever part you played – to you I say thanks.

Maybe yours was only a supporting role. You know, like maybe *you only listened* to other peoples' negative talk, and then you *automatically* decided to hate me. *Never mind that you and I had never clashed with one another.* **You didn't even know if what you <u>heard</u> about me was true or not, but still your mind was made up. How pathetically immature is that? God help you!**

Like a cashier ringing up miscellaneous merchandise, you looked only for my outer markings. This you did for the mere purpose of scanning me, so that you could willfully toss me aside, as though I were some sort of unidentifiable object, instead of a human being with real feelings. Some of you knew absolutely nothing about me, but yet you hated me without a cause. Perhaps you carried out the dirty work of another simply because you lacked the backbone to stand up in my defense. Never mind defending **me**, you didn't even have the guts to think for yourself, so instead you blindly went along with the opinion of the crowd. Whether you wrongfully accused me, talked about me, just didn't like me, went along with the others or suddenly stopped speaking to me, *for reasons that make absolutely no sense at all,* even to you - I say thanks.

I would like to acknowledge and thank all of the people at work who never saw me as being worthy of promotion - *ever*. You did your best to keep me back, and guess what? It worked! No matter how hard I tried to advance, you were always there to make sure that I never got selected. Your constant ignoring and overlooking, gave me the fortitude to strive even harder. The hot salty tears that rolled down my face, each time you denied me the opportunity to advance, were just the motivation that I needed to do something for myself. *Most especially to you - I say thanks.*

I suppose you feel I am being cynical. On the contrary, really, I'm not. It was however extremely important to me, that I let you know just how significant *your* contributions have been. Because *you rejected me,* I found myself in God's company. I re-discovered, "What a friend I have in Jesus." At one time, not only did I *want*, but also, I thought that I just *had* to have your friendships, your jobs, your ministry, your admiration, your love, your blessing and your acceptance in order to survive. I really thought that I *needed* you, to feel good about myself. Thanks to *you*, I have discovered something much better. My Father already accepts me just as I am. He has **always** been there for me. He has **always** accepted me, **and** He has **always** loved me.

It was I who could not see Him clearly because I was too busy looking for *you.* I have refocused my gaze to where it should have been in the first place. I have only *you* to thank for snubbing me and for rejecting me, so very much that I finally got a clue. Now I ask you, why on earth, would I have a reason to still be mad at *you?* Once again - even *to you I say thanks.*

❧To The Family❧

To my deceased biological father Joseph Godley who gave me the best gift that any man could ever give to a child – his very own last me. And my goodness, what a name it is - "GODLEY." It is a name that I am especially proud to wear. I shall forever cherish it, as a badge of honor, because therein is contained the name of my true father – "God", my Heavenly Father.

To my stepfather Deacon Neville R. Clarke who took on the difficult tasks, of being a husband and a provider. Although we did not always get along or see eye to eye, still we made it through. There were days in which I gave you a real hard way to go, just as you gave me (smile). Still, deep down I knew that you cared. I can fondly recall the times when you would go fishing, and would not come home, until you had caught at least three fish. In fact, you absolutely refused to return without *at least* one for each of us – even if you eventually ended up having to purchase them. There were times when it didn't seem as though you would ever get a bite, but you continued to labor anyway. That's what a real father should do – he is supposed to persevere and stick it out even when the going gets tough. Thanks for all the years of nourishment and for always cutting my grass in the summer (smile). Thank you for being there.

Thanks to my mother Juanita Clarke who gave birth to me. What can I say? She endangered her own life, trying to get me here. Thanks for all the years of love and financial support; I could not have overcome many of my monetary dilemmas were it not for your help. Thanks mom! I appreciate you for affording me a "stress break" whenever I seemed to have been at my wits end. You give so much to so many, but seemingly, you get little in return. I just want to say thank you, from them, and also from me.   Mom, you have overcome so much during your own time of trials and testing. It is now time to step up, higher into the realm of The Spirit and there lay hold onto the work assigned to *your* hands. There is so much more, if only you would dive in wholeheartedly.   The time for you to start taking better care of yourself is right now! You know exactly what I mean. Let The Spirit of God take you upon His Mighty Wings, to ministry [or to whatever] it is that He has reserved especially for you. There remains much work to be done!   So what are you waiting for? Arise! For somebody awaits your testimony and your service.

To my Grandmother Hestine Jenkins Hi "Meema" I hope that God is allowing you to peer over the banister of heaven for a little while (smile). I want you to see that your teachings on "Hell" and on "The Lake of Fire and Brimstone" have been paying off immensely. I don't plan on being cast into *that lake* for any reason.

I was only 5 years old, yet I remember <u>everything.</u> Because of your early warnings about "Hell", the charge to "Be faithful" and to [remember] to strive to "Get my crown", I now use the same words for you, as I did to honor your last earthly leader. Jesus admonished the faithful church of Smyrna to, "Be thou faithful unto death, and I will give thee a crown of life" (Revelations 2:10). Because of your *living* example as a, "Good Soldier", as you strove hard to receive your own promised reward, The Apocalyptic Book of The Revelation of St. John The Divine has always been one of my favorites. For one day, I too shall also wear a "Golden Crown." I hope that one day you will be proud of me.

To Dennis What can I say "Poppy?" The Lord obviously had to have planned this one, when He put the two of *us* together, "Oh boy." It is very scary, but in many ways, we do seem to be two of a kind. *I once asked The Lord, if He chose to send me a mate, how would I be able to identify him; <u>thereby knowing beyond any doubt that it was indeed He who had done the sending? The Lord said, "You'll know, because when you look into his eyes, you will be able to see yourself."</u> "Oh, ok" I thought, as I puzzlingly pondered His reply.*

Well, little did I know, it would not be very long after that inquiry, that I *would* have the opportunity to meet you, *and* on Holy Ground at that! Indeed, I have looked, and I did see. I pray He gives us many years to make up for the deluge of loss and disappointments that have plagued us both. As we painfully persevered, and revealed our struggles and even our hurts one to another, we discovered that our lives have paralleled in so many ways – even from the very beginning - wow! I pray that God will help us to pick up the pieces of our shattered hearts, tuck them away for safekeeping, and then build us anew. May we only call upon the memories of the hurtful fragments, as a testimony to others, so that all who look upon us will say, "Look what The Lord has done!"

I pray that we will follow the plan that He has mapped out for our lives, individually as well as collectively. Together I pray that we will always desire to walk the paths of righteousness as "Instruments" of God, to be used in His service. Not only do I thank you for telling me that you love me, but I thank you even more, for never ever failing to show me. Thank you for believing in me; the time has come, for you to also believe in yourself. "Forgetting those things [and especially those people] which are behind, and reaching forth unto those things which are before [us].

"Poppy" it is now time for us both to, "Press toward the mark for the prize of the high calling of God in Christ Jesus."

(Philippians 3: 13-14).

Love Always – Jonita – AKA -   "Mommy", "Momma" and "Mommita"

Lo, children are an heritage of the Lord: and
the fruit of the womb is his reward!
Psalm 127:3

❧ To "K" ❧

Kenita, my darling daughter, you are so precocious and so full of life. At times, your flashes of wisdom far exceed your years. Thank you for reminding me on May 3, 2004 that, **"It only takes one distraction to cause me to lose my dream."** Mommy really needed to hear that. I have been surrounded by distractions and dream killers for much of my life. *They* have had access to me and to my vision for far too long. The sad thing though, is that I have only myself to blame for not believing in me. I settled for trying to fit in with mere chickens and buzzards; and as a result, they nearly plucked me to death.

Quite often I found myself stuck and unproductive, because I had become too afraid to fly high or because I had allowed *THEM* to convince me that *THEY* were the ones who were *ALWAYS* right and that *I was not supposed to ever fly at all*. At other times, I found myself grounded, because my wounds had left me too darned paralyzed to soar. Thanks for reminding me that I am still an eagle.

Thank you for confronting me and for challenging me to dream yet again. Kenita, I pray that you will never allow anyone or anything to ever rob you of your unique identity nor of your dream(s), ability and aspirations - not even for a moment, because time is too precious and all too short. Don't ever let other people, (NO ONE AT ALL [but especially church folk who lack a higher calling than you]), rob you of your purpose, simply because they cannot discern their own, and neither can they [properly] discern you. If you are not careful, just like theirs, your life will also reek of regret. You too will be grounded, unfulfilled and stuck, just as they are. <u>Never allow it to be so! You and God alone must take control of your destiny</u>.

"K" mommy loves you so very much! I thank God for loaning us to one another and for allowing us to share a brief moment in time upon the earth realm together. Besides working for The Lord, you my daughter are my number one reason for living. I am curious to see what you will make of yourself, and not what others will make of you. *I adjure you, as I say unto thee my child – Be thou courageous and strong! LIVE! <u>Live YOUR OWN life!</u>*

Live life to the fullest my dear, but NEVER EVER leave The Lord out! Follow hard after His Son Jesus and you will not have time to follow foolish men and women [like I did], who will only lead you astray. Any thing that you need to know, ask Him. Any problem that you may be facing – tell Him.

He is "El-Gebor" – The Almighty God! Always allow His Word to guide you and to order your every footstep – allow it to become your guiding light, with Jesus as your best friend.

*Always do your very best to walk upright before men and circumspectly before The Lord. Do all that you can, to become a "Proverbs 31 Woman." But even when you fall short, [and at times you will; the shame is not in the failure or in the falling], BUT, GET BACK UP! Re-dress yourself in dignity and then, "Go forward!" Be warned though, many will dislike you, because of your strength. Therefore, you must always ask God for the wisdom to harness it properly – He will show you how to walk the tightropes of strength and humility! Make Him proud. Never let them change you, nor strip you of your self-worth, simply because they are intimidated by your "presence." **Use their rejection as your stepping stone and your gifts as God directs.** Be it from the earth, or even from the clouds, remember Kenita, I will be watching and cheering you on. I am so proud of you and I always will be – no matter what. I am honored to have been assigned by 'The Master', the awesome privilege of being your mother. Next to Jesus, I am your biggest fan! For you darling daughter Kenita, are indeed, "The wind beneath my wings."*

From this day forward, let us both dream as big and as vividly as He allows us to. God created you and I with the ability to soar and to fulfill a mighty purpose. That ability has been present since the moment of our conception but it was we who suffered it to be veiled through the eyes of **THEM and THEY SAY.** Well my darling, our veils have been lifted; it is now time to fly higher than ever. For God has created us, as His own unique vessels, and we know that everything "He" creates, is "Good" and "Very good."

Hear me clearly my beautiful, unique, talented daughter, in what I say. Never, ever forget that you are a smashing creation of The Most High. Until the day we depart this life, always remember - you have a mother who loves you very much, but even better than me, you serve El-Olam (The Sovereign, The Everlasting Father, The Eternal God of the universe and beyond). The Lord Jehovah is His name, and He will 'ALWAYS' ALLOW YOU TO CALL HIM YOUR 'FATHER'.

Love, Mommy

❧ G-d's Love Is A Bastard's Refuge ❧

Upon His throne,
He looks below. He
feels the pain, our hearts
now know. He saw the
tears, as we all cried. He
knows the truth, will
come with pride .

Rejected souls from ages past; our present sadness, will not last. Rejected souls, the pride of men; for G-d alone, is our one true friend. As we all cried, for those who died, rejected souls, no more to hide. As G-d returned, He saw the flock; rejected souls, no more to mock. Denied by envy, the greed of man; in G-d we trust, for He has a plan. Rejected souls, denied to speak; by satan's lies and from those who preach. As fame and fortune, control the world, the truth of G-d, will one day unfold. Denied by pride, which set to rule, a world of lust and sinful fools. Rejected souls, denied by men; but called by G-d, a loving friend. No father to know, no mother to grow, the broken heart, is all alone. The Lord is there, to show He cares; for those who hurt, and have been used, for those

who suffer, and are
abused. The wisdom
of G-d, for those
who know, rejected by
men, the truth untold.
Justice will come, in
glory and strength, to
remove all the pain, and
in Christ we'll remain.
His love is for all, no one
refused. The love of
G-d is, A Bastard's Refuge.

Written by: Minister Dennis Gideon Ramos Copyright 2004

***In keeping with ancient Hebrew text the 'o' in God has been purposely omitted.

✥Foreword✥

As I grew in ministry, quite often I would hear the term **"bastard"** applied to an individual within the ranks of ministry. However, there would never be a reason or clear explanation as to this labeling. Regardless to where I would find myself in ministry, this would always come up, but still without explanation. There came no clarity on the matter and therefore no concrete understanding had I ever gained.

One day I researched this word for myself. Of course, most of us understand and know how it was or is used in the secular world, but I wanted to know how it applied in ministry. Upon my research, it stated that, "A 'bastard' was one who is illegitimate." Furthering my research on "illegitimate", the word was broken down to mean that a person would be recognized as "unlawful offspring."

If this term was to be applied to the <u>offspring,</u> I couldn't help but wonder what label should be applied to a <u>father</u> who is unwilling to acknowledge the child that desires to be fathered? What is to be the title assigned to that individual? Can somebody help me please?

Well, there is some help in Gilead; Jonita has released a word for God concerning this very issue. This vessel of God has an inside track to the loosely used term.

This book should be a 'must read' for all leaders. God is releasing direct instructions for those who dare to be different, and who are willing to be called out, go through the fire, and come out with a dogmatic determination to make a difference.

I do not believe that God is pleased with some of the situations we have placed His people in when such were some of us. Prepare yourselves for a *challenging journey* into the life of a woman whom I unhesitatingly classify as a genius and a prophet for the times.

Travel with her as you read and learn. I thank God that the desire, which was placed upon my own heart more than twenty years ago, has found its reality through Jonita Godley-Ramos; to God be the glory.

Enter into *"A Bastard's Refuge"* with an open heart and an open mind. Expect your understanding to expand in a mighty way, and be prepared to experience a challenge, so that you will emerge having been changed.

Pastor Michael A. Robinson
Resurrection Life Christian Cathedral
East Orange, New Jersey

❧*Introduction*❧

This book had been burned into my soul long before the first letters were ever penned to paper. I knew on June 23, 2003 that this was the beginning of something much more than only the jotting down of a few notes. *These notes* would never find themselves amongst the myriad of papers that would eventually be crumpled up, and thrown away without having been used. In a feverish attempt to ditch my frustration and my pain, I wrote and talked to God – a lot. The more I wrote, talked, 'preached' into the air, or even into the 'mic' of my hand-held, 'silver', mini tape recorder, the more evident it became, that *this* was an assignment from *The Lord*.

I am merely the "clay" that The Potter has allowed to bring forth that which troubles His heart at this season. Looking back, I am certain that it was God, who ordered my steps even into the various situations that would play a major role in *"my making."* The treacherous trappings unleashed by my adversaries would nearly pound me into the dust of nothingness; but God in His mercy and "divine providence", kept a watchful eye over every single event. He eventually used everything that the enemy meant for my destruction, to instead become the catalyst, which would help to mold me into His instrument – "God's Instrument."

After having endured *so much* disappointment, brokenness, heartache and pain, God put me back together, and prepared me to walk in His will. However, *before the rebuilding process* could take place, and though stumbling at times, I would *first* have to fight my way through religiosity, the wasteland of other people's opinions, the crucible of affliction *and* the "church folk" experience. I would have to make my way out of a place that I refer to as, *"Rejectsville."*

I eventually did make it to a place of safety. For it would be there, in "The Secret Place", that I would *finally* obtain wisdom and understanding. There I would once again discover, that He, whom I call God, has *always* been the Father and friend for whom I'd been searching (for much of my life). Yes, it would be right there, in our own "special little meeting place", that The Father would *formally* introduce me to my purpose, which heretofore, He had chosen to reveal *only* in 'snapshots' and 'snippets.' Before this, *("my illumination"),* the 'finite' mind through which I thought, marveled, wondered and reasoned, had not afforded me the necessary, priceless 'spiritual eyesight', that would have allowed me to *'get it.'*

Exactly what was at stake as well as <u>why</u> *certain things kept happening to me was a complete mystery.* I did not understand; therefore neither was I able to see *clearly enough* to fully embrace my destiny, my purpose or the [true] reason for my very existence. Little did I realize, in those darker days, that the mental anguish, turmoil and depression, from which I'd suffered, (after having been emotionally devastated, neglected *and* rejected), would serve as the very tools, which would catapult me into a higher realm of spiritual existence, and even into a deeper understanding of His grace.

What I encountered is not unique to The Body of Christ nor is it uncommon in the secular world. The one major difference however, is that people in the secular arena have never hedged when it comes to being vocal about the things that ail them. The church however, has been too silent on too many issues for far too long, and God is tired. My deepest wounds did not come from an enemy, but rather they came from such a one that I would have deemed nearly impossible. Never in my wildest imagination had I expected to suffer such heartache at the hand of a spiritual leader. There are millions of unsuspecting followers, who have been spiritually assassinated, by the very leaders who instead, should have been imparting words of wisdom and life.

Many sheep have suffered because of the absolute negligence of those who were supposed to have been caring for them. We had been taught and admonished to obey leadership at **all** costs. As we attempted not to rock the boat, but instead to be totally compliant, the price proved to be steep indeed. Following *them* seemed to have cost us nearly everything, including our sanity. So many people have stopped short of their God given potential because they were trying to be obedient to their shepherds. We were duped into believing that the agenda of man was more important than the assignments of Almighty God. Because of this misconception, we have often fallen way short of God's very best for *our* lives. You know, we were always told that the "pastor's vision" is the *only* vision. We in turn began to see, breathe and speak the vision of the *house*, but to the neglect of God's plan and vision for our own personal lives.

They tell us that God will bless us if we obey *them. They* often quote the passage, which says, "Obey them that have the rule over you" (Hebrews 13:17). This they use in an attempt to keep the sheep in check. While they are quick to sputter off and lash out at the people, rarely do they expound upon the rest of that *same* passage. Hardly ever do they tell the congregation, that they have *an even greater* responsibility towards us. *They* are supposed to watch over *our* souls, not the other way around. *They* shall give account to God for what *they* fail to do as shepherds. This is the part that *they* always conveniently seem to omit.

Anyone daring to speak out from under the yoke of tyranny and/or neglect, risks the danger of being preached at, (or about) from the pulpits - and I know I'm right. Such an individual is said to be in violation of Scripture and is considered an enemy to the congregation.

How is it that someone can suddenly become an enemy to the pastor and to the church family with whom he or she has served for years, simply because the person is telling the truth? Moreover, who ever said that once people connect themselves to a local assembly that they must then automatically disconnect from that which God is speaking directly to them? God still does speak to individuals you know.

The gathering of people into one particular building, could never be *the only* representation of what the church is all about. If that be the case, then God help us! The authentic church of God is living, ever breathing and always moving. The *true church* is forever endeavoring to reach the hearts of men and women everywhere. God's church is never stagnant; neither does its leader, The Lord Jesus Christ, ever set out to *purposely wound people or to limit the ability and potential of those who are committed to the building up of The Kingdom. T*o be part of *man's* church, it is almost inevitable that we undergo a form of mental debriefing. We must be willing to forget nearly everything that we already know, and be taught *their way.* You are expected to forget what you know to be right, and do everything they tell you, even if their way happens to be wrong. If not, you will likely have to find yourself another church.

It matters not if what *you* know is correct; you are still subtly (and sometimes out right) told that you are wrong and out of order. Go along in order to get along is the clear message. Conform or get out; stay in line and keep quiet. Do what you are told and not what *you know* to be right; if not, then you must find yourself another place to go. Be warned though, changing your church home, could set you up for yet another mind-altering experience. For depending upon the mindset of the pastor and the leadership at the new church, the rules and the teachings of the former, may not be applicable at all, so please be prepared.

For your sanity's sake, you should not even try to figure this out. I know it can be tricky but you will save yourselves a lot of unnecessary aggravation, if you simply accept as fact, that in many places of worship, thinking for yourself is an absolute no-no. Using one's brain is not usually encouraged and in many instances, will simply not be tolerated. Should you be courageous enough to brave the elements, by attempting such a feat anyway, then just know, you will be dealt with accordingly.

The consequences may be extremely severe. For as the saying goes, "The nail that sticks out <u>must</u> be hammered down." It must not appear to be different – because others will also begin to think for themselves. They too may start "Thinking outside of the box." In other words, they too just might get free. Of course, your taskmasters cannot allow that to happen. Get in your place and stay <u>only</u> there appears to be the mantra of many churches today.

While we are taught to remain faithful to our congregations and to our leadership, we should also be taught that a pastor and his or her [pastoral] staff have an even greater responsibility to be faithful, first to God and then to *us.* They are after all, supposed to be the head, and claim to have been charged by God to operate in their positions. They are *supposed* to have *our* best interests at heart. By virtue of their very position, they are obligated to feed the flock, and not to bruise the members thereof. They are *supposed* to care for *us.* I know many of you have wondered about this, because I have asked myself this same question.

How can my pastor possibly be concerned about *me,* when he doesn't even know *my name?* I am only one person in an audience of hundreds, maybe even thousands. How could he or she 'really' know me as an individual? For the most part, the people in our congregations have become nothing more than a system of numbers - or more accurately stated they are nothing more than "Tithe envelope numbers." Some of the highly sophisticated corporate churches have even implemented an upgrade.

In many of these mega infrastructures, *income tax statements* have become the primary identifier of its parishioners. No names, and no personal touch; the members' identities have been reduced to nothing more than a system of digits. In some churches, the handing over of a person's personal financial portfolio or income tax statement is in fact, an actual prerequisite for membership. No statement – no can join.

Today's church is like unto a revolving corporate door, people in, people out. Often the masses come and go without any *real* caring transpiring one for the other. Hurry up! Get this lot out so that the next batch can get in here. After all, "We don't have all day you know." We dare not go a minute over the allotted time or else the two groups will likely collide.   God forbid if The Holy Spirit appears to be hovering at the precise moment that the preacher is trying to rap things up. The people are admonished to, "Calm down now, calm down", as the pastor checks his timepiece. Heaven forbid that The Spirit should shake things up a bit! Sometimes a congregation can find itself being 'driven' and not at all shepherded. Yet, in other churches, there seems to be no pastoral concern whatsoever.

If I were missing from church for several weeks, I doubt that anyone one would even care. The majority probably would not even notice. *The same leaders who lord their positions over us, should also be concerned about us – and not only when the offering plate is low, but also when we are missing in action.* How does a pastor know if whether or not a member is home, gravely ill, with no way of reaching out? He (or she) doesn't! A senior could be homebound without any means of transportation. A letter or a visit from *someone* would be nice. The missing member could very well be at home dead for all anyone would care. Okay, okay, perhaps I am exaggerating just a bit, but you get the idea. Some churches should actually post warnings on their marquees. There should be a word of caution for potential members, letting them know well in advance, what they can likely expect to encounter upon joining.

At the very least, some churches need to display these warnings in a "Membership Handbook." Here are just a few important things that we are not always made privy to, prior to joining some congregations…

WARNING: "You are Welcome, as long as YOU have no opinions about ANYTHING." *WARNING:* "Being anointed could intimidate our pastor, which in turn will cause you to be disliked, because this is pastor's church." *"WARNING:* "Following God instead of our pastor will be considered treason." "Depending upon the severity of your offense, you will be punished by being talked about, shunned or banned from all ministry participation." *WARNING:* "Asking questions may get you excommunicated for life." *EXTREME WARNING*: "If your prophesying tells us the truth about our wretched selves, we then have no choice but to consider you as a trouble maker and a false prophet (we really can't handle the truth)." "We are just like the church of Laodicea, for we also base our value on riches and large numbers." "Image is everything you know!"

"Jesus calls *them,* wretched and miserable and poor and blind and naked" (Revelation 3-14:18). "We may be blind and not realize it." "Some of us do however, know of our wretched status, but *YOU* are not allowed to point that out to us because, WE ARE ABOVE YOU IN POSITION – we are the leaders and you are not." "Your job is to stay only where we have put you." "Although you appear to have great insight and wisdom from above, we can take it better if a visiting pastor tells us the *same exact* thing that you have been saying all along." "You are not allowed to point out our faults, because we have to see your face each week, but we can soon forget about the visiting minister who has called us out." His/her rebuke or correction can be ignored and forgotten. "We can go right back to our trifling ways, just as soon as our initial guilt wares off." "A visitor does not serve as a constant reminder of our wickedness, but you do."

"But for the most part, *we really don't want to hear the truth from anybody at all. And why would we want the truth anyway? As long as we are oblivious to our real selves, we can keep right on believing that we are, "Blessed of The Lord and highly favored." I believe we already told you that we love having our ears tickled; this is what we major on in here – only good prophetic utterances." "Please don't bring us any bad news or words of correction." "We never want to feel convicted – even if we are wrong."*

"One last thing that you should never forget while you are here; "We are not really concerned if you do not show up, because we have so many clones that can easily replace you, and so we really don't have much time to care about you anyway." ***ADDENDUM:*** "Excuse me brother, sister, we forgot to add this new clause to our hand-book." "We *will* take the time to care about you, only if your name should appear on the pastor's preferred list of pets."

"Now then, if you can adhere to every single rule, and can remember above all else, to STAY <u>ONLY</u> IN THE CORNER THAT <u>WE</u> HAVE DESIGNATED JUST FOR YOU, then we welcome you with open arms. "Jesus loves you and so do we." "Welcome to your new church family and by the way, <u>feel free</u> to participate."

Beloved it could take years before a person realizes that he or she is in a church just like this. By the time, we realize that we have been brainwashed, it may be several years and several missed opportunities later. To our dismay, we may eventually discover that while *we* have groped in the darkness *with them*, we have totally missed God. The vision of "the house" is without a doubt, very important. Please keep in mind however, that *God also has a plan and a vision for your personal life for which YOU alone shall be held liable.*

I am not suggesting that anyone leave his or her church. Neither am I implying that people should disobey their pastors. What I am saying though, is that you had better be quite sure that where you are is where God wants you. Do take care that while you are busy fulfilling the mission of your pastor and of your church, that you are not neglecting God's mission and call upon your life.

Because of fear, and/or out of a need to belong, even well meaning servants, can be hushed into a "Holy stupidity." We have been lulled to sleep; I have learned first hand just how costly spiritual complacency can be. It was we, who almost failed in our assignments because we did not want to be *the only one* to stir up the dust by taking a firm stand for righteousness.

Sometimes God is looking for and is depending upon someone who He can trust to make a difference. And yes, sometimes He empowers just *one individual* out of an entire crowd. Beloved, all you need to do, is to look in the nearest mirror, because *that someone,* for whom The Master is looking, could very well be you. It has been my pain and it is now my pleasure to share my story with you. It was by The Father's design that I *had* to walk the road less traveled. Perhaps you now find yourself on the same path that gripped my feet not so very long ago.

God wants you to know that the date of your deliverance has been set. He desires that you be free from the chains that bind. The clutches of the oppressor have gripped you for too long already. I declare unto thee, by The Father's command, that in The Name of The Lord Jesus, you are hereby loosed, and made free! If the Son [of God] therefore shall make you free, ye shall be free indeed (John 8:36). *It is the deeper truth of Jehovah that "makes" us free, and not merely sets us free (John 8:32). Jesus 'sets' the captive free, but after initial freedom, comes the higher learning associated with the 'making' process.*

If a [caged] bird or a slave, had bound for years, and were suddenly set free, one would have liberty to fly away, while the other would have the privilege to live life as a free individual. However, because neither has been **inwardly liberated,** they would still possess shackled mentalities. The bird would probably remain grounded, while the freed slave would still possess tendencies and thought patterns of one who is yet enslaved.

When a person has been *"made free"*, from the inside out, even if he or she ends up behind bars, as The Apostle Paul had, (on many occasions), this same person could yet be totally free. Indeed beloved this is the freedom that Jesus wants for us all. He wants you and me, to experience – "A Liberation in Theology" as well as in our personal lives.

The Spirit of the Lord is upon me, because he hath anointed me to preach the gospel to the poor; he hath sent me to heal the brokenhearted, to preach deliverance to the captives, and recovering of sight to the blind, to set at liberty them that are bruised, To preach the acceptable year of the Lord.

Luke 4:18-19

God's Instrument:
Gutter to Grace to Glory Ministries Int. Inc.

❧ A Little About Me ❧

My desire is that this book will set the record straight for many who are in spiritual bondage. Although I am not "formally ordained by man", I have been ordained by the hand of God. I am not against formal ordination, but neither will I put off doing what The Lord has commissioned me to do, simply because I have not had one - yet. I know that God has ordained, equipped, appointed and chosen me, for whatever tasks He has assigned to my hands. I have experienced His school of wilderness training and have received my instructions from above.

The call of God has been something that I have suspected since my teens. It was also evident to various enlightened people who would cross my path. It was most unfortunate however, that during my younger years, the *enlightened people* only seemed to be around for a fleeting moment. They were there in passing but never had anyone *stuck around* long enough, to help cultivate the prophetic gift that brewed within my soul. The one person, who did remain a constant, was The Lord Jehovah. Bless His Holy Name!

My life was not always an easy one, and I would commit many sins, and fall way short before finally gaining an understanding, of that which The Lord wanted to accomplish through my life. As a youngster, The Lord would often commune with me. However, there came a time (at age 19), that He began speaking to me through prophetic visions and dreams. These visitations would come without any prompting or effort on my behalf. They were not "dreams" [or something] that I could conjure up at will; I did not control them, God did. I never asked for them, and neither did I ever try to manipulate them, in an attempt to change their meanings.

In fact, I never even knew when they were coming. I did not have them every night nor did I have them each week. Sometimes lots of time would pass in-between the "Night Visits", as I referred to them. If I received a prophetic visitation on a particular night, it might be 4 months or even a year later before another would come.

One thing was for sure though, whenever they revealed something, they were *always accurate* – never once did they lie. I saw things, I saw situations and I saw people, not even once had they ever lied. Even if at first I did not quite understand the events of the dream, or why it was that God had chosen to show me a particular thing, eventually something would happen and the dream would make sense. As I grew older, The Lord would sometimes send, "Words of knowledge." Communing with The Lord, or receiving night visits have been something that I have grown accustomed to over the years. At one point (very early in the experience), because I did not quite understand, I started thinking that, I must have been 'psychic' or that something was wrong with me. *I thought this <u>before</u> I knew better.*

By age 21 someone had finally given identity to these visitations; and had informed me that, "This was the doing of The Lord." Later there was confirmation of a "Prophetic Mantle" being upon my life. Although words of knowledge and night visits were a part of His method in preparing me for the prophetic office, these things as I would much later discover, were also designed to teach me how to distinguish *His Voice and Spirit* from that of the enemy's.

Keep in mind that satan is also a spirit and that he too knows how to send visions, messages and people into our lives, whose primary assignments are to foil the plan of God. In no way could I have known, just how valuable my early visitations and training with Jehovah would prove to be. The knowledge that I received from God's training, has come to my rescue on many occasions as I wrestled with that which has tried to take me out over the years.

Why am I bothering to tell you this? I am sharing this with you now, so that you can avoid some of the pitfalls that I encountered, as well as many of the mistakes that I made while on my journey. Kind of like Joseph, I would tell people about my dreams. (Don't do it). It wasn't that I was trying to brag or anything, but rather I shared them with people because I was excited. Also, I told because I was searching for comparisons.

Finally, I had gotten "it", I thought. In those days, The Holy Spirit (or Holy Ghost) was often referred to as 'it." "Did you get it yet", I would hear people ask as they inquired of one another; always referring to Him as "it." We know now, that "it" has never been an "it" at all. I thought that God, The Holy Spirit operated in the lives of *every professing Christian – and in the same way.* I thought that it was only a matter of who got "it" (Him) first. As a young child, I remembered praying to and talking with Jesus. I didn't know *as much* about "The Father" in those days, but "Jesus", Him I was very familiar with.

By 15, I suppose in my heart, I was approaching my personal age of accountability, because one Sunday morning, as the preacher asked the question, – "Who is on The Lord's side?", I felt the *need* to "give Him my life again." Something moved in my heart and I felt the urge to stand up and to make public confession. So with my little boyfriend "Ray" (smile), I stood up. In fact, we were the only two teenagers who took a stand for Jesus that day. Ok, he actually stood up first – but I still felt Jesus in my own heart. Soon, I was seriously considering my need for, and had also become desirous of a closer walk with God.

By age 17, I had begun my own personal quest in search of the **deeper** things of God. It was at age 19 however, that I noticed He began to reveal Himself to me through dreams – the "night visits" that I mentioned earlier. I honestly thought that *everyone in church* was doing the same thing. I thought that walking and talking with The Lord was common amongst *all saved people.* I never knew that not all Christians received these visitations. Therefore, when I realized that The Lord had seen fit to visit *me,* well, I suppose that I just had to tell *somebody.* I mean, we're talking about "THE LORD" – not just any visitor. *I had to tell it!*

These "night visits" seemed to be His primary way of communicating with me, besides His written Word The Bible. During those days, I did not yet have a whole lot of peoples' opinions to sift through, which made hearing from God, and believing Him a lot less complicated. I suppose even then, I could have been considered a "God Chaser" without realizing it. In that day, I had never before "heard" of the term, "chasing God." Nevertheless, I felt as though my "heart" had already begun the pursuit of deity. To me, He was more than just some "man in the sky." I mean, God was *always* available. He was someone to whom I could tell my innermost thoughts, and not be laughed at, made fun of or scorned to embarrassment.

God was someone in whom I could trust; I could talk to Him whenever I wanted to. I could confide in Him, and He would not think of me as odd, no matter what my questions, comments, or concerns. Neither did He ever laugh at any of my replies to His comments, requests or questions that He often posed to me. Simply put, He was my friend, and yet He was God. As I grew older, I came to realize that I had not started the chase with Him at all, but in reality, it had been He who had pursued me. We played our own little version of spiritual freeze tag! Just God and me, alone together. "Where are you God? – got ya!"

I also discovered that I had not been so far off [in my earlier years], when I referred to Him coming by as, "Night Visits." Much later, I found out that in The Bible, there were others who had them too. I realized that I had been in good company all along.

They however referred to them as "Night Visions" or "Visions of the Night" - Genesis 46:2, Daniel 7:7, Daniel 7:13, and Zechariah 1:16. I found myself really getting use to His friendship and also His fellowship. After a while, I simply *had* to have more. For some odd reason, He loved *me,* a sinner who would later on look for "human" love in so many wrong places. At that time, I had not come to know God as "Father", or as a "companion" such as a husband, but only as "El-Gebor", God The Almighty One – who just happened to be my friend.

Much later on, I allowed myself to become involved in situations and with people that *I knew* were no good for me. But because I wanted to belong and to be accepted BY PEOPLE, I sold my own self short and I did many things that I am not proud of. My self-esteem was near ground level by the time *people* finished stepping all over me, yet *God* had always seen fit to seek me out. I have in my lifetime, violated just about every single one (if not in fact all), of His "Thou Shalt Nots." I was a sinner and the biggest reject of them all. I did not quite understand why The Lord had chosen me in the first place. I almost felt like saying that the only reason, He wanted me, was because nobody else had, but that isn't exactly true. He chose me, because He loved me. The Mighty Apostle Paul said that he was the "Chief of all sinners" whom Jesus Christ came into the world to save. Well, he and I must be in a tie for *that* position. We certainly will have much to talk about when I meet him (smile). How he could have possibly sinned worse than me totally blows my mind.

I have often been the brunt of jokes, put-downs and cruelty inflicted by others. I scarcely seemed to fit in anywhere. Yet The Lord Himself has *always wanted me.* Imagine that! *I* had found a place on Jehovah's list for visitation. Why it is that He loved me so, has always bewildered me, but I am so glad that He did – and that He still does. Moreover, I am extremely happy that I eventually learned how to love Him back.

At first, I did not know that I could love God *like that*. I had no idea that He could be so many things; a friend, the lover of my soul, a husband, my counselor, my shelter, my constant companion, someone who understands my pain and so much more, as I came to later found out. He was God, how could I, a vile sinner, love and have such an attachment to a Holy God that I could not see? Even as a youngster, I could look up and talk to Him. It was easy really, for I had no brothers and sisters. Though I did have a few friends here and there, still they paled in comparison to Him. He never laughed at me nor did He think that I was stupid, dumb or ugly. He never thought that I talked [to Him] too much. Most of my family lived down south and in other areas. So for the most part, I had no close relations besides my mother and my stepfather. Who wants to hang around parents all of the time?

I spent a great deal of time alone in my room, watching television, playing my music, and talking to God – a lot. No matter where I went, I knew that God would be there and that I could always communicate with Him. Even as I frequented places, doing things that I had absolutely no business doing, I knew that I could always slip Him an S.O.S. I've always felt as though He were watching me – because indeed He had been (and still is).

It was not until much later that I truly "learned of Him." I had to learn of His manifold attributes and of His ways. I *knew* that He loved me and I loved Him back, still I had to learn how to worship and adore Him. Most of all I had to "LEARN HIM." From my earliest existence, I often sensed that, "God must have something awfully special for me to do, because the devil was sure trying hard to stop me [from doing it]." Little did I know, that I would utter those very words for years as I awaited my turn to be used by The Master.

I have always known and so do you. If you have an abiding relationship, with The Lord, you know when His hand is upon you. You really do not need a human being to tell you that. God will confirm your call, by using other people, but not always. You just have to know, that you know, **what you know**. Little did I realize how difficult my battle would be, neither had I understood what would be expected of me and what I would have to overcome before my purpose and I could finally meet.

Because the waiting period was soooooooo long, I began to place more stock in what others thought and said about me than what I knew God had already made plain (so many years prior). People had seen fit to deem me as a somewhat, "less desirable" and so I became discouraged. I could not always 'see' the good things that God had already predestined for my life; I only began to see what *they* said.

They said that I was ugly, so I began to see ugly. *They* said that I would never amount to anything and that is what I also came to believe. *They* said that I talked too much, so I became discouraged (because God had given me much that needed to come out), but I tried to shut up and not say anything at all. Each time as I would inch forward in hope, *they* would escort me right back to the end of the line. I could take it if only worldly people were this unkind to me. However, a lot of my pain came at the hands of *"church folk"* too. I did not realize it back then, but even in *this* lurked a divine set-up. Hindsight being 20/20, I can clearly see that there had definitely been glimpses of the prophetic office.

But during my "making" process, it became extremely difficult to verbalize exactly what it was that I felt, or to even imagine this very necessary process as being something "good" (Romans 8:28). Growing up in the Baptist church, one did not hear a lot about prophecy or the gifts of The Spirit. So even with the brewing of a prophetic anointing beginning to rage within, it would be quite some time before I would allow myself to *publicly* acknowledge *it or to* fully *accept it.* It would be a long time before I could totally push pass the voices of people and their opinions and finally realize unequivocally, that this indeed is the primary gift, that The Lord has bestowed upon me and has commanded that I walk in. It is one of the most unaccepted and hardest of the, "Five-fold ministry" gifts.

Not being accepted can be very difficult, if in fact it is acceptance that you desire. It was easier to believe that God had called me as an Evangelist, because I could handle that better. They did not seem to be hated nearly as much as the prophetic folks were; so this seemed tolerable to me. As I grew older, the call to the prophetic ministry that often intrigued me, quite honestly, began to frighten me. Besides being fearful that others wouldn't accept me, I also felt totally unworthy to acknowledge such a call, because I knew in my heart, that I could never, ever live up to it.

I did not want to disappoint God; neither did I want Him to kill me for neglecting the anointing or for taking it for granted as I engaged in sinful activity. *I certainly did not feel "clean enough" to acknowledge such a calling. I was unworthy and I knew it – BUT GOD!* The very thought of this scared me to death, because I do not believe in playing with God! I have since learned that being frightened and/or unaccepted often comes with the territory. God is able to help us through our most difficult areas in life. He is able to guide us through our worse fears. As far as me disappointing God, well He knew upon choosing me, what type vessel I was, and He chose me anyway. He also knew what I would become if I held fast under His tutelage.

Let me repeat that. God knew of my sloppy condition, as well as what He was going to make of me; He already knew what the end product would be. *Someday I will be a jewel in His Kingly Crown.* None of us are worthy to be of service to Him – and ministry is exactly that, it is a service. It is only due to the mercy of God that we have not all been consumed already. I know you see people who claim to function in this office, go on to predict cars, riches and wealth, *only good things.* However, those are not typically the kinds of messages that He gives me. The challenges connected with the prophetic ministry can be quite difficult. More often than not, people who *truly walk* under the prophetic anointing are often perceived as being 'strange', or 'different.' They can also be very direct [bold] in their speech and at times quite 'stand-offish.'

Other people often perceive them as being 'weird.' I didn't want to be any of those things. I did not want to be classified as being "different."

Typically, they are not well liked and oftentimes they are hated or totally avoided. Unless The Lord has already prepared the heart(s) of the recipients(s), the words of the prophet are not always welcome. Unless you are prepared to tell the crowd what *they* want to hear, do not expect to be well received. So sorry, but God would not be pleased if I did that. This is why the journey has been so difficult for me - I *always* desired to fit in and I wanted to be liked and well spoken of. I wanted others to view me as being a nice person, and as someone who *really* loved The Lord. This dilemma concerned me for years. When one tells the truth, he or she will not always be accepted. Whenever *a true prophet* shows up, one of three things often happens: Either the devil will run for cover, or he will launch an all out attack. If the heart(s) of the recipients receiving the word has already been softened, then the prophet's job is that much easier.

People might just be compelled to look into their own hearts and repent at the 'sound of truth' (the truthful word) given to them. No matter what the outcome, it is never an office in which to tread lightly or to take for granted. Neither does it make any person better than another. Each of us is very valuable to God; and He uses every one of us in a different capacity – a capacity of HIS CHOOSING, NOT OURS. Functioning under this anointing will oftentimes entail being misunderstood, while at the same time, one desperately tries to harness that which burns within. This particular calling is not something about which a person should brag or use as a reason to exude actions that reek with pomp and arrogance. While prophets have been designed to walk with kings, more often they must walk alone [with God]. The prophetic ministry is not at all like the fabulous showcasing we witness on television or in some of the more charismatic churches.

Check out the prophets in The Bible, and then ask yourself, why on earth, would anyone in their right mind, <u>ask God</u> for this type of an anointing?

While prophets of old were often revered and well respected, they were also hated, which led to them being very lonely. Again, assignment to this office is not something about which to brag. Those who 'truly' walk this road will not have a choice in the matter. They are expected to do their very best to live it – no, in actuality they *are* it. The person is bound to it, because God has chosen them for it. *They* (the wolves) know it, and so do you.

Now, on the other hand, if someone has chosen himself or herself, then he or she can tell the crowd whatever it wants to hear. An individual such as this can do as he or she pleases – but that is a different story altogether. It seems as though God has *used* the tragedies of my life, to teach me how to cope with loneliness, rejection and displacement. I did not say that He caused them or that He brought them on, but even in our struggles, there is purpose. These things toughened me up, and taught me how to walk alone! (with God).

By the time He decided to take me off the shelf, I would in no way be swayed or hindered by the opinion of man. By this time, God would have already taught me how to walk through (spiritual) fire, without being burned. This I had gotten use to, as opposition *always* seemed to track me down. By the time that destiny and I were scheduled to 'kiss', the acquiring of human acceptance would no longer be a major concern of mine. Had God chosen me to be His sewer worker, His engineer, or even His house cleaner, I would have taken pleasure in doing exactly that. I would be perfect for the job, because it would be that for which I had been created. I would be the best house cleaner, sewer worker, or engineer available, because I would be doing it for Him, and the job would fit me perfectly. I am not saying that I would necessarily *want* to be any of those things. However, I would more than likely, have "bent" towards them if either [or all] of them were part of my destiny.

Once people stop running, they tend to follow hard after that to which they have been called. Titles and offices do not impress me because I already know who I am, as well as to whom I belong.

However though, while titles and offices are not be the main objective, still I refuse to allow peoples' twisted agendas to constantly push my face into the dirt because of what *they* refuse to acknowledge – or because of what they cannot see. I am *who and whatever* God has called me to be, regardless to whether or not people see me as such. I cannot be anyone or anything other than whom and what He has made me. It is impossible for me to be truly content, if I am living an outright lie. As my time approached, it got increasingly difficult trying to pretend not to be me. It became too painful to hold back, simply because they could not handle it. At this point, I no longer plan on settling for less, than to become a vessel of The Master, and to be used in whatever capacity He chooses.

My primary desire is to have a relationship and to continue in fellowship with Him, rather than acquiring titles or friends. For this reason, I simply refer to myself as "God's Instrument" and I will be used if, and in whatever capacity, He sees fit.

Prior to undergoing the seemingly unending period of "wilderness wondering" there had *already* been a "word of prophecy" concerning my life, awaiting its time of fulfillment. This Word had been 12 years in the making. At least seven and a half of those years were spent on the backside of the desert, so to speak. Honestly speaking though, there were times when I felt as though I was literally *under* the desert, as He *taught* me how to wait. Just when it seemed as though my time had come, guess what? I had to wait some more, back into the furnace of affliction I went. God let me know, "You're close, but not yet."

At this point, He began a process of purification through sanctification and purging. I came to know Him as Jehovah M'Kaddesh (The Lord who sanctifies). He also revealed Himself to me as Daddy (ABBA) and as Jehovah Shammah (The Lord who is there). Sometimes we must trust Him although it seems like He has abandoned us. In our hearts, we know that He hasn't, but sometimes it sure feels that way. He tests us to see if we remember the lessons that He has already taken us through. It is during those times, that it seems as if He is not even listening to our pleas for help.

Beloved, these are the times when you just have to **KNOW THAT HE IS [STILL] THERE.**   Be still and know, even beyond a doubt that Jehovah Shammah, is yet God – fear not, for He has not forsaken you. We may get only one word on which to go and nothing more. Sometimes we must rely on what He taught us as He showed us how to walk through the valley, through the fire and eventually on top of the water. During my sanctification process, He told me to hang on to these Scriptures for comfort. Believing them with my whole heart would one day assist in saving my very life. They have served me well as faithful companions, as I traveled my wilderness.   The Scriptures are Isaiah 43:2, Philippians 1:6 and Jeremiah 1:5, 1:8 and 1:17. These He burned into my soul.

He instructed me to pay close attention to each of them, but in particular to Jeremiah 1:17. It is imperative that we obey God even in the face of our adversaries or we will answer to Him.
Sometimes it can be extremely difficult to go on, in the midst of people that we already know hate us, and have absolutely no problem displaying their feelings of hatred or ill will towards us. Yet we are compelled and called by God to persevere anyhow!

I invite you to look these passages up for yourselves. For one day, these nuggets of gold may also preserve you. Perhaps He has already given (or will give) you your own Scripture(s) upon which to cling. He spoke to me and told me in October 1996, in the year of Our Lord – He said, **"I filled you [with The Holy Ghost] last year, but I'm going to sanctify you this year.**

"Oh boy"! Did the testing ever begin!

I would eventually have to learn new lessons as well as review those from long ago. The Lord was calling my spirit unto Himself and He was preparing me for *His* ministry. A few years later, amid much deliberation, numerous promptings from The Holy Spirit as well as confirmations through those that He would occasionally send; I knew that God was summoning me.

I was neither anxious nor eager. For by this time, I had been so spiritually beaten up, and dragged through the wilderness, that I was determined to wait for God's timing - forever if I had to. At this point, I was safely tucked away, and hidden in obscurity, and for the most part, had become happy to work behind the scenes. It was sometime during *this point* that The Holy Fire began to burn and God beckoned that I should come forward. I'm thinking to myself – "Oh no, not again! More tests?"

"How much was one person expected to endure?" "What's He going to do this time kill me?" "Oh No!" "Why in the world did I ask that?" All kinds of thoughts ran through my mind. If God has ever fingered you for any reason at all, you will know it. Repeatedly He summoned me. I *finally* accepted the call that continued to burn within my soul. At first, I hesitated; I felt afraid for one thing, but also I simply had to make certain that it was He and not *my flesh.* I wanted to ascertain that desiring the spotlight or vein glory through self-promotion was not on *my* agenda. I also found myself halting because I honestly do not like a lot of attention. I had been so use to not being man's choice that I really did not care to be around many people anymore anyway. I had received a closer walk with God as a trade off to my being rejected by people; and frankly, I had grown to like it.

Not that I liked being rejected you understand, but I did like having a close relationship with The Lord – just thought I would clear that up. I am not a masochist and neither do I like pain, but I do love basking in the anointing. I wasn't looking for fame and I did not enjoy having my "God space" invaded. I like my atmosphere free and clear of a lot of peoples' 'spirits', opinions and religious clutter. I had really gotten use to "God and me." It isn't that I didn't like other people, but I had been so wounded, hurt and deceived by them, that desiring to be around a lot of them was no longer what I needed, especially since I already had God as my Dad and as my teacher and friend.

When I could no longer ignore or deny The Fire, I realized that this was it; God was not letting up this time. I had to be who He wanted me to be, even if it meant coming out of hiding. No matter what it cost, my soul became determined to answer the inevitable call that has been present since [and even before] my birth into this realm.

The closer I came to doing *His* will, the more resistance from outside forces seemed to multiply. The doubts would once more rush in and invade my mind. In the process of time, coupled with assurance and very, very patient counseling sessions from The Lord, I was able to dispel every doubt ...except one.

God would instruct me to remember certain events.

"Remember the prophecy." "Remember who said what to you." "Remember the night visions." "What did you do after I spoke?" "With whom did you share your heart?" "What did they tell you?" "Was what they told you different than that which I had already spoken?" "What was the outcome as a result of adhering to their counsel? "Why do you continue seeking fleshly validation?"

On and on The Lord and I hashed out my doubts, fears, and the reasons for their resurfacing. He even took me all the way back to my childhood. In *that process,* I would discover many things, including where the majority of my paralyzing thoughts and the *need* for flesh approval had originated in the first place. There were tears, repentance, and apologies. Sometimes we have to forgive people who will never ever even apologize to us. I first had to forgive me, for having allowed myself to roll over and to play dead in the first place. I forgave myself for having lacked the guts to fight back spiritually. He had [already] fortified me; He had given me my tools long ago [during the night visits]. However, because of my devastation and my low self-esteem, I could not seem to use them, perhaps I had forgotten how. *I had <u>nearly</u> allowed people to <u>permanently</u> take away that with which He had equipped me.*

I had to forgive me for not loving and valuing myself enough to say no! I had to forgive me for wallowing in the sheets and with the hogs! I had to ask God to forgive me, for calling myself ugly, just because other people had called me ugly – even though God had ALWAYS told me that I was beautiful because I was fearfully and wonderfully made by Him and in Him. I asked God to forgive me, for ever having allowed mere humans beings to make me doubt that which He had already spoken so many years prior. Just because *they* could not see it, did not mean that God had not said it. Just because they could not see me, did not mean that I had no purpose!

The prophecy and my very own set of "Spiritual keys" had not been for them anyway; *they were for my life's assignment(s).* Of course, [the] envious people refused to acknowledge anything good for me. I had to seek forgiveness for not following through with what God had said.

I never doubted God's *ability* to bring things to pass, but the fact remains, that I brought into the talk and into the lies of the people - both clergy and non-cleric alike. One day while at work, The Lord told me that I was operating in unbelief. How so I wondered? "I believe You can do whatever You say", I answered.

The Lord said to me,

"You are operating in unbelief, because when I speak, you don't need to ask anyone else's opinion." (End communication).

I was guilty. I did seek validation and confirmation from others - a lot. I did this even *after* already *knowing* the voice of God. At one point, I began to doubt my own ability to hear Him clearly. Somehow, His voice seemed distorted, as the leaders continued to program my mind into thinking that I *had* to check with them, because *they* knew more than I did and that God would want it that way, *because they* were God's shepherds.

I am so thankful for grace! It took the longest time to learn my lesson and to finally rid myself of the need to validation hunt. It took years to reclaim my spiritual keys and to deprogram myself from *warped counsel and tainted theology.* I had already been accustomed to hearing *Him* speak, long before ever listening to another's tainted message. So how was it that I ever started double-checking with mere mortals in the first place? Many from whom I had sought counsel were not even in my dimension, as I later discovered. Though I am not trying to sound like a know it all, but the reality is this; sometimes we seek counsel from others, based purely upon their position.   Unfortunately, we oftentimes later find out that *they* are actually less qualified than we are.

Often, the very people who try to teach *us,* haven't even ascended to *our level* of *'revelatory dwelling.'* They are not even in "the loop", but yet they try to counsel or preach to (and at) us. This is particularly the case if God happens to be grooming an individual for a *prophetic ministry.* With this in mind, the individual must ask him or herself, "How could <u>*their counsel*</u> be sufficient for <u>*my life*</u> (or for my set of circumstances), when <u>*they*</u> really don't have a clue?

A shepherd (or anyone for that matter), can only counsel from the highest level, that he or she has aspired to. If you beloved have managed to gain higher insight than those to whom you turn for help, then you really should not expect *them* to have the wisdom, to give counsel from *your* realm. Simply put, they cannot! If they don't understand, then beloved, you must realize that *they really don't understand - get it?*

They may be trying to give you counsel from 'a level', – when *God* has already got *you* rubbing elbows with dimensions and stratospheres!

But...because of *our own insecurities* and *their consistent mangling and misappropriation of Scripture,* or because of their higher "earthly" title or position, we have constantly found ourselves in a tailspin. This is especially the case if we have ever been [previously] victimized, or if we have suffered from [or are prone to battling with] feelings of low self-worth.

I can speak from first hand knowledge on this subject because I lived it. Because people were Christians, pastors etc., I would discuss things with them. I did this without realizing that they may not have even known how to help me. Then of course, there were those who would automatically give me their opinions, without even being asked. No wonder I had been so confused about things.

It was I who allowed them, to convince me that I had not really heard from God. God, they said would never tell me such things without first telling them, particularly because I was not in a position of leadership or authority. They told me to wait, and wait, and wait; wait to be sure. Even when I told them that I WAS SURE, they would dismiss me by telling me to wait some more. To go against their counsel, they said, would be considered disobedient to Scripture.

I HAD ALWAYS BEEN AWARE OF GOD'S VISITATIONS AND ALSO HIS VOICE. MY PROBLEMS DID NOT BEGIN UNTIL I ALLOWED "THEM" TO VOICE THEIR OPINIONS. I felt just like Peter, who while in route to Jesus, was literally [already] walking on the water just fine, as long as he kept his eyes focused on The Master ONLY. He didn't begin to sink until he looked around at the waves and the water, too. The Lord had not confused me, the people had!

Always had there been some Christian cleric or "prophet wannabe" who would come along and confound me, by convincing me that he or she knew better than I did – usually based upon their supposed rank or position. Nevertheless, just as The Lord Jesus saved Peter, I thank my God in Heaven that He also graciously extended His hand and rescued me.

Before my rescue and deliverance from "people dependency", I would however face one more round in the abyss of theologian mishap. F-I-N-A-L-L-Y, this was to be the last battle - at least for this particular demon anyway. Although I truly desire to respect fellow clergy, I have concluded after much deliberation and turmoil that no pastor is ever responsible for calling and compelling people to do the will of God, as we have been forced to believe for all these years.

Some of them act as though they are in the same stratosphere (space above the earth realm) as God, but they are not. The searing into the heart of an individual, the desire to preach The Glorious Gospel of our Lord Jesus Christ, has always been God's business. God is the one who does the choosing, and never a pastor.

The desire to work in God's vineyard or to preach The Gospel does not go away simply because a pastor will not confirm or ordain an individual. The fire is indwelling and 'in-burning'; no mere mortal can snuff it out. The church did not call me, and the church cannot take the call away. When my destiny and my set time are introduced, I intend to be present and accounted for with or without anybody's permission. God has already ordained me, and I will not allow a paper that man has not given me, to be the thing that causes me to miss hearing The Lord say, "Well done."

God knows my motives and the intent of my heart. Although I do not want to be out of church order, but more importantly, I cannot afford to be out of God's order.

Throughout the pages of this book, you will walk through the madness of my emotions and thought patterns prior to my deliverance. No longer do I beg like a pup for anyone's crumbs. God is ordering my steps even through this. There exists no person or manmade system that I am going to let steal my crown. Neither will I allow anyone to make me forfeit my own reward by not showing up.

For this decision, the mainstream church will likely deem me a rebel. They can say what they will, but unlike some others, <u>this rebel</u> has a cause. My mission is to do to the best of my ability that which The Lord assigns to me. I am quite clear as to who runs my life these days. I am "GOD'S INSTRUMENT" and not the instrument of any man.

If the acknowledgement and the stating of this truth, should henceforth classify me as a bastard, as a rebel or as one worthy of being rejected and/or shunned; then I say, so be it! And to God be the glory!

❧Psalm 91❧

He that dwelleth in the secret place of The Most High shall abide under the shadow of The Almighty. I will say of The Lord, He is my refuge and my fortress: my God; in Him will I trust. Surely He shall deliver thee from the snare of the fowler, and from the noisome pestilence. He shall cover thee with His feathers, and under His wings shalt thou trust: His truth shall be thy shield and buckler. Thou shalt not be afraid for the terror by night; nor for the arrow that flieth by day; nor for the pestilence that walketh in darkness; nor for the destruction that wasteth at noonday. A thousand shall fall at thy side and ten thousand at thy right hand; but it shall not come nigh thee. Only with thine eyes shalt thou behold and see the reward of the wicked. Because thou hast made The Lord, which is my refuge, even The Most High, thy habitation. There shall no evil befall thee neither shall any plague come neigh thy dwelling. For He shall give His angles charge over thee, to keep thee in all thy ways. They shall bear thee up in their hands, lest thou dash thy foot against a stone. Thou shalt tread upon the lion and adder: the young lion and the dragon shalt thou trample under foot. Because He has set His love upon me, therefore will I deliver him; I will set him on high, because he hath known My name. He shall call upon Me and I will answer him. I will be with him in trouble; I will deliver him and honour him. With long life will I satisfy him and show him My salvation.

Part 1
The Journey
Begins...

➷Words For The Wolves & The Wounded➹

Woven into the gigantic tapestry of our congregations, are sincere, anointed individuals who have been, "Chosen by God" to birth great works, and to do mighty exploits. The primary problem seems to be unanimous, as I am *constantly hearing the same* complaints from so many. This situation must be exposed and immediately corrected so that the church will not continue to be made mockery of, thus rendering its great work, to be of little to no effect. There remains much to be changed and/or to be done away with, so that The Body of Christ can commence to functioning, as it ought to.

Many are being "held back" by those in various positions and ranks of authority. This book has not been written for the purpose of "leadership bashing", as I have no time for that nonsense. Besides, if I really *wanted* to bash anyone, I would have written with the same ruthless vengeance, to equal the magnitude of depth that so many others and I have suffered at their hands, for all these years.

If you are a pastor reading this book, please know that if I truly *wanted* to personally bash *YOU*, then I would openly include *your* name as well as the names and locations of *your* particular church(s). I would picket and inform every form of Christian media of *your* despicable and demeaning practices being unleashed upon the people of God. I would have absolutely no problem pointing out the predators who attempted to devour my soul, because not only did I feel, but also, I had to recover from, every single blow of their vicious word venom.

Pastor(s), if I really *wanted to personally bash you*, or call you publicly, then that would mean that I am still angry or that I am holding a grudge. Alas, *bashing* is not what God has ordered for me. I have been delivered from you *and* from your emotional shackles. My assignment however, is to set the record straight. It is my duty at this hour to inform you, that the sheep are not always at fault as you claim. You need not attempt to guess which church or pastor I am referring to. Again, this is not about bashing, but about sending a clear direct message to all concerned parties throughout the ranks of Christendom.

This book is not about one church or a single pastor only; this word is for everyone who claims to be a follower of Jesus Christ, but in particular, it is for the leadership, and is written on behalf of those who have been brutally accosted by them – including myself!

Of course, as I refer to occurrences, they are written as referring to *"My pastor", because I am telling My story.* Let us just say that at some point during my nearly 28-year walk with The Lord that I sat under a pastor, who wounded me so deeply, that I no longer wanted to be bothered with "church folk" at all.

The person's name is not important because, *"My pastor"* could easily represent any number of clerics out there who have done the same thing to other individuals. This world is filled with people who have their own, "My pastor" stories to tell. The Spirit of The Lord will actually convict some clerics to the degree that they *will have* to identify themselves. If you are a pastor reading this book, I admonish you to go to God with your hands up in repentance. I pray you see yourselves and repent *before your own personal* exposure is wrought by His Mighty Hand. I don't have to identify you; He will do that if He chooses to! Whether or not your deeds stay between you and He will be up to Him.

The Spirit may drive some of you into public confession. Again, that is God's department. He has only charged *me* to write the book, not to expose you. You who are guilty must, at the very least begin to acknowledge your mishandling of authority as well as your mishandling of The Word of God. There exists something known as, "Pastoral abuse" but *your* offence is much greater than that.

This is about YOU declaring whom YOU deem fit to serve our King, when it is not your business to make that determination in the first place. Pastor it is not YOUR place to appoint any person to the five-fold ministry. GOD GIVES these gifts to the church, not YOU. Many individuals whom you promote and deem to be, "A real prophet." "An awesome man or woman of God." "A fantastic "bishop." or "A prophet to the nations"; may not be at all, like you proclaim. This is only what *you* say. Do you even know if this is how God sees them? For that matter, what does He really think about *you*? So many of these people are nothing more than shysters, charlatans, hypocrites and thieves. How easy it is to promote people who are just like you.

So many that you hold in such high regard, only claim to operate under The Anointing. In reality, they have done nothing more than major in learning how, to swindle the unlearned and the ill advised. The Holy Ghost calls both you and them out this day!

The Lord is calling *YOU* to attention. This is about those of *YOU* who are perpetrating a fraud. You claim to operate in gifts for which you have neither the ability nor the authority. *Some of you claim to have every gift that The Lord has given to the church - nobody has them all!* It would do you good to focus on being who *you* are in The Body, if indeed you are actually even in it. Many of YOU have appointed YOURSELFS as judges and as jury over anyone whom YOU perceive to be a threat to YOUR little empire.

Let me be the first to inform you of something pastors; <u>you</u> don't have an empire, but God does have a Kingdom; and guess what? YOU are not in charge of it!

YOU do not have an ancient formula on God. Jehovah does not belong only to 'you' or to 'your' church! In fact, He does not *belong* to anyone. He has graciously *chosen* to be our God. The same God who loves *you* also loves EVERYBODY and He is just as concerned about all of those whom you have snubbed and written off as He is about you. He is particularly mindful of those who you are trying to keep stunted.

The question is WHY? Who do you think you are, anyway? You are not Him! The trumpet is blasting and I counsel every <u>Christian cleric</u> to acknowledge their mishandling of God's children as well as their misappropriation of His Holy Word. You are hereby charged to acknowledge the part that *you* have played, in the bastardization of many who were placed under *your* care. Many there were who came to you in sincerity, but you however, did not love them nor did you invest in them as people; instead pastor, you made the choice, to spiritually assassinate them.

You know exactly to whom I am referring. The people who were so traumatized that they have altogether dropped out. You know the millions of people who no longer attend *any* church at all, because of you! Should you repent, then forgiveness is available and deliverance shall be yours. It is only God's truth that shall make you free, not mine and certainly not your own warped sense of truth.

The truth that you have conjured up in your mind is nothing more than a blatant lie. Just because you have not been confronted, does not mean that you have gotten away. Just because He has withheld judgment or exposure, does not mean that you are in His will. I don't care who you are, or how popular you are, God always has a Joel in the land awaiting His Holy command to, "Cry loud and spare not."

Preachers, you shall not escape this time, because too many have been wounded. Your *sincere* repentance along with the bringing of sacrifices worthy thereof is the *only* offering that shall suffice.   What sacrifice you ask? Yourself! Bring your wretched selves to repentance!

Thus Saith The Lord God: "YOU ARE THE CAUSE OF MANY WHO HAVE STUMBLLED." (End communication).

It is time for God's little ones to go free, from the oppressive masters who have enslaved them, through the use of lies and bonds of wickedness. The time has come for them to be loosed from the nasty slime pits of name-calling and also from the slanderous labels that YOU have imposed upon anyone who has been brave enough to question or to stand up to the dogma and hypocrisy, that YOU AS LEADERS, have allowed to take up residency in the local assemblies.

For now has the time come, wherein the hearts of the children, shall turn away from you, and instead turn [back] towards their Heavenly Father. Pastors, for far too long *you have* been running the show and attempting to steal God's Glory. Be it known unto you this day that your time for showboating is just about over! There are many pastors out there, some famous and some whose name the world will never ever know, but indeed they are doing wonderful work for The Master.

Many there are, who's names will never grace the pages of a newspaper; neither will their faces ever appear before the camera of a nationally televised Christian broadcast, but yet, they are some of God's finest and bravest soldiers. These men and woman have one objective only; and that is to see The Kingdom come, as God's will is done in the earth. At some point in their own lives, most of them, had also found themselves in situations, just like a lot of people in The Body of Christ, are in right now. They too were once 'stuck' because of the wolves.

These brave souls have since gone free and now they help to liberate others. To these courageous men and women of the faith, on behalf of The Remnant and in the name of the harvest to come, The Lord God Jehovah commends you for your service and your gallantry. I your fellow maidservant, in the midst of my tears would like to say thank you. I love you and God needs you to keep up the good work. For your reward is secure.

But again, I say unto the "wolves"; and you know exactly who you are. YOU who think more highly of yourselves than you ought. I am talking to YOU, who overstep your bounds when it comes to the handling of God's people. While we may be willing to sit in your congregations, we want to remind you that you too are only sheep. As leaders, you are to be servants of all, and not the other way around; please get that fact straight.

You may be a lead sheep, which makes you an "under shepherd", but YOU are still obligated to, and will bow to Him who is THE SHEPHERD and The Bishop (as in overseer and covering) of all our souls, including your own.

'Wolves', be informed, that we recognize *your* work – we see you. Through the eyes of The Holy Ghost, you have been detected. With all due respect, Madam Pastor, and Pastor Sir, the individuals in your congregation as well as the gifts and callings in their possession are not yours to disperse. Neither have they been given for you to receive capitol gain by prostituting them. These gifts of God are to be used as He sees fit. If it is by *His* mandate that individuals are 'called' or 'chosen' for Ministry or for various other duties, it then becomes His responsibility to lead them, even if in His leading, He leads them away from you.

The Lord God Almighty is the one who births all ministries that He approves of. Who are YOU to impose YOUR human 'opinion' and your stubborn will over the mandate of an infinite and all wise God? Just because you do not care for a person or for a certain group of people, does not give you or anyone else the right or the authority to deny them the privilege of obeying God.

It is Jehovah only who summons and burns into the heart of *His* creation a passion for ministry. It is He who does the leading and the drawing, not you! *Your* job is to feed them the unadulterated Word of The Lord, which in turn will equip them for service. Then you are to let them go, if God calls for them. He will lead them; and on occasion (if necessary) He will even *drive* them forward so that they cannot turn around, even if they want to. He knows better than you do what He has placed in each of His people. He knows in what capacity each is best suited and equipped to serve and He knows their limitations – you do not.

While you as pastors do have an awesome responsibility to execute, nurture, oversee and lead (to a certain point), the fact remains that, we are God's children and not your property.

How dare you bark out labels, threats, put-downs and insults? You know absolutely nothing of the emotional, physical or spiritual make up of most of the people in your congregations. A lot of preachers don't know *anything at all* about half the people whom they have snubbed and altogether written off. Like unjust magistrates, they have slammed their gavels and have belted out their ruling, sentencing people as dispensable and as easily replaceable. They are very often quite oblivious to the help that has been dispatched to them, and are unaware of the many blessings, that they have already turned away.

Sitting in the pews are a host of anointed individuals who are just waiting for you to look in their direction. They are eager to help and in many instances, they are more than capable. But yet pastors, many of *you* who do know, still turn a deaf ear, and continue to cock your head in that lofty position that you know all so well, as you refuse to even acknowledge them. Well guess what? God *has* looked their way and He does see them. He is now bidding *them to come to Him for instructions.* God is again heralding the great commission of "Go Ye." So why are YOU *trying* to stop them?

Again, I am not addressing *every* pastor. However, if you as a pastor are guilty, then *I am indeed speaking directly to you!* If you are purposely attempting to block His anointed, for the purposes of building up your own church so that *you* can boast about *your* numbers and brag about how many services *you* have, then yes Pharaoh, I mean you!

IF YOU CLAIM THAT ANY CONGREGATION IS "YOUR CHURCH" AND THAT YOU ARE ALWAYS THE ONLY ONE TO WHOM GOD SPEAKS, THEN YES ABSOLUTELY, UNDER THE DIRECTION OF THE HOLY GHOST, I AM SPEAKING DIRECTLY TO YOU! YOU MAY BE THE PASTOR OR FOUNDER, BUT BE AWARE OF THIS ONE THING:

IF YOU ARE CLAIMING TO FUNCTION UNDER THE LORDSHIP OF JESUS CHRIST, THEN <u>IT IS NOT YOUR CHURCH. IT IS GOD'S CHURCH. AND IT IS HIS BUSINESS WHEN YOU WOUND HIS PEOPLE!</u>

What you need to do, is to get some humility. Perhaps then, you will be able to understand what your position is, as well as what it is not. You need to get out of the way and let The Lord have His way. The Holy Ghost calls you out this day! The time has come for a showdown in the House of God, because the destinies of too many babes now hang in the balance.

You have no business telling someone to sit quietly (almost forever) in the back of the church, in some corner, doing some menial task of *your choosing,* when their set time has come. God may be trying to lead them into a very different arena; but you are causing them great confusion. The main reason pastor, that you try to keep *them* in the lower chambers, is because the anointing on *their lives,* intimidates you. But this is not their fault – it is you who has the problem. If for some reason you are feeling angered or intimidated, then this is something that YOU need to work out with God! There are times when God will call for those in the hinder parts to stand front and center, whether you like it or not. Just because he or she may not be someone of *your* choosing, does not give you the right to spiritually cripple the person.

Perhaps it is you preacher who lacks proper insight; therefore you cannot correctly discern when God is on the move. Maybe your own leadership capabilities should to come under question.

Stop sizing up people with *your* finite minds, because you could never know them in the same manner that God does. You *honestly* should be seeking the wisdom and counsel of God's Spirit and not that of your own mind. When God says that a person's time has come, who do you think you are, in your audacity, to *try* to overrule His decision, just because you would rather have your "yes people" and "kiss-up's" on board? And yes, many of you are guilty of doing exactly that! You are ignoring what God is saying by making believe you do not hear Him speaking concerning certain individuals, when you know that you do. You then have the gall to complain about your congregations having deficits in certain components of ministry. The much-needed elements are missing, because *you* have pushed them out with your verbal assaults.

Don't misunderstand me; I see nothing wrong with moping, cleaning, and faithfully engaging in behind the scenes ministry; many of us started out doing such things, and some may continue to do them for a long time to come. This is perfectly acceptable. Personally, I would have no problem picking up chewing gum from the parking lot if that is what my pastor required of me. I would even be willing to do windows and bathrooms, if needed. Not everyone has been called to pulpit ministry; again, I am clear on the matter. Neither am I denying the fact that people should 'sit' and be taught. I know that there must be only one leader/pastor of a congregation - again, this too is also clear. However, what I am saying pastors, is that you are absolutely out of your jurisdiction, when you try to restrain anyone, upon whom there is undeniable evidence of an anointing, as God is beckoning him/her (or them) to come forth. You are out of order when you blatantly refuse to acknowledge this truth.

Notice, I did not say that you *do not or cannot* see the anointing; you see it; but because you are so obstinate, most of the time, you simply refuse to acknowledge that you do. Because many leaders are festering in their own insecurities, they would rather overlook others who God is calling. They are stewing in their own juices and are yet licking the wounds of their childhood but will not admit to it. Their own pride and/or sin will not allow them to acknowledge (or to admit) that *they* are hurting; so instead, they are angered if others in the congregation are free. Pastors your crafty evil is exposed this day! God forbid it may tarnish your image to acknowledge your own transgressions. So instead, any person who tries to be obedient to God, despite not receiving *your* approval, is considered by you to be un-teachable or troublesome.

Sometimes you automatically chalk people up, as being those who are unwilling to yield to authority. And of course let us not forget the pulpit classics - they are accused of being rebellious and/or in sin. **Why must people be classified as being in sin simply because they are trying to obey GOD? Can somebody explain this to me? Perhaps I'm a little slow or something, because I just don't get it!**

I suppose it is always easier for people to create something derogatory about others, rather than to fess up to their own evil doings and/or insecurities. Leaders also need to admit <u>by verbally confessing</u> that they have been wrong, and that they have been guilty of playing favorites. Many have been operating out of a spiritual deficit, and are themselves, unable [or unqualified] to lead by example. Pastors, if you cannot confess this to people (right now), the very least you should do, is *confess* it (say it out loud), before The Lord. (He already knows anyway). I understand that a leader's position can be quite challenging, as pastors must deal with all sorts of individuals and personalities, many of whom can be extremely difficult to handle. Of course, there are those who will *have* to be put in place, kept in check or maybe even asked to fulfill duties that they will not be happy carrying out. A leader may even have to sit an individual down due to his/her blatant misconduct.

Some members will be disruptive, or even worse; they may actually try to take over. Every pastor must know how to stand strong and bring swift discipline to those who purposely try to upset the order of things. There must always be leadership and thusly, there will always be those who follow. As leaders, you must require submission, obedience and loyalty for carrying out the mission of the church. Pastors I do understand this, and I do recognize your very difficult task. I also salute and respect your awesome God appointed role as leaders - [those of you who *have been appointed by Him* that is].

However, this is not to what I am referring. What I am taking about is your purposeful stigmatization and writing off individuals because you are being controlled by the devil. Let me make it perfectly plain. As I said, many who are now in positions of leadership are themselves in need of deliverance. But, because of insecurity, pride and plain old being dumb, these same leaders refuse to acknowledge what they are doing. And, they are dumb indeed, if they believe even for one moment, that they are capable of successfully thwarting God's plan. Do you not realize that God's chosen will accomplish His will, no matter how hard *anyone* tries to block them?

You openly talk about people from your pulpits. It matters not that The Lord has need of them. No, that's not good enough for you. Because *you* are not 'convinced' or because *you* do not see *them* as worthy candidates, *you* refuse to bestow upon them the "fatherly blessing" that you continue to criticize them for not having. Who are you anyway? Oh yes, it is all coming back to me now. You appear to be just like someone else, who also thought that he could exalt his knowledge and power above that of Almighty God.

As I recall, he and his wicked host were kicked out of heaven. Do you suppose that some of those destructive imps have found embodiment and are currently operating from behind our pulpits today? If this be you Mr. or Madam Clergy, then The Holy Ghost is indeed right now calling YOU out!

Dear pastors, it is my sincere prayer that you do not let these things be said of you. If you find yourself guilty of committing any of these heinous acts, I pray that as The Holy Spirit pricks your conscience, you will repent and then go, and wound no more! Some of you have become so callused that you will claim not to hear Him when He speaks. Need I remind you of Pharaoh and the 10 plagues? God has no problem getting your attention, no matter how hardened your heart may be.

To those of you who have been victims of neglect and bastardization, please know that you are not alone in your plight. It is for this reason, despite the possibility of 'wolf leadership' backlash, that I have taken the liberty to drive the steak exceedingly deep. I need you to understand, beyond a doubt, that you are not alone, for there are many who know your pain even now. As you read this book, you may even identify with some of the things told to me, and to others by well meaning Christians who 'thought' and who truly 'believed' that they were conveying the will of God. The craziness that goes on in a lot of churches is almost identical to the mind-altering dynamics of an abusive relationship.

It is very hard to be content or to be of service to The Kingdom when you are suffering from the pressures associated with abuse and/or neglect. The difference between our spouse and our leadership is that, we feel at liberty to tell our husbands or wives off. Sure we do. You know that we speak our minds and that we argue back at our spouse. However, we dare not disagree with our pastor or with anyone operating from a position of authority. For the most part though, I really am not talking about being argumentative at all. But we dare not even let our countenance *appear* to be in disagreement with *anything* that we have been told – even if we have been told wrong. We certainly cannot have the rest of the congregation thinking that we are not "really saved."

The truth of the matter is that, we really don't *want* to say anything negative about a man or a woman of God, even if he or she *is* wrong. So as usual, we do what we do best. We stuff *our* feelings and we suffer in silence – all alone. Certainly, you cannot share what you know with anyone else in the congregation. Many people who are *spiritually blind*, do not even realize that they are.

Surely, they are not able to identify if whether or not their pastor is a wolf. If you say anything to them because you are hurting, they tell you to, "Suck it up and pray harder." They will hardly ever acknowledge the possibility that *there could be something wrong.* For the most part, they cannot even see the problem. On the other hand, even if they do happen to know of wrong doings, they are not likely to engage in any extensive conversation with you about it. They don't want to hear what you have to say. They have been ordered or trained by leadership not to "feed into negativity." "When someone comes to you, talking about *your church and/or about your pastor,* do not listen", the congregation is admonished. In reality what the leader has done is, issued an edict which he/she has for the most part, managed to camouflage under the guise of, "Warning the Saints to stir clear of gossip."

Translation: Do not listen [to a wounded brother or sister], because you might just learn something. You may even stumble upon "the truth." Of course, they don't want you speaking to anyone, who may actually say something, which might [purposely or accidentally] expose something that the leadership is trying to keep hidden.

In no way am I even vaguely suggesting for anyone to become a gossip or a listener of trash. The Bible warns us about being busybodies. I hope that you are mature enough to discern for yourselves, that I am not advocating such nonsense. Still I feel compelled to make myself perfectly clear – particularly for the haters who will [try to] twist what I actually am saying.

Sometimes if we listen objectively to the story of another, something that the person has to say, may in fact, save our own lives. We may receive great insight or better understanding of a matter. We might just get our own questions answered about something, which heretofore, even we had been hard pressed to understand or to figure out. Even if some in the congregation *do know* that you are correct in your suspicions, still, they are not likely going to acknowledge it; neither will they admit to it. Why not?

In most cases, these same people are hopeful of gaining a position or of achieving some level of popularity with the pastor. Because of this, more often than not, they are not likely to confirm the truth, even if they do know [that you are right]. Hence, the wounded brother or sister feels trapped, and all alone. The hurting member seemingly has no one "in there" to whom he or she can turn. There appears to be no one who understands. The lone Saint (or group) will likely continue to experience feelings of isolation and bewilderment, until somebody helps them make sense of what has befallen them. Without some sort of resolution, he or she may find it difficult to function. If this sort of thing has ever happened to you, than dear reader, you know exactly what I mean.

Likely, it is not you who are at fault; and no, you are not crazy either. Abuse of any kind, will almost always leave its victims in a state of flux and/or confusion. It is not uncommon for someone to vacillate between 'normality' and a feeling of "the crazies." If you have ever walked in the shoes of an abuse victim, then you are no stranger to the accompanying mental anguish. For the most part, you will likely have to sift through events that seemingly make no sense at all.

You know exactly what you have seen and/or heard. You've felt every pang and have endured every hurt connected to your experience, but somehow they still managed to convince you, that YOU were the one who had the problem – they tell you that, "You're crazy."

"It must be you, after all everyone else simply adores the pastor" (or so it seems) – you think to yourself. You need to realize, that more often than not, it is not you who is in the wrong. I pray not only will you earnestly seek the truth, but that you will also learn to discern error.

I adjure you to seek the counsel of The Lord. Did not Isaiah tell us that one of Jesus' roles is that of a Counselor? The God that I serve is neither the God nor the author of confusion. The Lord wants to take you higher. He wishes to reveal even more facets of Himself to you. The Lord is more than capable of speaking to your heart – and He is also willing.

When He does speak, I pray that you will no longer fear what mere man can do to you, but rather that you will ***immediately*** begin to stand in faith, for *whatever The Good Shepherd has spoken. You are to do exactly as He says...*

No longer should you be afraid, and no longer should you take counsel from a wolf.

❧*When Dad Is Unavailable*❧

Anytime that a child grows up without a father, society will usually label such a one as being destined for failure. This does not however have to be the outcome as expected. Plenty children, who although have lacked a father's presence or godly influence, have not only grown into healthy adults, but have also gone on to make great contributions to their communities and even to the world at large. I must give credit though, to the myriad of single parents (male and female alike), who have stuck it out for the long haul. These brave men and women stayed planted and stuck it out in order to fulfill their parental obligations.

Rearing a child and managing a household, [particularly one where there are multiple children present] is a tiresome feat and an on-going responsibility. No child is ever at fault for having been born. I commend all [biological and step parents], who have consistently and bravely borne the battle, never running away but who instead carried out their responsibilities as caretakers – to them I say thanks. Today there seems to be an increasing influx of single parent homes. Children born to and reared by a single parent, quite often tend to view their circumstances, to be as normal as those who have both parents present. Single parenting *seems* to be a normalcy, only because it has become acceptable *in our eyes.* But, I know that God certainly did not ever *intend* for it to be this way.

When The Lord God formed the first family, it consisted of ONE MAN and ONE WOMAN, (one <u>created</u> as a male and the other <u>created</u> as a female; neither same sex, nor sex-changed individuals were in the garden. <u>AND, THEY WERE LEGALLY MARRIED!</u> The husband and wife eventually took on the role as parents. In the same home, together they shared the responsibility of child rearing. <u>This ladies and gentleman was God's original design for the family, and HE has not altered it.</u>

Adam and Eve were both parental guides to their children - Cain, Abel and Seth. This is a far cry from what we see today. When either parent is missing (regardless to the reason), children are forced into the painful position of filling in the blanks for themselves.

A mother cannot teach a child the exact same things that a father can. Neither can a father ever, totally take the place of a mother. For obvious reasons, single parenting has *never* been the best plan for humanity. There are bound to be questions that deserve answering. Unfortunately, when a parental guide displays inappropriate behavior, or abandons a child altogether, that child is then left to figure things out on its own, as best as he or she can. A troubled youngster will usually turn to peers, who for the most part often know little more than he or she does. So then, the search for answers will more times than not, lead to frustration. As a result, such a one may find him or herself engaging in deviant behavior. Some children may not even understand why they act out, or why it is that they display such wayward behavior or signs of emotional distress. We are each products of *both* our parents.

We have been ingrained with many of their thinking patterns and habits. Each of us is a mixture of both their good as well as their bad habits and traits, whether we like it or not, God help us! Sometimes we can be in a family with both parents present, and yet find ourselves in a state of dysfunction.   The presence of both parents is no guarantee that a child will grow up in a healthy, loving, accepting environment. More often than not, when *dad* is the missing parent, children seem to be at an even greater risk. Dad, who is supposed to be the family's backbone, is very often the one who abandons it. The door is then left wide open for the destruction of the children, and quite possibly for the dismantling of the entire family unit. Children are most vulnerable during their developmental years.

Kids who are products of dysfunctional homes, i.e. those filled with abuse, or those that have been split by divorce and/or abandonment, or one that has been plagued by drug addiction, alcohol usage or sexual immorality, will likely turn to outsiders for help, as they search for a sense of acceptance and belonging. In a word, they are looking for love. Sometimes their searching will only leave them even more empty and unfulfilled. I once heard a preacher on television say, "So as it is in the natural, so is it also in the spirit." This pastor was talking about how children ought to obey their parents. Who can argue with that statement? This is Scriptural, children *are supposed* to obey their parents; for this *is* the will of God.   However, as I listened intently to the preacher's message, I also began to ponder his words. It was during my pondering that The Holy Spirit started speaking to my heart about fatherhood.   As The Lord ministered to me, I revisited the relationships or lack thereof with my own father figures (biological, step and spiritual). Suddenly, I began to see things more clearly.

The preacher on the television had been correct when he said, "So as it is in the natural, so is it also in the spirit." If our natural lives are chaotic, messy and out of control, so then will our spiritual lives be in a state of disarray. If we were not at least willing to obey our own natural fathers, then what makes us believe that we can, or even that we would consent to being obedient to a spiritual father or even God our Heavenly Father, for that matter. We know that God has absolutely no problem 'making' us obey if He chooses to. We need not look far for examples of this.

The great Apostle Paul; was knocked clear off his beast as he journeyed on the Damascus Road. God had no problem persuading this, "Chosen vessel" to fulfill His will. In addition, how could we ever forget the "run away" prophet named Jonah? I have no doubt that after spending 3 days and 3 nights in the stinky belly of a "great fish", (The Bible does not say whale), that he could not wait to get himself to Nineveh and preach the word of The Lord. ***Therefore, we can agree that God, The Almighty, The Sovereign of the universe can 'make' us do whatever He wants, if He chooses to.***

For the most part, He however, grants us the freedom to choose. Sometimes we choose to be disobedient on purpose and then we must suffer the consequences of our own actions. There have been many instances wherein men, women, boys and girls have been viewed and/or accused of being stubborn, insubordinate, or belligerent, because they have refused to obey their natural parents. Some say that such a person is in possession of a renegade or "bastard spirit." Society, and now even the church tends to write off such individuals; they are usually chalked up as being un-teachable, uncooperative, and as those who are despisers of correction. I certainly do understand how this can happen; as some people appear to be out of control, no matter what they are told and no matter what they are asked to do. They are like this, even though, someone may be trying to point them, in the right direction. It is unfortunate, but they might just have to learn the hard way.

The occurrence of a tragic event may be the only thing that will bring them to their senses. These kind of people must be committed into the hands of The Father for the taming of their spirit and for the development of their character. I am not referring to situations like these, but I am talking about children and/or adults who act out or who exhibit emotional insecurities, largely due to the necessary ingredients, that they failed to receive during their upbringing. For them there was no tuck into bed, no kiss on the cheek – not even a bedtime story. Their parents simply were not around.

Although lots of people <u>have</u> children, they are not <u>willing</u> to be parents at all. For those of you mothers and fathers who *are* at home and who *have not* forsaken your calling to parenthood, I applaud you. Congratulations you are the best and "all that." I am not addressing you at this time. I am however, confronting those who have been blessed with a precious child, but who have instead, made the choice to abdicate responsibility. As a result, the child [or children] suffers the consequences.

It breaks my heart to know how many orphans there are in our world. I cannot even imagine, being given away to a stranger. Human babies have actually been discarded with the evening newspaper. This writer cannot even fathom the idea of placing a baby into a trashcan and leaving it for dead. Yet more than we know, this has been the literal and unfortunate reality for millions. I personally know people who have endured an almost identical set of circumstances. The conversations that I have had with men and women, who were not wanted by their parent(s), are too numerous to keep track of.

In some instances the parents are still alive, but because the now 'adult child' never knew one [or even both] of its parents, while growing up, there had never been the forming of a bond or the establishing of a relationship. Consequently, the now adult child refuses to have anything to do with him or her. Thus when questioned, such a one will say that his/her parents are dead. Because of the parents' refusal to partake in the child's life, [when he/she was younger] the adult child has now turned its back. It should not be difficult for anyone to understand, why a person in this situation is not likely to *want* a relationship with an estranged parent – particularly not after so many years have gone by. It is almost like reopening a wound after the healing scab has already been formed. Who wants to bleed again?

Have you any idea what it feels like, to exist for nearly a lifetime, having full knowledge of the fact, that you were never wanted, and constantly having to deal with the feelings that accompany this knowledge?

There is no guessing about the matter; and neither has there been a mistake. The person must live with the horrible truth of *knowing,* that his or her parents, actually gave him or her away, *on purpose.* While some were given over to *legal* means of adoption, others were simply tossed out the door with the rubbish, taken to a beach or dumped on a stranger's doorstep. Unless such a one manages to overcome feelings that stem from these tragic events, he or she will likely carry the painful memories for a long time – some even for life.

Always in the heart of the now adult child, lives the constant reminder that he or she indeed was *that baby* whom the community, or perhaps even the nation, once read about and referred to as, "Baby doe." Such a one must learn live with the stigma of abandonment. Like a cementing compound, this labeling appears to be a permanent fixture. *Now imagine yourself as that child.* Everyone including you, remembers you as the once famous infant that no one wanted. You made the headlines and the evening news. You are the discovered infant that had been left for dead, because your, mommy and/or daddy, threw you away. Nevertheless, even though you were thrown into the garbage, pushed out of a window or dropped at the curb like a trash pick up, the one thing that they never thought of, was the fact that you would survive. Your parent(s) never even for a moment considered the possibility that you would make it out alive.

Your caretakers thought that they and the world would be rid of you forever. However, what they did not know was that God had another plan. So as it is in the natural, so is it also in the spirit."

Because of divorce, death or other traumatic circumstances, children are sometimes forced to teach themselves. This of course can lead to a whole new set of problems. Children who grow up with missing elements and the lack of proper guidance must fight their way through an emotional wilderness. Sometimes they are fortunate enough to make it safely to adult-hood and sometimes they are not. I have discovered that many who *have* "made it" and who *are* actively seeking help to cope, do very often carry lingering residuals from their past. Even so, these brave men and woman have decided to face their fears and even their hurts head on. Many are hoping for closure so that they can get on with their lives. Although I speak to people of all ages, I find many who are well into their 40's, 50's and even 60's, that are yet broken due to their painful pasts.

Some people have purposely chosen to live out their lives in a state of denial. For *them,* I suppose refusing to acknowledge their reality hurts far less than facing the pain. A significant number in this category, refuse to make even the slightest effort to cope with what has transpired, even though, their past continues to rob them of quality of life. They instead choose to "make believe" that they are perfectly ok. Statistics have shown that individuals (minority males in particular) who go on to live lives steeped in thievery and debauchery are often linked to a tumultuous childhood. This is especially true, if dad happened to have been the missing element.

On the other hand, females are likely to turn to prostitution or to some other form of sexual misconduct. There exists any number of ungodly avenues, whereupon people can turn, as they attempt to escape their pain. Unless they actively seek help, they will likely remain scarred for life. It is no coincidence that many people with missing parental figures (especially fathers), have similar stories. A lot of people have grown up with at least one parent missing; sometimes both were gone. On occasions, I have spoken with someone who had the good fortunate of having both parents in the home – but not many, let me assure you. In the majority of situations, it was however, the dad, who had for whatever reason, decided to remove himself entirely from the picture. Dad simply decided to bail and in most cases, he has <u>never</u> returned. Some kids *did* have a dad in the home, but even they were not always better off. Many of their fathers proved to be lousy when it came to nurturing and being there emotionally. On the other hand, others were extremely overbearing and all too smothering.

Remember, while children are supposed to obey their parents, these same parents are also bound by Scripture, and are admonished not to exasperate their children or to provoke them to anger. Some parents constantly 'nit pick' children to death, as a result they are left with a child who absolutely resents them. Sadly, the majority to whom I have spoken, *whose fathers were present,* have had dads who abused substances like alcohol and/or drugs, or they had been physically or emotionally abusive – oftentimes both. Some parental figure(s) ruled with an iron hand and proved extremely overbearing and authoritative. They ruled the home in such a manner, that the children were more *afraid* [of them] than anything else.

Sometimes the exact opposite proved to be the case, as some fathers were so 'wimpy' that the child could scarcely muster up *any* respect for him at all. They were not very good [or strong] examples of what a father (or a man in general) should be. In such instances, the boy child is/was often forced into assuming the role as, "Man of the house." When dad refuses to take *his* rightful place, then somebody has to take over. Still other children have had to endure the [*painful*] *pleasure,* of having a father in the home.

Unfortunately, dad became *a little too loving*, if you know what I mean. Certainly, he may have been a great provider, and not at all a wimp but still, he did not know his place. For you see sometimes in the middle of the night, dear old dad would make his way into the bedroom of his sleeping youngster. As the child lay silently asleep, he or she suddenly [sometimes violently] would be rudely awakened. Innocent images of sugarplums dancing in the child's head; were often interrupted by the shadowy figures of a father's (or a mother's) lurking silhouette. And then, the vicious attack or intrusive invasion would commence.

Not only would dirty, perverted father penetrate the child's body, but this wretched excuse of a parent would also bribe the child. In some instances, he (or she) would even threaten the child, swearing him or her to secrecy. Because of their innocent nature, [younger] children are often gullible, and can for the most part, be easily persuaded or frightened into submission. It would not be difficult for a conniving adult to obtain a child's secrecy or even his or her cooperation as he or she is forced or tricked into engaging in sexual [or other perverted] activity. Even after a child has been violated, he or she may still trust its parental figure and though confused, may yet remain completely loyal. The molesting parent will sometimes lavish the child with gifts, and with "special promises" in return for the child's silence. This the pedophile says, is to be, "Their own little secrete."

The parent (or any other person) committing these egregious acts will sometimes actually manage to convince him or herself that, "The child had been asking for it all along" and that "He or she got what it deserved." This line of thinking, allows the perpetrator to feel a sense of justification, while the poor victim, on the other hand, is left to suffer all alone. Mommy or daddy never settled for a one-time act of the egregious and the abominable. Oh no, as if that weren't criminal enough, father or mommy dear decided to keep up the disgusting brutish attacks and would accost the child at will. In many households, rape, sodomy and the like would go on for years, randomly and seemingly without end - Lord God! Years of unwelcome touching, groping and penetration not only pierced deeply enough to damage the child *physically*, but often, the same had led to emotional devastation as well. The silencing of the child/children would create within each victim a hell from which there seemed to be no escape.

After all, whom *could* the child tell? If the child were to tell, would anyone even believe him or her? I mean after all (the child reasons silently), "I would be telling on my own father – he's still my daddy." "My father is supposed to set an example for *me* – isn't he?" "He is an adult, and the leader of the family." "My father is a shining pillar of the community." "He is a pastor; to whom could I go?" "He is my covering and my provider." "He wouldn't do this to me!" "Not to me, not to his baby."   "Not to his little boy." "Not to his princess; I'm daddy's little girl." "Why did you rape me mom?" "No! *My* mother wouldn't do such a thing - would she?" "My mommy wouldn't take me to the crack house with a jar of Vaseline." "She wouldn't let those men do mean and nasty things to me – *would she???*"   "Who would ever believe me if I told?" "I'm only a child and my mom, is a great ambassador for The Lord?" "Oh I know what's happening, it must be my overactive imagination telling me things; at least that's what my daddy told me last night when he got into my bed again; yeah that's got to be it."

"Surely I've misunderstood my dad's actions - right?" "Dads are supposed to love us, and not hurt us kids." "One thing I can't figure out though." "If it is my imagination like mom and dad say, then why am I in so much pain?" "Why am I bleeding and hurting *down there?*" "Imaginations are not supposed to bleed." "Am I making this whole thing up?" "Maybe I'm going crazy; surely that must be it."

"Daddy's right, I watch entirely too much television, and now it is driving me crazy." "How could I have even thought about doubting my own father?" "Boy am I glad that's all cleared up. I am the one who has the problem, not my mommy, and certainly not my famous daddy.

This writer has listened to people, who have poured out their hearts, as they have dared to express their nightmarish ordeals. Not only did they speak of the vile acts of affection from their *biological [and step] fathers,* (or mothers) but also many spoke of the violent intrusions inflicted by their *so-called, "Spiritual fathers."*

Men and women who wear white collars and long robes are not guiltless of seducing members of their congregations and even those of their very own households. This they do spiritually and yes, in many cases, even physically. Millions of clerics have taken advantage of the weak and unsuspecting. These pastors are a far cry from being innocent, as they literally prostitute the Saints. Not so long ago, only sinners would have been accused of such horrid atrocities. It is unfortunate, that these crimes have not only trickled, but have literally bulldozed their way into our assemblies.

Some of you may have your own stories to tell or even to write about. You are probably not a stranger to somebody's horrific act of physical or spiritual rape. Perhaps you are aware of something that has remained hidden and locked away behind the secret chambers of perverted quarters. If you yourself have never been a victim, you may at least know of someone who has been. For even at this very moment one could be sitting right next to you. Someone in your very own home or congregation could be under attack, even as you read this book.

Just as some parents have abandoned their biological children, many pastors have also abandoned their spiritual sons and daughters. They have negated their original call to fatherhood and have instead opted for the perverted. Not only have they raped the masses, but they have also turned many from the faith. This ladies and gentleman will happen when dad is unavailable.

It happens when the original design for natural and/or spiritual parenthood is altered. These things also happen when our parental figures choose to become entangled with sin, perversion and gross darkness. It manifests when our parents and leaders give themselves over to the influence of evil and negligence. Some may have started out with intentions of only 'dabbling' in the perverted - still unacceptable. Nevertheless, because of their 'dabbling', they were instead [literally] overtaken by it. Many were too weak to withstand the draw of the enemy's enticements and their minds became altogether seared. Because so many are 'unclean', they are no match for satan's powers.

A father's (or mother's) presence in the home does not automatically denote availability. Dads, your children do not need you to be available in their beds! They don't need you scarring them for life, by taking advantage of their trust and of their innocence. They don't need you raping them! They do not need you making whores, rejects, homosexuals, addicts and derelicts out of them because of your own sick a*s perversions!

They don't need you prostituting, and pimping them. They do not need you to strip them of their innocence, and self worth. After you have raped the very life out of them, depriving them of their childhood and of their innocence, you then have the audacity to turn your back, leaving them "lost and turned out." Because of this, many childhood victims have come into adulthood as flawed and sometimes as extremely violent individuals.

They have been neglected, raped, molested, and sodomized, physically, emotionally, financially AND spiritually. People who have been violated [in any form], are often left to cope with the pain of it all, as their abusers on the other hand, live life as though they have done absolutely nothing wrong. So as it is in the natural, so is it also in the spirit.

Prostitution, rape, rejection and abandonment are thriving in many congregations right now. The church has become a breeding ground for sex, lies, cover-ups and gluttony. Enter in the fad of "Spiritual character assassination." This appears to be the latest trend amongst the 'redeemed', as they often accuse the victims instead of confronting the real culprits. Some of you will never know just how deeply the wounds of a victim can run. Neither are you able to show empathy for people who have found themselves derailed, due to the sinful actions of another. Critics cannot even begin to imagine the tears that many including myself, have shed in the midnight hour, as our soul's calling and the bitter chiding of church dogma have violently collided.

Reader, this is something to which you could never bear witness, unless you have had a soul's cry of your own, one in which you and God alone could understand. The complexities of the situation are far too intricate to comprehend without having firsthand knowledge. Like other victims I too have experienced feelings of failure, suicidal thoughts, self-loathing as well as having a near hatred for [some] people because of the gaping wound that once existed within the parameters of my own soul. Can you even imagine having lived for nearly 40 years before realizing the value of your own life? Does anyone know what it is like, never fitting in and all the while always wanting to? Have you any idea what it is like to constantly take 'crap' from those who you could literally run circles around, but because they occupy a *'position'*, you are instead forced to hold your peace and to stifle your creativity?

Not all self-loathing is brought on by a person's *own* bout with low self-esteem. *People don't simply _choose_ to be that way.* They don't just decide to commit murder or suicide. They don't nonchalantly, one day _make the choice_ to go insane! People don't all of a sudden, choose to not give a damn! More often than not, there are always warning signs before any person, throws in the towel. Rarely do individuals ever, "out of the blue", make the decision to no longer care. Oh no! Many, who do not wish to partake in the events of life, have at one time earnestly sought involvement, as they longed to fit in, but were repeatedly scorned and negatively received – as a result, they no longer even try. It is bad enough when a person carries an inferiority complex, originating from the home front or from the world's system, but when a person is victimized in a place that is *supposed* to be a representation of God's house, it may prove to be the final straw.

People who are violent or confrontational have often had negative experiences throughout their entire lifetime; seldom do people ever "suddenly" go off the deep end. They have been screaming for help all along, but nobody has been listening.

It has been my own experience, to suffer some of the greatest wounds at the hand of fellow Christians. You know the ones who claim to be *'saved.'* You know – the supposedly 'redeemed' crowd. A lot of them have been more of a pain than they have anything else. I mean it is bad enough that we *already have satan and his crew to contend with*, while living in a world system that despises us because we love Jesus, and at the same time being sniped at by people [both sinners and saints alike] who are either jealous of us, don't like us or who don't understand us so they have decided to hate us [usually because their friends hate us]. Let us not forget those who have been rejected by their own biological families, as if that weren't bad enough. But my goodness must we be at enmity when we come to church also??

I am Black; I am a woman; I am a *"female preacher"* of The Gospel of Jesus Christ (A Christian) and until recently, also a single mother. In today's society each of these things are usually frowned upon or viewed with some sort of negativity, hostility or prejudice. Having to contend with all of this, must I now *have to fight* my fellow brethren also? I find it quite discouraging when I am forced to engage in warfare with those of like faith. Seemingly, I must love them, fight them, pray for them, and beware of them, all at the same time, *while still* maintaining enough strength to do battle with the enemy. Whew! What a difficult and exhausting task that can be! Certainly many of you can relate to what I am saying. Though the details of our circumstances will vary, the dynamics and the feelings associated with our pain will likely be identical.

In the natural, there exists a nation of orphans, as well as those who are regarded as illegitimate or as inferior (bastards), because fathers have abdicated their responsibilities. So as it is in the natural, so is it also in the spirit. The church is no different from the world, when it comes to cranking out its share of the orphan and bastard population. Oh sure in the church we have spiritual leaders and pastors, but where are the TRUE FATHERS? I will tell you where they are. They are either missing in action or have become perverted. At one time, I actually longed for a "spiritual father" or mother.

I wanted nothing from him or her except to be nurtured and instructed in the things of The Lord. My objective had not been to glory seek; neither was I desirous of the pulpit; I wished *only to be included* as a daughter. I did not care if I ever preached in my pastor's church, because I knew that God would open any door that He has ordained for me to walk through. God's pulpit is not limited to the four walls of any particular building. I am not ashamed to inform you that what had been missing in the life of this writer, was the "spiritual parent" (pastor) that everyone continued to bash the masses for not having. The only thing that I wanted was for someone to put their arms around me and say, "Daughter, I will vouch for you." "I don't want to have sex with you, neither do I want your money, nor do I intend to keep you stuck and under my feet."

Was that too much to ask for? I wanted someone who would not try to hold me back from doing that which The Lord required of me, but rather a mentor who could and who would show me how to get there. And no! It does not take 20 years to get there either (unless <u>God</u> has you waiting for some reason). At one point, I truly desired a mentor, a leader and a "spiritual dad." I longed for someone who would sit down with me and show me how to get from point A to point B in ministry. I had hopped for someone to pray with me, that I might indeed, "Grow in the grace and in the knowledge of our Lord and Saviour Jesus Christ (II Peter 3:18).

While I still desire *nurturing relationships,* my expectations are now quite different. No longer am I willing to simply accept someone else's opinion of me over my own. Neither will I give credence to any person's opinion or plan for my life unless what they have to say, lines up with what I know God has already spoken.   Never again will I follow anybody's skewed advice, including that which comes from a pastor, who puts me at risk of hurting myself, by not following God's plan. I refuse to grant anyone that much access into my head or heart. I must guard with my life that which The Lord gives to me.

If someone's counsel and advice comes from their own head, and not from the wisdom of God, I back away. If they are speaking from the flesh and not by The Spirit, again I turn a deaf ear. Trust me when I tell you, I do know the difference, and I don't want to hear it! If you are taking pot shots and stabs at people from the pulpits (as do so many preachers), it becomes quite difficult to receive your counsel. Because The Lord is retraining and re-sharpening my hearing, I am no longer willing to listen to you. Perhaps some would consider me as "damaged goods." To a large degree, they would be correct. I once possessed many goods, but I allowed other people to damage them. I found myself damaged at both the spiritual and emotional levels.   I take responsibility; I allowed other people's opinions to damage me.

These days, I no longer accept human opinions of who I am. There are no more applications for mortal approval or for the position of "Spiritual Dad" being handed out by me. Sorry folks, but my Heavenly Father has permanently filled that vacancy.

If on occasion I find myself slipping, by feeling as though, I simply *have* to have this father of the flesh, I quickly remind myself of what I have already been through. I dare not forget that it was my submission to a "spiritual father", which was largely responsible for emotionally and spiritually paralyzing me in the first place.   This time, I am content to dwell under the wings of The Most High until He leads me to the right person and to the right church. God is not going to place me under the care of some scoundrel or "pimp pastor" who is merely pretending to be a shepherd – for He loves me entirely too much to do that. If

God never sends me to a natural man for spiritual mentorship, I am enjoying the fact that He Himself has taken an interest in teaching me. In no way am I outright refusing to be under pastoral supervision, I am not saying that at all. But in terms of a "father figure", well… let's just say that it will be a cold day in you know where, before I seek out another one, unless God speaks to me about the matter.

I use to watch people on television who said they had been (or currently were) privileged to have a spiritual parent, and how they reverenced him or her. I listened, intently as they had nothing but good things to say about their mentors. I often watched in awe as I admired the many high profile evangelists, bishops, prophets and the like. Joyfully I watched as they promoted their 'spiritual sons and daughters' up the ranks. What about you beloved? I know you saw the broadcasts too. Others would be promoted, while the rest of us continued to look on in hope, that it would one day be our turn. Well, for the great majority of *us* that 'one-day' has not come yet – and for many, I am sad to report that it never will.

The mentors would gleefully announce to the world his or her allegiance and support of the newcomer. There I sat as I watched with longing anticipation of one day receiving the same thing. I wished that someone famous [or even not so famous], would had selected me to be his or her pupil. Would to God that *someone would have sincerely* reached out to me. Their popularity or lack thereof would not have mattered, so long as they had genuine concern for me. After a long time, I found myself becoming jealous because I longed to be nurtured too. I needed validation; I wanted to be loved, and I wanted the blessing of my pastor, so that I could be free to do the works of The Lord too! I was pleased to cooperate and would have done things the way *they* said I *had* to. I needed someone to hone into, and help cultivate the prophetic gift, because spiritual leadership capabilities had began awakening in the realm of my soul.

How I *use* to long, passionately, for this. I wanted a mentor so badly, that I would have done just about anything he or she required of me – I said "almost" anything. I wanted what I use to see in my late pastor. He had been like a father figure and I had a very good relationship with both he and his lovely wife. Unfortunately, when he died, the leadership ran amuck and the church eventually split. I have not been fortunate enough to find a pastor like him. He was my Shepherd, and a very prominent leader who I could easily view as a "spiritual father figure." He was someone whom I could respect.

No matter how well known he might have been; my late pastor Reverend J.C. Crawford was neither too big nor too busy to be concerned about those who needed him. He took time to 'hear' the concerns of the people in our congregation, AND – he worked outside of the church. He had a job – just like Paul! He and his wife both seemed to take an interest in me, and I actually *felt* loved; at the very least, I felt as though I mattered, to someone. They saw *something* in me, that at the time, I was not sure existed.

Since the death of this great man, it has been extremely difficult for me to find a pastor of this magnitude, who is willing to father me, and not wound me. Father me, and not swindle me. Father me and not try to have sex with me! He was the type of pastor that I could respect as a Shepherd and as a father figure – because he cared! I found none (at that time) to be genuinely concerned about me. I met no one who had been truly willing to guide me into the 'deeper' things of The Lord, or to sit down long enough to hear my questions and concerns, without having some ulterior motive.

I am certain that Paul would also say the same thing to us today that he said to the church of Corinth so many years ago. He was about to send Timothy, who was faithful to The Gospel of Jesus Christ, and one to whom Paul had become a mentor or spiritual father. He was sending him to the Church of Corinth. Paul had a handle on *that,* which may have served as the source of their many problems. Lord knows that the Corinthian church, was not without its share of issues. Paul said, "For though ye have ten thousand instructors in Christ, yet have ye not many fathers." Never has a truer statement been uttered (in Christendom). Where are the pastors who truly care about people? A person does not have to look far in order to see and feel the very noticeable deficit of true shepherds and/or fathers.

Oh sure, THEY TALK a good game, but where are they when WE need them? The REAL fathers seem to be missing in action.

Yeah, we see them in the pulpits and on television, but besides making guest appearances for popularity's sake; just where else are these spiritual parents that everyone continues to rave about? Remember back in the day, when we were younger? Just as there were, "Church Mothers", we also had men of God who were *real* fathers. Of course, they had their flaws; but many of them also had warmth and a genuineness of character, which actually made people *want* to overlook their shortcomings.

My late pastor Rev. J.C. Crawford was not a perfect man, after all, who on earth can claim to be? However, during my 16 years under his tutelage, I do not recall anyone in the church ever having anything [really] negative to say about him. Our church had its issues too – but again, as our shepherd, we knew that he loved us – ALL OF US! We had a large congregation and the church was well known throughout. As I stated, pastor had his flaws, (because he was human), but at least he was sincere when it came to the preaching of THE GOSPEL, and he was faithful to the keeping of The Master's flock. Being a good shepherd and father, he actually took the time to care. I remember having a healthy fear and loving spiritual reverence for both he and his wife.

Prior to serving under Rev. Crawford, I had been a member at my parents' church, Little Friendship Baptist Church of Newark, New Jersey. Reverend Martin LeGree served briefly as my pastor. Unfortunately, Reverend LeGree came aboard during a time of transition. At the time of his arrival many of the young adults, (ages 16-19), myself included, were just beginning to test their own "spiritual wings." Most of us were branching out. With our parent's blessing, we were venturing out to join churches of our own choosing (or wherever God seemed to be leading). You know how it was back then. Parents brought their children to church with *them,* so that is where the children stayed until they were old enough to make their own decisions. Although that entire crowd has since grown up and are living in different states or have become members of other churches, many do go back to visit.

Pastor LeGree *always* seems glad to see us, and he never ever hesitates to acknowledge our presence. Even though we have long since left his shepherding, we are welcome at any time, – what a blessing. To this day some 27 years later, I am still welcomed with open arms. Here you have leader who is actually concerned about the people he shepherds. Although his church is small, [in comparison to many] it is filled with warmth and with the type of genuine concern that is rarely felt when visiting many of its larger counterparts. After leaving Little Friendship Baptist Church (at age 16), I established my roots in the Beulah Baptist Church under the leadership of the, "Late Great Reverend J.C. Crawford", as he is affectionately remembered.

It was there, under the direction and tutelage of he and his lovely wife and wonderful "First Lady" Sis. Doris Crawford that I remained for more than a decade. Boy could Sister Crawford pray. I have fond memories of her praising The Lord with all of her might. She praised Him even more, whenever an anointed individual happened to belt out her favorite song – "He Touched Me." That song seemed to catapult her into an even 'higher' dimension. As I grew older, I too began to understand why *this particular song,* had always moved her so. I have since come to appreciate and to know *for myself,* the treasure she endeared. Brothers and sisters, you have not *really* been touched, until you have been touched, by the Hand of God – Halleluiah!

Sister Doris Crawford, now known as "Mother Crawford", is a woman in Zion par excellence; she is a woman and "First Lady" whom I shall never forget. To this day, she embraces me with warmth and compassion – as though I were her very own biological daughter. I love Mother Doris Crawford and I shall never forget the kindness that she has ALWAYS shown me.

As a youngster, I held membership at the Washington Temple Church of God In Christ, where the distinguished late Bishop F.D. Washington and his wife Songstress Ernestine Washington were the leaders. Although only a child, I can *still* remember the times spent in *that* church as I attended with my grandmother. I remember my first baptism ceremony. (I was later baptized [again] by Reverend Crawford at my request). I even remember singing in the choir with my little gold blouse and my navy blue skirt (smile). Compared to some of the mess that we have going on in our churches today, Saints let me assure you that, we have much to weep about. Sure, we have more dramatics to entertain us, and more knowledge than ever to impress people with, but where are the fathers who possess real Holy Ghost, yoke destroying, demon demolishing, [without all of the gimmicks], power of God?

These men, of whom I spoke, seem to have existed in an era (not that long ago), when being a Pastor really meant something. The position of a pastor was well respected, because the cleric walked worthy of his/her calling – or at the very least, the majority of them underlined actually tried to. While we have dynamic speakers, pastors, leaders, comedians and authors, there certainly remains a deficit of true fathers. Seemingly, we are now bombarded with more taskmasters, ringmasters and predators than ever before! I have heard many SAY that *they* are fathers and mothers. I am certain that *they* have managed to convince themselves of that. But, have you ever tried to get an appointment with some of these so-called fathers? Have you dear reader ever sat down and *really* talked with some of the pastors who *think of themselves* as parental guides? Have you ever tried reaching out to them in sincerity? What a freaking joke!

While "the pastorate" is an honorable part of God's five-fold ministry, "the office" does not automatically (and neither does it necessarily) qualify one as "a spiritual father." Too many are claiming to be something that they absolutely are not, as they give themselves such a title.

A huge percentage of them are so caught up in financial gain and popularity; that they could not possibly have time to father *anyone*. So as it is in the natural, so is it also in the spirit. How many times can you recall hearing the bad news of a family splitting up because one (or perhaps even both) parents opted for the pursuit of financial gain instead of childrearing? Men and women have left families, marriages and children, in order to seek material wealth. Scores of leaders have no problem projecting stimulating words from the pulpit, which keep us dazzled and coming back for more. We may even witness them operate in various gifts but does that mean, that they can or that they even should be trusted or looked upon as 'fathers'? Are they planning to stick around for the long haul, as a real father ought to or what?

Dad, where are you? Where are the pastors who really care about people as individuals? Where are the shepherds who love people and who care about them, without first, having to examine their financial records and/or real-estate portfolios? These fake fathers continue to hold people hostage by telling them that they 'must' have a spiritual father or covering; yet THEY are often unavailable. Real fathers with Holy Ghost conviction, (and guts) can you please identify yourselves because we need you? Can you please come out of hiding long enough to be whom and what you say you are? Is this too much to ask of you? Can you take a break from your albums, CD's, video tapings and photo shoots long enough to see that many are falling by the wayside, and that you are no where to be found? Why are you abandoning us?

I heard a prophetess on television one night, as she announced to the world the coming out (so to speak) of her spiritual daughter. I found myself deeply moved as she told all who tuned in, that this was someone whom she had nurtured. She was announcing on national television, that her 'daughter' had at that very moment, moved from the office of an Evangelist to that of Prophetess. She then took what appeared to be a white "Tails" (A Jewish prayer shawl also spelled "Tallit") that she herself had once worn and proceeded to drape it around her "spiritual daughter's" shoulder. This was symbolic of her having, "Passed the mantle."

The prophetess, not only acknowledged the young woman, but also she prayed for her success. She announced to the entire world that this was her daughter "in ministry." She then asked that the newcomer be accepted throughout the ranks and that doors would be graciously opened for her daughter, just as they had been for her.

As I thought about the younger woman being vouched for by this famous woman of God, who also happens to be someone that I truly, admire; I found myself literally moved to tears. The ceremony was beautiful. In fact, the entire program that evening was touching. The theme had to do with, "Mentoring mothers of the faith." While I praised God for and with the individual who had just been "birthed out" (as they put it), still I could not help but feel a slight bit jealous.

It was not that I felt envy or jealousy because of the person's advancement in ministry, gosh no! I applaud that and I praise God for her. I am happy for anybody who can advance, live his or her dreams or make a difference in this world. Nevertheless, my feelings stemmed from the fact that I had been left out – as my pastor had (just very recently) rejected me; and so for a moment I felt saddened and slightly envious.

It had been my heart's desire that my own pastor would have taken the same such interest in *my* spiritual well-being, aptitude and development thereof. Like I have already mentioned, at that time, I too desired nurturing and I am not ashamed nor am I too proud to confess this truth. There was (or so I thought), a piece that was missing in my life and I wanted it. My heart desired my pastor's blessing. At that time, I would have given just about anything for someone of her caliber to have presented me to the world as one of her own. I heard this same prophetess discussing something one evening, with another prophet. They were having a conversation [yet again] about this "birthing out process" and being 'fathered', in ministry as well as in the natural. At length, they discussed the role of a father and what that role consists of.

The thing about fatherhood, as one of them put it, is that, "Being a father (or mother) requires much." "Fatherhood costs something." They were right indeed. Being a parent in any capacity requires much sacrifice. Parenthood is definitely not for the selfish! It requires so much, that not everyone who *claims* to be one is even capable of paying such a high, but very necessary price. Parenting involves constant impartation and commitment. It takes energy, time, and sometimes much heartache to be a good parent.

Giving birth in the natural can sometimes bring about unexpected complications. The process of birthing a child, can bring about extreme pain and discomfort, elevation in blood pressure and in some cases, childbirth can even result in death. Just getting a child here can result in fatality for mother, child or both! However, should both survive, the position of parent will entail a lifetime of commitment and sacrifice. The challenges will be even more demanding should a parent endeavor to raise 'godly' offspring in this less than godly world.

Parenting of any kind can be an awesome and rewarding experience, albeit the job will still be tedious. It is an *ongoing* responsibility, which may at times prove extremely overwhelming. Commitment does not end for a custodial parent. His or her job is not at all like the absentee or non-custodial parental guide, who can on a whim decide to make an appearance a few times out of the year - if he or she bothers to show up at all. Custodial parents cannot just pick them up, drop them off and go on living life as usual. I have a daughter and I know first hand how difficult parental assignment can be – particularly as a single parent. A parent who has been blessed with a physically or emotionally challenged child or one that has "special needs" will have it even harder. My daughter, who was diagnosed with Attention Deficit Hyperactivity Disorder, when she was younger, use to present me with quite a challenge.

Although her case was not an extremely severe one, still there were times in which coping with it had become extremely difficult, not to mention terribly exasperating. It was quite difficult keeping up with her, while also trying to carve out some form of life for myself. She is doing so much better now – Thank You Jesus!

In the earlier days, I can recall thinking to myself – "If God chooses to heal or to deliver my child, I'll take it - boy will I take the healing for my overly active, excessively talkative, EXHAUSTINGLY ENERGETIC (but very beautiful, loving and extremely talented child that has been loaned to me [smile]) - Thank you God Amen!" The Lord may not always choose to heal. Contrary to popular belief, I am so sad to announce it, but it just isn't true. Not everyone will receive healing in *this lifetime.* I don't care who tells you something different. If it were true, then no one would ever taste physical death on this side. We would continuously be healed, and healed and then re-healed some more.

Not all underline physical healing shall manifest itself *on this side.* God *does* perform miraculous healings if it pleases Him to do so. I have witnessed this in my own family. However, at the same time, I have also borne witness as The Almighty instead chose to take a loved-one or a friend home, and did so regardless, to how earnestly people prayed, fasted or laid hands.

We can consult our Bibles to settle the debate as to whether or not EVEREONE GETS HEALED ALL OF THE TIME. We need only revisit the thorn of the Apostle Paul. Whatever the exact nature of his buffeting thorn, he was not delivered of it. God may not always grant a physical healing, but His grace will always remain sufficient to help us cope with our most piercing ailments.

Even the account of King Hezekiah, shows us something about healing. Even though The Lord did lengthen his days by adding, an additional 15 years to his life, yet at the end of that term, the King still died. I have accepted the fact that my lovely, child whom I adore does sometimes present great challenges in my life. However, I have also come to realize that The Lord would not have blessed me with her, if He did not already know that He and I were capable of handling her - together. Just as some children in the natural, have special needs, likewise so do a lot of spiritual sons and daughters.

People often show up in our congregations, after having been torn, bruised, battered, and beaten up. While I cannot imagine that being a spiritual leader is an easy task, still God has given pastors precious sons and daughters to shepherd.

If He did not think they could handle the responsibility, then certainly The Holy Spirit would not have led them their way. God would never have trusted him or her with such an awesome task. So as it is in the natural so is it also in the spirit. A child with special needs will require a great deal of attention, which can be extremely difficult for anyone to handle. Because of this, many parents simply decide to abdicate responsibility, and instead turn deaf ear to the cry of their children. This is not the child's fault. So why are the children always having to shoulder the blame?

NEVER IS IT THE FAULT OF ANY CHILD WHEN DAD (OR MOM) DECIDES TO JUMP SHIP AND ABANDON HIM OR HER. NEITHER IS IT THE CHILD'S FAULT FOR BEING BORN TO A FATHER WHO REFUSES TO CLAIM HIM OR HER AS HIS OWN! IT IS NOT THE CHILDREN'S FAULT THAT THEY ARE NOT WANTED – THEY NEVER ASKED TO COME HERE! WHY THEN MUST THE CHILD BE THE ONE FORCED TO WEAR A LABEL – LIKE BASTARD OR ILLEGITIMATE? DO YOU HEAR ME ADULT CHILD OF GOD? IT IS NOT NOW, NOR HAS IT EVER BEEN YOUR FAULT!

Hardly ever is there a mention of what *they* do to the children or to the sheep. Just as pastors expect us to work together and to grow with them, God requires that our leadership work together and grow with us. Every child of God should be evolving. Those of us who have desired, but have never had a mentor can easily find ourselves becoming jealous and envious or even critical towards those who do. However, when our feelings are examined more thoroughly, and if we are totally honest with ourselves, we would have to admit that it isn't even that we are envious or jealous, but rather we are trying to process our hurts and the pain, which grips us so tightly. We may not always know how to express it, nor are we always able to admit it, but we are hurting. We don't want to appear as being too needy or too vulnerable, (because vulnerability often opens the door for people to wound us further).

The masses have suffered tremendously because nobody has ever deemed them as being worthy. Herein is the core of our wounding. Being looked upon and thought of as someone who is "less *than*", had become the source of my own emotional pain.   Because of the way in which my pain made me feel and sometimes act, people probably chalked me up as being angry, corky, antisocial, odd, weird or whatever. Many people have a call on their lives, but have no one to vouch for them. For us there has been no coming out party. Never had anyone thought of us as candidates who were worthy or deserving of their time or of a surprise cotillion.   We have been cheated out of the opportunity to make our grand entrance into the ballroom.

There has been no one to announce our arrival into spiritual adulthood. Never have we been the honored guests or the recipients of the nurturing that we so desperately desired and longed for. Never had a banner been strewn across the room, bearing our names as the honorees. We have never been on the receiving end as the baton of "fatherly blessing" was being passed. Instead, year after year, we were forced to watch from the sidelines, as *they* admonished us to stay put and to keep quiet. We obeyed them as we struggled to hide our tears. We gave quite a performance as we clapped and cheered for all of the others.

And though our hearts broke into a million pieces, we dared not let on that we were in pain. We stuffed every hurt, every painful longing, and for a long time, we have felt incomplete. Because we were never afforded our right of passage, there has remained a breech deep within. For many of you, the wound continues to fester sore, even to this very day.

Never before had we realized the magnitude or level of depth to which we had been wounded. But, with so much talk lately about fatherhood and about "having to be birthed out", mentored and covered, we have now become even more [painfully] aware of our injury and of our lack. For the sleeping giant that we had <u>somehow</u> managed to put to rest, thanks to them, has now been fully resurrected.

Like many of you, I wish that I too had been afforded this opportunity, but alas, as I pen this book, I have yet to receive the human mentoring that I so once desired. There are many in The Body, who desire mentorship, yet there is no one to fulfill that role in their lives. As a result, they continue to be at a spiritual loss.   They have never been told that not having an earthly and/or spiritual mother or father does not make them any less valuable in the sight of God.

Because of the pain which once existed in my own heart, as well as the hurt endured by so many others, The Lord God made it quite clear to me that writing this book was to be my current assignment. Of course, the doubts came as He told me 'exactly' what I was to write about. As usual, I waited and I procrastinated, but God did not relent. At one point, I began to feel like, I can't write this book, for how could I disagree with those who I hold in such high regard. I recalled vividly, one evening as I listened intently to a well-known woman of God, who said something on Christian television that took me on a spiritual tailspin. (See "The Making of A Bastard). Anyway, this particular time, she and another well-respected Bishop were having a conversation. It was during this segment that they kept going on and on about people without a spiritual covering and about how those who had not been properly "birthed out", were considered bastards.

This had not been my first time hearing this same female (who I absolutely love in the spirit) say such a thing. Shortly after the first time that she said this on national television, I noticed that a few more people jumped on the bandwagon *and of course,* started saying the same thing.   As I again contemplated the possibility of the controversy ahead, once more I became fearful. I did not want to contradict someone who I admired. I personally have great respect for both parties to whom I am referring. For years, I have been extremely blessed by both their ministries. It is not my intention to cause further conflict in The Body; Lord knows satan already has that position on lock down.

Yet the problem remained, in that the very servants, who I so deeply admired, had become the primary source of my spiritual discontent because of what they continued to spew out. How then I wondered, could a nobody, (unknown to the world), dare to write in direct opposition of these two great servants? One day as I agonized over this, my (then fiancée – now husband), spoke to me and said, "Not everyone was born with a sliver spoon." "We would all like to have had mentors and people who cared enough about us to have nurtured us, but not everyone has the same story." I considered all of the horror stories that had been shared with me about leadership gone amuck. I also thought long and hard about *my own* devastating reality. Not everyone has had the privilege of being under a leader who actually cared enough to teach him or her *the right way* – if in fact the person was 'taught' at all.

We did not all have someone who chose to be committed to our growth and to our personal and/or spiritual development. Some of *them* did not even think that we were worth the effort. Had it not been for The Lord on our side, *many of us* would not have stood a chance – believe that! A lot of leaders, who *were* willing to father us, often anticipated some form of financial gain or sexual gratification, as re-payment for their 'spiritual' *deposits.* No matter how hard we may try to gain the approval and the blessing of our pastors, the reality of the matter is, sometimes we never will. They choose not to see us and they may never adopt us, simply because they do not want to be bothered. But why were we ever trying so hard to gain *their approval* in the first place? We were trying because that is what *THEY* told us we needed in order to carry out the works of The Lord. Because it had been drilled into our heads for so long, we came to believe, nearly every lie we had ever been told.

No matter how much we may desire a father or a mother, the cold facts are these – sometimes our parents just don't want us around. So as it is in the natural, AND sadly, dog-gone-it, so is it also in the spirit! <u>And somebody out there in the leadership pool, should have been telling this side of the story too!</u>

I wish that people would get their facts straight, <u>before</u> they begin the name-calling and <u>before</u> they begin their nationally televised rebuking of the masses. Before throwing out blanket statements, leaders of The Gospel need to first qualify them. They don't know who may be listening to them as they spew out what <u>THEY BELIEVE</u> to be the truth. A lot of people look up to those who appear on the airways. <u>The least that they can do is to make very sure that what they are saying is "SCRIPTUALLY CORRECT" and that what they are spouting off about is coming from the direct counsel and wisdom of God and not from their enthusiasm or from their own need to publicly assert themselves or look good.</u>

Finally, as I thought about what my fiancée said, God also reminded me as to how that one skewed statement has managed to serve as a deterrent and as a source of discouragement to many of HIS servants who were, *at that time being prepared by Him* in the wilderness. More than anything else, I REALLY thought about what The Lord told me during my procrastinating.

God simply said to me:

"If you don't write it, someone else will." (End communication).

After that word from Jehovah, how then could I not follow through? I did not want to disappoint God and I certainly did not want *Him* to be mad at *me.* Besides, I have been writing this book for most of life without even realizing it. Imagine, out of all the people in the world, that The King could have chose, He picked me. He told me that I am to be, "The voice of the bastard" [because they have no voice]. People speak out for, "Women's Rights", "Civil Rights", "Gay Rights", "The Right to Die" and "Rights for the Unborn." For every "Right" society can think of (even if the right is wrong) there stands ready someone who is wholeheartedly prepared to represent and/or to defend the population thereof.

The entire conversation [with God] came about one Saturday morning, as I literally poured my heart out into my tape recorder, after having been so wounded by my own leader. There I was preaching to my tape recorder and agonizing over why it was that people were so cruel. Why did they have to call people such despicable names? "Who will be their voice I inquired in earshot of my recorder?" "Who (out there) will represent The Lord's people who have no voice? "Who shall come to their defense?" "I need a spiritual father, because *they* say so."

"But who can I turn to that will represent those of us who have been misrepresented?" "To whom can the people go, as they seem to have no voice on the earth realm?" Father please tell me to whom I can go? I wanted to know, who was going to be *their* voice, because I needed to find and to speak in detail to such a person.

I needed that person's help in order to understand my own dilemma; I am the one who had need of something; but…

The Lord swiftly replied and said, **"You are!"** **(End communication).**

I gulped, my eyes simultaneously widening – Ohhhhhh nooooo, uh oh! *Who? Me??* "Lord I was just venting into my tape recorder." "Lord you know how we do; I was just talking to you (like I always do). *"Oh man, why did I ask?"* *Oh! – oh my goodness, not me!??*

I wasn't applying for the job or anything; rather I was hoping that He would point out and then send me to somebody who could help me! How can I help anybody? I'm the one who needed the help!

He said:

"You are to be the voice of the Bastard", [the left out, the scorned, the reject and the outcast]. *(End communication).*

Shocked, I gulped again. I immediately started shaking in my boots because I knew that God had spoken. I know *that voice,* oh god how I know it! Certainly, I had no trouble relating to the subject matter. I mean, who better to know the heartbeat of a reject than someone who walks in those same shoes? Surely, I had not planned to write *this type* of a book, another perhaps *but this???* *You've got to be kidding.* It wasn't as though I had ever planned to be a bastard or reject representative you know.

Lord?? "You are going to help me – right?" "What are you doing to me?" "Lord, I don't know how to tell these people about this." "What am I supposed to say anyway?"

How many of you know that it does absolutely no good to argue with God, because *He will always win?* Looking over my life, rejection seems to have been a close companion. Because I was a member of a church, I suppose that officially speaking, I already had this flesh and blood covering that everyone continued to yelp about.

YET I SUPPOSE SOME WOULD CONSIDER ME A BASTARD BECAUSE, I FULLY PLAN TO OBEY THE VOICE OF THE LORD WITH OR WITHOUT ANYBODY'S PERMISSION OR BLESSING.

I NO LONGER CONCERN MYSELF WITH WHAT PEOPLE SAY, OR WITH WHAT THEY THINK OF ME. THE FACT OF THE MATTER IS, I CAN NO LONGER AFFORD TO CARE. IF THIS MAKES ME A BASTARD BY THEIR STANDARDS, THEN I SAY, FINE WITH ME!

If this is the price that I must pay, in obedience to the command of The Lord; then I will faithfully bear the stigma of spiritual illegitimacy. Just as God gave me my precious daughter, He has also assigned *me* the responsibility of spreading the word to *"His babies"* who have been wounded. I am privileged to be on His mission, speaking hope and life into the hearts of those whom the world and the church have tossed aside. God still loves them and He yet loves me. If taking the backlash from those who may not understand is the price that I must pay at this point in time, then I say, be it unto me according to His will. I will not fail the bastardized or the outcast as long as God allows them to cross my path. More importantly, *I refuse to fail GOD even if that means disobeying EVERYONE ELSE.*

Like I once heard a well-respected theologian say, "If God tells you to do something, you must do what He says and you must do so in the manner that He instructs." "If God is doing the leading, He is responsible for the outcome." "God would never instruct us to do anything that does not line up with Scripture." "If He gives you a message, you had better bring it." "He further stated that even if we do make a mistake, but our heart and our motives are honorable, The Lord [he says] is able to take even our worse foul ups and turn them into something good for His glory." "God already knows *why* we are doing everything that we do."

The birth of this book has been ordained and blessed, not by an earthly mentor, but rather by my Heavenly Father. I had to write it. For me to do anything less would have been to disobey Him. Along with my disobedience, would have come the possible short-circuiting of my own blessing. I had to obey God, and I will NEVER apologize to anyone for that.

Many are "out there" who have never had a proper "birthing out", so now what? If we believe that we have heard from The Lord and thus begin to pursue our calling, we are thought of as bastards. While I do understand to a degree what some well-meaning clergy may have intended to communicate, because there really are people who are disagreeable and rebellious and these people love to take over and to stir up strife; but still, what they managed to do was, to inject uncertainty into the hearts of an entire host of end time servants. Many of the babes have literally gone into hiding and some, into deep hibernation.

*I need to stress that what they did say, was not entirely accurate.
It is not always our fault that we fall into the bastard category. I cannot
think of anybody in his or her right mind who would purposely "want" to
wear such a title.*

This derogatory label has been assigned in error to many, who frankly
did not ever deserve to wear it. Some people have been called 'bastard' by
leadership, for no apparent reason, other than for pursing the call of Jesus
Christ, The Chief Shepherd.

*I am sick and tired of people getting on television and behind the
pulpits, rebuking everybody without having full knowledge of individual
circumstances. I am sorry, but one word simply does not fit all!*

From the pulpits, they rave on and on about how they are fathers, and
about how much they love everybody. They admonish the people to come to
them because they truly care. As soon as an individual does speak to some of
these "pastor-fathers", he or she often encounters a shepherd who is not at all
like the person behind the Sunday morning pulpit face.

*I am not judging; neither am I declaring this true of every pastor or
leader. Fortunately or not, depending upon how you look at it, but if you
as a leader are now finding yourself to be offended as you read this book, it
may be because the shoe is fitting YOU just right. If that is the case,
perhaps it is because God is telling YOU TO WEAR THE DARN SHOE!*

I stand firmly upon my conviction and am willing to tell you to your face
the things that many in your churches and the traditional "Jesus clubs" will not. I
can boldly proclaim this, because "He whom The Son sets free is free indeed!"
And I for one intend to remain free. Understand, it isn't personal; but I made a
promise to God, that if He ever chose to use me, or if He ever scraped me up off
of the gutter's floor, that I would say whatever He tells me to. I have a vow to
God that I must pay. Many of The Lord's servants, who when sent to certain
congregations have been met with everything but kindness. All a person has to
do in many instances is to show up, never mind operating in a gift.

An individual does not even have to open his or her mouth, before he or
she has already been scanned by leadership, and is officially branded as the one
to ignore or to dislike. "This one shall never be promoted in *our church* they vow
amongst themselves. It is bad enough when other parishioners are spiteful,
hateful and envious, a person can often overlook them. But, it is quite a different
story, when it is *the pastor,* who is intimidated by a member's presence.

I cannot tell you how grateful I am for leaders like Bishop Jakes, and others, many of whom the world has not even heard of. These men and women are secure enough in themselves, as well as in their own God given assignment(s) that they do not have to crush the life and spirit out of everyone else, neither are they in competition with anyone. Many people have benefited from the guidance of this mighty weapon of God whom we call Bishop T.D. Jakes. (Like him or not, agree with him or not [I do not necessarily agree with EVERY THING that people do just because I *admire them*] but the fact of the matter is, he does not seem at all intimidated by those serving under him or by the many he has helped). The *average Christian* unfortunately, is not always privileged to find him or herself under the tutelage of a shepherd, who is secure enough, to allow and/or encourage him or her to be what (and all) that God has called him/her to be.

If a pastor even *suspects,* that what God has for the other individual, could in fact, one day surpass his (or her) own ministry, (whether or not the *suspicion* is accurate), more often than not, the trainee will be hated and/or shunned, (many times without the individual ever knowing why he or she is being treated in such a manner). Insecure pastors are never able to allow God, to simply be God, in the life of anointed people. It is with deep regret that I inform/remind you, that hostility and unnecessary friction are the order of the day, when serving under hostile, jealous or insecure leadership. The "Saul mentality" is still very much alive and functioning today!

Should the fact that our pastors do not like us force us now to bury *our own* heads in the sand? The fact that *they* are intimidated will never negate the call on our lives. If the anointing is present, it will not go away just because *they choose* not affirm us. It is not that simple and leadership has backed us into a very tight corner indeed. We can find ourselves in a bind that we do not want and neither do we deserve to be in. For if we pursue the leading of The Holy Ghost, without their fatherly blessing, we are then deemed as being out of order.

Pastors you really should ask your selves a few questions:

How many times has someone showed up in your congregation, whom you felt to be unimportant, thus you blatantly overlooked them? How many people have you purposely ignored simply because you were too caught up in yourself? Exactly how many have you held back because YOU FELT them to be a threat to your self-built empire?   Who have you held back, because you wanted your clones around, instead of someone who would dare to give you the whole unadulterated counsel of God? Who is it that you have merely shooed away and written off simply because you did not like them?

No one wants to openly admit that clerics are not exempt from feelings of pettiness. The church is reluctant to acknowledge that pastors and leaders have issues with jealousy and that they too carry unjustifiable "aught" (in their hearts) towards many of the brethren. They have their own set of ill feelings towards selective individuals, and in turn they do their very best to keep them "held back" and oppressed.

Pastors are human beings who are also capable of *having* and who do *exhibit* the same "isms" that are presently devouring our society. Pastors are not exempt from acting upon feelings that stem from sexism, favoritism and even racism – yes, boys and girls all of the various "isms" are alive and well, even in our churches. Some leaders will not give people the time of day, just because *they* see no value. They tend to overlook the "plain Jane" attendee while willingly catering to the well-dressed big spenders who make *them feel like little gods.* Many pastors today are treating us in the same exact manner that King Saul once treated David.

Initially, Saul *truly* loved David. It was he who asked Jesse (David's father), if young David could come to live with him in the palace. Through David's skillful playing on his instrument, Saul would always find relief from the evil spirits that often plagued him.   Much earlier in his life, Saul had demonstrated his disobedience and rebellion by refusing to obey the *entire* counsel of God as spoken to him by Samuel the prophet. Rebellion will always lead to evil spirits attaching themselves to people. Much later in life, Saul would even seek counsel from a witch, which I am positive (by the end of his life) had caused him even greater mental distress.

In the beginning, the king loved David and David loved the king. Not only did David have love for Saul but also he revered him and honored Saul's position as the reigning monarch (and probably even as a surrogate dad). When David came to live with Saul, he was just a lad. Immediately he won Saul's heart and also his respect, because of his victory over a giant named Goliath. David's victory over Goliath reclaimed the honor of Jerusalem, as the entire host of the King's [yes] men were cowering in fear, being too afraid to fight.

As David grew, he served as Saul's armour (or armor) bearer and became even as his very own son. He went wherever the king sent him. The Bible lets us know that, "David knew how to behave himself wisely in all things." Saul trusted David and put him in charge of his warriors; the people also accepted David.   Eventually though, the same loving king (and father figure) would be the very person that would make and attempt to slay him, as sometimes love lasts but for a season.

SAUL HAD GENUINE LOVE FOR DAVID UNTIL; <u>HE BECAME</u>
<u>INTIMITATED AND BEGAN TO GIVE IN TO HIS FITS OF RAGE. IT WAS</u>
<u>SAUL'S OWN FEELINGS OF JEALOUSY AND HIS OWN EVIL SPIRIT THAT</u>
<u>EVENTUALLY DROVE HIM TO A PLACE OF NO RETURN. IT WAS NOT</u>
<u>DAVID'S FAULT THAT GOD HAD CHOSEN TO ANOINT HIM! NEITHER IS IT</u>
<u>YOURS NOR EVEN MY OWN! JUST AS THE LORD CHOSE DAVID HE HAS</u>
<u>ALSO CHOSEN YOU – IT IS NOT YOUR FAULT MY BROTHERS AND</u>
<u>SISTERS. REJOICE IN KNOWING THAT YOU ARE THE ANOINTED OF</u>
<u>GOD!</u>

Personally, I believe that Saul may have been on the brinks of an emotional breakdown by the time he died. (He was later killed in battle). Let us now examine The Word of The Lord to find out exactly how it is that this loving "spiritual father" turned into a would-be assassin. What could have driven him to such madness? We will find our answer in the book of I Samuel 18: 6-12. Remember, this could happen to you!

And it came to pass that as they
came, when David was returned
from the slaughter of the Philistine,
that the women came out of all
cities of Israel, singing and dancing,
with joy and with instruments of
musick (music).
And the women answered one
another as they played, and said,
Saul hath slain his thousands, and
David his ten thousands.
And Saul was very wroth, and the
saying displeased him; and he
said, they have ascribed unto David
ten thousands, and to me they
have ascribed but thousands: and
what can he have more but the kingdom?
And Saul eyed David from that
day forward.
And it came to pass on the
morrow, that the evil spirit from
God came upon Saul, and he
prophesied in the midst of the
house: and David played with his
hand, as at other times: and there
was a javelin in Saul's hand.
And Saul cast the javelin; for
he said, I will smite David even to
the wall with it. And David
avoided out of his presence twice.

And Saul was afraid of David,
because The Lord was with him,
and was departed from Saul.

Wow! That was a mouth full, and for many of you, it may have been a real eye-opener. You see, just because *you love your leaders and submit to them,* does not mean that they will not harm you. Saul seemed to have been driven mad by his own Jealousy. The Spirit of The Lord departed from Saul *after* he tried to smite David twice with the javelin. He became afraid of David – because The Lord was (obviously) with David and he, (Saul) knew it. But, did you also notice that Saul yet had the ability to prophesy in the midst of the temple, just before attempting to murder David with his javelin? He that hath an ear to hear "sho-nuff" better listen up now! You need to know what God might be communicating to you at this very moment. Today's leaders are not exempt from becoming envious or believing that they are being conspired against and that someone is set on wrenching away their self-made kingdoms.

What did David eventually end up doing? He ran for his life that's what! During the course of Saul's assassination attempts, David found himself in hiding. Even as he was on the run, the opportunity to kill Saul had presented it self on more than one occasion. God will sometimes give *us* the opportunity to bring great harm or even shame upon our enemies. What will our response be? He wants to test what is in *our own* hearts concerning those who have wronged us. Will we now behave just like the people who tried to take us out? Or on the other hand, will we behave in a manner in which God would be pleased? What have *we* learned from our own experiences? God already knows, but He wants us to know. **He wants you and I to see what is in our own heart.**

David could have easily retaliated and slain the king. Instead, he chose to leave Saul in the hands of God. He decided to, "Touch not The Lord's anointed." David did not even realize that the anointing had departed from Saul, but still he considered him as The Lord's anointed because of Saul's position as king. But also, David really did love Saul. It was a real unfortunate situation to say the least. David could resist the urge to take matters into his own hands, because of his even greater love and respect for His God Jehovah. He did love Saul, but the fact that David did not take revenge, was largely due to his relationship with The Lord. He also knew that God could and would remove Saul in His own time – and later on, He did exactly that.

Many of us have also chosen not to publicly expose or to humiliate our leaders. Like David, who could have easily brought harm or even open shame upon the very person who tried to destroy him, but did not; we also have instead decided to leave their fates in the hands of YHWH.

Speaking of not touching God's anointed; let me take a moment to clear something up for a lot of you. This mishandled verse of Scripture will be dealt with in a later chapter. But for now, just to let you know, "Touch not mine anointed and do my prophet no harm", has absolutely nothing to do with pastors and leadership being exempt from correction or from appropriate confrontation. (See: Your Life May Depend Upon You Getting It Right).

Anyway... David had been anointed by God and was destined for the throne, long before his encounter with Saul. This was God's doing – it wasn't David's fault!   At the command of God, The Prophet Samuel was told to go to Jessie's house because there he would be instructed to anoint the next king of Israel.

From David's childhood, we get the impression that even then he may have been the "black sheep" of his family. For when the prophet came to the house to anoint God's future king, David's very own father [obviously] had not thought him worthy to even be in the line up. It seemed as though Jessie had not even remotely considered the possibility that David could be the one. Samuel looked at David's brother, Eliab and thought, "Surely The Lord's anointed is before us." God said, "No, not him." Eliab was tall and handsome; from the outside, he appeared to fit the bill, as he exuded all of the characteristics that people seemed to like in a leader - he merely *looked* the part.

God told the prophet, "Do not look upon his countenance." The outside means nothing as many people are often fooled by what they see. Remember, Saul had also *looked* the part. God said to His Prophet Samuel:

> **Look not on his countenance, or on**
> **the height of his stature; because I**
> **have refused him: for The Lord**
> **seeth not as man seeth; for man looketh**
> **on the outward appearance, but**
> **The Lord looketh on the heart.**

> *(I Samuel 16:7)*

Next came Abinadab and Shammah that they too might pass before Samuel. On and on the procession of Jessie's boys went until finally, Samuel *had to ask Jessie* if he had any more sons left. Surely, he had not heard wrong; this *was* Jessie's house, and his assignment *was* to go there and to anoint the next king of Israel (I Samuel: 16). Jessie told Samuel, that he *did* have one more son. He had the youngest son left, but that he was out attending the sheep. You know the rest of the story. The prophet bid the man of the house to send for David.

Here we even get a foreshadowing of David's future kingly status. People are never allowed to sit in the presence of a judge or in the presence of royalty until they are given the ok. Whenever a judge or a reigning monarch enters a room, he or she will sit down first. Only afterward can all others take their seats, and only if granted permission to do so.

Samuel the prophet said, "Send and fetch him: for we will not sit down till he come hither." As soon as Samuel beheld David, The Lord told him to "Rise!" (Rise as in 'go' [not as in get up], because he was already standing) "Rise, anoint him, for this is he whom The Lord has chosen." I do not know what Jessie could have possibly been thinking. If I were him, and there existed even the remotest possibility that any one of my sons had been chosen, by God, I would have had each of them dressed and standing before the prophet. From the least to the greatest, the oldest to the youngest; every male child in my home would have been present *from the very start.*

Why wasn't David there [as a son], to begin with? I do have my own theory about David and Jessie's relationship. Nevertheless, to give explanation would require that I write a completely new book. The one thing that I do know for sure is that those sheep would have had to care for themselves for a while. I mean, I know that sheep should not be left alone, but really, couldn't a servant have watched them for a few short minutes? Jessie could have watched them himself, in order that his son might appear before the prophet. His father had not even considered that young David might possibly be the recipient of the blessing. He had been a mere afterthought. Only at the prophet's bidding, was he finally "fetched" [from the pasture].

From the account of David's life, we have witnessed him first being overlooked by his biological father, to later becoming a hunted prey, having to run for his life or stay and be killed by his spiritual father (Saul). Oh but bless The Lord! David had yet one more Father. It was God his Heavenly Father who would one day promote him to Israel's throne, in spite of everything that he had ever encountered before. This examination of dad's unavailability has brought us full circle in the natural and also in the spirit.

Some fathers, as we noted, are out of the picture all together. While other dads *are physically* in the home, but they do not "really want" to be fathers; they simply do not want the responsibility. Others are present, but they play favorites and are willing to nurture only *some* of their children. Yet there are those who really *do want* to be fathers, but may not know how, because they themselves lacked proper parental guidance, as their own fathers may have been absent or unavailable. And of course there is the "predator" dad – enough said.

We have seen how a father can turn on us. A dad can love us in one moment and attempt to kill us in the next. As I continued hearing comments regarding the matter of spiritual fatherhood, I was again provided with a staunch reminder of what I did not have. As leaders continued to belt out the same message from pulpits, radio, television or in person, they would constantly admonish the masses, to be sure that they would be bastards without one. Except YOUR pastor makes public confirmation, the person, or in some instances even an entire congregation would be considered "bastard."

Across the airwaves leaders continued with their slandering of peoples' character, and made clear, their blatant opposition of anybody who did not have what *they* considered as "proper covering." This entire matter confused me for a very long time. Around and around I went with my thoughts, as I continued to process my own painful ordeal. Still trying hard to figure out what had happened, I became even more confused. I tried hard to be obedient to my pastor and could not figure out, nor could I understand exactly what had gone wrong between him and me.

As I continuously sought The Lord, and pondered my dilemma, I was reminded about how in the book of Jeremiah, that God deemed Himself, to be married to the backsliding nation of Israel. The same nation that The Father loved, had denied Him, disobeyed Him and even disowned Him repeatedly. Even after God embodied Himself in flesh, in the form of Jesus, they still refused Him.

The Bible tells us in John 1:11 that, "He (Jesus) came unto His own and His own received Him not. Even as He made the ultimate sacrifice on the cross, they still did not receive Him as the promised Messiah, never had they been convinced. Surely if God was married to, had obligated Himself to and died for a backsliding, stiff-necked people like Israel, who turned their backs on Him, then certainly He must have *some place* for us who have been called unworthy and inferior by our fellow brothers and sisters of the faith.

Not only did Israel turn their backs on Jehovah, but also like a spiritual tramp, many in the population literally went "a whoring" after other gods. They were doing then, much the same as we are doing right now. Throughout Christendom, there are many who have become just like spiritual whores.

We have been programmed seek pleasure and to feel good. People often turn to the god of the moment. Many of us are guilty, as we too, tend to drool over and follow behind whoever is the most charismatic and the most popular. If someone is 'convincing' enough, then we straightway take his or her word about anything - without launching a thorough investigation for ourselves.

As Israel, God's chosen people started taking their eyes off Jehovah and putting them on gods of stone and calves of gold that could never satisfy, so are we also doing today.

They wanted a god of their own choosing instead of The Lord God Jehovah, who had even chosen them while they were yet in their unrighteousness; just as He later chose us. Surely, I thought if God could still love them, then certainly those of us who have NOT abandoned Him but wish only to do His will, must have some hope.

If God keeps a watchful eye out for the wondering prodigals, and receives them back with a festive party, a fatted calf and a ring of son-ship then certainly, He must care for you and me. If God listens to the voice of just one sinner who is desirous of making a change for the better, then I *know* that He hears my cry and yours too. If He loves the backslider, then certainly those who the world and now even the church continues to call bastard, must have *some* chance of gaining acceptance.

The Father loves us all and in equality, we shall each stand before Him to give an account. The church, which should be in the business of nurturing and protecting its own, has instead become notorious for ferociously chewing them up and spitting them out. NOT ALWAYS, but often I have found sinners to exhibit much more compassion than the born again sect. Christians are usually the most arrogant, smug, non-feeling, clueless, ruthless, insincere, conniving and hypocritical of all. (Of course I do not mean EVERY SINGLE CHRISTIAN, but a great number of them are indeed just that way). God help us!

I remember something that was told to me, as I conversed briefly with a physician. The Dr. shared with me something that had been told to him. He said that another person had made the comment to him that, "There was nothing wrong with Christianity, except for the Christians." Wow - Now check that out! The teachings of Jesus are fine, but the people who claim to be HIS followers, are quite a different story the person expounded. Because so much damage has *already* been done, I believe that The Lord Himself has stood up. He is saying time out, hold up, and wait just a darn minute!

"Man's attempts [to instruct] have caused many to be out of My perfect will [says Jehovah God]. The hirelings have destroyed many of My babies, and have even plucked them up by their very roots." (End of communication).

There came a point, in the midst of my deep despair, that The Lord reminded me about going to school. He had been quite specific already as to where I should go. He told me that, "There (at the school) I would find what I needed." I wasn't sure whether or not to tell the pastor. By this time, (after the 2nd time that I had spoken to him), it had been made painfully clear, that this man did not have my best interest at heart. (See: One Wounded Sheep: My Story). Still, for one split second, I found myself agonizing over whether or not I should (or indeed if I had to) inform him. Was I crazy or what?

I agonized because of those darned "church folks", who continued to tell me that letting him know would be the proper thing to do. They insisted that they always let their pastor(s) know what they were doing. I would often hear them make comments about how they had obtained "pastor's permission" to do a thing. I wasn't sure what to do. What about God's nod of approval I thought? I already had HIS permission – it was His idea in the first place. Besides my pastor did not care about me anyway.

Still, I took this concern to The Lord. I did not feel Him change His mind about the school so I signed up, all the while asking The Lord to close any door that I wasn't suppose to walk through. I continued checking with Him and telling Him that, if He did not want me to go, then I would not. In addition, I vowed that if He wanted me to consult with my pastor that I would, not knowing that later God would instruct me, that **"There is to be no more meetings"** [with my pastor].

Because He was the one who told me to go in the first place, I did. If The Lord tells me to do a thing, why do I always feel obligated to check with someone else anyway? He had already called me out on my apparent need for flesh validation and people-pleasing. I certainly did not want to go back down that road again.

If I were walking down the street and The Lord told me to pray for someone, would I be out of order for not calling my pastor to get his permission? Of course not! Would I not be able to pray for lack of formal credentials or ordination? What do you think? If I were to start a business, must I consult my pastor? Does my pastor consult me about his personal life choices? I wish I had the kind of relationship with my pastor wherein I could feel free to discuss certain things with him, and to ask for his input or spiritual insight, but I did not. He wanted nothing to do with me! For this writer, that type of relationship simply did not exist. I have always had to rely upon my own ability to hear from God – thank goodness, He has never led me wrong.

Dear reader, if you have a close relationship with your pastor (spiritual father) and you desire to share things with him or to get opinions about school, business decisions, or life in general, this is perfectly acceptable. If you would like to have your cleric pray with or for you as you ponder answers to your basic (or not so basic) questions that too is fine. My spiritual dad was unavailable to me, but my Heavenly Father has always guided me from above.

Through my own experiences and from those of others, I have discovered that, while many pastors may not care at all, there are those who care a little too much. In a word, they are nosey! In some churches, pastors *tell* the members that they are not allowed to visit other churches, without first obtaining pastoral approval. Some leaders actually prohibit their members from visiting unless; the entire congregation can go together as a unit. *Some even 'forbid' [grown] members, to go on family vacations, without them first sharing all of their personal details and/or itinerary, either with the pastor or with the leadership staff.*

I am not talking about informing someone out of common courtesy so that posts are filled and duties are carried out. No, instead I am talking about grown people *having* to check in as though he or she were on parole or on "spiritual lockdown" – *the hell!* In some congregations, the people are even forbidden to follow the leading of The Lord, without first obtaining permission from *them.*

Once again – the hell!! No one besides God should ever have that much control, authority or influence over anyone's life. Been there and done that! It will not happen again!

Beloved, whether or not you believe me, please know that there are churches that do operate exactly like this – no kidding! Instead of being taught by shepherds and fathers, many have found themselves to be under nosey busy bodies and/or cruel ravenous dictators.

For lack of knowledge, and from fear that comes through [sometimes] *purposely* erroneous teachings, parishioners are viewed and treated as cleric property, rather than as fellow believers and co-laborers, [who happen to be grown men and women], who are capable of thinking for themselves., as well as hearing God FOR THEMSELVES (I'm talking about mature Kingdom people here, not just people who want to hear what they want). Woe unto anyone unwilling to be brought under subjection *they say.*

What they really mean is woe unto anyone who refuses to allow them to control their lives. However, of course they disguise their control tactics as "being concerned." They claim to be watching out for you. Don't fall for the hype. You are not obligated to any organization to such a degree, that you must allow that entity or the leadership thereof, to run your entire life. When it becomes like that, then baby you are no longer in God's house, but rather you are under a ton of hierarchal flesh.

Be very aware that this is how most cults are formed. Leaders of churches and organizations like these are notorious for isolating its members for the express purpose of gaining control over their lives. Seek not to be controlled by any spirit or by any person other than The Holy Spirit.

He SHALL ALWAYS lead you and guide you into all truth. Remember though, not even God totally controls us or makes it His business to run every aspect of our lives, although He could! However, even He gives us freedom of choice! [Free will] He doesn't treat you as though you are a puppet on His string, so why would you allow someone else to? Don't do it!

I know you think, it is the "in thing" to be approved of by pastor and to have his or her spirit, but why would anyone settle for being like a mere man or for having the spirit of any human being, when having The Spirit of God is what you really need? You cheat your own selves when you strive to be a clone of anything or of anyone. Rather, why not focus on being approved unto God? The more I thought about what I continued to hear preached, the more I inquired of Him. During one of our many talks, He asked and then answered His own question:

"Since when do I need permission to use anything that I have created?" "I created and formed you and ordained you before you took your first natural breath." "Before you even knew you existed, you were already ordained to be whatever I have declared you to be." "I am Almighty God and I don't need permission from anyone to use anything that I have created." *(End communication).*

My steps had been ordered long before ever making contact with my pastor – or even before I nestled into the protective covering of my very own mother's womb. God had been my Father, long before I discovered that my pastor did not want to be. But, you know what's strange though? Deep down, I knew this already– but still I allowed them to convince me otherwise.

Do you not realize that the seeds of greatness were implanted long before you were even born? The book of Genesis lets us know that, long before fruit is manifested outwardly [on a tree], and its formation has already begun. Long before the natural eye even sees it, the fruit is grown. It lies embedded within its carrier, in [growing] seed form until the appointed time. Although the fruit is present deep within, still it requires proper nourishment, together with the passing of time. Only then, can it manifest and present its true form (or self) to this present environment.

God Himself has securely planted your seeds. In fact, not only are you *carrying seed,* but also *you ARE seed!* You are a living seed awaiting your time to burst out of the soil! You have been equipped to produce and to bring forth everything that He has ordained for your life. Everything that you need is already on the inside. Who or what is it that keeps trying to hinder your growth and spiritual (or emotional) development? Who is trying to kill your spirit before you are ready to give birth? Who keeps trying to snatch you out of your incubator before the "set time" so that you fall to the ground and spoil?

"Who or what is it that keeps trying to postpone or tamper with your scheduled date of arrival? Worse still, who is it that is trying to keep you from arriving at all? Could it be someone with whom you surround yourself? Who has the enemy assigned to [try and] keep your seed(s) from making it to their expected end called fruit? Do not let others cause your seeds to die or far worse; don't you die as a carrier without first making a deposit into the rich soil of someone else's life.

Why should people be called bastards just because there is no <u>man</u> who wishes to bestow a blessing upon them? How is that the person's fault? Why do they blame you or me? It *was they* who did not want us remember? In the natural, a child is considered a bastard because of the *parents'* sins not because of the child's. Natural bastardization occurs whenever parents are not committed in a (male/female) covenantal partnership called marriage.

Illegitimacy is also brought about when a mother has no clue as to who her child's father could be. Yet in other instances, even if the mother and father do know, the father may not claim the child as his own. Unsanctioned (illegitimate) births often result from extramarital affairs. The children are then riddled with questions and are plagued with feelings of guilt. They are forced to carry a heavy burden and bear an ugly label that rightfully belongs upon the shoulders of another.

At times questions about a father's identity or the circumstances surrounding the birth of a child will remain a mystery. This is particularly true if the one person, namely momma, who does know all of the details, has passed away or is herself unavailable and nowhere to be found.

A child left without resolution will often grow up with a bastard complex and with a real need to belong. Unless it is dealt with or unless there is closure, that need can last well into adulthood. – or even for a lifetime. Millions are still scarred as their gaping, festering sores continue to go unnoticed, or unattended. Bastardization is realized when a person has no identity with which to identify. Although a lot of us are wrapped in adult bodies, the reality is that many of us are still children. There are many right now, who are aimlessly wondering throughout society, in search of a dad who will never claim them. They continue to carry the pain of knowing that they were not wanted. So as it is in the natural, so is it also in the spirit!

Illegitimacy in the church is forced upon people by leadership, when precious souls, make up their minds to pursue the will of God, despite the fact that their pastors refuse to bless them. It is as though we are made to await a blessing (which often never comes) or to worry about not accomplishing that which we know God has spoken. What is it that we are guilty of anyway? We were guilty of seeking the permission of our leaders to bless us and to vouch for us so that we can do the work of our God freely. Yes, I admit it; many of us are guilty of wanting to do the will of YHWH.

We too desire to answer His call. If this is the crime for which we have been accused, then absolutely, we are guilty indeed. I mean really, is it wrong to *want* God to add purpose to *our* lives just like everyone else claims He has done to theirs? Is it so wrong to desire life above the realms of mediocrity and status quo? Speaking for my own self, if this makes me guilty, then yes, I suppose that I am, and have been so for quite some time now. After having heard this bastard thing just one time too many, I wanted to know, if there were any "real life" examples in The Bible, of people who had been considered as a physical or spiritual bastard. I simply had to know who they were and what became of them. And trust me when I tell you, in light of today's teaching, there are many in Scripture who <u>should</u> have been classified as such.

I needed to know, how it was that <u>God</u> dealt with such a person. Moreover, I really needed to know what they had accomplished throughout the course of their life – if they had accomplished anything at all. Is there hope for the physically & spiritually illegitimate? First off, I discovered someone who had a slightly different set of circumstances, but who none-the-less, still found himself banished to the illegitimate population pile. I found Jephthah, who would not necessarily, be a bastard because of his *father*, but he had been considered "illegitimate" because of his *mother*. Now there's a twist for you. You can read about him in The Book of Judges, Chapters 11-12.

In those times, a person's lineage meant *everything*. Because of his mother, Jephthah should have been doomed right from the start, as he was the son of a harlot. For those of you who are not familiar with this term let me break it down. Mom was a prostitute; she sold her body for money. The younger people would probably describe her as being a 'hutchie', a 'slut' or 'chicken head.' Plain and simple – momma was a whore. While Jephthah may have loved his mother, certainly he could not have been very proud of her lifestyle and choice of profession.

If people in Jephthah's day, were anything at all like they are today, then I am certain he suffered much ridicule and rejection because of her. For Jephthah's sake, thankfully he had more positive role models on his father's side. A father's background was extremely important, even more so than the mother's. Whether or not a person was considered important or would be given respect etc. rested primarily upon the father's ancestry. Jephthah was from the lineage of Manasseh, who was the son of Joseph (Jacob [Israel's] son). Joseph begat Manasseh, Manasseh begat Machir, Machir begat Gilead and Gilead begat Jephthah.

Jephthah's "½ brethren" literally put him out. Gilead's wife, who was not Jephthah's mother, had given birth to other sons. These 'legitimate' sons of Gilead grew up and "thrust Jephthah out", and said unto him, "Thou shalt not inherit in our father's house; for thou art the son of a strange woman" (Judges 11:2). When his brothers put him out, he fled and dwelt in a land called 'Tob.' While there, he met up with and formed an alliance with some unscrupulous henchmen who were strong and warrior like.

As time passed, Jephthah's brothers went to war with the children of Ammon. His brothers, (The Bible calls them Elders) came looking for him in *their* time of need. They were no match for the enemy, and as a result, they were losing the battle. It was then that the brothers realized their *need for Jephthah*. They not only sought him out, but he also became their captain and their leader. Jephthah, whose name means, "He opens", was referred to as, "A mighty man of valor." Some scholars say that they literally referred to him as, "The Mighty Jephthah" (Harper's Bible Dictionary). His circumstances were very similar to those of his great, great grandfather. He too had been hated by his half brothers.

They not only put him out, but they actually sold him [out of the family]. Years later, because of a famine in their own land, the brethren of Joseph were forced to make a pilgrimage to Egypt, in order to obtain food. Just like Jephthah's brothers, their need would bring them face to face with the same brother they had gotten rid of so many years earlier.

This reunion would also test Joseph, as he would have to lay eyes upon those who had hated him. In no way could Joseph's brothers have possibly known, that the one they had ridded themselves of years earlier, would be the very person to whom they *would have* to ask for food in order to save their lives. Here it was generations later that the brothers of Jephthah also had a problem *that* only their 'hated 1/2 brother' could help solve. The unloved half brother who had once been put out was now being sought out.

The Spirit of The Lord rested upon Jephthah long before they ever went to war. According to one source, the brothers must have *"seen something" on Jephthah,* and remembered that he was the man for the job. Jephthah had what it took to help them defeat their enemies, because The Spirit of The Living God moved through him.

As I read Jephthah's story, I could not help but once again think about his mother. While I am in no way glorifying or condoning her way of living, still I want to make mention of the most famous of all harlots in Biblical history. Her name was Rehab (Sometimes spelled Rachab).

Many of you know her story and some of you may not. She is initially found in The Book of Joshua and was responsible for helping him and his men defeat their enemies in Jericho. She hid the two men who were sent by Joshua to spy out the land. This she did, because she had heard of Jehovah and of His mighty works. The fame, of The Lord God of Israel and how He had fought for and defended His people, against their enemies had spread abroad.

Rehab believed everything that she had heard about His greatness, and she knew that He would not hesitate to fight for His people again. She and Joshua's men struck a deal. Because of her kindness and her faith, she and her father's household would be spared when they came back to destroy the city. She was to hang a scarlet cord form the window, as a sign to Joshua's men, who in turn would know not to destroy that section of the city. Rehab's house, which sat high upon the wall of Jericho, would be the only one safe from destruction, and would remain standing as the rest of, "The wall came tumbling down."

Rehab, as well as everyone with her was guaranteed safety, as long as they were inside the house. They had to be under the covering of The Blood. Her scarlet (red) cord was similar to the instructions given at the Passover in Egypt. The destroyer or Death Angel had been instructed to "pass over" every Blood marked lintel and doorpost.

Do you know something else about Rehab? She became part of our Saviour's lineage. Because of her faithfulness, this mighty woman is listed in Matthew 1:5, Hebrews 11:31 and in James 2:25. She is a direct descendant of The Messiah. I tell you her story because, I want you to understand, that it does not matter what *they* have told you. Be assured that regardless to what sins may line your past, if you give your life to Christ, then God will use you as a vessel of honor. No matter what sin or curse may serve as your family's backdrop, know beyond a doubt, that God loves you.

Don't listen to *them*. **READER, DO YOU UNDERSTAND ME?** Take this word that comes straight from The Father's heart and allow it to penetrate and to minister to your broken heart and wounded spirit. The Lord can save your life spiritually and physically.   Rest assured that if God mightily used Jephthah, who because of his mother, had been labeled as illegitimate, then certainly, He will use you. If He cared enough to save one harlot from destruction, how could you doubt that He will also save you?

Many people were saved because of this woman's faith. We are not exactly sure whom she had in her home, as The Scripture states that "Her father's house" would be spared. Perhaps it was indeed only she and her family. But who knows, The Lord being merciful, could have allowed her to have friends or even customers there - who can tell? Jehovah not only honored the promise of Joshua's men, but He also engrafted her into the royal biological lineage of His only begotten Son. How much more could she have been blessed? Certainly if He did all of that for one lowly Madam, then there has to be hope for all who ask.

Would anyone dare consider The Apostle Paul to be a bastard? According to that which is being preached in our times, he very well should have been. This Apostle wrote much of the New Testament and at times received divine revelations of such great magnitude, that he could not even speak of them.   Yet he had neither traditional ordination nor an earthly "birthing out" ceremony. Paul, who had never been covered by the traditions of men, had certainly been birthed and covered from above.

For this reason, much of what we have been taught, is at the very least suspect and warrants explanation. Clerics tell us that we are wrong if we do not have *their* permission to do the will of God, but yet we read of this very great and very outspoken Apostle who after receiving <u>a</u> <u>direct</u> <u>word</u> <u>from</u> <u>The</u> <u>Lord</u> <u>made</u> <u>it</u> <u>a</u> <u>point</u> <u>not</u> <u>to</u> <u>confer</u> <u>with</u> <u>flesh</u> <u>and</u> <u>blood.</u>

In the book of Galatians, Chapter 1, Paul makes it quite clear that, "He is an Apostle not of men neither by a group of men [nor by the will of man] but by Jesus Christ and God The Father, who raised Him from the dead." In other words, Paul had not been voted into his Apostleship by a man, neither had a group of elders, held a board meeting to discuss the matter, but rather God Himself had voted him in. He then goes on to affirm doctrine and revelation that he passionately states was not received from man. Man did not reveal to Paul what he knew, God did.

The one thing if nothing else that we must admire about this "chosen vessel" of The Lord, is the fact that, never once had he ever been a man pleaser. For Paul, it was not about being liked, by trying not to rock the boat. He did not purposely try to upset things, but he endeavored to do that which God instructed him to. If doing The Lord's will happened to shake things up a bit, then he stood flatfooted in his determination to obey The Lord anyhow. Never did Paul hedge on what Jesus told him to say or do, in order to save face with those around him. I'm sorry folks, but this simply was not his style. Oh how I wish that I had taken hold of this so very long ago. Oh well, better late than never I suppose.

> For do I now persuade men, or God?
> Or do I seek to please men?
> For if I yet pleased men, I should [and would]
> not be the servant of Christ
> (Galatians 1:10) – You go Paul!

When he gets to Galatians 13, he reminds his brethren of his past, and how he use to persecute the church of God. When I was growing up, we use to sing a song that says: "When The Lord gets ready for you, "you've got to move." Paul said:

> But when it pleased God, who
> separated me from my mother's
> womb, and called me by His grace
> to reveal His Son in me, that
> I might preach Him among the
> heathen: immediately I conferred
> not with flesh and blood.
> Neither went I up to Jerusalem
> to them which were Apostles before
> me; but I went into Arabia and re-
> turned again to Damascus.
> Then after three years I went
> up to Jerusalem to see Peter and
> abode with him fifteen days.

(Galatians 1:16)

Paul went to Arabia. Some critics say, that he was still confirmed by Peter and the other Apostles. He *did* appear to the other Apostles, but much later on. However, Paul did not need them to affirm or to approve of him. He began his ministry BEFORE ever gaining acceptance or confirmation from any human being, including the other Apostles. It was by the will of God that he preached The Glorious Gospel of The Lord. He was commissioned not at the hand of man and neither through a staff of ministerial hierarchy, but rather The Lord Jesus Christ, called Paul from the portals of glory and stamped him with His own seal of approval.

In Arabia, Paul preached and ministered to the heathen nations (the gentiles). He began doing exactly what God had instructed him to do. Unlike some of us, Paul never became confused or went "stir crazy", from going around asking people's opinions, and begging for permission or a nod of approval. Still, according to many theologians of our time, his ministry would be considered illegitimate. Yet this "Hebrew of The Hebrews, and Pharisee of The Tribe of Benjamin", had been "properly birthed" by his Saviour.

When The Lord sent Ananias to him immediately after his "Damascus Road" experience, it was so that he could receive his sight. At first Ananias was reluctant to go because of his "pre-conversion" reputation as "Saul of Tarsus". It was no secrete that Saul who would soon begin using his real name "Paul", had been well known, and was notorious indeed for terrorizing the Christian Believers. Yet in obedience to God, Ananias went and prayed for him. Immediately, "Something like scales" fell from his eyes and he (Saul who we now know as The Apostle "Paul") received The Holy Ghost as well as his sight.

He   immediately began to preach Christ in the synagogues, proclaiming Him to be The Son of God - Acts Chapter 9. Paul's later appearance before the other Apostles had absolutely nothing to do with him being commissioned to preach; Jesus Himself had already taken care of that. Once The Lord made His will known to Paul, he did not go running around asking people for their permission to carry it out. Moreover, while we are on the matter – neither did he have to attend seminary, or sit and be taught by a pastor for the next 50 years of his life in order to do that which he had been commissioned to carry out!

I see absolutely nothing wrong with going to school, BUT I do not, and hopefully no one else is, depending solely upon book knowledge when it comes to the things of The Lord. A person does not have to go to school in order to, "Learn how to preach" – the anointing takes care of that.

Certainly we indeed are to study, but to be told that a person absolutely HAS to jump through an additional set of hoops, namely man's educational requirements, in order to be used of God, well it simply isn't true.

PAUL NEVER ASKED A PASTOR OR ANY OTHER HUMAN BEING ABOUT HIS VALIDITY AS AN APOSTLE BECAUSE GOD HAD ALREADY SPOKEN TO HIM. HE KNEW THE VOICE OF THE LORD AND THE MATTER HAD BEEN SETTLED ONCE AND FOR ALL – PERIOD AND AMEN!

Do you not realize that later on, even Paul's very calling and validity as a true apostle came under scrutiny? There were many who <u>never</u> believed him, nor did they <u>ever</u> accept his appointment as an apostle – especially since he was not part of the original twelve, chosen when Jesus walked the earth. What did their opinions matter anyway? Once God, "The source", has already confirmed you, everything and everyone else is merely "a resource" and their opinions do not matter nearly as much as The Lord's.

Even the very location to where Paul goes is significant, as Arabia speaks of a dry place, or wilderness. While there, I believe that amidst the barren desert sands, Paul wrestled with God, as he hashed out the many questions and concerns that he may have had concerning his calling and assignment. It was there that God would once and for all solidify his authority as an apostle. Paul was God's chosen vessel. As he ministered to others in Arabia, The Holy Spirit in turn, I'm sure, ministered to him. The Lord Himself took an active role in the mentoring and in the training of Paul.

By the time The Father, Son and Holy Ghost finished with him, Paul's mindset had to be like – "Look, I don't care what you think about me 'cause' I know who I am, - I am God's Apostle." If Paul could speak to today's leadership, I know he would tell them, "Whether or not you believe me or accept me, I still know who I am." "I know that the hand of God has touched me." "I've been God ordained, God appointed and God sent." "Like it or not, here I am by the will of God The Father." Paul, who was so full of God's Spirit, would have never been governed by the rules of mere men. By the time he returned to the mainstream, nothing else mattered to him, except, "Jesus Christ and Him crucified."

Certainly, it appears as though, what Paul learned in Arabia, (about Jesus and God The Father), was sufficient and would sustain him for a lifetime – I am sure of it. There with God he had likely been instructed as to how to answer even his most skeptical critics. No matter what people may have thought of him, they certainly would not have been able to stop him from preaching about Jesus.

If preachers were saying the same thing *then* as many are saying now, then absolutely, even Paul would be a bastard. This being the case, sill I am certain that he would have set out to be the absolute best bastard of all times. Why could he so boldly proclaim The Gospel of our Lord without reserve? Well let's ask him – he said it best in, (II Timothy 1:12B) "I know whom I have believed, and am persuaded that He is able to keep that which I have committed unto Him against that day." Paul knew that it was to God whom he would ultimately be accountable. He knew that God had called him, and that it would be God's responsibility to keep him. Whether it pertained to his Kingdom work or to the keeping of his soul, Paul knew that everything would be seen, kept and judged by God. He never concerned himself with the need to check in with anyone else, because he did not have to.

In today's lingo – Paul knew what time it was. And in case you are not clear about it by now, so do I. Thankfully, I too "Know whom I have believed and am also persuaded." For those who say, that was then, and this is now. I have only this for you: Does not The Bible clearly state, and in fact do *they* not preach it to us - "Jesus Christ [is] the same, yesterday, today and forever"? Well, if He is the same, and indeed, He is, then He is also sovereign and can speak to whom He pleases *whenever* He pleases.

DEAREST CLERGY, HE DOES NOT NEED YOUR PERMISSION NOR YOUR TAINTED INTERFERENCE WHEN IT COMES TO COMMUNICATING WITH HIS OWN CREATION. HE RESERVES THE RIGHT TO DO WHAT HE WILLS. IF THE LORD JEHOVAH DECIDES TO USE AN INDIVIDUAL TO CARRY OUT <u>HIS PLAN</u>, HE IS NOT OBLIGATED TO SEEK THE OPINION OF ANYBODY; NEITHER DOES HE <u>FIRST</u> HAVE TO CHECK WITH ANYONE AT ALL - THAT INCLUDES YOU!

Speaking with a co-worker one day, we began discussing the ministry of John The Baptist. Here was a man preaching in the wilderness, as he ingested a diet of locus and wild honey, while dressed in a leather girdle made of camel's hair. By today's standards, if *anyone at all* would have qualified as a candidate for excommunication, lunacy, church shunning, and bastardization, certainly it would have been John The Baptist. He would be the first to get the 'ax.' Surely, they would have put him out.

I am certain that not only would *his ministry* be considered illegitimate, but also the church would deem *him* a total nut case. He would be labeled as strange, weird and as one to stir clear of. John The Baptist did not associate much with mainstream clergy; he was completely unencumbered by the clerics of his day, and in no way had he ever been intimidated or inhibited by them. In fact, he had absolutely no problem calling them vipers to their faces. John knew who he was *and* he also knew what he had been sent to do.

Often the toughest assignments are given to those who are moved ONLY by God's Spirit and not AT ALL by man's opinion.

John The Baptist was filled with The Holy Ghost from his mother's womb. Those who are wired for the prophetic are not always well received. Their primary training comes from God alone. This does not mean that a prophet cannot take instruction from preachers or from leadership, but what it does mean is that God's instructions are the only ones on the forefront of the prophetic intellect.

Prophets are not moved by men, but by God's sovereign will. Who besides Jehovah could ever properly train a prophet anyway? Prophets do not easily (if at all) conform or adapt to that which surrounds them. Depending on the activity around them, they may at times appear to be extremely uncomfortable or agitated. Some might even consider them a bit odd or 'stand-offish.' For the most part, their spirit has been heightened and sensitized, and they may appear to be 'on edge' or as though they are on the 'look out,' – not crazy just alert. They must be ready to hear the voice of The Lord at all times.

John was the epitome of that which we call a prophet. He was led into the Judean wilderness where he preached the truth! Notice, he did not take over anyone's pulpit, nor did he ever try to, simply because he did not have to. He certainly did not lack, in audience appeal, *and without trying.* People went out into the wilderness to hear what this "strange great man" had to say. He was the first cousin of Jesus and would be His forerunner. John had the awesome privilege and assignment of announcing HIM to the world. People actually wondered if whether or not he (John) was in fact The Promised Messiah.

John *quickly* set the record straight. He let them know unequivocally that he was not the one who should come. He informed them that one would be coming after him, who was mightier [in Spirit and in truth] than he. "He of whom I speak, said he, I [John] am not even worthy to stoop down and to unloose the latchet of His shoe." Wow! The humility of John The Baptist is a far cry from the things we hear coming from the lips of leaders today, as they boast of *their* relationship with The Saviour.

I have heard pastors who claim, to have met Jesus face to face, and in so doing, have proceeded (they say) to **"tell Him"** what they were or were not going to do. Others claim to have had The Messiah personally appear to them, and in turn, the two of them proceeded to literally walk hand in hand down the street. Yeah, ok! Right! Sure, they did – keep right on believing that!

Though I am not saying that The Lord could not have appeared, as The Lord can do what ever He pleases, including walk the earth. But with their unclean and unworthy selves *they* make it seem though, if one were [really] to ever meet the embodiment of God, it would be like meeting some long lost buddy for breakfast, as they proceed to speak to Him as flippantly and as arrogantly as they speak to you and me. How dare they!?

If anyone of us were to have a face-to-face encounter, with The Master, I doubt very seriously if we would even be able to speak at all, let alone stand, walk or go skipping down the street with Him, as we dare to declare what we will or will not do. No doubt, we would be so taken back by His glory that we would probably forget how to speak. I don't know about anyone else, but as for this writer, just thinking about seeing Him physically (as some claim to have), it is enough to make me want to fall flat on my face in worship.

If my first response is not to prostrate myself, I would probably be too busy crying, trembling in awe or simply trying to breathe while in His presence. How on earth could I possibly do anything else in the face of His glory? I am truly baffled as to how modern day theologians with all of their filth and unholy loose living, could possibly *view themselves* as being so worthy and capable of 'standing' in the presence and in The Majesty of Christ. It truly boggles my mind.

I find this to be utterly amazing in light of the fact that many in Scripture, who when they beheld Him, would sit at His feet, fall down and worship, or fall down as though they were dead. These were their reactions as they beheld Him, because they were stricken in the face of glory.

Modern day pastors sound like a bunch of fools in comparison to John The Baptist who had been "womb sanctified" and yet he did not boast, but considered himself as not being good enough to even unloose the latchets of The Master's shoes. That statement alone still gives me the chills, every single time that I read it. *We* on the other hand seem to believe that we are worthy enough to do *everything*.

We are not even in the same league as John The Baptist! When was the last time you baptized The Messiah?

John was sanctified and separated *before* he ever saw the light of day or even before, he beheld, announced and baptized "The Light of the world." As iron sharpens iron, sometimes only those who have been truly sanctified can recognize another of like kind. John had taken the death walk long ago and was clear as to his mission.

This powerful prophet knew from early on that Messiah would be coming, and therefore he had absolutely no problem pointing the people to HIM. It was his duty to make the grand announcement of our Saviour. His job was to point the people to Jesus, – "Behold! The Lamb of God who takes away the sin of the world! He was not connected to a leader of flesh, but he *was* connected to Jesus. Moreover, Jesus made it His absolute business to be connected to John. The Bible declares John to be, "The voice of *one* crying in the wilderness."

I don't read of any church affiliation or pastoral covering. Never did he beg, connive or browbeat people into 'submissive giving', because he had no multi-million dollar building fund to concern himself with. Neither did he ever worry about church expansion, because he had an entire wilderness from which to preach. People came to hear him because *he* had something significant to say – his message came from God!

He did not [have to] plead for members or money, because *they followed him,* as in "These signs shall follow them." (Different subject same principal). Had John never gained a human disciple, I believe that the very elements of nature would have risen to the occasion. I am convinced that even the wilderness creatures would have stood at attention and "on all fours" would have listened to and applauded the words of this mighty man. Jesus says concerning John, "Among these born of women there is not a Prophet greater than John The Baptist (Luke 7:28A).

If John were here right now, certainly our leaders would not share Jesus' opinion of this unconfirmed, untamed vessel of the wild. I am totally convinced that He too would have been considered a bastard, absolutely no doubt in my mind. Now I ask, how much do you think he would care? When Jesus was baptized at the hand of John, who just happened to be His first cousin, The Father Himself parted the clouds and said concerning Jesus –"This is my beloved Son, in whom I am well pleased." Did you hear that? The Father was pleased with Jesus, and I happen to believe that He also wholeheartedly approved of and was pleased with the one conducting the baptismal service. Isn't He the only one who must be pleased with *us?*

We have not been left for dead. I don't care how *they* try to tell you that God does not approve of you, (or that He does not love you). How do *they* know? There are many of them that God does not approve of. He has, never authorized a great number of the clerics and 'gurus' that are preaching and teaching today. A lot of them are going straight to hell from behind the very pulpits, from which they stand each week.

In many instances, God is not even vouching for them because they are under the rulership of a different master. The saddest thing of all is that they do not even know it. In fact, on *that* day there will many, whom The Lord will command to depart from Him. Imagine all the while, as they preach using words of grandeur; and illusion (because many of them are liars); Jehovah is peering through the heavens, shaking His head in total disgust. They do not belong to Jesus now, nor have they ever. We see them all the time writing books, building bigger and improved edifices and preaching all over the world; yet in hell shall many of these same lift up their very eyes.

If I being mere flesh cannot take it, then I *know* that God who is Altogether Holy must be sick to His stomach. (And yes! I know that God is a Spirit and that He has no literal stomach). Far better, it is to complete just one task that God has placed into our hands, than to be involved with many that have been birthed from human effort and ambition with wrong motives.

I bet God is going to ask many a preacher, "Did I tell you to build a 100,000 member church? No, I simply asked you to feed the poor once a week. Did I ask you to feed people all over the world? No! I told you that your job was to take care of the 50 who sit in your congregation each week who cannot afford weekly groceries for their families. What were your reasons for disobeying Me? Just what did you expect to accomplish by doing something other than that which I had clearly instructed? – Depart from me!

Dear pastors, just because you have large numbers does not mean that you are a successful leader. If heaven were to take a census, it would be pretty darn interesting to note how many members under Your tutelage are actually going to make it in. Sure, they may attend your services but it is not church membership that counts for eternity. Need I remind you that anyone can go to church? Hell, even satan goes to church *and* he brings his family of demons with him! What Gospel are you preaching? Is the Gospel that you preach balanced accordingly or have you tilted the scale, by only preaching what you like as well as that, which tickles the ears and entices the people, so that they keep coming back for more? Is the Gospel you preach unadulterated or does it reek of you?

While we are on the subject of "your church" and the works thereof, tell me something. What exactly was your angle? What is your motivation for ministry, or for anything that you claim to be doing for God? Why are you trying to build these establishments anyway? Do you really want them to be monuments for *The Kingdom of God,* or are you erecting these as memorials unto yourselves? Are you interested in building a school because another pastor that you saw on television has a major Christian school?

MAYBE THAT WAS "HIS" ASSIGNMENT AND NOT YOURS! Are you only in ministry to make a name for yourself? I know, perhaps you are addicted to the spotlight and ministry provides you with a much-needed adrenaline rush. If you were not the pastor or the center of attention, could you remain happily behind the scenes doing the same work that you want to keep everyone else confined to 'forever'?

Do you really have a heart for GOD'S people or are you merely putting on a front? By the way, this <u>image</u> of yours happens to be something that many with a trained Spiritual eye can see straight through. Frankly, we are pretty darn sick of it! Although you may fool quite a few people all of the time, rest assured you are not fooling everybody. MOREOVER, it would do you good to remember that YOU NEVER FOOL GOD AT ALL!

Because of *your* ministry, would you say that people have been turned on to Jesus, or would they want to abandon Him and the faith altogether? Preacher, it will be a sad day when God requires you to give an account for all of the souls that have been derailed because of your ill treatment and/or neglect. It will be very sad to hear those three permanently stinging, irrevocable words – "Depart from me!"

For The Word states that many will ask, "Did we not prophesy, in Your Name?" "Did we not visit the sick and do all manner of services in Your Name Jesus?" Then The Lord will tell them to, "Depart from me ye workers of iniquity - I NEVER knew you." I once heard a theologian say that this passage could not possibly be referring to Christians having to 'depart' because Jesus states that He *"never"* knew them.

The preacher went on to explain that, if this passage were referring to saved people, then Jesus would have said something like, "I once knew you but now I have turned away from you." He said that this would have been a more appropriate statement for The Saviour to have made – *What?* As far as I am concerned, the bottom line is still – "Depart from me." Regardless to whom *we think* the passage addresses, I submit the following for your consideration.

For the most part, sinners are not going around doing work for Jesus. If a person is a sinner, it is not likely that he or she will have a lasting interest in the things of God. Therefore, I do not think that sinners would be bragging or trying to give explanation to Jesus about what he or she has done for Him or done in His Name. I do however recognize that there are those in the land who try hard to mimic The Power of God.

They use trickery, sorcery and witchcraft, and have actually managed to convince themselves (and others), that they are doing a great work for Him.   The passage could be referring to these people as they are only fooling themselves by *thinking* that their works are acceptable in His sight.   Also, let us not forget that there are pastors and lay people who claim to know The Lord, but the question is, does The Lord know them?   They will be in for a rude awakening. I pray that you dear pastor and dear reader will not end up in this category.

To their utter shock and amazement, they will witness the glorious procession of many whom they have bastardized, abandoned, snubbed and written off, being ushered into the presence of The Lord, while they, on the other hand, will be hell bound as they stand before "The Great White Throne", (for judgment). Some leaders will see many whom they have deemed unfit, go on to finally receive their long awaited acclimation of, "Well done!" God has the final word and His Word is the only one that matters.

If you KNOW BEYOND A DOUBT that God has told you to do something, then you had better get busy. We *want* the pastor's approval and a fatherly blessing, but if he (or she) refuses then I say, better to do what God says, than to face *Him* with *your* work undone.   Better to be unpopular and shunned by a congregation than to give an account to God for your disobedience to Him. God knows why you had no choice but to disobey *them.* He also knows of their ungodly reasons for trying to restrain you.   Many Christians are engaging in church work, but have yet to enter into their Kingdom Assignments. Are they in God's 'perfect' will for their lives? Are they so stuck on local church dogma that they are not mindful of the greater work that remains?

Pursuing the perfect will of God, may sometimes require that you depart from the mainstream. Sometimes God will assign you to Sharon for a season – maybe even longer. Sharon is wherein you may experience yet another dry place or wilderness adventure. Nevertheless, fret not my friends, Jesus who is "The Rose of Sharon", will meet you right where you are every time. If you are doing the will of The Father and mainstream clergy thinks you to be a bit unorthodox, don't even worry about them. You are in such good company you cannot even imagine. Do you not know that even Jesus could not escape the syndrome of illegitimacy?

The Pharisees and Sadducees of His day not only opposed the validity of His ministry, but also they questioned the legitimacy of His very birth. Joseph was not married to Mary at the time of Jesus' *conception.* Besides, we all know that technically, Joseph is not Jesus' father anyway – God is. Now try explaining *that* to a non-believer. The clerics of His day did not accept Him as God's Son.

The Bible lets us know that the conception, which had taken place in Mary, while she was yet a virgin, had been by the working of The Holy Spirit. Mary found herself impregnated with The Seed of God. Now how is that for having to believe God even in the presence and under the scrutiny of naysayers? Think of the faith that she had to have had - hummmmmm. And we think that we have it bad when someone doesn't believe us!?

Some things that transpire between you and The Lord will not always (or necessarily) be visibly evident to others. In many instances, you will have to let them say what they will so long as you know. The birth of Jesus has always come under accusatory fire. In fact, the entire Gospel message is questionable to a world that simply cannot understand. Think about it – an illegitimate Saviour, who came to redeem illegitimate, unworthy, sinful people who to this very day, continue to reject Him. In the words of the young people – *WHAT??* Think about that and tell me if you still believe? I do! That is why it is called 'faith.'

Your relationship with God is a precious treasure that can only be accepted and maintained by faith. The alternative would be to abandon Him altogether. There are some things that we will never be able to convince others of. But should we even try to convince them? Should we who have been summoned by The Master now try to convince our fellow churchmen, that our names have been called? Jesus did not have much of a problem with what clergy thought. He knew who He was. Sure, He submitted Himself to the authorities of his day, and to His earthly parents. Nevertheless, He also knew that His time was approaching, and that the day would come wherein He would submit only to the will of The Father.

One day as Mary and Joseph were leaving Egypt, they were unaware that the caravan had left Jesus behind. When Mary went back to look for Him, Jesus asked her - "How is it that ye sought me, whist ye not (know you not) that I must be about My Father's business?" (Luke 2:49). He knew that when His set time came He would accomplish exactly what He had been sent on earth to do. In John 4:34 when Jesus says, "My meat is to do the will of Him who sent me." While The Disciples were supposing if anyone had brought The Lord any meat [as in physical food] to eat, Jesus let them know that He had, "Meat that they knew not of."

Jesus was speaking not about the meat of cows and chickens, but rather sustenance from on high. The meat of The Spirit, the thing that sustained Him; the heavenly delicacy that kept Him alive. His sole reason for existence was to do the will of God. Jesus knew that His mission was not to give explanation to critics but to do the will of The Father. Later, Jesus and His rag tag team of 12 turned this entire world upside down. Twelve against the world;

now check out those stats for being out numbered!

Because we live in a natural realm, we must follow the order of things. God has established positions of leadership in the church as well as in the home. Yes, He established the positions, but it does not mean that He expects leaders to abuse people. Neither does it mean that He will not remove them. How many fathers and TRUE shepherds do we have anyway? How many are able to take time to care about all of the sheep under their watch? How many are *willing* to care even if they do have the time? Seemingly, there just are not enough, who are concerned about God's people to the degree that they should be. Yet they blame the flock for everything.

They are quick to sermonize and bludgeon us to death with messages on how they feel the sheep are no longer listening to <u>them,</u> but interestingly enough; they hardly ever speak about the many shepherds "gone wild." They never expound upon the thousands of heart breaking stories that give attention to the fact that there are ravening "wolf clerics" who are trying to eat the sheep alive.

If bootleg pastors were not an issue, then The Lord would not have stated so many times IN HIS WORD, that He would raise up shepherds after His own heart. If wolves were not on the prowl, (making them a serious threat), then we would not see constant warnings in The Word of God cautioning us to beware of them, neither would we read or hear about "shepherds who fleece [and rape] the sheep" and neither would we be warned about the many "false teachers", "false prophets" and "hirelings."

Functioning in the role of a pastor or leader [in any capacity], does not make that person better than everyone else. A high position is no indicator that the person is operating in obedience to the will of God; neither does it automatically or necessarily prove that he or she <u>has ever been under the influence of The Holy Spirit.</u> Even a pastor or priest can function <u>in the church</u>, and yet (all the while), operate under the influence of someone or something <u>other than The Lord.</u> Don't believe me? Allow me to introduce you to Hophni and Phinehas, who were '<u>priests in the temple.</u>'

Hophni and Phinehas were the two sons of Eli the priest. These two boys were priests who while serving in the temple, were helping themselves to the sacrifices, amongst other things. Not only were they stealing, but also they were having sexual relations with the women who came to the temple – uh oh!

They were very sinful indeed and not at all godly like their father had been. The Bible even says of these two that they were, "Sons of belial." "They knew not The Lord." (I Samuel 2:12) "belial", (even here he gets no capitalization from me), is the father of all wickedness. Do I even have to tell you to whom this is referring?

It is very possible to function in ministry without even knowing The Lord. There they were, serving people, counseling them and performing their priestly and "spiritual fatherly" duties, yet the entire time, they were literally operating under satanic influence. Not only had they not operated under the influence of God, but also it is God by inspiration of The Holy Spirit, who (as it is written), calls them the sons of the devil. Wow! They were sons of satan, but were in the house [of God], AND THEY WERE SERVING IN A POSITION OF AUTHORITY!

Many pastors today are themselves operating under that same influence. They are endeavoring to lead God's people, while functioning under the rulership of everything wicked, just as Eli's sons had done long ago. NO WONDER THE SHEEP ARE SO MESSED UP AND CONFUSED!

Pastors who are true agents of God would not purposely and maliciously wound people to the degree that they no longer want to attend church. They would not willfully crush the spiritual life out of people with prideful arrogance. Legitimate pastors would not try to hinder a "true movement" of God's Spirit. If you have never experienced such a thing, then this may be very hard for you to believe [or to accept]. Whether or not you believe it, does not mean that it is not a fact – IT IS HAPPENING!

What classifies a pastor as a "spiritual father" (or mother), anyway? Is it a position? Is it money? Is it the vote of the people? On the other hand, is it simply a title that people pin on themselves? In the Word of God, we are given the criteria for various offices. For instance, if you check out the qualifications for the office of a Bishop, we would all have to agree, that there are a whole lot of men (and now even women) who daun this title, who are a far cry from legitimately qualifying, but yet they occupy the position just the same.

How do the sheep know if their shepherd is trustworthy or if whether or not he or she has their best interest at heart? Pastors, Jesus knows His sheep by name – do you? A good shepherd is concerned about *all* of the sheep – even those who run away. In addition, He is concerned about the wayward ones, like the "special needs" crowd; the people who you never bother to seek after because you are too busy or because you simply do not care.

The Father never stops looking out for His prodigals.   He is constantly on the watch and is always hopeful of their safe return. Now, how many pastors can still claim that they qualify as a shepherd, a bishop or as a father – spiritual or otherwise?

If you *are* a pastor, do you display Christ-like love for all of the brethren? Are you connected enough to your flock to spot when one of the little ewe lambs may be in trouble, you know, like the one who has been missing for months at a time? Are you concerned enough to care about the lone choir member who once served faithfully but has suddenly begun missing in action? Does anyone bother to call and see if there may be a problem, or if such a one may require the congregation's assistance? Do you even care?

My goodness, you are not that busy, neither are you *that* important. Jesus, who is my Shepherd, is also a King, yet He still takes time to care about me.   Although Jesus had the 'juice', He made Himself of no reputation, but instead took on the form of a servant. Jesus did not glorify Himself, He Glorified The Father! He became a servant even unto death. But while He was here, my Saviour washed dirty, stinky feet. Woe unto you, fake shepherds and fathers!

If you are a pastor, can these things be said of you? Do you truly care for your flock? **WE DON'T WANT YOU TO THINK SO IN YOUR OWN EYES,** but can those who serve under your leadership detect that you are concerned about them? Let me rephrase that. Can people who serve in your congregation, (THE ONES WHO ARE NOT SPIRITUALLY BLIND); detect your genuine concern for them also?   Pastors are you out there? Can you please come forward and identify yourselves?   We need more of you who really have a heart for the things of God.

We need those who <u>truly want</u> to care for us. Who amongst you has been assigned to care for the bastard and reject population? Can you please come forward and claim your calling? We're waiting!

Even if some of us are a little high-strung or rough around the edges, can we please count on you to work with us anyway? Can you be patient enough to help us until 'we get it?' Where are you? If you have a heart after God, can you please come out of your hiding places? There are many who desire to learn from you.

LET THE CRY BE HEARD THROUGHOUT THE LAND; WE NEED TRUE FATHERS!

WOLVES, HIRELINGS, GOATS, PIMPS, PLAYBOYS, PEDOPHILES AND CON ARTISTS NEED NOT APPLY. DO US ALL A FAVOR AND STAY HOME! STAY AWAY FROM ME! STAY AWAY FROM GOD'S PEOPLE! STOP DEFAMING THE NAME OF THE LORD! AND FOR GOODNESS SAKE STOP HARMING THE BABIES!

STAY THE HELL OUT OF THE MINISTRY IF YOU MEAN US NO GOOD!

We need true men and women of God to step up to the plate. We need you to help undo the damage already done by the wolves and pseudo servants. Is there room for the hurting and the broken in your congregation? Do you welcome the prophetic voice? Would a person such as myself be welcome to serve amongst you, without *you* becoming intimidated and straightaway embarking on a crusade to destroy my spirit? Remember I don't want nor do I need *"your stuff."* God will give me whatever platform He has assigned for me. I wish to serve under a leader who is Kingdom-minded and Kingdom-bound as well as confident and secure enough in His own position [in The Lord], to allow me to be who God has called me to be.

Ministers of the Gospel of Jesus Christ, the harvest is waiting. I heard Bishop Paul Morton once preach a message that asked a question. "Is there not a cause?" He wanted to know. To the bishop I say indeed, there is a definitive cause. The need is for the fatherless to be fathered. The cause is so that God's babies will not be left out. The cry of the bastard child has reached The Heavenly Father's heart. Not only has their cry touched it, but also their wailing has pierced it to the very core, and The Father is very, very concerned. Did not Jehovah indeed say that He is a Father to the fatherless? He did not say that He *was*, but God said He *is*. *When The Lord says a thing, we can certainly depend on it.* His 'is' means that a thing is eternally so. Because pastors have neglected their responsibilities to fatherhood, it has become necessary for The Lord to once more take back the reins.

Do you know how many grown people there are who have no one to be their covering, but they love Jesus? Have you any idea how many physical orphans and illegitimate children exist in our world today? The unwanted and unloved are all over the land. When their needs go unmet, throughout childhood and even during their teen years, guess what happens? They grow up to become adults who are still unwanted. Many of these precious people have NEVER known *anyone* whom they could call father. Some have no idea who they really are, or where they come from because momma refuses to tell them the truth.

In fact, because some women have slept around so much, without sufficiently spacing out their torrent "love triangles", they themselves are clueless as to who has fathered their now illegitimate child/children.

I once saw a young girl on a talk show, who issued tests to over 20 men as she attempted to establish the paternity of her baby. Not one of the men tested proved to be the child's father – Lord Jesus. Now let us imagine the same child [or children] all grown up, who one day comes to know The Lord. Let us further suppose that such a one finds him/herself in the ranks of Christendom, only to discover that once more there is no one who cares. Having been dealt a gut-wrenching blow, this person now struggles to deal with yet another deficit.

Reader can you even imagine what it must feel like, to live your entire life as <u>a human question mark?</u> Have you any idea how it feels, to have no clue as to who your father is, and at the same time wrestle with your emotions, as you attempt to understand, why it is that no one wishes to claim you as a daughter or son? So as it is in the natural, so is it also in the spirit. Well Pastors, there are people just like that in your congregations, and each week you continue to snub them.

Thankfully, because Jesus is The Good Shepherd and God is a loving Father, these precious souls can still be covered and loved. God has a special place in His heart for widows and orphans and yes – even for bastards. Woe unto you pastors and priests who offend the children and widows. For Jehovah has said:

Ye shall not afflict any widow, or fatherless Child. If thou afflict them in any wise, and they cry at all unto me, I shall surely hear their cry; And my wrath shall wax hot, and I will kill you with the sword; and your wives shall be widows and your children fatherless" (Exodus 22:22-24).

I don't know about anybody else, but this writer has done a whole lot of crying. Think about how many times The Lord said that He would raise up priests that would say what He is speaking and not what their pride is compelling them to say. I long for the time when The Father Himself, begins to birth pastors who will feed HIS sheep with His Word, rather than oppress them, control them, and rape the life out of them. Our Heavenly Father desires for you and I to have a dad, and so He has adopted us. I cannot officially speak for anyone else, but I know that God is my Father. I am not anyone's bastard, spiritually or otherwise. Jesus surely knew that our fathers would eventually run amuck. For even in Matthew 23:9 (read the entire Chapter) He tells us to, "Call no man father upon the earth: for [only] one is your Father, which is in heaven."

Now pastors, do you still think that *you* deserve the title of "spiritual father?"

I had a biological father and a stepfather. I tried to have a spiritual father. Not one of these has ever treated me better than my Heavenly Father. I personally believe that God has a Remnant to whom He alone will play Dad and I for one could not be more delighted. I believe that God will soon pay a mighty visit to this earth realm.

What happens when God comes down? He finds the underlying cause of things. He solves problems. He puts some up, and takes some down. He plucks up even by the very root! My Father handles His business. If necessary, He cleans house and starts from scratch! God said concerning the wicked cities of Sodom and Gomorra, (upon hearing of their blatant sin of homosexuality), "If it is true, I will know it. And if it is not, I will know" [that also].

He is on His way to visit our churches. He will press His ear against the wall of our hearts to see whether or not He can find anything that resembles His own. He's going to know who has been good and who has not.

He has heard the voice of the reject. He has heard the cry and has seen the heart of the illegitimate and rejected, as well as their longing to belong. God will nurse us back to health as only He can. He has seen it all and has witnessed everything as the hot tears have rolled down our cheeks. He is quite aware of the restless nights wherein we have tossed and turned.

Hallelujah! We who have been called bastards *have* gotten His attention. For He has loaned us His ear; and we have been granted access. For God has extended His golden scepter; and we have gently touched Him who has so graciously first touched us. He has granted us permission to enter the throne room and to submit our petition and our request.

"We want fathers", say the children. "Request granted," said He. God is well able to be whatever we need Him to be. Mr. Vandross penned the words exactly right as he expressed his longing to dance with his [biological] father, again. My Heavenly Father came to see about me and we have begun a dance of our own.

For years, I put stock into what *THEY* said. Some were well meaning, and others were cruel on purpose. I messed up because I became more concerned about what *THEY* thought. In actuality, it had been the people in the "*THEY CLUB*" who had led me astray.

Like Peter who I told you was *already* walking on the water *before* he began to survey that which surrounded him. He did not begin to go down until he took his eyes off Jesus, who had bid him to "Come" in the first place.

Perhaps I could have made it to my purpose a lot less confused, scarred and beaten up, had I kept my gaze upon the one whom my heart adores. Had I kept focused [on The Father], I would not be the bloody mess that I am today. Nevertheless, I am stronger and better for having survived each experience – whew! Of a truth, I have rediscovered something of old, which remains true to this very day – "Can't nobody do me like Jesus."

I am delighted to be back at the place with my Dad, wherein deep again calls unto deep, and the depth (deeper spiritual things) in me, respond to the infinite depth in Him. Once more the frequency is unhindered and I hear Him with clarity, because *finally,* I have stopped tuning in, to everyone else.

Locked in His strong embrace, once more, we have begun to dance! Engaged in a Spiritual tango with my Dad, I dance with He who loves me best. Swept off my feet, by the one who led me to the dance floor so very long ago – I am now safe in His arms. He knows every 'numbered hair' on my head as well as which 'hair numbers' fall into my sink, each time my hair is combed.

I am dancing with He who knows *everything* about me and yet loves me anyway. Because His love is eternal, we are in it for the long haul – for life! He has seen the good, the bad, *and* the very, very ugly and has yet called me to worship and also to "the dance." He has seen all my (spiritual, physical and emotional) scars; and has kissed and anointed each one. He saturated them with the oil of Himself – *for He, The Lord God, is love.*

He has witnessed my shortcomings and even my pain. He has joined me in lament over every traumatic event. Never once has He ever turned away from me, but to this day, He continues to embrace me. He is there all of the time just for the asking. I can call Him when I need Him as well as when I simply want to say, "Hello Dad." But do you know what the best part is? It is *He who often calls for me.*

Imagine that, The Father often summons one who has been rejected by others. Wow! The most awesome thing about my Father is that no matter how many children He has, He always has time just for me. Never have I ever felt neglected. If the truth were told, it is I who have often neglected to spend quality time with Him – sorry Dad.

So you see hirelings and humans, <u>you</u> <u>can't</u> <u>hurt</u> <u>me</u> <u>any</u> <u>more.</u> Things with God and I are back to normal. No longer can I afford to be fathered by earthly hands because they hurt too much, and too often, they lack the wisdom necessary to guide me into my purpose. I suppose this works out exactly the way you intended it to. Dad, pastor, you were always unavailable, because you never wanted me in the first place.

Dearest Father(s), (biological, step, and/or spiritual): Having a nurturing earthly male figure to call 'Dad' would have been wonderful during my younger years. Unfortunately, your presence is no longer something that I continuously crave.

I am all grown up now with a family of my own to care for. There once was a time however, when I really needed you. I longed for you, and I waited patiently for you, but you refused to come. For so long I held out hope that you would change your mind, but instead you remained aloof.

I would have respectfully submitted to you as I solicited your guidance and advice. Unfortunately, my waiting proved to be in vein, because you <u>always</u> let me down, as you <u>never</u> even bothered to show up.

I no longer have the same desire to see you, or to even talk to you. I've had to learn so many things about life and about myself, without you being there. I had no <u>earthly</u> role model to look up to, no one to call my hero! As a result, I have made terrible mistakes, many of which I am dreadfully ashamed to acknowledge – but I have.

The good news however, is that I did <u>eventually</u> learn from my poor choices. Through it all, I have also grown spiritually, more than you will ever know. Fathers, do not be too angry with yourselves. I am certain that you had your own reasons for being aloof, apathetic and in many instances, altogether absent.

Many of you were lousy nurturers, even when you were in the home. Dad, for the most part, you were simply unavailable. It is not yet too late for you to be a father <u>should you decide to be.</u> However, I think it is only fair to inform you that you have showed up at a time <u>when I no longer need you to be.</u>

For you see, it was not so long ago that I stopped looking for you altogether. In fact – it was only yesterday.

Lovingly submitted,

From all of the children who survived without you – and in many cases, we survived even in spite of you!

P.S. God bless you dad!

❧*Whom Shall We Blame Anyway?*❧

For the pastors who see *us* as bastards, perhaps you should ask yourselves a question. Do you honestly think that God will hold the sheep responsible, for the atrocities that you have committed? It was by virtue of your own neglect, that so many were forced to walk away. All we wanted from you was your love; at the very least, we had hoped for your respect. We submitted to your authority, only to find ourselves trampled under foot with our hopes and in many cases, even our dreams dashed or snuffed out altogether.

Most of us desired only the crumbs from your tables, but instead, you purposely left us starving to death. We hungered for your acceptance and were desirous of your fatherly blessing, but you pushed us away. Are *we* to blame? Or on the other hand, will the charges be laid to your account? Fathers and Shepherds you need to think about that. In fact, many of you should repent even now for the collective millions who have turned away from the faith because of your ill treatment.

Upon whom do you suppose the greater sin shall be? Does it rest upon our shoulders for pursuing the will of God despite your withholding of the blessing, and the nurturing relationships that we so desperately needed and longed for? We looked up to you. We admired you, but you tried to keep us from accomplishing that which we had been clearly destined to carry out. Looking up to you is what we have been taught to do for most of our lives. In fact, it really wasn't that difficult, because we *wanted* to believe in you. We wanted your guidance because we trusted you; we wanted to be just like you. We were always taught to be, "Good little Christian boys and girls."

Never were we permitted to ever ask questions or to talk back; nor could we dare voice our opinions on your ability to lead. For that matter, we were not to have much say at all, about anything! Pastors and fathers, not even once did we ever disrespect you, or question your authority. For even when doubts arose in our minds, we remained obedient. And in all of this, you still pushed us away. Perhaps it really is our own fault for putting so much confidence in our leaders to begin with.

Many of us believed in *them* and as a result, our spirits were nearly beaten to death. Not until we had suffered a near fatal wounding, did our eyes finally come open. We have come to see, that in many instances our leaders have never been who or what they pretended to be. Because of them, many of us have had difficulty even seeing God. We listened to their counsel, and became more bewildered. At one point, during my own ordeal, The Lord pointed out to me that, "I had been operating in unbelief." To my utter dismay and shock, I inquired of Him. I knew that I believed what He had spoken and I knew that God could do anything that He wanted to. I also knew that I had heard His voice and that He had an assignment for me to carry out. This would be something for which I had been groomed for much of my life. What was I lacking? How could I now be in a state of unbelief?

God said to me, **"When I tell you something, you don't need to ask anyone else."**

He was right - God was God. Who else's permission did I really need anyway?

Because I kept halting between two opinions – HIS AND THEIRS, God was right; I had literally been straddling between what He said and what they thought. I <u>was</u> in unbelief and as a result, I had become terribly confused. Although I knew God's voice, I yet found myself hesitant and always stopping way short. He was right (as usual); my own unbelief had kept me from moving forward. I became my own stumbling block, because I had started listening more to His representatives, then I was to Him, (because they said that, they knew more than I did). I stopped short because I did not want to appear as a renegade or as someone who seemed bent on doing my own thing, [as pastors often accuse people of].

Doing what I wanted had indeed not been the attitude of my heart. It was my desire to do only that which God had assigned to my hand. Like I said before, a position was not what I sought, but rather it was The Lord who had sought me [for the position] – oh God. Yet the anticipated backlash from *them* kept me in a state of flux, confusion and instability. I suppose James said it best, "A double minded man is unstable in all his ways." (James 1:8). I am in essence largely to blame for having wasted so much time, because GOD HAD ALREADY SPOKEN TO ME. Of course, I did not listen because *they kept telling me that I would be out of order. They said that <u>God would always speak to my pastor first and that if my pastor did not approve, I would be out of the will of God, and that He (God) would not be pleased with me. Of course, I did not want God to be displeased, so I listened to those who claimed to be His shepherds.</u>*

Howbeit they fail to tell of their own selective memory. They never preach about the fact that they are often guilty of not listening to God speak because they don't approve of the person or group of people that He may be speaking to them about. They do not share with the flock how that they have been guilty of convincing themselves that they do not hear what they know they do. They will never admit that they have on many occasions, completely ignored the counsel of God, simply because they did not like certain individuals. This is the portion that they so conveniently [love to] leave out.

They have selective hearing, because if they do not like a person, they will never truly receive such a one (in their congregations), neither will they ever support him/her in ministry. So now dear one, because your pastor has not released you, you sit, and sit, and sit, and sit. God is still calling, but yet you sit and sit and sit some more.

You need to ask The Spirit of God to demolish the destructive systems of "them and they say."

You should always ask God, if you are not sure who is doing the speaking. If you are not certain that you know His voice, please do not be afraid or too embarrassed to admit it. Even if you have been in church for many years – please do not be ashamed. *It is far better 'to learn' a little late, rather than 'to be' too late!*

The Bible says that God's sheep hear [and know] His voice – they are not "into strangers and hirelings." Perhaps you feel as though you are not one of His because you are not sure whose voice you are actually hearing. I know it can be tricky, especially when the wrong voices keep coming from places that we should be able to trust, like from behind the pulpit. Because we respect our clerics, we have subconsciously come to see them as those who have an edge, with The Lord. A lot of people have even come to view their pastors as being some sort of 'God-men.'

I suppose that this would be equivalent to how a great number of people in the Catholic Church (and others) view their pope. Some parishioners actually believe that their leaders reign in equality with The Almighty. Know they not that their leaders are mere men of flesh, just as they are?   Even the blessed Mother of Jesus, who should be held in high regard, (as she did carry The Christ Child in her womb), but still, she is not equal to Him, neither do we have to pray to her, in order to reach Him.

The Bible lets us know that, "There is only one mediator between God and man, The Man Christ Jesus" (I Timothy 2:5). While The Pope, a bishop, a pastor and even The Blessed Mother of Jesus are to be revered, and given proper honor and respect, certainly, they are never to be worshipped. Neither of their names is the one upon which we must call for Salvation. It is not necessary to have more than one mediator, but it is imperative that you know HIS voice. If you cannot determine when it is He who is doing the speaking, why not ask Him?

Ask The Lord to teach you how to hear Him. Do not let your admission of not being sure you can identify His voice, be the thing that hinders you. Instead, why not let this be your very first step in learning. For goodness sake, don't be too proud to ask Him for help *and/or for clarity!* The very fact that you *are* concerned and *are* seeking His will, indicates that you WANT to belong to HIM and that you REALLY DO want to do things His way.

Ask God to train you to distinguish His voice above ALL the rest so, that YOU will stop being misled. Remember God is NOT like man. He knows exactly what has led to your confusion – He won't hold it against you. He knows why you have held back. Still, I am not sure though to what extent our "reasons" for not obeying will matter to Him. We have our Bibles and we should be searching The Scriptures FOR OURSELVES, regardless to what anyone else tells us.

Therefore, I do not believe that the 'reasons' (or excuses) we offer for not knowing His will, are going to hold up. We are not supposed to totally rely upon our pastors to tell us what God has said (or is saying) anyway. If we do, then we are at fault. For even The Saints in Berea did not blindly accept the words of Paul and Silas, but also they searched The Holy Writ <u>for themselves</u>, to see if whether or not they were being told the truth (Acts17: 10-11). This beloved is also, what God expects of us.

I found out the hard way, that God is not bound to do something in the same manner all of the time. *He can, and does speak to His creation at any time that He sees fit. GOD DOES NOT ALWAYS WORK THE SAME WAY WITH EVERY INDIVIDUAL EACH TIME THAT HE DECIDES TO DO A THING.* He did not first consult with Eli the priest when He decided to call Samuel. God went directly to the boy, and stood [over his bedside] and spoke directly (and only) to him. Because Samuel was not use to hearing the voice of The Lord, he thought that Eli had called him. Read it for your selves in I Samuel Chapter 3. It wasn't until the third time that Samuel had run to him, that Eli perceived that The Lord must have been calling the child. Unlike many of *our leaders,* I must at least give Eli credit for pointing the boy back to The Lord.

Although Eli had not done such a great job in rearing his own boys, who were now grown, (remember Hophni and Phinehas – the priests, who The Bible declares were the sons of the devil), at least he did not get jealous of Samuel, when he suspected that The Lord was calling for him. Neither did Eli purposely steer him in the wrong direction or try to discourage him altogether, like so many of our clerics do. Though Eli had much to lose, still he did not tell the boy that, "God couldn't possibly be speaking to him, because he was just a child." Had Eli been like many of our pastors, he could have easily convinced Samuel that he was only "hearing things"; or that "satan was trying to confuse him" and that; "God had not called him at all.

In addition, he could have told Samuel, that it was "Only his [own] flesh" calling. You know how *they* do. Eli could have easily discouraged Samuel, in an attempt to thwart the plan of God; for His plan would include some major changes. In fact, these changes would drastically affect Eli's ministry. The time for the changing of the guards grew closer and Samuel would become his successor as Priest. (Additionally, Samuel would also be appointed as "Prophet"). Eli could have easily led the boy astray *on purpose.* God's ushering in of the new order would have signaled that the time had come for the old to either move over or to move out. Eli had been Samuel's only mentor, and was in the best position to do exactly that.

Samuel, the boy who would be Prophet, looked up to Eli, who had been the closest thing to God that he had known up to that point in his young life – and he trusted Eli. Eli must have known in his heart, that the time for change had come; but even so, never did he ever mislead the boy. He instead told young Samuel to go back and "lie down." Eli told him how it was that he should answer if "He" (God) should call again. Little Samuel was told to say, "Speak [Lord], for thy servant heareth." The Lord "Stood over the bedside of Samuel"; and indeed, for the forth time, He called his name. This time, young Samuel was ready and prepared to give the proper response. Although Eli had been given the privilege of instructing Samuel, the time had come for God to take over.

God did not even share with Eli that which He had spoken to Samuel. In fact, The Bible lets us know that it was Eli who asked Samuel the following morning, to share with him all that The Lord had spoken. He literally went as far to admonish the boy, that he should hold nothing back of The Lord's sayings. Please read the entire story; in its context for yourselves. Check out Eli's response after Samuel discloses all that The Lord told him. Eli said, "It is The Lord: let Him do what seemeth Him good." I Samuel 3:18. In other words, what Eli said was – "This is The Lord's doing, I submit to His will; let Him have His way!"

Keep in mind that Samuel was only a boy. He did not yet know The Lord (neither could he discern His voice); as The Word of The Lord had not yet been revealed unto him. Because Samuel was not acquainted with His voice; or with hearing HIM speak, he did not know that he was being called. What of you and me? I know that many of you, by now have got to know the Lord's voice. We have The Bible in its entirety to refer to – His Word is now complete! AND HIS Spirit should be abiding in your heart. Surely, God has called your name and has asked something of you.

Who or what is it that has hindered you from giving Him the proper response? Who *is* responsible for listening and for hearing the voice of The Lord? We may not have an Eli to help us, but we do have someone much better. We have The Holy Spirit. Our pastors are not God, but we fail to heed God's voice because we are too busy listening to *their* words. Just as The Lord did not first consult with Eli about Samuel; He will not *always (or necessarily)* consult with your pastors about you. Unfortunately *they* will not [usually] inform you of this very pertinent piece of truth. It really is God's doing, not yours, not theirs and certainly not mine – GOD ALONE DOES THE CALLING.

We need to know this! We also have The Bible, Jesus, prayer, and fasting. Each stands readily available to assist us and are just waiting to be accessed. Our "holy tools" are more than capable and are indeed willing to help us learn of Him. With this arsenal at our disposal, there is neither valid reason nor excuse for any one of us to be roaming around in ignorance and in uncertainty. Will The Lord blame the sheep for honoring the opinions of mere mortal men above His own? Will He blame the shepherds who have purposely beaten the sheep with tainted doctrinal jargon and ecclesial trappings? This *they* did as we sat idly by in our stupor. This *they* still do as many continue to fall way short of God's best for their lives.

Whom *will* The Almighty hold accountable for this mess anyway? Perhaps the blame will be of equitable distribution. The pastorate hammers into our psyches the necessity of a "fatherly blessing", while simultaneously, admonishing us not to make a move until, and/or unless *they* say so. I certainly cannot see by Scripture that this is always the norm.

Is waiting on them necessary or just preferable? Most of us do prefer to have a father or mentor. However, does the absence of such totally disqualify someone from fulfilling the purpose of God? Is the fatherly blessing ALWAYS required in order to move forward?

We certainly cannot argue that Paul mentored Timothy, as did Elijah [mentor] Elisha. On and on throughout the pages of Scripture, we can find examples of the fatherly blessing and of the mentoring relationship. Still inquiring minds want to know why *they* do not preach more about people like John The Baptist, Moses Gideon and even Mary the mother of Jesus?

These people, (as did most throughout The Bible), received a direct mandate from The Lord without the presence of a confirming voice, mentor or earthly blessing. They did not have to go through a pastoral clearinghouse.

Mary's mission was to give birth to The promised Messiah. Although the circumstances regarding His conception had to have been less than believable (in the natural, as you have already read) still she received the word joyfully and she believed (and obeyed) God. What about clerics of old who opened store front churches and ran tent revivals? Sometimes, with ***only one word*** to go on, these courageous men and women stepped out upon the foundation of faith, under the covering of Jehovah.

Fearlessly taking a leap, many went on to do mighty exploits for The Kingdom. This they did, long before Christendom became filled [and bogged down] with all of the knowledge that we have today; which by the way, seems to be accompanied by more rules, than the ones Jesus left on record.

Were all of these great men and women bastards too?? Many there were who stepped out after having received only a single word from The Lord; often it was the word GO! For the most part, they had no one to bless, birth or to believe neither in them nor in their vision [one that God had given]. He Himself took care of the most intricate details. For He blessed, He birthed and He bound them to accomplish that which He alone had beckoned them unto. He even bestowed upon them everything that they would need to carry out the assignment.

WARNING: STEP OUT ON FATH. BUT "ONLY" IF YOU HAVE A SURE WORD FROM 'THE LORD'. NEVER MAKE A MOVE BASED SOLEY UPON WHAT YOU (OR OTHER PEOPLE) THINK. ONCE YOU HAVE GOTTEN A DEFINITAVE WORD FROM HIM THEN YOU MUST STOP WAVERING AND GET MOVING

I told you that for much of my younger life He had trained me to recognize His voice and many of His ways. I knew that He was with me. In addition, I knew that God talked to me, but because of my lagging self-esteem and desire to *'fit'*, I allowed public opinion to get the best of me.

Guess what? After all was said and done, I still didn't fit in. It would not be until much later, that I would *finally* discover [realize and understand], a startling truth about myself and also about The One who had created me. Never was I made to 'fit' – for God did not fashion me in that manner.

The practice of *blind conformity or simply blending in,* had never been encoded nor programmed into my DNA. Simply put – I did not fit, *because I wasn't supposed to!* I should have known better, and have only myself to blame. Often I feel as though I have failed God on a much deeper level than I care to admit. I messed up by allowing people and fear to hold me back; I wavered instead of operating in the solid trust and pure belief that had been placed into my heart so long ago. You also have some choices to make. I pray you choose wisely. For goodness sakes, don't do as I did! Don't wait until you have become ill from the instability of popular opinion. I can only hope that it is not too late for me.   Now that I have **finally** come to my senses, I pray that there is still something left for me to do. I am relying on Him to restore the years that I have allowed the enemy to steal, many of those years I gave him for free, because I never fought back. I failed to use my spiritual tools.

One thing is for sure, as I have already shared with you, - in the natural, a child is never considered a bastard of his or her own accord. Likewise, in the spiritual scheme of things there exists only one real route to bastardizm, as you shall soon discover.   Yet the question remains, who *will* God blame?   Our parents can be blamed for not properly fulfilling their obligations as our caretakers. Likewise our pastors may be blamed because they did us wrong. Some gave us wrong information on purpose, while others simply did not know any better themselves. In the final analysis, however, it is *we* who are ultimately responsible, for hearing and obeying, the voice of The Lord *for ourselves.* We are responsible for doing exactly what He tells us to do, no matter the outcome and no matter who may be telling us [to do] something different.

Perhaps the real question should not be about blame. Instead, maybe we should set our focus upon discovering how it is that each of us can begin making a difference. Everyone in The Body must be willing to make amends. We must apologize, first to one another, and then to The Lord. I know it seems as though, we should first apologize to Him and then to our brothers and sisters. I'm not saying that you absolutely cannot go to God first; but in some instances, He will not even listen to us, until we have first made things right with the person, whom we have offended – or who has offended us.   Each of us must be willing to do our own part, so that together we can advance our Father's Kingdom. Only then will we be able to stand before Him [being] blameless.

&Getting On With It&

Thankfully, I have overcome my pain and have forgiven those who wounded me. For I realize that they are only flesh, just as am I. Thinking about the pain is no longer an activity of regularity. Sill, I must admit though that on very rare occasions, I feel somewhat angered and quite saddened as I in hindsight survey *certain aspects* of the ordeal. Even though I have forgiven them, (at least I honestly believe that I have), I no longer trust them to hear from God for me, as they claim to be their job. Neither do I seek the approval of any man, when it comes to carrying out the assignments of The Lord. Honestly, I can no longer afford to be hindered because; I have a promise to keep to Him. I promised God that if He spoke to me again, I would do His will to the best of my ability. I told Him that if He called my name, I would come running and would not allow myself to become sidetracked.

If I KNOW the voice of THE GOOD , why then should I feel obligated to check with people anyway, only to be met with more discouragement, and humiliation or to be totally ignored again? I am not going to keep being wounded by the same imposters who are merely posing as pastors.

This time should The Master have need of me, I will not bail from the war. I refuse to be AWOL (absent without [permission to] leave. God is not in the habit of speaking just to hear Himself speak. He already knows the sound of His own voice as well as what is on His own mind. If He speaks a word into the earth realm, it *always* has purpose. If God speaks a word <u>directly to you</u> my friend, that too is for a reason. He expects <u>*you*</u> to take action. You are hereby charged and obligated to do something with what He speaks to your heart or places into your hands. Countless times had The Lord God spoken to me concerning a matter of significance for a season or about something that would soon unfold throughout Christendom. The lessons or messages seemed to be ahead of their time, because many people surrounding me would often appear puzzled if I shared them. For this reason, I could not always share the revelatory words of knowledge that The Lord would give to me. Instead, I resigned into a place of meditation; I pondered them mainly in the annals of my mind and in the confines of my own heart.

Many things that The Lord spoke were not necessarily being preached or written about at the time. This served as even more of a reason for my uncertainty as to whether or not I had indeed heard Him correctly [or not]. Because it seemed as though I was the only person in my particular circle, hearing these things (not audibly, but in my heart and spirit), I allowed the enemy to make me wonder if whether or not I simply possessed an over-active imagination. I wondered, "Why had God persisted on doing this to me?" On occasion when I did try to share, the person (or group) with whom I'd speak, would usually nod politely in the spirit of agreement and camaraderie; but by the end of the conversation, the person would say something that would immediately indicate that he or she really had not gotten it at all – the individual wouldn't have a clue.

When the clerics finally did catch up, and started preaching about some of those same things, it would be nearly 2 to 4 years later. God had prepared me and/or had already taught me, well in advance as I spent time alone with Him. Neither a teacher nor pastor had made such a personal investment in my spiritual training, but The Lord had. Although deep down I knew that God was speaking, yet at the same time, I had no physical being with whom I could discuss these matters, without being branded a weirdo or something.

Sometimes I would be told that, what I was saying could not possibly have come from God – "because it was too strong", or that "it didn't sound right." (Because it was different). For this reason, I suppose it was easier to go along with popular opinion, rather than to stand all by myself. Brothers and sisters, how many times do we do this to ourselves? How often do we allow the enemy to prevail over our creativity as well as over our spirit? We are guilty of going along, in order to get along, simply because we do not want to rock the boat.

There I was inflicting that same old self-doubt; the very thing that had initially surfaced because of other people. And yes, sadly enough once again, I brought right into it. One day I wondered, "Who it was that had planted the notion in my head that I ALWAYS had to be "the wrong one." From whence had this garbled line of thinking come anyway? In my heart, I knew that I could not have been wrong ALL OF THE TIME; but still, because of my (then) low self-esteem, I seldom acquiesced. I suppose even as you read along, things seem a bit confusing. You must be asking yourself, how is it that I could have been definitive, in knowing the voice of The Lord, yet [at the same time] allow myself to be sucked into an abyss of doubt and confusion by mere humans - duhhhhhh! Either I knew (His voice and that which was right), or I didn't. A bit of a paradox to say the least - right??

I know *it sounds* bazaar; I suppose you just had to be there, (in my head) in order to understand the entire mess. There were many forces at work, and each one of them managed to do a major job on my mind. I found myself many times literally becoming as one who is double-minded. This remained my reality for a very long time, simply because I had not been strong enough to take a stand. My worth as a human being had plummeted, because I did not fit. And in turn, I became unable to assert myself, or to stand flatfootedly upon the things that I knew to be true.

If just reading about my ordeal confuses you, can you even imagine how I must have felt as I lived through these things?

This was the vicious cycle, in whose clutches I would remain for nearly 40 years. Off I would go again cowering under the weight of fear, confusion and self-doubt, while deep down inside, I knew that *somebody was calling my name.* At times, I felt as though I were embarking on the pursuit of Christian education, but at a much higher level than many of my surrounding [spiritual] peers. Seemingly, I took regular and advanced courses, while those around me were enrolled only in the non-credit course curriculums.

If you are familiar with non-credit courses, then you are aware that they are "brush up" or refresher classes. Their purpose is to familiarize the student with a subject matter or to bring him or her "up to speed." They are actually designed to <u>prepare,</u> and/or to equip a person to better handle <u>the real thing.</u> I once took two such courses during my college years. Algebra – "oh boy!" Never had I excelled in mathematics during high school and I could not wait to rid myself of everything having to do with equations, fractions and the like. Therefore, by the time I attended college, 'nearly 12 years later', I had no choice but to enroll in beginner or non-credit math.

Concerning the things of The Spirit however, I seemed to excel in comparison to those around me. But because I had no peers with whom to compare notes, it was difficult for me to blossom - still. Although it was I who had the advanced courses, people still managed to convince me that it was I who lacked. They treated me like an outcast and somehow, they actually made me believe, that I really did not know what I did. For many years, I held out hope, still longing to fit. However, in the process of time, it became difficult to discern truth from error (because of their many lies). I in turn, became quite confused and no longer knew me! Outwardly I went along with *whatever* they said, simply because they were the majority, while inwardly my soul raged on.

All the while, they were too blind to see that it was themselves who actually operated from a lower level. But alas, still I must take the blame, because it was I who had "played dumb" in order to gain acceptance. So as it is in the natural, so is it also in the spirit.

At the church of my wounding, there were a few times when I actually learned something from the pastor's messages that I didn't already know; but more often than not, I would leave with a deficit. Even so, I really did enjoy going there (because it was different from the type of church I had grown up in). Different, does not necessarily mean better (or worse) – just new. However, the fact of the matter is, there came a time when I simply required more.

The call of God began to burn more intensely in my heart, and I sought Him constantly for spiritual sustenance and reassurance. As I eagerly awaited His next move, many of my fellow congregants seemed content to dine on day old spiritual bread; more like 2-4 year old bread to be exact. I would often marvel at the level of spiritual immaturity exhibited, as the congregation would go into a frenzy, if the pastor preached something that <u>they thought sounded good.</u> I suppose *for them, anything was very good.* But for me, it just did not satisfy. I simply had to know *if there was* <u>*any more word from The Lord?*</u>

Again, I am not sharing this with you in an attempt to brag, for honestly I have no boast except in Christ. I share these things because you need to realize, that the same gift, which does eventually make room for you, can also become your greatest nightmare, or hindrance. It can lead to your demise if it is not properly harnessed while you are waiting on The Lord. The very gift, if not embraced, cultivated and 'tapped' can serve as your greatest source of discontent. In a word, it will drive you mad if never utilized. But until the set time of your unveiling, you must rely totally on God to help you maintain.

Never before had I realized, that the 'raging restlessness' inside of me, had only *persisted,* because *my soul* hungered for a substance, that *my senses* had not [fully] experienced; yet my heart and my intellect *knew* that such a delicacy existed 'somewhere.' The gifting in me needed *more truth; and more nourishment.* It needed 'to feed' on a 'higher manna', if it was expected to remain 'content' while awaiting its time of unleashing – and unveiling to the world.
     Oh God! *"Fill my cup Lord – I lift it up Lord." "Come and quench this thrusting of my soul." "Bread of heaven, feed me till I want no more." "Here's my cup; fill me up – and make me whole."* Yes children, – this [song] mirrored everything that was in my soul and had become my desperate cry!

What could I do? I could not talk to my pastor about these things, because he didn't like me. In addition, because I had received so many discouraging words and emotional assaults early in life, I allowed this to keep the gift and me at bay. Throughout much of my early life, I allowed people to keep me back and I never utilized the gift. I never prophesied (in that church), nor had I ever stood up in a disruptive manner in an attempt to "bring a word" – not even once. This is exactly what the enemy had [always] hoped for. The adversary has attacked me since my earliest existence. Beloved of God, you need to realize that he never even wanted this book to reach you. Each time that God saw fit to restore me, it would not be long before my spiritual legs would be kicked from beneath me.

Because I really wanted to be right, (with God) and in no way did I desire to be out of order, (with my pastor) the call as well as the words of knowledge would be something that I purposed to keep to myself – or so I thought anyway.

Although there seemed to be much vision in "the house", still I knew that *something* was missing. It almost seemed as though they were operating from an entirely different realm. One night as I inquired of The Lord, He showed me a vision of people in my church, clawing and scratching at one of the walls in the sanctuary. I did not see faces, only arms and hands of various hues.

Upon my inquiry as to *what* was wrong, The Lord's answer was quite simple, only two words, in fact – **"No depth"**, came the reply. He then explained to me that many in that church (and certainly in others too), are only at the surface level. They are still in the "outer court" and have never entered into "The Holy of Holies" – Blessed Be His Name. I then asked The Lord, what could a person do if he or she already had *some* level of depth but needed more? Do you know what He said? Yet again, only two words – He said, **"Go deeper."** Well gee, that sounded simple enough I thought, *but how?* My yearning for "something more" would remain constant and unfulfilled until one day...

I received an invitation from a friend; finally, I hit pay dirt – YES!
There I found people who seemed to be on another dimension – just like me! Also, I stood in awe because there, I was privileged and blessed to meet many who had far surpassed me in the things of The Spirit and I wanted some of that too. My desire increased even more, because now I had an opportunity to learn something new. I wanted more meat and *finally* I knew where to find some. This was the place for me I concluded.

Alas, I had found my people. Finally, I knew beyond a doubt that there *were* others like me - I had not been so spiritually odd after all. There were those present who prostrated themselves as they prayed and worshipped – just like me. They too were in harmony with The Spirit of God and they too were "free." The messages would so resonate with my spirit. This was exactly what I had hoped for. I could finally be myself! The Lord seemed to be speaking and confirming things just for me. I felt liberated and with that came the realization that I had not been inept or spiritually delusional for all those years. Where had I gone? To a Convention! Never once have I ever left a Praise Power Convention feeling anything less than spiritually charged, edified and ready to take on the world. I am so very grateful for my friend named Shirley, who saw fit to introduce me to this awesome event.

But...Oh no! Had I really found them? You see this was only a yearly convention and not a local church home. The spiritual food received during The Praise Power Celebration would often keep me feasting for an entire 12 months. I never got anything like this at my home church. Even with my newfound knowledge, never once did I act or behave unseemly. I continued to fellowship with my local church, but with a renewed sense of vigor and inner peace. I knew of a certainty that there *were* other people "out there" in Christendom, who had already gone deeper – and I wasn't far behind!

The Praise Power Celebration had been equivalent to discovering a whole new spiritual world. It truly helped me a lot. And my daughter, oh my goodness! She loves it, and with her energy, she fits right in. Major highlights for her include "Midnight Madness" (sessions for the youth). They praise The Lord – ALL NIGHT LONG! In addition, recording artist and pastor, Tonex conducted her baptism ceremony! For her, it could not get any better than that. Thanks again Shirley.

Anyway, I continued to show up on my posts at church, and was content to be a good little church member. There had been something about my encounters with other spiritually mature Saints that had given me a sense of peace and inner satisfaction. It had been just the reassurance that I needed to sustain me. Still, I knew that destiny was approaching. How did I know? – Because God had already told me. Since I had finally realized that I was not "some spiritual nut case" after all, it became much easier to be content. I could be happy serving as I waited in peace for God to move. When my time eventually did begin to grow near, I noticed more and more that God started to tug at my heartstrings even more so than usual. He would speak more frequently and His words would be wrought with swifter confirmation.

I would like to have shared many of these things with my pastor, but what could I say or do? To him, I was to <u>forever</u> remain in the choir, in the pews or behind the scenes with the children. I already told you, that the man did not like me. His dislike of me was something that I had sensed, quite early upon joining; but honestly, I had hoped that this would blow over, because I really did want to be part of the [church] family. I very much looked forward to going there (in the beginning). In addition, I did not want there to be even *the slightest* possibility that I had been wrong concerning his ill feelings towards me. I am not an individual who simply throws in the towel. I was not going to allow him or satan to run me out of the church, and so I hoped for the best.

As my set time drew near, it became increasingly difficult to understand *exactly* what God was doing. While destiny loudly beckoned, my pastor's disdain also seemed to heighten, as his ill feelings towards me, became even more evident. I really did not understand (at the time) exactly why it was that he did not care for me, especially since I had never operated in "the gift." Neither had I done nor said anything to let on that I had it. Still I knew that he just did not want me around.

In fact, I tried extra hard to stuff it. I did my best to conceal the gift, attempting not to attract attention, because attention [for me] often meant being hated.

On quite a number of occasions over the years, I'd notice him looking directly at me, and then frowning. He would scan the congregation, all the while with a huge smile on his face, until... he spotted me. Whenever he got to me, he would immediately become noticeably agitated (or something). His countenance would quickly change, and his smile would turn into a grimace. This really did do a number on me to say the least. It definitely was not the best thing for my spiritual self-esteem that's for sure. This happened a lot and it hurt. I became even more painfully aware of the fact, that my presence really did irritate him for some reason. And no! – it was not my imagination.

Only a few times in the entire eight-year period, had he ever looked at me (with a shred of decency) in a manner other than his classic expression, which brimmed with contempt. When he wasn't frowning at me, he seemed to watch me like a hawk, as though he were somehow trying [hard] to figure me out or something. Sometimes he actually appeared to be wrestling with himself in an attempt to not feel hatred, or to hide the contempt that he did feel. If I walked into the church, his eyes would follow me and he would literally frown up – I know he did, because I saw him! I felt his spirit towards me! Again, like I said, I have eyes and I SAW HIM!

I remember very vividly one night in particular, how he watched me as I made my way to my seat. His expression of hatred, disapproval or *whatever*, was soooooo darned obvious, that people <u>literally</u> turned around to see who he was looking at. Honest to goodness, his disapproving glare could have burned a hole straight through me. Seemingly all eyes were upon me. It was so embarrassing. As I prayed silently to God (trying hard to hurry and get to my seat), I couldn't help but wonder what the others must have been thinking. I kid you not; his disapproval was just that noticeable. He was not preaching, so I had not interrupted the service or anything. Nevertheless, his eyes seemed intent with hatred – he did not want me there!

Have you any idea, how hard it was to play that off – him staring and frowning at me, as the people looked on? A wealth of emotions ran through my body as well as through my mind. I'm thinking – GET ME OUT OF HERE GOD – *PLEASE!?* I tried hard not to notice the faces of those who had turned to see the sight. They simply *had* to see for themselves who had warranted such an icy stare. Who amongst them could have possibly been the object (more like the target) of the pastor's ruthless glaring? Who was it that agitated him so? The experience was intense and very uncomfortable to say the least – but still God helped me through it. Eventually I did meet at least one other person, who told me that he treated her pretty much the same way. This person supposed herself to have been alone in *her* suspicions, just as I had.

Although I have always known on some level that he did not care for me, I remained baffled as to the reason why. Most of the time, I tried to ignore what I knew, by telling myself not to jump to conclusions. You know; I told myself that, "It had to be my fault" - as *usual.* It would not be until June of 2003 that finally this would all make sense. I would finally be forced to see that which I had tried so hard to ignore. Maybe this all seems a bit childish but remember, this was not high school, this was my pastor! This was church, and this was about doing God's work! I attended faithfully, gave regularly, kept quiet, but was still hated. Also keep in mind, this was the man who I thought HAD to bless me; this is not just some childish rant, I really thought that any chance for future ministry hinged on his approval.

I now understand everything much better. Friends, you must realize that regardless of their positions, a lot of leaders do not have the same close relationship with God as you do. Pastors, who are themselves insecure or who are held captive by their own imaginations, will *always* feel threatened by anointed or gifted individuals. Because beloved, they are not as "spiritually high", seeing you calls their attention to that which they lack in themselves. They can pretend, but God knows. The strange thing is that many of you also know.

You probably find yourselves thinking things like –"Who me?" "I'm just a bench member?" "Why me?" "Why doesn't he or she like me?" "My pastor has no reason to feel threatened or intimidated by me." "What reason does he have to hate me?" "He has churches, members, cars and cash." "He has everything; why would he possibly have it out for me?" "I'm not even operating in my gift, for what reason does he hate me?"

Let me help a few "Josephs" that may be reading this book. Like I once heard a pastor say (on a tape) - "The Father has placed something [valuable] inside of you." *"Oftentimes the enemy will detect your gift long before you do."* "Just like Joseph's coat was colorful and brilliant, so is the anointing on your life – it's *"LOUD."* "It attracts attention." "The Father designed it that way" [on purpose].   He went on to say that, "You've got to know that the same anointing that attracts favor is also going to attract opposition." You may not even be aware of your own gifts (and or talents). Honestly, you don't even have to be [officially] <u>functioning.</u> But just the fact that you have it (the anointing) "on", is enough for people to hate you or to feel intimidated or uncomfortable being around you. (Do not take it personal, they are the ones who have the complex).

God has securely planted something inside of you, be it a gift, an anointing 'a presence', etc. Your adversary knows this, and he absolutely hates you because of it. Another person's refusal to acknowledge you (or it in you), does not negate its being there. The enemy knows this too; he is very much aware that he cannot remove it and neither can he snuff it out. Your enemy will never be able to remove, anything that The Father has placed inside of you; but what he can do however, is to try his best to keep you from ever tapping into and utilizing what you have been given. Many anointed/gifted individuals do not even realize that they are. They are a threat to hell! The pastor went on to say that, "Some people are going to be mad at you [intimidated by you, jealous of you, throw darts at you or absolutely hate you] just for wearing the darn thing (the coat; the anointing; the mantle)." You did not place it upon yourself, God did.

He said, "The enemy is often aware of what you possess long before you are." "Many times he tries to destroy you and your gift(s) while you are young" (before they are fully developed).

In my case, he tried to destroy me *before* I could even get here. Had the devil had his way, I would not be alive right now. (See: Oops Wrong Fold). Here are the nuts and bolts of the matter. This man of God said that the enemy knows, that "If you ever get to where you're going, [in God], you have the potential to, do his kingdom some major damage."

He said, that the devil will always *try hardest* to destroy [or to discourage you] while you are young – especially if you are to be a ***"deliverer."*** He tried to destroy Moses while he was an infant; you know the story. If you don't, go to Exodus and read it, see for yourself. He tried to snuff out our Saviour, long before He could take his rightful place. Don't forget about King Herod, who wanted the Baby Jesus dead – but God intervened via a dream to the Magi who had come to worship Him. They were supposed to report His whereabouts to the king, who *only pretended,* that he also wanted to worship Him, but was actually planning to kill The Saviour. However, the magi following orders from God, were instructed to go a different way. Many of you may also be deliverers of sorts. An entire generation might just be waiting on *your* arrival. *You* could very well be 'inwardly housing' something that has yet to come on the scene – who knows.

Could it be that you possess something of great value, like a cure for a disease? Perhaps you are the carrier of a great end-time message that will be of vital importance to The entire Kingdom! Think it not strange that your enemy will try to take you out, long before you ever manifest to those who await your anticipated arrival. To the pastor's statements, I will also add this. If satan and those employed by him, are not successful at destroying you during childhood, your fierce battle with him will continue well into adulthood.

It will not be over until YOU finally realize who YOU are in God and until YOU know that The Lord has always been with YOU and that He is still with YOU.

Although the battle may persist you can rest assured, knowing that you are a vital part of God's plan. The enemy and his imps will always try to assassinate you until the fulfillment of your purpose. Even as God prepares to unleash your gift into the world, the fight will rage on. Depending on what you have been assigned to carry out, the battle will be almost continuous and at times very intense. Sometimes you will certainly feel like giving up, count on it!

Beloved, you will have to fight in order to survive – and I do mean fight hard. However, the good news is, by this time you have discovered the truth about your self; you have also learned how to use, "The weapons of your warfare, which are mighty through God... (II Corinthians 10:4). The enemy's job has always been to destroy your self worth, and to kill your confidence by confusing you, thereby making you an emotional and or spiritual basket case. If he gets your mind, then you can hang it up. More than likely, you haven't a clue as to what lies in the balance, but your enemy does.

Not only must you fight to preserve your own destiny, but also you do not know who else's life is depending on your victory, so that they also can overcome. Who knows if whether or not like Joseph, you may be the very link to the preservation of a generation to come – maybe of an entire nation even. No wonder the adversary wants you dead; at the very least, he wants you out of commission and non-functional. He does not have to kill you physically, but if he can wound your spirit to such a degree that you give up or "hold back", your gift will not be effective for The Kingdom, and it will never reproduce. If satan can make you abort that which God has placed inside of you, he knows that you will no longer be a threat to his darkness.

The thing that catches most of us off guard and hurts us so badly, is the fact that the enemy often uses prominent, respected individuals, who we revere. These same people who are viewed as role models to thousands, maybe even millions, are often the very people he targets and employs to aid him in wounding and/or silencing us – because we look up to them, and often out of respect, we believe them even when they are wrong!

It is bad enough to witness them on television or to listen to them on the radio, but it is far more devastating when the near fatal blow, comes from someone who we thought to be trustworthy, like our own spiritual leader whom we see each week. When a person's very own pastor is responsible for inflicting the paralyzing wounds, it hurts far more than anyone could ever imagine. It hurts a lot – a whole lot. Ok fine, it hurts a hell of a lot! Is that honest enough for you?

As the years came and went, it was apparent that God wanted me for *something and it became increasingly more difficult to ignore His call*. How many of you know that, if The Master has chosen you for something, He is not going to take 'no' for an answer? So there I was; on one end with God calling, while on the other, my pastor had chosen either to ignore me or to oppose me. Talk about torture! In the midst of it all, people were steadily preaching the same thing –

"Your pastors know better than you." "He/She knows how to hear from God better than you." "God will ALWAYS SPEAK FIRST to leadership about anyone He is calling to the ministry." "Sheep nowadays think they know more than their shepherds." "All of a sudden everybody in the world thinks they've been called!" "The people just don't want to take correction." "This is a generation of bastard and rebellious sheep." On and on these messages filled the airwaves. We were either spiritually whipped, with the switches of bastardizm and rebellion or we were clobbered over the head with a 'prosperity' cattle prod.

Although I would receive reinforcement from people who I met during my travels, yet at my home church, I received no encouragement whatsoever. Because I did not want to disrespect my pastor, I kept quiet and went along with the program. In spite of how he felt about me, I stayed, and continued to do my very best to overlook his dislike.

I prayed and asked God to help the both of us. I asked Him to search me, to make sure that I had not done something wrong without knowing it. I asked The Lord to help me not to run away, but to stay on the [potter's] wheel until it was over. My daughter was young and I did not want to uproot her. Also, I had sincerely hoped that my pastor's ill feelings towards me would change and that I would eventually be allowed to advance in the ministry.

To some, my staying would no doubt be thought of as stupid or as self-sacrificing. At the time however, I simply could not help it. I hung in there, because I did not want to be accused of being a church hopper, and because I wanted to make sure that I was not moving ahead of God or taking the easy way out, by running away. I kept quiet and went along with the program. I determined that I would be obedient to my pastor, and that I would submit to his leadership. *I made up my mind that I would stay - until doing so darn near killed me.*

Eventually enough was enough. There came a time wherein I had no choice but to get on with the business of answering the call of "The One" who had summoned me. I had to get on with living my life and that included taking my rightful place, in the grand scheme of The Master's plan (whatever it was). I had to follow He who had called my name, whether I wanted to or not. Even if I had no earthly approval, and whether or not anyone else understood; God had already apprehended me for life, and to Him I had to surrender. For some of us, obeying The Lord does not come with an option.

The eagle-like talons of The Holy One of Israel had placed a firm grip upon my soul. For I had been tagged long ago, and now He was giving me no choice but to finally comply. Blessed Be His Holy Name!

❧One Wounded Sheep:
My Story❧

I don't mind letting you know, that after my pastor snubbed me, I felt so hurt that I could hardly sleep. Sometimes I tossed and turned all through the night, trying hard to figure out just why it was that my spiritual father did not want me as his daughter. After much deliberation, crying, counsel and prayer, there came a point when finally, I understood the dynamics of my entire ordeal. I remember one day, as I felt hopelessly depressed - yes, even Christians can get depressed.

Can we please stop pretending that we are so sanctified and so unattached that we are totally unaffected by the painful events that touch our lives? I was hurting – real bad. The devil is not playing; he's trying to destroy us all. We hurt because we are human. The church would be so much better if people would get real and stop pretending as though they have never found themselves, emotionally destitute and in the valley.

Deliverance will never come, if we cannot (or will not) be honest. At times, we get depressed and there is nothing shameful about admitting it. God still loves us even when we are hurting. We can even ask David and Elijah about depression. There came a time when the people who were with David, rose up and spoke of stoning him. This they contemplated, as their hearts were grieved, because the Amalekites had invaded the camp (Ziklag), burned it with fire and had taken their wives and children captive. The Scripture declares that David had to, "Encourage his own self in The Lord." I Samuel 30:6 David did not always have a cheering section and neither will we.

Elijah, prophet of the Most High; the same prophet who had raised the dead also succumbed to fear and depression, just after calling down fire from heaven at Mount Carmel. He became fearful and depressed, because of one evil woman named Jezebel, who had threatened to take his life. This mighty anointed vessel of The Lord ran away and commenced to throw a major pity party for one. Who then are *we* to pretend as though nothing could ever shake our faith or rattle our frail emotions? Even our Lord at times had hurt to the very core – for even "Jesus wept." I don't mind telling you that my 'saved' world has been rocked quite a few times because of some mood-altering event.

The key is however, that when these situations arise, (and they will) it is imperative that we meet with The Father. I found myself in a deep depression because my very own pastor had flat-out refused me. I knew that the man had issue with me, but never had I expected *this*. It was not so much his disapproval that stunned me, but it was more so the lofty manner in which he spoke to me. His prideful exhibit of speech had succeeded in both spiritually and emotionally paralyzing me for over a year.

Yet today, I am here to tell the story. Did you hear what I just told you? – ALTHOUGH HIS WORDS MANAGED TO TEMPORARILY PARALIZE ME, THEY DID NOT KILL ME; AND NIETHER WILL YOUR ENEMY'S VERBAL VENOM DESTROY YOU.

I had to wait a long time for my turn. When my time finally did come, I thought surely that my own pastor would jump for joy at the very thought of one of *his* congregants, (someone under *his* tutelage) receiving *"The call."* I thought that he would be proud of me. I was after all, a member (in good standing); if I were blessed of The Lord, so also would he be blessed at least that's what *I thought*. Little did I realize at the time, that consulting with him would be one of the worse mistakes that I would ever make in my entire life. Before I tell you the *final* incident of 2003, that left me totally baffled, I feel it necessary to *first* take you back two years earlier to October 2001.

Here goes…

The Lord had previously given me a vision, of which I had already received numerous confirmations. I never make a move unless God confirms something several times through a variety of circumstances.

I need to make absolutely sure that it is He who is speaking a thing, and that it is not only my idea. I make sure that I simply do not <u>want</u> to do or to pursue something and then try to convince myself (and others) that it is God's doing.   OH, YOU KNOW HOW SOME PEOPLE DO IT; THEY EXPECT GOD TO CO-SIGN THEIR CRAP BECAUSE <u>IT IS WHAT THEY WANT TO DO AND GOD HAS NOT SPOKEN AT ALL!</u> LET ME ASSURE YOU, THAT THIS IS NOT MY STYLE.

After numerous biddings from The Lord, I finally called the church office and inquired as to how I might make an appointment to speak with the pastor. The secretary gave me a time and a date to come in. I remember very vividly the evening of my appointment. Initially I had been quite happy and excited, as I was about to speak with my pastor about God's idea, wow!

I remember it like yesterday, because there was a guest Evangelist present in the building and from the pastor's study, we could hear her teaching in the adjoining room. Some of the Saints were involved in a fellowship class, which was always held prior the main service. From what we could hear, they were having an awesome time in The Lord, and we made mention of the same. Anyway, my pastor seemed pleasant and asked me what it was that I wanted to see him about.

After thanking him for seeing me, I began explaining to him, how it was that I truly seemed to be sensing the call of God. I went on to share with him, the vision that God had given me as well as how I had received numerous confirmations. I remember telling Him how afraid I was, and how unsure of myself in terms of being 'qualified' I had been. I explained to him that I wasn't quite sure to how to go about doing certain things, but that I, "Did not want to drop the ball", because this was for God and I just wanted to get it right.

At some point, I began reading from my paper, as I simultaneously explained the idea to him. I had written everything down because I did not want to make a mistake on anything that The Lord had given me. Just in case my pastor needed specifics, I wanted to have them available for him to look over. Besides, we are always admonished thanks to Habakkuk 2:2 to write the vision down, so I did exactly that. In fact, The Holy Spirit had insisted that I do so. When The Lord paid me a "night visit", I woke up.

At first I started to go back to sleep because I was sooooo tired. I figured that I could or would remember, and that I would write it down [later] after I got up. Instead, I felt compelled by The Spirit to get up and to write everything down ***"Now!"*** Writing things down <u>immediately</u> after you receive the word or the vision is always best. Ask me how I know that you will not remember if you go back to sleep…that too has happened to me, so I should have already known better. Also you know how the enemy is. He is a master at stealing the word, revelation or communication that has been released to you. The adversary never takes a break from trying to steal, to kill and to destroy.

Anyway…

The things that I had written down, is what I used in my presentation to pastor for his consideration. I had hoped it would be a ministry that would perhaps spark his interest. He seemed to be open to new ideas, (if he liked you) anyway. Seemingly, he wanted our church to be on the "cutting-edge" of ministry. Therefore, I figured that if he were interested, perhaps he would implement it and that I could be in charge of it or *at the very least,* he would allow me to assist in getting it started.

You see, in 2001 there was not a whole lot of talk about the church going, "Beyond the walls and into the community." We did not really start hearing about this (a lot) until around 2002/2003 and now, it is all we hear. The Lord had laid this on my heart long before it became, "The new direction for the local church." He began dealing with me about community ministerial outreach in the late 90's in fact – it wasn't very popular back then.

The second part of the ministry though, would deal directly with those who were in The Body [already], but who were yet struggling with serious issues, that kept them from excelling in the things of The Lord. My pastor asked me, what was to be my end result; what was it that I hoped to accomplish? In a word, I said – deliverance. I wanted people to know that they were not alone in their plight. So often, people of God suffer in silence because they are either too ashamed or too proud to admit that they still have struggles.

Receiving Salvation does not automatically free a person from the binding shackles [that in many cases] have gripped them for years. After initial Salvation, a person still needs deliverance. Some people struggle for years, even after they have been 'saved.' I am not saying that this is right or wrong, I am only letting you, the readers know that struggle, even for the Christian, is real. I myself have been in the position of struggle and I truly wanted to help others. I wanted to have people come in who could and who would minister to specific areas – particularly to the deeper ones that we so love to keep hidden. The goal was to get the people delivered. I was not trying to muster up yet another "support group" which would continue to do exactly that – only "support" or provide a platform to entertain that which aileth the people."

Instead, my aim was for <u>total</u> deliverance, and therefore <u>total</u> freedom in The Lord. I wanted this to be more than just another group of people coming together to share their sob stories, while simultaneously continuing in their pacification of one another's demons. While I certainly did want the people to have a "safe place", for the open expression of their pain, sill the main objective was for them to go free. I was so excited and I just knew that my pastor would be all for the idea especially since it had come from The Lord.

During one of the rare moments, when he actually looked at me, he said, *"That sounds like a church."* I was not trying to form a church, I assured him. I wanted to work in *his* ministry. I am not called to be a pastor (at least I hope not). *"A church"*, is what *he said,* the vision sounded like *to him.* Starting a church had not been at the forefront of my mind – believe that! Anyway…

Throughout most of our meeting, he seemed rather preoccupied. In fact, he rummaged through the things on his desk and read his mail for the majority of our meeting and my presentation. Undaunted by his preoccupation I continued - trying hard to overlook the fact that I lacked his undivided attention. *When he finally did look up at me again,* he shared with me that his wife was being used in that *same* capacity. He said that, "She ministers to people struggling with all sorts of problems – you wouldn't believe." "Some of them even famous people in ministry", he said.

Therefore, in my heart I'm thinking, "Yeah, yeah, I'm on the right track; even he knows that there is a need for this type of ministry." This is a good sign I thought. My hope heightened, as I thought that he was about to give me a chance. Finally, I was in the right place to make a difference, to do something meaningful in ministry and to obey God.

I thought that maybe he would consider letting this be a newly formed ministry in the church, because he has always been receptive to new ideas. Besides my pastor had always stressed the need to win souls, so I figured this would fit right in. Besides being instrumental in community soul winning, [which he loved and often made mention of]; it would help my fellow brothers and sisters who were already saved, but who may have also been in need of a little extra help. The kind of help that is not (or cannot be) offered during a regular Sunday morning service, i.e. participating in dialogue and receiving practical and spiritual feedback to their various questions and concerns.

In other words, this was to be a participatory ministry with the people becoming proactive in helping themselves, not just getting "preached at" (or about). At that time, there were various new ministries being formed and approved by him. I began to get excited as I felt like my time had come. I became hopeful; It was my time yes? NOT!!! He said, "I'm not going to tell you what to do, but if The Lord speaks to you, then follow Him."

He continued – "If I were you I would fast and pray, make sure it is The Lord and then do whatever He tells you to do." "But in the meantime we have a telephone ministry here that requires people to do follow up work." "It's behind the scenes work, but people are dealing with all sorts of issues." I knew that what he wanted me to do was not exactly what I had in mind. I mean I did not mind doing behind the scenes work – that was not the problem. However, calling people on the telephone twice a week had not been what God had spoken. I became confused, because I know that I had heard Him correctly. The other reason for my hesitation was that my pastor had clearly stated, "If God speaks to you, then obey God." (I should do what God says - right?).

Okay, that would be great, but that is only what he and other pastors say, while at the same exact time, they continue to bash us with the "God speaks to them first" routine.

So did I [also] need or in fact, did I actually have *his* approval or what? Was the pastor going to help me or not? Did he just want me to work in the telephone ministry for a season and would perhaps consider the other ministry later? On the other hand, was the ministry I proposed to him, not something that he deemed appropriate for our congregation at all? Do what God says? If God always speaks to the pastors first then why did he tell me to just follow God without saying whether or not I also had *his* blessing, support and approval?

Had God spoken to him [first] or not? He really had been quite vague and nonchalant throughout the entire meeting. I could not tell where I stood as far as counting on his support as my leader. I felt somewhat uncomfortable and because he did not offer his support, it was difficult to know for sure, whether or not I had it. I could not tell if the ministry would even be recognized if formed.

While he [and others] may in one sentence, tell us to 'follow God,' these same also penalize us when we do exactly that. Many pastors, mine included tell us to "obey God", but in their very next sermon they warn us not to be like those who "just went" without *his* [or their] approval and blessing as opposed to those who were sent (with *his* [or their] approval and blessing (the blessing which my pastor <u>always bestows publicly,</u> in the presence of the entire congregation).

If he trusts that people have the ability to hear from God – (and most do), then why is it, that with his next breath, we are frowned upon for following God's lead? As usual, I went where I always do, right back to God. Was my pastor telling me what he did, his way of giving me his blessing?

This was not the way he blessed everyone else – he always blessed the person as well as the newly formed ministry in a public forum, so that the congregation would know that he had sanctioned it and that the person or group had not merely acted as a "lone ranger." In other words, the public ceremony would let everyone know that HE had OFFICIALLY authorized the new ministry and that those who wanted to, could feel free to participate.

I wasn't sure what to do. I wasn't sure if he was giving me the go ahead by saying, "Do what God says", only to later rebuke me with the, "Some just went" crowd that he often mentioned and frowned upon. I remember being confused and depressed about the entire matter, so much so that I didn't even go to work the next morning.

Instead, I drove my vehicle to a local park, where I sat and cried. By that time, I had also become a little angry with God because I had not gotten the anticipated response. It was He who had sent me in the first place; it is not as though *I asked Him* you know. What gives, God? What's up with this? I know what you said God, but this is not what pastor is saying – for that matter what *exactly* was he saying anyway? After all, if YOU gave me the vision in the first place, and by YOUR Spirit YOU urged me to go to my pastor, why was he telling me something totally different, like calling people on the telephone?

I felt as though I were in limbo; my pastor had not clearly stated whether or not he was indeed for or against my proposal. He really had not said much at all. In fact, I became very confused and somewhat depressed (sort of in a haze) right after speaking to him come to think of it - hummmmmmmm. Speaking one day to someone from a different church about the matter, I was told that pastors sometimes test those who "claim to be called", by giving them the "brush off." This was supposedly a primary test of obedience. Their theory being that, if a person could remain humble and obedient, working in ministry outside of the spotlight, then they figure that such a one may truly have a heart for the things of God.

I thought about what was told to me, and agreed that perhaps this could be some sort of character test or something. Well, working outside of the spotlight would not be too difficult, I thought to myself. For most of my life, I had been shoved to the back anyway. Being in or out of the spotlight has never been a key issue for me, but I did <u>at least</u> want to serve in the capacity for which I had been created. Although quite honestly, calling people on the telephone, was not something that I really wanted to do; nevertheless, out of obedience, I did it anyway. After all, the pastor had announced on more than one occasion, that there really was a 'need' in that area. In addition, someone else reminded me that I should not despise small beginnings. I would still be working for God after all, which *was* the primary goal anyway, so…

On New Years Eve 2001, I said yes. I signed up for the telephone ministry and became happy to help. In fact, I actually began to look forward to it. This was the beginning of a new year and I had a new task to accomplish for The Lord. While I did speak to a few nice people, for the most part this venture proved very unfruitful. Many of the people that I contacted were never home or if they were, there seemed to be a language barrier of sorts. Mainly though, the majority of them just didn't seem interested in receiving the calls. But, because I am no quitter, I tried to remain faithful to this task (for about a year). There *was* at least one person who did seem to enjoy our weekly chats; so for this reason, I became content to serve in this capacity – for a while anyway –until…

It happened again! Or more to the point, I should say, 'He' happened again. God again started tugging at my heart; and this time His Fire refused to be quenched. The passion and The Holy Fire came with much more intensity as it began to capture my soul, so much so that there was no possible way for me to ignore it, no matter how hard I tried – and God in Heaven knows that I tried real hard.

This went on for a long time, as I fought hard trying not to give in, because I no longer wanted to be disappointed. I was tired of being hurt. This time, an intense struggle would take place. I did not want to be as those who were constantly being rebuked for _wanting_ to go into ministry. "Everybody thinks they've been called." "Everybody wants to go into ministry", the pastors would sarcastically snipe and accuse from their pulpits. Sheep have been verbally ripped apart, for nothing more than *wanting* to serve.

The wolf pastors and their leadership always seem to view everybody, (except themselves of course) as being incompetent or being only desirous of the 'spotlight.' They accuse everybody, labeling them as those who only "want to be seen." For some reason they seem to feel as though they alone are the only people who God has called and that they alone, are the only ones capable of working for The Kingdom. Like they say in the hood, "Somebody done told them wrong!"

After returning from my convention in May of 2003, deep in my soul I knew that the time had come, to once again make contact with my pastor. It had now been nearly 2 years, (20 months to be exact) since our initial meeting. I had gone through a lot more in the spirit since that time, and had grown by leaps and bounds. God was calling, and this time He was not letting up. I *HAD* to talk to my pastor again, because The Lord would no longer allow me to run, to make excuses or to ignore Him.

I really wrestled with the thought of contacting my pastor, because I remember how dazed and confused I had become after our first encounter and I definitely did not want to go through that again. Not to mention that his stares and frowns had not subsided; the man still did not like me. Anticipating what was to come, as I had no choice but to call him, I turned to people in different ministries, to get some direction. I called ministry hotlines for prayer and for guidance. I spoke to clerics, both local and national. I talked to people in (and out) of ministry.   As The Fire of God burned intently, it seemed as though I would lose my mind. Upon contacting one local pastor, he and I spoke for a long time; he (confirmed what I knew) by telling me that he also sensed "some sort" of call on my life.

Speaking with him, I discovered that he actually knew my pastor. He assured me that it was ok to approach him and that he (my pastor) was, "A cool guy." In fact, he was "Cool cool cool" as this preacher put it. I had always noticed how my pastor handled others and how supportive he could be, if he liked you. In addition, he had often stated from the pulpit, that he loved us "ALL." Certainly, as a faithful member in good standings (AND FAITHFULLY PAYING MY TITHES); so I figured that "ALL" meant me too.

I thought (and hoped) that since I was part of the family, I would also be included in the crowd that he claimed to have so much love for and that he wanted to see excel in the things of The Lord. When he said that "he loved us all", honestly, I thought that ALL meant exactly that (ALL OF US). I thought he meant everyone, – INCLUDING ME.

I figured that I would pray and ask The Lord to first search my own heart, and then I would give it another try. I would talk to my pastor. For I suppose that I must have been taking just a little too long for The Master's liking, because He began to turn up the heat. It did not seem as though He were ever going to give me any rest. There were numerous promptings from others, confirmation from circumstances, while at the same time, the relentless prodding of The Holy Spirit continued. My goodness as He doused me, The Fire seemed to almost chase me at times.

I am very serious about what I am telling you. At one point, I thought I was going to have a heart attack, or lose my mind, because The Holy Spirit pursued me so. When I could not take it any longer, (AND I DO MEAN COULD NOT TAKE IT!) I finally HAD to make contact with my shepherd again. After gathering up enough nerve to make the call, I spoke with a person who has since been ordained and appointed as a minister there.

As we spoke on the telephone, I being nearly in tears, proceeded to explain everything that I had been experiencing up to that point, including how I knew beyond a doubt, that God was calling for me. I also mentioned how I had been putting things off [for a while] out of fear, but that The Lord had pressed me so, until I finally had to make a move.

I DID NOT WANT TO DROP THE BALL FOR GOD. I FEARED THAT IF I MESSED UP, PEOPLE WOULD LAUGH AT ME – AGAIN. I DID NOT WANT TO MAKE GOD LOOK LIKE A FOOL FOR CHOOSING ME IN THE FIRST PLACE. (We know that cannot happen. God knew of my issues well before He chose me). WHAT IF I LET HIM DOWN I THOUGHT?

I DID NOT WANT HIM TO REJECT ME OR TO CAST ME AWAY LIKE PEOPLE HAD. (Humans do things like that, but not God). I DID WANT TO WORK FOR GOD BUT I DID NOT FEEL WORTHY. (Of course none of us are). Excuses, excuses, excuses! It was like knowing that I had been born to complete a mission much later. The only thing though, was that "much later" had finally come, and the time was 'now.'

I felt like I had one foot on this realm, and the other planted firmly on the rung of destiny's ladder out in the 'stratosphere.' I felt as though the universe was simply standing still, just waiting for me to step out, and upon it. My moment of decision had finally arrived. What was I going to do? The moment for The Master's use of my life was here. My tattered beginning would finally make sense. The Lord of Heaven and earth had called for me. It was now my turn to report for duty; and I had no choice but to show up.

The sister to whom I spoke, suggested that I write the pastor a letter because, "He loves read," she said. By the way beloved, do you think that I should send him a copy of *this* book? – Just kidding (smile). Anyway, she had me speak to the pastor's personal secretary. This same woman had made our initial appointment nearly two years earlier. She again took the standard information – name, telephone number and my reason for requesting to speak with him. When I hung up, in no way could I have been prepared for what happened next.

The secretary told me that *she* would get back to me. I figured in a few days, she would call me with an appointment date, as had been the procedure last time. I returned from lunch about one half hour later, (I was at work); my supervisor told me that my pastor had called. I began working on a project, as I struggled for the confidence to call back. There was a lot at stake and once more, I started shaking in my boots. Imagine knowing in your heart and in your soul, that the very purpose for which you have been placed upon this earth, is now even at hand.

Knowing that events are about to unfold which could be the beginning of a ministry, or the carrying out of an extremely significant assignment which will be swiftly completed [and so might you be]. Standing on the threshold of something that could be the start of a whole new beginning or the beginning of an ending is truly a frightening place to be. My insides were trembling because I really wanted God to be pleased as well as proud. I just could not let *Him* down again – not this time. The very thought of meeting with pastor again, made me wonder what I would say when the time came.

I knew that I had to get hold of myself. I had to collect my thoughts and I had to have sufficient (honest) answers for the man of God. I had to be prepared to answer questions like, how did I know *for sure* that it was God who was doing the summoning, versus satan trying to trick me, or if in fact, it was out of my own ambition that I desired to minister. I needed to be prepared to answer his questions, as well as to give an account of my motives. In addition, was I willing to serve and to work hard? How did I know the difference between God's voice, satan's, man's and my own?

I really thought that my pastor would require me to give an account of my call. I figured he would want to know how it was that I could be positive that this was The Lord's doing. I felt it imperative that I be prepared for this moment in time. I began taking deep breaths and I asked The Lord to help me. Nervous and all, I *had* to return that call - finally. For I had promised The Lord and I could not back out now. Oh God I thought again as I panicked and shuttered in anticipation. The Holy Spirit's presence became increasingly more evident – Jesus! "Okay God, this is it," I thought! "My entire life is about to change." I suppose in my stalling, that once more, I had taken just a little too long.

Before I could exhale, the deep breath that I had taken in, my telephone rang. On the other end was my pastor. I felt myself trembling as I explained to him, how I had come to recognize the voice of The Lord, and how I was certain that He had called for me. I told him that I was not interested in "a position" but that I wanted only to be that which God had called me to be. I explained to him, about the many things that had transpired, which had caused me to know beyond a doubt that He was calling. In addition, I shared how I had known for quite some time but had been afraid to answer. I wanted my pastor to know that I had *some* level of maturity in The Lord.

Our church was large and everybody had to be on different levels. I wanted to assure him that I *did* have some experience walking with Jesus and that I was not a new convert, who may have only been 'excited' about a newfound relationship with Him, as opposed to someone sensing a call and the wooing of God's Spirit. So many times when a person is "young in The Lord", it is quite easy to mistake zealousness with a 'call' to ministry. So many times what a person is actually sensing, may not necessarily be a 'call', but rather a heightened sense of enthusiasm for the things of God. I wanted to assure my pastor that this was not the case. I assured him that, "I know when The Lord is speaking [to me] and when He is not."

I made sure that I shared with him, how God did not seem to be letting up; for this was not simply the initial call, before going back into the wilderness or into the furnace. No, I had already survived that process. This was not the "get ready"; but rather this was "it." I explained to him how that on several occasions, I had spoken in churches or to different people and had always been encouraged to speak with him because he was my pastor. Many of The Saints, including a number of clerics had long sensed and/or confirmed a call. Although I knew what they meant (because I felt it too) still I usually played it down.

The older folks and elders would say things like, "Honey God has gifted you." "You need to go to your pastor and talk to him." Some people would ask me, "Did you go to your pastor yet, if not why haven't you?" "What are you waiting for?" "You can't ignore God honey."

Through fear and trembling, I told my pastor that I wanted to submit myself to his leadership and to his authority. I even shared with him how someone from a well-known ministry in Atlanta Georgia, hand sensed the "the gift of prophecy", as had others stated that they perceived/believed there to be a "Prophetic Mantle" on my life. When he spoke, what he said not only wounded me very deeply, but it literally shocked me and nearly shook my very foundation. He very arrogantly stated, and I do quote, *"Anybody can prophesy, (humph); I once had a bird that prophesied humph!"*

I further explained [yet again and as humbly as I could] that I was not interested in position because that would be easy. (I know too many people in ministry, so it would be easy to have that). I explained to my pastor that all I wanted to do was to be whoever The Lord was making me, and nothing more. *I told him that I did not want to drop the ball for God;* I even shared with him how afraid I had been to speak with *him* concerning the entire matter.

Overlooking his *"bird comment"*, I continued by saying – "I don't know how long I'm going to be here pastor, but for how ever long I am here, [at his church] I am willing to submit myself to your leadership and to your authority, as well as to the authority of this house." "I just want to be who God is making me into." As Jehovah God bears witness – that is all I said to the man.

He in turn he <u>*smugly*</u> *replied: "Well first of all, I'm not a leader, I'm a father." "I'm for women preachers and all that." "You know how we do it here; I'm for sending out sons and daughters in the ministry." "The problem is that most people just don't want to endure the process." He said: "David was anointed to be king, but he didn't take that position for a very, very, very, very, very long time."*

He continued: "Then you know, you said something about not knowing how long you're going to be here." (Humph!) "We can't sink our teeth into something like that, and you're saying you don't know how long you're going to be here (humph – ya know, so)."

My response was, "Oh pastor, I understand about process. I sat under my last pastor for almost 16 years and am very familiar with process and with serving [in the church/under leadership]." "Unfortunately my pastor died and our church ended in a split." I told him that "I have been here in your church for the last 8 years, I sing in your choir, and teach children's church" [in the back]." He asked me the name of my former pastor. I named him - I told him that my late pastor was named "Reverend J.C. Crawford" from The Beulah Baptist Church in Newark. Before I could even address his concern about "not being sure how long I was going to be there", he rudely interrupted me.

At the time, I had not planned on leaving – it wasn't as if I even wanted to jump ship or anything – honest. **However, none of us knows how long God will allow us to stay in any one place, be it a job, school church or even in relationship with people. For that matter, we do not even know how long we will be alive. That's all I meant and nothing more; honest to God.**

The Bible instructs us to say that, "We will do this, or we will do that, if The Lord allows." We must always leave room because sometimes His agenda [for us] might just change. I grew up with the phrases, "God willing" or "If the Lord says so" embedded in my psyche. Saying this is like second nature. However, before I could even open my mouth to clarify the matter, (since he had brought it up), he interjected. Immediately after I answered his question, concerning the identity of my former [late] pastor, he bluntly and very nastily snorted:
"Well, perhaps we're just a little too slow for you here; but right, wrong or indifferent (well, humph) that's just the way it is" (humph, so).

I'm thinking to myself WHAT?? His speech was both smug as well as arrogant. I tell you, I felt almost like satan himself had just slapped me in the face. Even as he spoke through the telephone, my entire insides had taken a turn for the worse; my spirit and gut had made a serious shift. The burning sensation of The Holy Spirit had instead turned into an uneasy churning, that seemed to be doing flip-flops in the pit of my stomach. I felt like crying, I felt shock and I felt dread all at the same time. Honest to God, I could not believe what I had just heard. After my initial shock wore off, feelings of anger began to surface.

After his first comment about the "bird prophesying bit" I already knew who and what I was dealing with. Calling this man had been a terrible mistake; I felt it in my gut. Depending on how you view it though, I suppose God used even this, to show me the man's true colors. (He really had showed me all along). Anyway, I am not exactly sure how I did it but honestly, I managed to contain my feelings.

It isn't as though I could not have said something mean, but I was too stunned to reply. Also, I made the decision to hold my piece, because he still had something that I needed and I was trying very hard to respect his position as my leader. In spite of his prideful tone and insulting mannerism, I thought that I still needed to obtain his blessing. So I figured I should let his comments roll off my back and not say some of the things that I could have, neither did I want to totally break down like a baby and start blubbering over the phone; I was not about to give satan that satisfaction.

He really had been quite rude to me and I would have been perfectly within my bounds to answer him back (or to tell him off) but I managed to show great restraint. My emotions had gone from feelings of awe and trembling (a healthy fear sort of like the butterflies or jitters that one gets as he or she embraces the pulpit). You do still have a healthy sense of reverence and fear; as you presume to speak for God, do you not? (If not, you might want to check that). Anyway...

The reverence for him as my pastor had instead turned into a feeling of sickening dread. I felt as though I were on the telephone with the devil and that he had verbally dropped-kicked me. ***The only time that I ever experience feelings like these is when I encounter "satanic interference" or some form of "strange fire."*** When you have experience walking with God, you eventually learn to identify when God is moving and/or speaking, as opposed to when the enemy is at work. As God is my witness – like Job said in the face of his accusers, "Behold my witness is in heaven and my record is on high (Job 16:19).

I was immediately taken back by his curt and very nasty response. My stomach felt sick, sick, sick at the pit. From the very first moment of his stinging comments, it seemed as though I had immediately began to experience a sickening, sinking, ominous feeling deep down in my belly's reservoir. To this day, I do not know how I managed to choke back my tears, contain my anger, snap out of my stupor and handle my disappointment all in a matter of seconds but I did. I dug so deep that I even surprised myself – so help me God!

Still trying hard not to disrespect the shepherd of the house, I figured that maybe I could somehow salvage this entire mess and yet obtain "the blessing from my spiritual father" that I so badly needed. Because he had said those things to me, I thought that perhaps this would be a good time to clear the air. *Something had gone wrong somewhere. This certainly was not spiritually healthy or beneficial for either of us. "Maybe we just needed to talk", I supposed [to myself].* Perhaps there had been some grave misunderstanding that I was not aware of. Perhaps I could reason with him I thought. Remember, I still needed his approval - *THEY SAID.*

I confided in him about how afraid I had been to speak with him. I also stated that I was trying to be obedient to elders who had urged me to speak with him – promising me that it was God's protocol and that everything would be ok if I did. Moreover, I explained to him, how I had always sensed for some reason, that perhaps he did not like me, but that I wasn't sure. (I was sure, but I did not have to tell him that).

Please exercise wisdom at all times. No need to blurt out everything you know, or everything that you feel). I told him of the times, that I had shared this with my mother, my fiancée and sometimes even my child. "I don't think my pastor likes me", I'd often whine with a sigh. "He looks at me and just frowns up, "I don't understand why", I would often whine to them in bewilderment. Thankfully, my family was patient with me. I know that I got on their last nerves, as I burned each of their ears 'on a regular.' This I did because at one point, his very obvious disapproval had really started to bother me, especially since I did not know what, (if anything at all) that I had ever done to irritate him so. Sometimes I would be so discouraged over the matter that I could not even sleep. I mean, I just wanted to be a part of the church family and be used of God, nothing more – that was it. In an attempt to clear the air and to open up the lines of communication between the two of us, I pointed out to him how I realized that satan could plant things into the minds of people.

I told him that perhaps the enemy had been trying to create a rift between the two of us in an attempt to thwart the plan of God.

If satan can successfully create strife or division between two parties, more than likely they will never speak. Instead, each would go on thinking ill of his/her brother or sister, with both individuals believing that the other is at fault and that he or she is not. *Meanwhile, both persons have played right into the enemy's hand; an enemy who of course, desires nothing more than to prevent God's plan from coming to fruition.*

You think he would know by now - God <u>will</u> <u>never</u> be out done, but yet the enemy still tries. The adversary loves it when the people of God are at odds with one another. Many times brothers and sisters misjudge and/or make snap decisions only to later find out, that what they <u>thought</u> to be the case, had never been that way at all.

With this in mind, I asked my pastor if he had ever heard of Dr. Rebecca Brown. She deals a lot with witchcraft and with spiritual entities. She says that demons are the primary forces that are responsible for causing strife and all types of dissension between people.

Dear reader, I just wanted to be certain [in my own heart], that satan was not using <u>him or me</u> as a harbor to host bad feelings. Also I wanted to rule out that there had been perhaps the use of a third party, to create a rift between me and my pastor – you know like another member telling him something about me or telling me bad things about him (without the two of us having a clue as to what was really going on). Think it not strange beloved, these sorts of things do happen! The enemy will do anything and will use anyone to cause division; and oftentimes he does it quite subtly!

My pastor acknowledged that he *had* indeed heard of Dr. Brown. However, what he said next not only shocked me even more (as if that were possible), but at the same time, his words freed me.

With an absolute smugness, true to himself, he said: "How can I not like you? (Humph), I don't even know who you are, but you know (Humph), if you want to meet... (He was smirking and sort of giving me the brush-off while being very snobbish and really uninterested in meeting for real– sort of like a – "Whatever, just leave me alone" type response). Stunned again, I said: "Oh [ummm] pastor, may I ask you just one more question? He said: "Nope! Nope! Gotta go, gotta go; (as in "I've 'got to go"), you'll have to call the office."   And then...dead silence.

Oh, ok I said, (having heard the click *before* I could even finish saying "ok"). I don't think he even heard my last words of – "Oh ok", because I did not hear him say anything after the word "office." I never heard him say "good-bye." Once I *finally* put down the receiver, I immediately began to revisit the entire conversation in my mind. I had literally held on to the phone and sat motionless with my mouth open, trying to figure out what in the world had just gone down.

Purposely I relived every second from beginning to end. I replayed the entire conversation; paying extra attention to the tone of his voice, as well as the repugnant arrogance with which he had spoken. I paid especially close attention as to how agitated and filled with *dread* my own spirit had become almost immediately upon beginning our conversation. What had my own responses and tone of voice been like? I replayed those too, as well as my choice of words. Had I said too much? Had I left anything out? Had I been out of order? For the life of me, I could not figure out what I had said or done that would have caused him to be so rude, smug and arrogant. I mean he was haughty, with a capitol "H."

Like an arrow, his words shot straight through me. Not only was it *what he* said that hurt, angered, frustrated and confused me, but mainly, it was the arrogant and snappish manner, in which he had said *EVERYTHING*. It was the way he had spoken to me throughout the entire conversation that left me totally bewildered. Look, the man treated me like a piece of 'crap.' He spoke to me as though I were a piece of garbage ok - as if I were totally beneath him – like I was nothing at all. He totally "dissed" me. Never had I expected to be treated *like that*! His demeanor had been less than compassionate. There I was, darn near groveling (out of respect for his position as my leader, or even as a human being for that matter), to only be met with sheer arrogance, smugness AND rejection – again.

Just in case my critics are wondering, how it was that I approached him, like was I being proud or coming off like a know-it-all or something? Let me just say this for the record. If my mindset has always been to respect my leaders (even when they are wrong), as well as having had the belief that I absolutely <u>had</u> to have this man's blessing for ministry, then why on earth would I approach him in a negative manner?

That would not have been a very intelligent thing for me to have done. Common sense (which I do have), would dictate that if a person needs something from another individual, certainly the best way to obtain it would be to approach him or her with a spirit of humility and kindness – in a word respect. I would have been well deserving of what I got had I approached him in a nasty manner. Remember, it had been drilled into my head that he was the link to my being approved for public ministry.

I 'wanted' him to like me and to be accepting of me. It would not have been very wise of me to have approached him in a less than honorable manner. Let me just say it real plain – It would have been down right stupid of ME to have been nasty if I needed something from him.

Remember, the goal was for him to like me and to bless me, not for the man to hate my guts! As I told you, I knew that he had something against me long before this conversation had even taken place. I have always sensed it in both the spirit and in the natural, and now it had become even more evident. My suspicions were confirmed. STILL out of respect for <u>his position</u> as MY PASTOR, (and as a man of God in general), I attempted to give him the benefit of the doubt, by darn near kissing his you know what! Besides, everyone else thought so highly of him, so I figured it had to be me who had the problem. I allowed his position and the messages that came across my television set about respecting "spiritual fathers" YET AGAIN to paralyze me, even though in my gut, I knew that I had done nothing to this man and that I had been right all along.

It was not I who was at fault – not in this situation, not this time! Absolutely no way! I am not stupid. I know when someone does not like me. People who knew me, including other pastors, not only perceived but also confirmed the call of God upon my life <u>long before</u> I had ever become a member of his church (and since joining too). <u>Not only that, but I have known God much longer than I have known my pastor. God has never had a problem communicating with me in the past, so why would He have one now? He was calling me and I knew it!</u>

I went to my pastor because I wanted to be obedient to everyone who kept telling me, suggesting to me, and aggravating me to death about doing so. I went because they assured me, it would be all right. This, the leadership says, is how God has "things set up." This they said was proper protocol – fooled again! If I were un-teachable and had not intended on listening to my leader, then why would I have gone to him in the first place? I have enough knowledge and resources to get things done without having to ask to beg or to grovel at the feet of a mere human.

I told you I went out of reverence and respect for my leader, because this was the way THEY instructed, not because I did not know how to hear from God for myself. "Your pastor is a cool guy, I'm sure he'll help you." "You want to make sure you do things the right way honey." I agreed. I did not want to be stubborn. Neither did I want to be accused of being un-teachable, or of thinking that I knew everything. I obeyed their instructions to give him yet another chance. I was tired of the looming possibility of being a "spiritual bastard." I did what THEY said. I did not do it for my pastor, but I did this for God. Because God's people told me that, this was the correct procedure.

I did not want any part of my future ministry, birthed from God (if I am to have a ministry), to be tainted in any way because of my own foolish disobedience to leadership and so, I obeyed. And No! I was not trying to prophesy to him! Operating in a gift was the furthest thing from my heart and my mind at that moment. I was too busy trying to be respectful and agonizing over not dropping the ball. I was too scared out of my wits to even think about trying to prophesy to somebody. In obedience, I humbled myself in submission to my pastor. Boy was I sorry; boy was I ever!!!

We are admonished to ALWAYS respect and to cover our leaders. What are we suppose to do though, when those same leaders are the very ones who are trying to kill *us?* What then is our recourse? What (if anything) is to be our line if defense/action [for ministry], when our leaders try to sabotage us because *they* themselves are blind, insecure and are unwilling to yield to God's plan? That one conversation with my pastor set the stage for what would be yet another round of spiritual mental torment. Here I was twice confounded and totally befuddled and rejected by the *same* leader. I did not deserve that from him. I humbled myself and I got dropped even deeper into the pit.

Shortly after that, I found myself asking God to [please] take the call back, and to remove the anointing from my life altogether. Because of this entire ordeal, I had become more confused, saddened and angry not to mention tormented and depressed. After all, it *was* out of an act of obedience to answer *His* call that had started this whole mess to begin with. I didn't ask for this!

The pain of rejection and the confusion that came with it seemed to be more than I could handle. Who needs this mental anguish?! I mean like, what was my crime anyway? The only thing I had done was followed *their* procedure. I remained obedient to the very things that *they* kept teaching – that was all I had done! I did not want anybody's job or position; I only wished to be mentored and spiritually nurtured so that I could carry out my own God ordained assignment(s). I could have continued to wallow in my stupor, depression and desire to fit. Oh but bless The Name of The Lord; today I can say that I am no longer trying to do that.

How glad I am that The Lord Jehovah did not answer my request to remove His call from my life. How thankful I am that His anointing yet abides. Looking back, I now realize what a very stupid prayer that had been, but at the time, I just wanted to stop being rejected, and I wanted to stop hurting. I probably would have said just about anything. It was a desperate plea born out of hurt and spiritual exasperation – so glad He overlooked that one. Thank You Jesus!

Brothers and sisters, you never want to be without The Anointing of The Lord, not under any circumstance; not even for one moment. It is your empowerment to do that which He bids you to. Never ever, attempt to function or to do *anything* for Him or in His Name, unless you are operating under the unction of His power – The Holy Ghost. Again, I cannot stress enough how grateful I am, that God turned a ear to my stupidity, as I made that desperate request. I have a charge to keep and work to do; I owe Him my very life. As I focus on His plan, I no longer have time to concern myself with whether or not people accept me.

I refuse to keep dwelling on the past or on those who choose to hate and/or reject me. I know that I sound redundant; please forgive me, but I must stress it once more. *The only thing that I wanted was the blessing that they continued to preach about. I am repetitive on purpose, and will probably be that way throughout the entire book, because I really want you to get this.* Pastors say that their blessing is a requirement for any person to be publicly/officially acknowledged and released to function in ministry. Therefore, in order to do that which The Lord had assigned to my hand, I thought that I had to obtain it, and I did my very best but evidently, my best was not quite good enough for man.

At the time, I was not even planning to leave his church. In fact, I really wanted to be a part of it (still, I knew that God would eventually move me, because He had already told me so). I desired recognition of my calling so that the conflict would stop. I did not want to feel as though I were in hiding – as if I could not acknowledge my calling in front of my church family. I wanted what *THEY* said I needed to have, so that I could be ready to do The Lord's work when the time came.

Public acknowledgement was not for *my* benefit. I already know who I am, with or without anybody's confirmation or affirmation. However in keeping with *their* procedure and the ecclesiastical teachings and tradition, public blessing would have let the congregation know that pastor had approved of me, and that therefore I had officially received the blessing of the house (the leadership), and could thereby operate freely as The Lord would lead.

I did not receive "a bootleg calling" from The Lord, my relationship with Him was not unauthentic or disingenuous, so neither did I want some lame "back door" method of blessing to be bestowed upon me. IF IN FACT I REALLY DID NEED AN EARTHLY BLESSING, WELL, THEN I WANTED IT!

Desiring validation from my leader was neither for the sake of pride nor for vanity. Technically, I could not have cared less whether or not people knew – (well perhaps I cared just a little [smile]). After all, we should want our lives to count for something. It is desirable for each of us to *want* to leave a good legacy behind. I want to be remembered as someone who gave her best for The Lord. I don't want to go out of the world as a loser, nor as someone who was gifted, but who failed to make a lasting impression. Neither did I want to resign to being angry all of the time. Nevertheless, it is hard for a person not to be angry when he or she is constantly running into brick walls, knowing that he or she is unwanted and is never taken seriously, but is still expected to keep showing up wearing a smile. As a person who has been gifted, we should want for our talents and treasures to impact this world in a mighty way. How much more should we desire that they be used to the glory of God?

What would be the purpose of an individual becoming a physician, if he or she were banned from practicing medicine? If nobody but the person knew of his or her practice, the waiting room would be pretty darn empty. Please understand that this was not a vanity trip for me. It was more like a "coming out." To those who read my story and feel as though I sought recognition *purely for the sake of receiving glory and attention, to you I say, "Not so!"* But honestly, I no longer care what YOU think either. It is always too confusing when I allow myself to care and to focus upon what others think. In addition, I am sick and tired of hearing pastors say things like, "Some were sent (by pastor) while others just went (on their own)." I am sick of hearing those statements. Let me just put something on out there that needs to be said.

Pastors have sent a lot of people, but that does not necessarily mean that those individuals were qualified, approved of and sent by God. Some people sent by pastors, are afforded an opportunity simply because they fit [or blend] in. They fit the mold of men but not necessarily the requirements of The Lord. Often they are clones, position seekers or kiss ups. For the most part, they have absolutely no backbone and are usually the type that go along with the pastor's program, which may even include themselves [at times] being the recipients of ill treatment. Sometimes, they are even instructed to "keep and eye on" or to 'mistreat' others, whom the leadership may not approve of. Simply put – they will do anything to gain position or approval. Ignorantly they go right along, even if what is being said or done goes totally against the auspicious of God's will. If that is what I must do for somebody's blessing, then they can keep it! Most people in a congregation depend on their pastors for promotion. I can't speak for anyone else, but like the song says…

"My hope is built on nothing less, than Jesus' Blood and righteousness." My hope and my trust is in The Lord not in people!

If being accepted and affirmed means that I am expected to kiss up, sex it up, and forever shut up [in the face of evil doers ALWAYS], then the wolf clerics can take their blessing and shove it! I trust in Him for everything. My promotion or elevation if it is to be, shall come because of God's will and not because of man's approval.   While a lot of people have taken on the spirit of their church and their leadership, I for one am not striving to take on the spirit of any building or of any man. I don't want to be known as having the spirit of a particular church – but rather of "The church." The universal church – God's church. THE REAL CHURCH, as in, "The gates of hell shall not prevail against it" church; not the four walled buildings that they merely call a church.

Don't let me be known as one who has the spirit of my pastor, but let me be identified as having the Spirit of *my Master – The Lord Jesus Christ.* I have absolutely no problem staying in my place and not making waves. Nevertheless, no man owns me because I belong to God. At that time, my only hope had been that my pastor would have acknowledged and affirmed the fact that I too had *something* to contribute to The Kingdom and to the ministry. I wanted to avoid the stigma and the labeling of being something that I am not. I am neither rebellious, nor un-teachable, and neither am I anybody's bastard.

My hope had been that my pastor would have seen *something* of value in me. I was hoping for him to assign me some sort of responsibility. I need something to do; being idle is not my style, it simply is not good for me. I was hoping to have been given the chance to do something meaningful.   There simply is too much inside of me to let it die. **But, when my pastor said, "How could I not like you? I don't even know who you are (humph)."** I thought to myself – "Exactly!" "Pastor you are so right!" "You don't know me." My pastor did not know me, nor did he *want* to know me. He didn't even pray with me, or *for* me - nothing! He did not intend to try to know me, neither in the natural nor in the spirit.

As my shepherd, the very least that he could have done was to agree to seek The Lord with me, or to seek Him on my behalf, in order to confirm or to solidify the call, if he did not see it. He could have asked The Lord to show him or even to show me if I had been wrong. He could have suggested that I sit under him or take classes and be taught for a season to see if I was agreeable, teachable or *whatever HIS process* consisted of.

As far as "The prophetic" is concerned, it is something that I am finally no longer fearful to acknowledge or to embrace. If my pastor did not want me around, he at the very least could have suggested, that maybe I needed to sit under a "prophetic ministry" or under the tutelage of a leader who could help me walk this path through. He could have even recommended another pastor for me to talk to – anything. If he didn't want me there, he could have referred to a different church! There are a number of things that he could have done besides snub me. I would have felt better had he at least suggested *something!* Thinking about everything, I finally *accepted the fact* that he wanted nothing to do with me. He was right; he did not know me. He does not have a clue as to my identity. The same way that God asked Job a few questions, I would like to pose a few to my pastor and to anyone else out there who claims to be a leader:

Where were you PASTOR(s) when I was crying in the midnight hour? Who was it that formed me and placed me in my mother's womb? Who was it that filled me with His precious Spirit? Was it you?? Where were YOU when I could not pay my mortgage? Where were YOU pastor, when I as a little girl, a teenager and even as an adult would sit, and have my talks with Jesus? Where were YOU when I fell to my knees and began crying over the painful things that you said to me? Where were YOU when The Spirit of God who distributes the ministerial gifts <u>as He wills</u>, and <u>to whom He wills,</u> Himself decided what He would make of me?

Where were YOU as The Fire of God burned deep in my soul and commanded me to "Come"? Were YOU there as God and I tangoed the moments away during the fourth watch of the night? As we ceased not until the breaking of day, tell me pastor, where exactly were you as The Master and I danced? As I positioned myself prostrate in His Holy presence at dawn or as I prayed in the heat of the day or even at the midnight hour – where were YOU?

Where were YOU when my ordination took place? Oh yes, indeed I have been ordained all right! For you see pastor, I received my ordination long before The Lord ever introduced me to myself or to you. My ceremony took place before the framing of the world, as we both know it. From the portals of glory, with the "Signet" of The Lord, He stamped me "BLOOD APPROVED", long before ever birthing me into the earth! I've been permanently sealed until the day of my redemption.

When I sought counsel and a word of encouragement, but instead got kicked, tell me pastor, out of all the people in the world, why were YOU the main one doing the kicking?

Thanks for snubbing me; you have never been so right in your entire life. YOU COULDN'T POSSIBLY KNOW ME! Little did I realize, your vile nasty comments would serve as the very catalyst to deliver me from people-pleasing. Pastor, your rejection was the exact key that I needed. Your sniping served its purpose; as it fit the lock and unloosed my shackles. In fact, after the initial paralyzing effects finally wore off, the hastening of my emotional recovery from wolves who merely pose as concerned shepherds was inevitable. Upon careful inspection of the entire matter, I actually had to agree with my pastor's final remark. He *does not* know me. As nasty and as smug as he had been, he was right, and I owe him my gratitude. My heavenly Father is the one who made me. He created me with His hands. It is His breath that I breathe and no one else's. He is the only one who really knows me.

Jesus once told me in October 2001, "He's your pastor, but I'm your Master; you do what I tell you to." Oh, how liberating and what a feeling! As I thought back on the words of my Saviour, I felt even the residuals of my pastor's shackling verbiage drop to the floor. Jesus spoke these precious words prior to my second encounter with my leader. They however, served me best just when I needed them most.

Shortly after this, God commissioned me to proclaim that which I had learned through my life as a reject. I therefore must share this testimony with others who are now going through their own labyrinth of confusion (religious or otherwise). Since the looming bastard syndrome had come into affect and had *by that time,* made its way to national television, I am certain that thousands of others also began to be alarmed about their future in ministry. There was absolutely no way that I could have been the *only* person in all of Christendom, who had experienced this sort of thing. I also know that I could not have been the only individual who had listened and had become disenchanted as popular theologians spat out erroneous comments and issued crippling edicts over the airwaves.

The Lord wanted me to help others understand how they too could be free of the looming attachments pertaining to the spiritual bastard complex. Furthermore, He wanted them to know what He Himself has said about bastardizm. The reason for my pastor's refusal of me is no longer something that haunts me. Sometimes people are just selfish. Perhaps he could not deal with his own feelings of insecurity and therefore he became intimidated. Maybe he's still hurting from his own issues. Who knows? Maybe he was once deemed a spiritual bastard - or *something.* He might be hiding his own self-hatred behind the masks of pride and arrogance that he wears so well.

While I do not know his entire story, I do know that a spiritual leader once wounded him. I am not exactly sure what part *he* might have played; if what happened to him had been brought on by his own actions, because he does seem rather self-centered. Perhaps when he received the calling he became uppity and *TOLD* his pastor what he was going to do, I really do not know. I asked him; never once had I ever attempted to TELL him anything, but totally submitted to him as my leader. The only thing that I did TELL him was that, "I knew when God was speaking [to me] and when He was not." (By this time, The Lord had well trained me to recognize His voice). I wanted my pastor to know that I was not a new convert, so that he would not feel it necessary to treat me with "kid gloves"; he would not have to begin from "ground zero" with me. Who knows, I may never fully understand 'his' reason for rejecting me, or for judging me without getting to know me.

Albeit the good news is that, I no longer spend time trying to figure it out. To be perfectly frank about it, I no longer care. He chose not to receive me and that's that! All things work together for good! I have stopped crying and I have since moved on spiritually and emotionally. Even though I no longer hunger for spiritual validation or for a fatherly blessing, still the confusion surrounding the spiritual bastard syndrome remained, and God decided that the time had finally come for it to be addressed.

Note about the prophetic: At times, there were people who sensed that I possessed, as they called it "Something in the realm of prophecy" or the "Gift of prophecy." I usually kept it low-keyed, and I never made a big deal about titles nor did I feel the need to correct people when they were doing their 'sensing.' I already told you, I know who I am, and so does God. Besides, my pastor already hated me, and I was not fully ready to embrace that to which I had been called, because to do so would have meant subjecting myself to even more ridicule and/or rejection, because I would stick out even further and I just didn't want to.

Now that I am free of everyone's constraints (including my own), I feel it necessary to clarify something. People in The Body often confuse, "The Gift of Prophesy" to be the same thing as walking in the "Office of a prophet." What they were 'sensing' was "The Prophetic Mantle" on my life. (This too was later confirmed). My primary ministry gift to The Body of Christ is that of the prophetic office, and thus I do prophesy [whenever God commands me to do so]. However, not everyone who prophesies walks in the office. A prominent example in The Bible is that of King Saul. For instance, there were instances when Saul prophesied – but he was not a prophet.

<u>*ALL CHRISTIANS*</u> *ARE SUPPOSED TO BE SOUL WINNERS, THUS THEY ARE ALL CALLED TO EVANGELIZE. However, actively engaging in the works of evangelism, or obtaining a license, does not necessarily or automatically qualify an individual as an "Evangelist", as it relates to the "five-fold ministry." Never is a person supposed to seek an office (of the "five-fold"), but rather the office, or the God behind the destiny of the office literally apprehends the individual. When The Holy Spirit comes upon an individual, he or she may indeed prophesy. Yet the prophetic office is one that can only be appointed by God to the church (as is applicable to any office of the "5-fold" ministry gift).*

Also, because The Bible has already been written in its entirety, <u>the primary function</u> of the Prophet is not necessarily used to 'foretell' the future as in days of old, (as it pertains to Biblical events) but rather they "forth-tell". They are heralds of the knowledge that has already been given from above. But please remember, God can do ANYTHING that He darn well pleases - including show or have someone 'foretell' futuristic events; this is also applicable to the prophetic ministry.

WE HOWEVER MUST BE EXTREMELY CAREFUL AS THERE ARE A LOT OF MADE UP, SENSATIONALIZED (AND AFTER THE FACT) SO CALLED PROPHETIC UTTERANCES BEING COMMUNICATED THAT ARE NOTHING MORE THAN LIES AND HYPE! PLEASE BE DESCERNING.

I wanted to make this perfectly clear, since there seems to be so much spiritual ignorance in The Body, (I say this in love). A lot of people simply do not know the difference. Perhaps they do not know, because they have never been told, and since a vast majority do not study for themselves, but only rely on men, they may never know.

We need to start <u>ACCURATELY</u> teaching these fundamentals because there are many babies who have no clue. Likewise, there are millions of well meaning brothers and sisters who are eaten alive by satan and his crew, because someone has pumped them up or told them wrong. They think they have what it takes to function in a particular role or in an office, for which they have absolutely no authority – <u>because GOD has never assigned them to that office.</u> Many who prophesy, are running around calling themselves prophets (or whatever), but <u>God</u> has never appointed them to <u>that position.</u> Again, this is not something to be chased or sought after, but it will chase you – believe that!

<u>Many there be, that want to walk in this office, but they have not even come close to fulfilling the wilderness wondering, sanctification, dart ducking, strange fire extinguishing, costly sacrificial purging, which may include them being nearly spiritually beaten into the dust of the earth, part of the process that comes with the making of a Prophetic Instrument.</u>

I offer you this much needed clarification because there are so many false prophets and 'wannabes' in the land and <u>even in the church.</u> These pretenders have given the gift of prophecy and the "genuine prophetic ministry" a bad name.

<u>"TRUE PROPHETS OF THE LORD JEHOVAH", THE GOD OF THE "HOLY BIBLE", ARE NOT NOW, (AND NEITHER WERE THEY EVER) MEDIUMS, PSYCHICS, CLAIRVOIANTS, WITCHES, WORLOCKS, PALM READERS, MAGICIANS OR "SCRIPTURAL NUMBER RUNNERS!"</u>

Charging money for prophecies and words of knowledge; forming prophet clubs, (where <u>EVERYBODY</u> IN THE CLUB CLAIMS TO BE A PROPHET). (Or in reality none are, they just think that they are). These same use witchcraft, psychic powers, crystals, ouija boards (pronounced wee-gee or wee-ga), potions, powders "concoctions of various sorts", "seeds", "chicken feet", "roots", "stuff" (whatever 'stuff' is supposed to be), "tarot cards", "astro projection" (out of body experiences), "tea leaves", trickery and sorcery in an attempt to authenticate themselves (and their mess), as they claim that what they are doing is like unto the "genuine prophetic ministry" of The Lord.

THE DEVIL IS A LIAR!!!

Whoever you are – if you are a "witch", then be a damned witch, but please stop calling yourselves prophets of God! I believe you are looking for "the other camp   down below." If you continue to practice such things, then "Ye are of your father – the devil." "The Bible" does not support false prophets or witchcraft EVER – read all about it! (Read the entire chapter of each). Check out – Exodus 7:1-25; Exodus 22:18-20; Leviticus 20:6; Leviticus 20:27; Deuteronomy 18:9-22; Jeremiah 14:10-16; and Ezekiel 13:1-23; just to name a few. Oh, that's <u>OLD TESTAMENT</u> you argue...We are no longer under "THE LAW" but under 'GRACE' you say? Ok, fine. Why don't you check out Matthew 7:15-20; Matthew 24:11; Mathew 24:24; Acts 13: 1-13; Acts 16:16-19; Acts 19:13-20; 2Peter 2:1-2 and 1 John 4:1 for your reading pleasure.

REGARDLESS TO TESTAMENT OR DISPENSATION, GOD'S VIEW ON WITCHCRAFT, FALSE PROPHETS, FALSE TEACHERS, WOLVES IN SHEEPS CLOTHING, BOOTLEG S AND SIN HAS NOT CHANGED. HIS WORD NEVER CHANGES! CHOOSE YE THIS DAY – ARE YOU A WITCH OR A PROPHET? ARE YOU A HEIRLING OR AN APPOINTED SHEPHERD OF GOD'S FLOCK? ARE YOU A CHILD OF GOD, OR AN OFFSPRING OF satan?

YOU CAN EITHER COME TO CHRIST WITH THE INTENTIONS OF DOING THINGS GOD'S WAY, AND BE SAVED (FOR REAL) OR YOU CAN SUFFER THE CONSEQUENCES. IT WOULD BE FAR BETTER FOR YOU TO GET ON THE OTHER SIDE AND SUFFER YOUR PUNISHMENT LIKE A <u>REAL MAN OR WOMAN,</u> RATHER THAN TO KEEP <u>PLAYING WITH GOD.</u> CHOOSE WHAT YOU WILL, BUT STOP LYING TO THE BODY OF CHRIST, AND PLEASE STOP LYING TO YOURSLVES!!

<u>YOU   HAVE   BEEN   WARNED!</u>

Many there are in the land, who are spurious prophets, teachers and preachers. They are fake and phony <u>self appointed</u> leaders who in <u>His Name</u> operate from a power source <u>other than HIS.</u> These are they, who from their lofty positions, are right now, leading millions astray. But fear not little children, and flock of God, "Our Father" sees it all! For I declare unto you this day, that the terrorizing reign of the wolves and the beguiling false prophets and shepherds shall come to an abrupt end!

WOE BE UNTO THE PASTORS THAT DESTROY AND SCATTER THE SHEEP OF MY PASTURE! SAITH THE LORD. THEREFORE THUS SAITH THE LORD GOD OF ISRAEL AGAINST THE PASTORS THAT FEED MY PEOPLE; YE HAVE SCATTERED MY FLOCK AND DRIVEN THEM AWAY, AND HAVE NOT VISITED THEM: BEHOLD, I WILL VISIT UPON YOU THE EVIL OF YOUR DOINGS, SAITH THE LORD. AND I WILL GATHER THE REMNANT OF MY FLOCK OUT OF ALL COUNTRIES WHITHER I HAVE DRIVEN THEM, AND WILL BRING THEM AGAIN TO THEIR FOLDS; AND THEY SHALL BE FRUITFUL AND INCREASE. AND I WILL SET UP SHEPHERDS OVER THEM WHICH SHALL FEED THEM: AND THEY SHALL FEAR NO MORE, NOR BE DISMAYED, NEITHER SHALL THEY BE LACKING, SAITH THE LORD.

JEREMIAH 23:1-4

ᴓBastard:
*Webster's, Them & God*ᴓ

Since the day of my deliverance from the need to people please or to seek fleshly validation, I set out to understand what spiritual bastardizm was *really* about. I wanted to know why I or anyone else should have to wear such a derogatory title, for simply choosing to obey God. Because my pastor did not like me and was not likely going to bestow his blessing anyway, I figured that I had nothing to lose. I mean, there was to be no more meetings, asking, groveling, longing or begging to be blessed and accepted. God said there was to be no more meetings with this pastor. I had nothing more to concern myself with in terms of people's opinions.

It took me nearly 38 years to realize that there was something gravely erroneous with the entire practice of *always* having to seek opinions, [even from leaders]. Doing so had often resulted in my getting hurt and sidetracked - hardly ever had it helped! Oh boy, but by age 40, I finally learned the lesson real well. I got my fill, and had had enough. Since I obviously would not be "properly birthed out" by a man, I had no choice but to "step out" at the command of The Lord - Amen! I had only to gain, that which He would grant access to. Still for those who need to know; let me tell you what I have discovered about the true meaning of the word bastard and the standard application thereof.

To find the definition of most words, society has been trained since its youth, to head for the nearest resource. The first choice will almost always be to consult a dictionary. This writer decided to be no different, so here is what I found:

I have three such definitions or explanations as to the *official secular* meaning of the word *bastard*.

According to Webster's Dictionary a bastard is:

(1) An illegitimate child
(2) Something of irregular or inferior origin, kind or form
(3) Slang usage - a mean or disagreeable person

The history of this word:

In Old French *fils de bast* literally meant "child of a packsaddle." The phrase refers to the unsanctified circumstances in which a child was conceived. Travelers used packsaddles as beds; often no doubt, as impromptu beds. The word bastard was formed in Old French from bast, "packsaddle"; add the pejorative suffix - "ard"; which then gives you "bastard."

Because the first Webster's definition refers to a bastard as "an illegitimate child", I figured I would go ahead and give you their definition of 'illegitimate.' No brain buster here; most of us can certainly figure this out without even reading the definition. It seems almost juvenile to bother with the explanation, but it is necessary for those who *may* not know. I don't know how many books are out there pertaining to the subject matter, so I want to be as thorough as possible. In addition, because I have no way of knowing into whose hands *this book* may eventually land, I need to be clear. So…

When a person (or organization) is illegitimate, it is considered to be "against the law", "illegal", "illogical", "inferior or lower in origin and/or class. The person (or group) is considered "less than." Though not in the exact sense, but this word is as offensive as the "N" word. For someone to be called a "Bastard" in the rawest form, should evoke nearly the same level of concern as the word "Nigger."

It is not the fault of any black person, that a racist society classifies them as a "Nigger" based purely on pigmentation (skin color). NIGGER, WHICH ALSO MEANS TO BE IGNORANT, INFERIOR ETC. CAN APPLY TO ANYONE. THERE ARE PEOPLE IN EVERY CULTURE AND IN EVERY RACE WHO ARE THEMSELVES EXTREMELY IGNORANT AND VOID OF COMMON SENSE! WHY THEN IS THIS TERM ONLY ASSOCIATED WITH EVERYTHING BLACK???

Unlike the marking of a headstone with a favorable epitaph, signifying the ending of a person's life, the illegitimate child is unfavorably and undeservingly marked at the very beginning. "Bastard" should never be the identifying description on anyone's birth certificate. Like I said, it is not a child's fault, for having been born to a father who has made the decision to walk away! In my opinion, both the "N" and the "B" words are derogatory adjectives, which should be banned! Speaking of something banned…

Humanity is notorious for banning Christ from His own day; the one day of the year, designated to celebrate His birth. The holiday [or Holy Day] we call Christmas, has just about shut HIM out, but we cannot ban nor make an effort to dispense with the ignorance that runs ramped every day - go figure.

Christmas is supposed to be a Christian holiday – we should be saying MERRY CHRISTMAS! Or HAPPY BIRTHDAY JESUS! (NOT HAPPY HOLIDAYS). In our greeting, can we at least acknowledge the person whose birthday we are celebrating?

Dear reader, perhaps *you* were conceived "in sin." In this use of the term, "in sin" I refer to all persons, having been conceived in <u>any other manner than through a set of parents, (one male, one female), who were legally married (to one another) at the time of conception.</u> All offspring conceived outside of the covenantal male and female marital relationship would technically be classified as illegitimate or bastard. If this is your circumstance, then let me assure you, you are certainly not alone. There are innumerable others who find themselves in your same shoes. Perhaps you are the product of an incestuous relationship, rape or extramarital affair. According to society's standards, you would be classified as a bastard. This, all because of <u>someone else's</u> sick perversions and/or sinful activity.

On the other hand, if you were not raped, molested, invaded or in any way violated, but *you willfully* engaged in sex outside of the boundaries of marriage, i.e. fornication, and you became pregnant, then unfortunately, your offspring would still bear such a title.

<u>According to The Bible,</u> sex within the confines of a <u>legal marriage,</u> is the <u>only</u> way that intercourse is considered Holy and is legitimately sanctioned and acceptable in the eyes of God. EVERYTHING ELSE, AND I DO MEAN <u>ALL OTHER</u> SEXUAL ACTIVITY, IS CONSIDERED SIN! DON'T STONE ME – CHECK YOUR BIBLE!

Perhaps your own parents may have been teenagers who loved one another dearly but for some reason, the two never married. Maybe they were older but still unmarried; the exact circumstance of each case is not as important as the point that I am making. The bottom line is, the label for you would be "bastard." There just isn't any way around it. This is an ugly word that we must accept and deal with; and today we shall!

If you are feeling as though you are lacking in some way, or like you are unworthy, please do not. Facing this reality may be painful if *you* are the product that resulted from any one of the aforementioned circumstances, which by the way is occurring at epidemic proportion these days. Think not for one moment, that you dear one are the only person, who due to no fault of your own, must now legitimately, wear the title of illegitimacy. We are going to call it what it is. Today we call it out, and give it its proper identity. We are going to face the ugliness of bastardization head on. We will not run away! We are going to deal with it face to face, right now, so that we can be free from this day forward.

I want you to know that even if you have been stigmatized by the church and by society, there is yet hope for you. There exists no other name that is above The Name of Jesus. Moreover, if you have been washed in His blood, even physical bastardizm is only a name, that falls under The Name, which is above every (other) name. That at The Name of Jesus – I say you are bastards and unwanted no more! You are not throw-a-ways, but rather you are sons and daughters of The Most High.

Let not your bastardized mentality defeat you any longer. Instead let it lie as dead, let it remain as something that has been demolished under The Feet and under The Blood of Jesus. Today we give this stigma its proper burial, and don't *you* dare dig it up again either! And for goodness sake, do not allow others to compartmentalize you with their poison by digging it up for you. You can be God's child, and you are not limited to the constraints of anybody's stigmatizations, including your own.

There are not many today, including our leaders, who can honestly say that they have not in some way, been affected by bastardizm. Many of them have even had children who would rightfully be classified as illegitimate. Playboy turned preacher; you haven't always been saved. If the truth were really told, some of you pastors would have to admit that you are yet contributing to the bastardization of society, but this time you are doing it even from the pulpit. We know all about the pastors who run with the choir members, etc. etc. etc., as if they are fooling somebody. I 'sho-nuff' had better leave that one alone.

Remember, Eli's sons (the priests), were also sleeping with the women who came to the temple. Anyway…

With so many single parents in our congregations, I know that leaders have encountered a deluge of individuals who fall under the bastard category. Again, if you are a child (or even an adult) you need to realize that you are very valuable in the sight of The Lord – He loves you, regardless to what you have done and no matter what title hangs above your head.

Your "illegal" birth has never been due to any fault of your own. It was the sin of your ancestors that caused your legally documented status of [physical] illegitimacy to exist. So as it is in the natural, so is it also in the spirit.

If you are a parent who gave birth to a child out of wedlock, also know that you are not alone. Forgiveness for each of us can be found through Jesus – at the foot of The Cross. You are not the only parent in nor outside of Christendom who has engaged in sexual sins, which resulted in pregnancy and now, you are left to raise a baby whom the world tags as "illegitimate."

In no way am I condoning or glorifying unwed pregnancies, resulting from the sin of fornication. However though, I do want you to know that there neither exists any sin for which forgiveness has not already been made possible; total forgiveness is available for all who ask. God stands ready to forgive and to take each of us back, if we earnestly repent, and make every effort to turn away from our besetting sin(s). There are no sins for which God's prescribed antidote cannot forgive. "Earth has no sorrow [nor sin] that heaven cannot heal."

"What can wash away our sin?" "NOTHING BUT THE BLOOD OF JESUS." "What can make us whole again?" "NOTHING BUT THE BLOOD OF JESUS."

As I discuss the meaning of bastardizm and the causes thereof, in no way am I doing so in an attempt to discredit or to make anyone feel bad; for in so doing I would certainly have to include myself. Although my parents *were* [legally] married at the time of my conception, they later divorced. I too was once married. However, during the course of my own marriage, I suffered from the affects of being emotionally abused, to the point of nearly having a nervous break down.

My husband and I were not long separated before I found myself pregnant by another man. I know what some of you may be thinking. The answer is no! No, I was not having an affair, but I had suffered severe anguish resulting from a marital relationship that had been filled with mental and emotional torture.

Shortly before our separation, I had come to a critical point in my life. There I was nearly 30 years old and on the verge of breaking down. At one point, I actually considered committing suicide. My husband and I did separate (See Oops Wrong Fold). Instead of committing suicide or even homicide for that matter, I found refuge in a friend. Though it did not start out that way, and was never meant to head in that direction, still I found myself engaging in the sinful act of fornication, and as a result, MY SIN resulted in a pregnancy. Did you hear what I just said? *I SAID, 'MY' SIN!*

There I was, a Christian, half out of my mind and engaging in the sin of fornication. Just because my husband and I were separated, did not mean that I had the right to involve myself with someone else, because legally I was still married. No matter how horrible the circumstances, and regardless to who did what first, two wrongs never make a right. Here comes another very bitter but truthful pill, which I then, as well as many of you right now may have to swallow – so listen up.

Even if I had been legally divorced instead of only separated, and even if my husband did cheat on me first [and had moved out] STILL, <u>MY ACTIONS</u> WOULD HAVE BEEN CONSIDERED AS SIN, BECAUSE MY DAUGHTER'S FATHER AND I WERE NOT MARRIED!

Even Christians do accidentally and unfortunately do also willfully commit acts of sin. All have sinned and come short of the Glory of God; that is unless of course you are a part of that "special elite group", whose members claim to have never done anything wrong. Or perhaps you carry membership amongst those who say that they have nothing at all for which to be ashamed, as they perch themselves high upon their very own pedestals of pride. Give me a break!

Anyway, for those of you who *are* real, I will tell YOU what it takes to break free; at least what it took for me anyway. *It will require absolute honesty and a <u>sincere</u> desire and effort to stop doing what you are doing.* Please don't play God's grace cheap. He will not allow us to take advantage of His love, His favor nor His mercy.

We cannot keep pretending as though we want to be free. Pretence is exactly what we are doing if we continue to live the same lifestyle of sin. Stop saying with your lips that you want deliverance, while at the same time; you keep one foot still in the fleshpot with no real intentions of coming out. I am not talking about that foolishness; so don't try to play me out. For goodness sake, don't even think about trying to play God out!

I can't speak for anyone else, but I thank God that just as I willing engaged in my sin, and in disobedience, I also knew how to WILLINGLY CAST MY OWN SELF DOWN BEFORE HIS PRESENCE TO ASK HIM FOR MERCY AND FOR FORGIVENESS! Like David, I too have had lots of practice at this. I too knew how to climb on top of the altar for some serious spiritual surgery.

Though I am far from being perfect, still I can truly say like The Saints of old – [Most] of "The things that I use to do, I don't do no more." "The places that I use to go, I don't go no more. Why? Am I some super spiritual sinless saint? No! Of course not!! I <u>don't</u> <u>do</u> <u>these</u> <u>things,</u> because I <u>don't</u> <u>want</u> <u>to.</u> I <u>wanted</u> <u>to</u> <u>change,</u> <u>and</u> <u>by</u> <u>God's</u> <u>grace,</u> <u>I</u> <u>have.</u> He is still working on me, and I may have a ways to go but I can say of a truth, that I have indeed come a mighty long way. And for this I say, thank You Lord!

Prior to my sanctification and true conversion, there I was at the time, not even officially divorced and yet pregnant by another man just a couple months after my husband had left. (Before you judge read the entire story in "Oops Wrong Fold). So trust me when I tell you, I am in no position to look for fault, in someone else and neither do I presume to pass judgment upon anyone. For one thing, I am too busy trying to keep my own self out of the way of God's wrath.

Unless you have ever experienced abuse [of any kind], you could not even begin to imagine, let alone understand, the dynamics that are involved. Nobody knows for certain what will go through a person's mind; neither can an individual know exactly what he or she will do given a certain set of circumstances. In the garden of Gethsemane, was it not the same Peter who quickly defended Jesus by slicing off the guard's ear, only to fail miserably, as he later denied The Lord "thrice" (3 times)?

Yes beloved you can be saved, but depending upon your situation and your mindset, sometimes even *you* might find yourself taking a tumble. The strongest Christian can find him or her self in a mess. Not that I am God's best servant or anything, but I am a Disciple of Christ and I was in a terrible fix; I had not yet been sanctified. I did not know, neither did I understand [or care as much about] the things that I do now. It is called acquiring wisdom. It is called being purged, and cleansed. It is called growing up and making a serious effort to get right with God!

It seemed that from my earliest existence, I would become the victim of much emotional turmoil, rejection, and the object of people's disdain. At times, all I would have to do is show up, and immediately the eyes would start staring or people would begin whispering. I was a youngster and had not even been in society long enough, to have presented myself as un-teachable or rebellious. It was not my fault that kids teased me or that they did not like me. Resulting from years of trying to figure things out, trying to fit in or looking for love, at times I willingly engaged in gross acts of sin and fornication, all because I longed for fleshly validation and earthly acceptance.

In my heart I did not *want* to do wrong, I never *wanted* to be bad; but I suppose I gave myself over to these sinful indulgences because it felt good to be embraced, even if it was only for the moment, and I had many moments. How many of you know, yet again, that The Bible remains true when it says that sin is pleasurable – it seems good, it sounds good, it tastes good, it looks good and it certainly feels good too! Do I have a truthful witness anybody? Oh but children, take yet another glance at The Book; the pleasures thereof last but for a season.

The wages of sin is STILL death. That my friend has not changed. I know you don't hear it preached these days, but we know that in the end, our sinful acts will only bring forth death, disease and/or destruction.

Even in my sinful state, I still recognized that God was bearing witness to everything that I did. Frankly, knowing that He was watching me bothered me and I felt guilty a lot - a whole lot. OK FINE! *A WHOLE, WHOLE, WHOLE LOT!* In my quest for acceptance, I wallowed with the hogs. But GOD! GOD! GOD! GOD! GOD! - He loved me too much to leave me in the gutter. Hallelujah! When nothing else would help, not sex, not money, not men, not a child, not even church folk could or would help, it was The Father's love that lifted me.

Like the song says -

"I was sinking deep in sin, far from the peaceful shore." "Very deeply stained within, I was sinking, to rise no more." But The Master of the sea, He heard my despairing cry. "From the waters, He lifted me, now safe am I."

Thanks for allowing me my moment; I needed that (smile). Now, where was I?

Oh, yes – back to defining the term bastard: Next, we have the theologians' definition of what a bastard is. I have already told you what *THEY* think but here it is again: A bastard is said to be anyone who is engaged in ministry, without having received the fatherly blessing, or without having been "properly birthed out", (which seems to be the new term these days).

That means, if your calling and/or ministry has not been officially confirmed by the congregation or by the "church board", via the pastor, and yet you are "out there" engaging in ministry work, (no matter how fruitful or how significant a work, you may be doing for God's Kingdom), you my friend, will still be considered a bastard; simply because THEY say so. "Who is your mentor?" "Who else besides you, has confirmed your call?" – they ask. "Whose covering are you under?" This would be like having a spiritual mother, father or leader to say; yes, I can vouch for this one. He or she belongs to me, and to *my* ministry – they boast.

Like a stable of valuable thoroughbreds, some pastors love to display and boast about the numbers they have *"under them."* Like a two-bit prostitute, many in the house of God are being 'pimped' by the very preachers who are supposed to nurture them. Do exactly as I say; keep your talents under *my* ministry so that you can bring *me* some more money – you hear me!

Although our earthly parents have raised us, some preachers tell us that we also *need* spiritual parents to raise us as well. If someone does not have such a mentor, but continues to be about the business of ministry, then the bastard label is applicable. Christians who do not attend any local congregation are most worthy of the bastard title *they say.* I have been privileged to meet many brothers and sisters, who honestly love The Lord with all of their hearts, but who for one reason or another, no longer attend a local church [on a regular basis if at all] because when they did they were almost always met with blatant opposition, or with a fresh wounding from those who claim to be holy.

Still others have not quite overcome the *one* near fatal blow of arrogance, hypocrisy and/or neglect that almost killed them (spiritually), causing them to flee in the first place. Remember, I am not referring to 'sinners' who *never* knew The Lord, but rather I am talking about fellow Christians who use to be very faithful members. Also, please keep in mind that just because people attend church does not mean that they are 'really' saved. Wheat and tares *do* grow together; anybody can attend a service. THEY say that people who have no official church home are spiritually disconnected because they are not assembling themselves together with The Saints. They have no spiritual leader and are therefore said to be in total violation of Scripture, which in turn, makes them spiritually disobedient, and yields the end product of them being labeled as spiritual bastards.

Note: Scripture admonishes us, "Not to forsake the assembling of ourselves together with The Saints." (Hebrews 10:25). Would that make those who no longer fellowship at a local congregation eligible for bastard status, or would they simply in danger of missing the mark, as in the committing of a sin? I am not condoning sin, but I am making a point. There are thousands who sin directly from the church pews each week and yet they are not referred to as bastards. Some of the most egregious offences continue to be committed by pulpit clerics; but these sinful pastors are not classified as illegitimate. Why not? Why then must their victims be?

Is detaching from a church building enough to banish someone from The Kingdom or from a future with The Lord? On the other hand, should non-attendance be treated like any other sin? If it is a SIN, is it not also FORGIVABLE? Some people, who no longer hold membership in traditional churches, in fact still do attend prayer meetings, cell groups and other ministry gatherings with fellow believers. Although I am not suggesting that people leave or abandon their congregations as some are now preaching, but I will ask that you consider Matthew 18:20.

Jesus said – "*For where two or three are gathered together in My Name, there am I in the midst of them.*" *My personal preference is to be part of a local assembly. I rather enjoy the music (praise and worship) as well as the atmosphere of being in a church environment. However, I still believe that anytime you and others of like faith gather in The Messiah's Name, with Him as the center of attention, God is being glorified. He then promises to be there also. This did not come from a pastor, but this comes from The Lord. It does not take large numbers to constitute an entity, which we can officially classify as "a church."*

According to Hebrew law, there only needs to be 10 men present at a gathering for it to be officially recognized as a congregation. <u>In addition, the previous verse of that same passage states, that we also are to, "Consider one another."</u> We are indeed to be considerate of one another, by being concerned about each other's feelings; but also we are to consider one another's ages, aspirations, gifts, talents and abilities; but even more than that, we are to consider the fact that EVERYONE is valuable, and that we have ALL been brought by the same Blood.

Oftentimes, consideration of our fellow brothers and sisters cannot be seen or felt. As a result, a whole lot of people are injured instead. Therefore, instead of pointing an accusatory finger at a brother or sister who <u>use</u> to attend regular services, why not ASK, him or her what happened. Why do so many people no longer attend church at all, (or at the very least, why are so many reluctant to do so). Stop judging! Instead why not ask questions - the answers might just surprise you!

Alas, who does The Lord call a bastard and why?

What we are looking for is found in verses 7-8. But because it is all so good, I'd rather we read 1-11, so that *you* can get the proper feel of the text. You can know for yourselves exactly what is being said, by whom, to whom and why – I tell you, context is key.

Here we go to The Book of Hebrews Chapter 12, verses 1-11, read...

Wherefore seeing we also are compassed
about with so great a cloud of witnesses,
let us lay aside every weight, and the
sin that doth so easily beset us, and
let us run with patience the race
that is set before us, Looking unto Jesus,
the author and finisher of our faith;

who for the joy that was set before Him
endured the cross, despising the shame,
and is set down at the right hand of
the throne of God.
For consider Him that endured such
contradiction of sinners against Himself,
lest ye be wearied and faint in your minds.
Ye have not resisted unto blood striving
against sin.
And ye have forgotten the
exhortation which speaketh to you as unto
children, My son, despise not thou the
chastening of The Lord, nor faint when
thou art rebuked of Him. For whom
The Lord loveth He chasteneth, and
scourgeth every son whom He receiveth.
If ye endure chastening, God dealeth with
you as with sons; for what son is he whom
The Father chasteneth not?
But if you be without chastisement,
whereof all are partakers, then ye are bastards,
and not sons. Furthermore we have had
fathers of our flesh which corrected us,
and we gave then reverence; shall we not
much [more] rather be in subjection unto
The Father of spirits and live?
For they verily for a few days chastened us
after their own pleasure; but He for our profit,
that we might be partakers of His Holiness.
Now no chastening for the time seemeth to be
joyous, but grievous; nevertheless afterward
it yieldeth the peaceable fruit of righteousness
unto them which are exercised thereby.

Many theologians have chosen to say that if we are not submitting to *their counsel* or to *their chastisement,* then we are bastards. While The Bible does teach that we are to obey them that have the rule over us, it certainly does not mean that our pastors own us. We are not their biological children, and neither are we their property or personal possessions.

This passage can refer to, "Them that have the rule over us" as being the laws of the land, or governmental officials, and rules or authority figures. However, it is actually more applicable to those who are our pastors, because they really are SUPPOSED to be watching for our souls, but...

<u>As Christians, we ought to ALWAYS obey our governing officials as well as adhere to the laws of the land, EXCEPT WHEN TO DO SO IS IN DIRECT VIOLATION OF GOD'S COMMANDMENTS. We are not only to obey the written commandments of God, but we are also to obey any "rhema" that He makes known to us.</u>

<u>If obeying governmental law applies, unless to do so goes against the will of God, then this same rule is certainly applicable, when it comes to obeying our leaders. Certainly, we should listen to and obey them, unless to do so is in direct violation of God's word or His revealed will for our lives.</u>

<u>Surely, The Lord never meant for us to obey them to such a degree, that we allow them to lead us into a ditch or to fail in the carrying out of His mission! If they are supposed to be watching for our souls, certainly they cannot be doing a very good job, if they are busy bruising us instead.</u>

The majority of Christians have experienced the leading of God long BEFORE ever setting foot into a local assembly. In fact, in many cases The Holy Spirit may have led them to a certain place to begin with. Sometimes a person's stay will be temporary, it may only be for a season, or until he or she has learned a particular lesson or completed a specific task. Just as The Lord leads us to a place, there will also be times that He calls us out. Yet sometimes He may keep us there, but still require our services in an area other than the place we attend.

Mainstream clergy will hardly ever tell you to obey God's voice, even above *their own*. A lot of them want to be God in the lives of people. That simply is out of the question; this type thinking needs to be exposed, dealt with and done away with. Soliciting advice or the help of our clergy is fine. I can even go with having a covering or spiritual father (remember, at one point I truly desired one), but to allow someone *other than God* to be God in my life - absolutely not!

They always preach The Bible and what it says, when it comes to giving, as in the paying of tithes. They have no problem trusting *you and I to* hear the voice of The Lord (clearly) for ourselves, when He may be telling us to give, especially if He should command that we give a lot. "You ought to give whatever The Lord tells you to", *they say.* "If He speaks to you, obey God if He doesn't speak to you then don't", they admonish. Isn't it strange how they suddenly trust us then? They trust us to know His voice when it comes to doing anything that will line their pockets, promote their ministry or boost their reputation.

However, I find it quite interesting that they suddenly feel the need to hear from God "for us" when they do not stand to gain anything. Sometimes God may let you know that your time is up in a particular place. Your pastors will then tell you that God has not spoken to *them concerning you, [or about your leaving]. However, if you pursue anyway, the word is put out, informing everyone in the congregation, (and then some), that you are in a state of rebellion.*

While it is true that, many of us did have earthly fathers who corrected us; (the ones who stuck around that is); hopefully they recognized and accepted the fact that we would eventually grow up and would no longer be under their tutelage, or control. They watched over us and covered our mistakes for a while, but when we reached the age of accountability and when the time came, they let us go. They did not stop being our fathers (or mothers) just because we grew up (and perhaps) went our separate ways.

They had enough wisdom and common sense to realize that a child does not stay a child always. Progression is the natural order of things. A child is *supposed* to grow up, move out and eventually move on. As a natural parent, I know this can be difficult. I too will have to face this with my own child who is approaching high school age. I can still remember quite vividly, the day on which I brought "my little bundle" home from the hospital; it seems like only yesterday. The years have escaped me, as seemingly she has grown up all too quickly. While I may not like it, as the years have come and gone too rapidly – still, I must prepare myself to [eventually] cut the cord. This is every good parent's worse nightmare, but…

We are to grow physically AND we should be growing spiritually. If either of these areas has become stifled, then something has gone terribly wrong. Not even did Jesus keep His group of 12, at "the disciple" level forever. They became Apostles and in turn, *they* went on to win souls for The Kingdom. If we find ourselves serving under a leader who will not allow us to grow up and into the things of God, then that pastor is operating under an authority other than The Lord's.

If a member is fortunate enough to have a good shepherd, (one who happens to be [spiritually] insightful), then there really ought to be a collaborative effort, with the implementation of a plan, that will further equip the individual, *for whatever* The Lord may be calling him or her unto. Unfortunately, this has not been what a huge percentage of people in The Body of Christ have experienced. Instead, they have encountered pastors/leaders who have sought to ostracize and/or penalize them, for no reason other than the fact, that the individual(s) desired to grow and to be of service. How sad!

Never even once did I in any way presume to act unkind or unseemly towards my pastor. I desired only to obey God, and submitted myself to my leader. Had I allowed my pastor's stinging words to penetrate my heart on a deeper level, I can tell you right now, that I probably would not be a Christian today. I felt so bad after speaking to him; surely were it not for my own nearly 28 year relationship with The Lord, I would be well on my way to becoming a backslider.

After having been compared to a bird, which he claims to have heard prophesy, I felt totally dejected. How dare he! As if the gift of prophecy or the prophetic office is something that *everybody* possesses or walks in. In no way am I trying to portray that I am better than anyone else, neither is it my intention to imply that I have some sort of inside information *on everything* because certainly, I do not; but to chalk me up to his pet, by comparing me to a mere bird, whose only messages are limited to mimicking and imitating, what it hears from frail human beings, – well, the devil is a liar! Had YHWH not delivered my mind from that "strange fire" I too would have turned *totally* away from the church as some are preaching and as countless millions have already done.

How many ecclesial endorsements do you suppose I would have gotten to redeem the bastard, reject and outcast population? I had to obey God, because it is MY crown and MY eternal reward that hangs in the balance. Nobody is going to make me miss hearing The Lord say "well done", not even my pastor!

I have already experienced for too long where obeying man has gotten me. I am sorry if those of you in power think that I am out of line, but right now I am [literally] running for my own eternal life; it really isn't about *you* at all. I told you that my pastor compared me to some bird, a parrot that he claimed to have prophesied. To his comparison, I say the following: First off, I am nobody's bird. Humans train parrots, while I on the other hand, have been trained under the auspices of God The Father, God The Son and God The Holy Ghost.

Next, be it understood and allow me to inform you that, I do not now nor will I ever simply mimic what someone else teaches me to say. That includes some of those 'tongues' that preachers think they have the ability to **'teach'** people to speak in. **EXPOSED!! If you are not The Holy Ghost, then I don't think so.** I am nobody's clone. I desire to have only the Spirit of my Father. I will only prophesy, preach, write, teach and say that which The Lord gives me. If He isn't saying anything, [to me] then neither am I saying it to anyone else.

Never will I do what PEOPLE think I should or say what they want to hear, unless what they want to hear happens to line up with what He is telling me to say. Why, you ask? It isn't rocket science for goodness sake. The fact of the matter is that I am responsible and accountable to God if I lie to you. My neck is on the line if I purposely try to embellish what is or isn't being said, by attaching to it a "Thus Saith The Lord." Again, if He is not saying it, than neither am I.

Because my aim is not to impress anyone, and my objective is not to people please, I am not obligated to make anyone shout or feel good. I refuse to make up some fake prophecy for the mere purpose of whipping the crowd into a state of spiritual pandemonium. I could not care less if you do not like me, nor do I concern myself with whether or not you believe me. I am on God's time and on His assignment, and not anyone else's. Walking in the prophetic does not mean for an individual to rattle off something that sounds good just because it makes the people feel good. The prophetic office consists of much more than prophesying. If God is calling someone for His purpose and a pastor is trying to hinder the progress, what then should the individual do? Well, while I cannot speak for anyone else, I for one would certainly rather be wrong in *their* sight by letting them call me a bastard, renegade (or whatever) than to take *even the slightest chance* of not showing up for God, should He have need of me.

I would rather be kicked out of their crowd than out of His Kingdom that's for sure. This is a decision that you will have to make for yourself. One day when we each stand before God to give an account, (and we shall); we will not be standing as a collective group, as some would have you to believe.

We will each stand and give an <u>account</u> of <u>our</u> <u>own</u> <u>individual</u> <u>lives</u> and of the deeds that we have done (or failed to do) in the body [of our flesh]. Notwithstanding, God being sovereign, could very well call us to account for what we have done in the cooperate body, His Body – as in "The Body of Christ." What have we done with Christ since our conversion? I don't know about you, but this alone is enough to make me push past what THEY think and instead press forward towards everything that HE is saying. I must warn you though. Sometimes doing His will, may mean leaving where you are. At other times, it may mean for you to stay put, but to do His will anyhow. You and The Lord will have to decide what course of action is best for your life. If you are not clear as to whose voice you are hearing, or if there is even the slightest possibility that you could be wrong, making absolutely certain that you know and can readily identify, The Voice of The Lord, should be YOUR main priority and very first assignment.

God is not going to tell you anything else, until YOU FIRST get to the place of knowing whether or not it is He who is doing the speaking. Remember, YOU are NEVER to approach any leader in an authoritative or negative manner, regardless to how empowered you may be feeling at the time. Liberation may be power, but still I cannot stress enough, how important it is to do ONLY what HE tells you to. <u>YOU</u> HAVE TO BE AS RIGHT AS HUMANLY POSSIBLE. Keep in mind that being right and experiencing a feeling of liberation because you are, does not give you the privilege to act in an ungodly manner, even in light of what your enemy has tried to do to you. If you were to retaliate or to approach him/her in a negative manner, you then would be no better than those who have wounded you. Granted this is not easy because humanity can be tough to deal with, gosh how I know this. At times, I still have problems in this area. Nevertheless, we must do our very best.

First, be sure that YOU are right, then leave the rest to GOD. In addition, when you do error in any area, then just like David, you need to fall into the hands of The Father. He is more merciful than man will ever be. Don't be too stubborn to say <u>I'm sorry</u>. Those two little, but very powerful words, go a long way. Do it <u>before</u> you "get caught" or <u>before</u> God "has to expose you." I am not talking about perfection, but the best thing that you could possibly do, is to stay as spiritually pure as humanly possible. If YOUR hands are clean, then you won't have to worry about Him exposing you – right??

When I am out of line, God knows exactly how to correct me without wounding me. He can break me, without permanently destroying my spirit; man cannot do that. Humans are simply not that skillful. I pray people do me a big favor, and just leave me in the hands of Jehovah. We must be willing to endure the pruning process, His preparation of us, as well as the prescribed wilderness period for our lives. We do not have to *like* the process, but it is of a surety that we must submit to it if we are truly going to walk with Him. Our 'making' process is one that is best overseen by The Father. If we despise His chastening then The Bible says that we become bastards and not sons. We will be as those who have no father. The preachers don't tell you that they too are subject to this same process, and that they too are also at risk for bastardizm, should they despise chastisement and/or correction. They must also endure The Lord's chastening. They too must be broken, tested and put through the fires of God's choice. Many pastors have at one time found themselves exactly where we are right now and have failed miserably. Yet for some reason, they now feel as though they are free to hurl their accusations and insults as they continue in their misappropriation of Scripture.

It is God's process and chastisement to which we are bound. We are not admonished to endure some lame process, conjured up in the minds of sinful, power-stricken, perverted "wolf clerics", [or other people] whose process by the way, has been designed [for the most part], to keep you and I bound, gagged and chained to them forever.

Like Job's friends, (or even like satan) they take pride in pointing an accusatory finger. Job's friends probed and prodded as they tried to *make* him confess or acknowledge some trespass or sin that *they felt* he was trying to hide.

According to their judgment, <u>sin had</u> to be the reason for his ongoing calamity. They continued to drill him based purely upon something that they thought. Job's friends, (if you really want to call them that) had absolutely no idea as to what was at stake or what was going on behind the scene. They were clueless, yet they slandered and railed on anyhow – just like we do! When it comes to the sentencing of anyone as a bastard, it is God's call and no one else's. He will deal with you as with those who have no father; but according to Scripture, YOU beloved are the only one capable of bringing this sentencing upon yourself by despising His chastening and/or correction. So do not be fooled by what you hear anyone else say. Let God's Word serve as the <u>final</u> authority in your life.

Although at times God has been known to employ the hardened hearts of others to help carry out His plan, still He alone decides when the process is over. He is the judge of us all, including those who have taken such delight in judging you. I do not believe that God would ever assign such an intricate and delicately detailed process to the hand of a mortal. Human beings simply do not know what to do with that much power. God help us, we have already witnessed what humanity does with *the little bit of authority* that it has been given – we often abuse it!

Even as we survey the suffering of Christ on The Cross, we must be aware that He too was enduring The Father's chastening, which should have rightly been upon our own wicked shoulders. He hung there dying for your sins and for mine. It was The Father's will that the sin penalty be satisfied. While His own people screamed for His crucifixion, Jesus knew and had already come to terms with this as being the will of The Father. His battle had been fought and won as He wrestled in the Garden of Gethsemane. It was Jesus' ultimate assignment to come to earth and to lay down His life. The Master did not ask anyone's thoughts concerning the matter.

Before His 'showdown' at Calvary however, He decided to share some of the details of his impending fate, with His beloved Disciples. Of course when the outspoken 'Peter' tried to *tell* Jesus, "Not so!, that He [Jesus] "would not indeed suffer those things" [being crucified at Calvary]; Jesus immediately and quite sharply rebuked him. We can certainly understand from a human perspective how the announcement of Jesus' approaching death must have grieved Peter.

After all, Peter did not *want The* Lord to die. Howbeit, Jesus was able to see straight through to the heart of the matter; for there was too much at stake for Him to fail. He knew that it was not really Peter who had done the speaking, but rather this was the work of the enemy. Unbeknownst to Peter, the devil was trying to thwart the plan of God and had attempted to use him as a pawn to help. Jesus knew that it was not really Peter's fault. For He did not say, "Get thee behind me" 'Simon Peter', but rather Jesus rebuked the real culprit. Although He addressed Peter, (only because it was his voice that satan tried to use), Jesus said, "Get thee behind me, satan: <u>thou</u> <u>art</u> <u>an</u> <u>offence</u> <u>unto</u> <u>me</u>: for thou savourest not the things that be of God, but <u>those</u> that be of men. (Mathew 16:23).
AND AGAIN, YOU WILL FIND THESE WORDS IN MARK'S ACCOUNT...

"Get thee behind me, satan: for thou savourest not the things that be of God, but the things that be of men (Mark 8:33).

With full knowledge of the agony that awaited Him at Calvary, Jesus yet sought and obeyed only the will of The Father. The Cross, which would soon be laid upon His shredded, blood stained, back was Jesus' assignment and He knew that. His life's calling had been to first profess The Father, and then to die for a sinful, undeserving humanity, which totally lacked the power to save itself. Beloved the day of reckoning will surely come; when you will also realize your need for The Saviour, (at least I hope so anyway). And yes my brother, my sister; Jesus willingly laid down His life, because He knew that too.

He had you on His mind, as they nailed His wrists to The Cross. He died so that you would never have to be a bastard, unless you choose to be. He hung there; He bled and He died. He gave His life freely. He decided not to come down, just to keep <u>you</u> from having to be nailed up!

❧Discerning The Time❧

Because I finally understand my calling, I realize that it had never been by God's design, that I walk two paces behind *everyone else forever.* My Father designed me to be somewhat of a trailblazer. Oh, that doesn't mean that I cannot (or that I should not) be under the teachings of another. What it does mean however, is that I must be free to do God's will, regardless to whose leadership I am under. I feel the need to further explore my reasons for allowing others to have oppressed me in the first place *and* for so long. Why is it that the impostors usually overshadow the very people who possess much wisdom and spiritual insight?

Those who have made a name for themselves by kicking and clawing their way to the top, are often revered and looked upon as possessing much power and esteem. Society will likely deem them more worthy than the rest of us. For too long, those who have real strength of character, ability and power, not to mention necessary survival skills, have constantly found themselves lagging behind. Don't get me wrong; I am not suggesting that *everyone* at the top has gotten there illegally. However, it does appear as though a great many if them, have indeed climbed up, at the expense of those upon whom they've seen fit to trample.

The time has come, [for us] to reprogram the tape that has played in our heads for most of our lives. We owe it to our selves and to The Kingdom, to ask for God's help in deleting every negative "put-down" that has been told to us. These destructive communications in many instances have been the primary source of our problems, as we have allowed them to penetrate our spirit, and in turn, they caused our self-esteem to hit bottom.

In some cases, we may even have to reexamine our feelings and opinions about *Him.* Many of you are angry with God, because you feel like He should have done something [more] to help you out of your pit, or that He should have done so a lot sooner. Some of you right now view God, in the same light as you do the abusive parent who left you or physically hurt you. While others of you see Him as an uncaring, oppressive leader who rules with an iron hand. You see God this way because it is the only style of authority you have ever known.

Let me assure you that God is nothing at all like sinful man. He truly does love you. However, you beloved must get to know *Him* as well as His ways. Although I do not always understand Him, for surely, at times He has bewildered me; heaven knows I have even been angry with Him, but never have I viewed Him as being even remotely similar to the authority figures that I have known.

We must now be 're-born' from the snares of traditions and religiosity. Although we have been born again and are <u>now in Him,</u> *it is imperative that we also have our minds* <u>renewed by Him.</u> "Let this mind be in you which was also in Christ Jesus (Philippians 2:5). The time for renewal is right now. This process will help you dispel the erroneous information that you have heretofore taken at face value. Whether we have been duped by their crafty suggestions, or whether some fancy pulpiteer has thoroughly bashed our heads in with warped theology, the time has come for renewal and for the refreshing of the minds of the masses.

Unfortunately, many clerics have purposely spewed venomous lies into the ears of the people. This they did in an attempt to keep others at bay as they alone continued towards their own advancement. This they did at our spiritual expense. We have been brainwashed for far too long. The time to revive [or to begin], your own personal relationship with The Lord is right now. You must arise from your slumber. Wake up! You must rid yourselves of both popular opinion and your oppressor's bonds. You must then pursue wholeheartedly that which He has spoken to you.

This is our finest hour. It is the time of the underdog! The children of God must now overthrow everything that desires to keep them chained. We must denounce all advice, counsel and instruction that in no way could have possibly originated from the wisdom of glory! The hour of visitation shall soon be upon us and we must do our very best to rid ourselves of all emotional and verbal shackles, they are simply too binding.

We can no longer afford to take chances as we have wasted much time already. I know that God has a plan for each of us. He has enough work for all of His children. The thing that I do not know though, is how long each of us has to complete our individual and/or collectively assigned tasks.

The time has come for <u>everyone</u> who claims to name The Name of Christ, to begin making his or her way forward in order to be counted. Nobody is obsolete; He needs us all!

God will often share things with His friends and with His servants the prophets that others may not be privy to for a season. This does not make anybody better than anyone else. However, the fact remains that some people have a much clearer understanding of what may be transpiring at a given time because God has made an impartation.

For example, Abraham knew that God was on His way to destroy Sodom and Gomorrah, before Lot did. As Lot slept or went about business as usual, he had absolutely no idea of the great intercession taking place on his behalf and on behalf of the wicked city that he dwelt in. Even though Lot actually lived there, he had no idea that Abraham and God were about to strike a deal on his behalf.

Not even Sarah or anyone else living in Abraham's home had an inkling of the judgment that loomed just over the horizon. These two wicked cities reeked of sodomy centered and other sexually perverted activity and God had finally had enough! Abraham was the only person with whom The Lord shared what He was about to do. The others merely witnessed the aftermath of the explosion. No one knew that Abraham had been forewarned (informed) of the imminent destruction. Neither had anyone known that Abraham had received a promise from God and that the city would be spared for the sake of just 10 righteous people. There were not even 10 people, out of the entire population of two major cities that were *at least trying* to live right. Wow, now that's scary!

Some of the very pastors, who ridicule you, have absolutely no idea that in many instances, their own churches and in some cases, even their very lives have literally been spared because of you. Maybe you interceded on their behalf, (although you may not have [really] wanted) to, but in obedience to The Lord, you did so anyway. You may have suffered pain at their hands but still you prayed for them.

People who have acquired true humility, do not normally go around bragging about who or what they are or about who and/or what they know. For they have enough wisdom to realize, that all that they are and ever shall be, is made possible purely by the benevolence and the mercy of God.

With the exception of Salvation through Him, what could we as sinful creatures possibly have to brag about anyway? We need not brag, but neither should we have to keep denying who we are. Why must we feel compelled to hide the fact that we have been gifted from above?

Why should anyone be forced or controlled into denying that he or she is who or what God has chosen or called him or her to be, just because others cannot handle it. Why must we stick our heads in the sand?

Stop depending on pastors and other people to do only what The Lord can do for you – He *wants* you to thrive. He wills that you grow! He wants you to listen to Him! Children of God will you please stop kissing up and begging mere men of flesh to promote you? Your Father never designed you to be beggars, spiritual paupers or followers of men.

God knows who you are and He stands ready to assist you. Why would He gift you, only to keep you stunted and hidden forever? You must stay closer to Him, now more than ever, so that you will not continue to be fooled by every voice that you hear.   You cannot afford to trust every person that you meet, simply because that person claims to be a Christian. You must realize where we are on the calendar of events. Inquire of Him as to where it is that you fit.

He alone knows if it is YOUR time yet. Ask HIM; better yet, you will not have to ask, because God has a way of making it quite clear when He is ready for us. Some of us may even be behind schedule, but you need not fear either. God even knows how to redeem the precious time that we have squandered and let slip away. It will soon be your turn to unveil and to unleash that, which burns within your soul. For others, your time is right now; God has already given the command.

"CHARGE!" "ATTACK!" "PURSUE!" "OVERTAKE!"   "RESCUE!" "WARN!" "CRY LOUD AND SPARE NOT!" "PREACH THE WORD!" "SING!" "WRITE!" "INVENT!" "CLEAN UP!" "GET IN THE BATTLE!" "GO TO WAR!" "WHAT IN THE WORLD, ARE YOU WAITING FOR NOW??"

Follow hard after The Lord and do ONLY what HE tells you to. Your lives may depend upon it. No matter where we are in life, God always has the means by which to rescue us. So as it is in the natural, so is it also in the spirit. If He tells you to move then dog-gone-it, you need to move. What are you waiting for anyway? Don't let *them* keep you stuck. Likewise, if He tells you to wait, then you had darn well better wait. But for goodness sake, please know what time it is –

And don't miss your turn!

Do something – get in prayer, go on a fast. Get in shape; you'll need that second wind. Worship and prayer are <u>always</u> in order. If you are a babe, and cannot enter into intense high worship, then why not give Him some praise? For goodness sake, make a move! Believe me; there will come a time in which you will no longer be able to do anything at all.

PLEASE REMEMBER THAT YOU ARE NOT BOUND TO ANY HUMAN, BUT YOU ARE BOUND AND SHALL WITHOUT FAIL GIVE A THOROUGH ACCOUNT TO THE ALMIGHTY. He expects every one of us to seek Him through His Word, through prayer, meditation and fasting. We are responsible to know <u>for ourselves</u> what is pertained in The Holy Scriptures. We are responsible and must learn to discern the times <u>for ourselves.</u>

This is a time of good news my fellow end-time warriors. We have no cause to fear. For The Lord our God is sending out a "war cry." In this season, the call is going out to all who have been bastardized, rejected, orphaned, bedraggled, cast out and left behind.

The trumpet is blowing in Zion – Bless His Holy Name! You have not been forgotten! For it is your turn to Bless Him! Know that you are not rebels just because you no longer grovel at the feet of oppressive leaders, whose only desire is to see to it that you are kept quiet and locked down.

We are not in any way trying to be rebellious and/or belligerent to leadership. But we are however, rebels for The Kingdom, and we have been inducted into the Army of The Living God. We have been brooding in the background and festering in righteous indignation because The Kingdom has been suffering. It suffers, because the leadership have not been doing their job! We are suffering because our pastors are not obeying The Word of The Lord, but have flagrantly aligned themselves with the works of wickedness!

Our pastors are angered if we refuse to listen to them, but look what they have done. They have turned the church into a circus. They have excluded the beggar and have instead embraced only those who line their pockets. They have welcomed the world to come in, as we continue to hurt. They have defiled themselves with the filth of the ages. They have allowed satan to rip into The Body and now, we are all bleeding! We are a hemorrhaging bloody mass of confusion. But fear not Remnant of The Most High. God shall never be out done! BEHOLD! The time has come to fester no more but to instead cry loud! Hallelujah!

The time has come to take back The Kingdom <u>of God, for God.</u> Not only are we taking it back from satan, but also we will assist God, by doing our part to wrench it out of the hands of the impostors, who are merely posing as HIS children and as HIS shepherds and priests. The Trump of God is further blasting to alert the end time prophetic voices. Come out with your songs, with your harps, with your wailings, with your dancing, with your words and with your lanterns. Out from under your hiding covers!!! Fill up with oil! Trim the wicks of your candles! Go! Speak ye the word of The Lord. Play skillfully upon your instruments. Strike the timbrels! Blow loudly the trump in Zion; prepare ye the way!

Make ready for the Mighty blast of "The Seventh Trumpet" – Blessed Be His Holy Name! Come from beyond the desert sands with your praise, with your worship and with your Sword. Up from behind the willows! Get thee hence unto the mount of The Lord! Prepare yourselves to receive further instruction! There yet remaineth many babies to round up – for The Lord told me so! No more peaking from under the covers; come out! Prepare yourselves and make ready to rescue the babes! Preach HIS Word! Come out of the deserts! Go into the deserts! Do what you must! BUT GET READY!

Hosts of The Lord Most High, the time has come to ready yourselves for war and for service. We wait on God and not a man. The Father is shifting some things. He will set in motion that which is soon to come. He will place into the churches leaders of *His choice*, not of others' choosing – are you ready? *THEY* have hurt the sheep, as many have fallen for hype and charismata and have likewise perished. We have witnessed all of the attractions and all of the performances and we have had enough!

Be it know Madam, and be it known Sir; God says that your days are numbered. It has been a long time coming, but this time WE tare down YOUR strongholds, which heretofore had nearly choked the life from us. We are coming back, but this time we come in the power and with the strength of the arm of Jehovah Sabaoth - The Lord of Hosts is His Name! We are going to dismantle the wolf dens that you so love to hide out in. Imposter do you hear The Spirit of The Lord talking to you?

Every time you made us cry we took it up, and we learned how to wield our Spiritual Sword, as our pain helped us to gain strength. Be warned, we are no longer afraid of you; for this time we fight back! At the command of God, we stand ready to whip you even in the midst of your own self-proclaimed dynasties.

THIS TIME THEY WILL CRUMBLE AND THIS TIME, "DAGON" SHALL FALL DOWN!

The TRUE WORSHIPPERS shall soon take over; for I can hear them assembling even now. They are even on this very realm awaiting the command of The Father and of The Captain of His Mighty Host. They have come down to help the children fight. Beloved, will you also be counted in the number? Not another time should you relent out of fear and hide your head in the sand like a sniveling coward.

Never again should you allow ANYONE to convince you that God no longer loves you. Whoever who tells you that is lying to you, no matter whom he or she may be and regardless of the person's position. Anyone spewing out such garbage is an enemy of your soul. GOD HAS ALWAYS LOVED YOU AND HE STILL LOVES YOU EVEN NOW!

Beloved of our Father, the time has come to stop lying down as road-kill and letting yourselves be crushed by your enemy or under the weight of popular opinion. Through the eyes of The Spirit, The "Unseen Captain" has been revealed. Just like Him, we are neither for nor against [our leaders], but we have come to do battle along side the "Captain of The Host" of The Lord – Joshua 5:13-14a. We too have a one-track mind. We too are on the side of The Lord. And we too have come to do His bidding.

I've got a message for all of you hirelings:

Allow me the honor of informing you and let me make it perfectly clear.

This time we stand alert with <u>our</u> [Spiritual] Swords drawn, fully prepared and ready to do battle, as we await our orders. This time we see you for who and for what you really are. This time impostor, we will not fail Him! No longer will you rape the flock and get away with it. We will not sit idly by and allow you to molest The Holy Word of The Living God. YOU WILL NOT DO IT ON OUR WATCH!

The Remnant is now gathering for the great confrontation. At His command, we will come against you if we have to. Fake preachers, get out while you can! This time He will come down and fight for us! This time The Father shall lead all of His children! This time He will rescue the babes!

AND THIS TIME WOLF CLERICS - '<u>WE</u>' <u>WIN</u>!

Checklist For Every Christian Soldier

☒   **Breast Plate of Righteousness**

☒   **Belt of Truth**

☒   **Shield of Faith**   *Ephesians*
                              6:11-18

☒   **Helmet of Salvation**

☒   **Sword of the Spirit**

☒   **Feet Prepared With the Gospel of Peace**

Don't Leave Home Without Them!

Your Life May Depend Upon You Getting It Right

Many of you reading this book are hopefully old enough to remember the Jim Jones fiasco. My younger readers may have to do a bit of research. This reverend was *so* convincing, and he [obviously] had so much influence over the people, that he single-handedly managed to hoodwink nearly every one of them. He fooled mostly all if not in fact, every single member of his flock and convinced them to partake in the drinking of a poisonous concoction. The world has seen others just like him who in their day, also managed to carry out diabolical schemes. They too had their own bag of tricks from which they produced enchantments that successfully seduced their sleeping congregations.

Just think of the lives that could have been saved if *someone*, ANYONE AT ALL, would have just spoken out. Perhaps someone *did* try to say something but in the end, the individual instead, allowed other people to convince him or her that he/she was wrong. The person's mind could have played tricks on him/her. Or more to the actual reality, perhaps the person was simply too afraid to stand alone. The individual might have been told [or warned] that to speak out meant that he/she would be "Going against "The Lord's anointed." Therefore, to avoid being ridiculed for taking action, the person instead opted for the poison and perished along with the rest. Remember, people are destroyed [they perish] everyday for lack of knowledge. Does not even The Word of God confirm this? It is often what you do *not* know, or that which you fail to confront and/or to correct that might just kill you.

As I told you earlier, not every pastor who oversees a congregation, possesses genuine love for that flock. Not all of them are concerned about the souls of people. How unfortunate it is that a lot of them are only concerned, when *their numbers* indicate a drastic decline. If your pastor is "image conscience" he or she may only care, whenever the body count is too low. In either case, giving will decrease if the number of members do. Yet there are some who seem to be on a relentless quest for power and prestige. It is as though they are trying to achieve some super studded stardom status or something.

If the members would ever wise up and <u>really study The Word of God for themselves</u>, they would soon realize that they have been lied to for a very long time.

Once their eyes are open, they may decide to leave where they are. They may even attempt to speak out. At the very least, they will (or at least they should) begin to examine things just a bit more carefully.

Of course, the less than honorable pastors cannot afford for this to happen. As a result, they tell the congregation only what they want them to know. Bootleg shepherds depend on the fact that the majority of members will never have the guts to question or investigate anything they say or do.

If a person (or even a few people) are brave enough to speak out, likely the same shall be preached about from the pulpit or worse, the entire congregation is alerted and told that the individual (or group) should be 'shunned.' They are to be avoided and given the silent treatment and/or cold shoulder.

Crooked leaders rely upon the sheeps' own ignorance and in many cases on their downright stupidity. Wolf clerics, are often very smart; they use the sheeps own lack of knowledge as their primary strategy to aid them in keeping the flock controlled and stuck.   I am addressing you who are seasoned; as this word may not be for the babes right now. I am talking to those of you who have already been through THE process and KNOW that God is beckoning, but you have stayed bound, gagged and regulated because of what you have been told.

Preachers often use the power of suggestion and/or mind control. The wolves are especially talented when it comes to invoking fear. They ought right tell the masses that, "To speak out of turn, means subjecting oneself to danger, to illness, or even to sudden death." To speak against *them,* means to speak against "The Lord" and to do so will result in him or her being stricken by God - *they say.*

God knows them that are His anointed and He does protect His own; but still that does not mean that His people are exempt from correction or from having their wrongdoings exposed. Most pastors and 'wannabes' will quote from The Book of Psalms 105:15 and from I Chronicles 16:22, as they attempt to inflict guilt or to inject fear into the minds and into the hearts of those in the congregation.

This verse includes a whole lot more than only the misinterpreted portion that THEY love to recite - "Touch not mine anointed and do my Prophets no harm." It is actually pretty frightening [when we really think about it], to realize how this Scripture, when read in <u>proper context,</u> does not say at all, that which we have been led to believe. Many leaders use this very passage as a silencing tool and as a gagging instrument, to keep people under their diabolical leadership.

They tell you things like, "You shouldn't say anything negative about your pastor." Or that, "God is going to get you." They tell you all sorts of things to shut you up. *They* have even been known to lie on God. They tell you that, "God has said this, and that God has said the other", when in fact, He has said nothing of the sort – *if* He has even spoken to them at all. So many of these same leaders are not even the slightest concerned about The Scripture's context. Like for instance, who is doing the speaking? Whom is the speaker addressing? To what or to whom is the speaker referring in this (or any) passage? What is the overall situation at hand? In other words, what events are taking place at the time?

In both accounts of this, [the same] passage, we find that it is in fact David, who is doing the speaking. Each time, He is giving God praise and thanks, for taking care of The Patriarchs - Abraham, Isaac and Jacob, as they journeyed towards "The Promised Land." David was literally thanking God for not allowing the enemies of the patriarchs (or the inhabitants of the land) to, "Touch The Lord's anointed" and for not allowing them to "do God's Prophet's any <u>physical</u> harm", as they sojourned throughout.

This passage has absolutely nothing to with nor has it ever served as an implication that leaders are to be above correction. "Touching" The Lord's anointed; as it relates to The Scripture means touching as in to inflict physical harm.

Just as David could have killed, (touched with the sword) Saul, who relentlessly pursued him, so could those of Abraham's day, such as King Abimelech, (and others) have done to him, Isaac and Jacob. ***"Touch not" in this sense refers to, no physical harm being inflicted upon God's anointed*** – (or upon those who we think are anointed. Remember, Saul had already lost his, but David did not know this). It indeed has absolutely nothing to do with being an instrument to detour someone from speaking the truth, against a leader who may clearly be in the wrong, as he or she is bashing the sheep instead of feeding them.

It does not mean that leaders cannot be corrected or properly approached and or confronted about their godless behavior or abhorrent activities that they carry out in God's house. (At The Lord's command of course). If this were true, then certainly God would have never commanded The Prophet Nathan, to approach this same David, [who himself was also anointed], about his ruthless sin of adultery with Bathsheba, (which lead to the setting up and the murdering of her husband Uriah). Read I and II Samuel – two great books!

Again, if a leader were totally above being confronted, neither would God have ever commanded The Prophet/Seer, named Gad to confront (yet again, *this same 'anointed' man* after God's on heart) David, for his senseless numbering of God's people (who by the way David had begun to see as being *his own* people).

God considered his numbering of the people to be a terrible act of pride. Some Bible commentators say that he did this in an attempt to determine his own power. He began to trust in the strength of his numbers rather than in The Lord, upon whom he had always relied from his youth.

For a split second, David began to depend upon that which he could see with his natural eyes. This sin greatly displeased and offended The Lord. In fact, Jehovah was so upset by David's actions that He handed down a swift penalty befitting of the offence. The Lord still being merciful gave David three choices of punishment. Read the entire account for yourselves in I Chronicles 21: 1-30.

Just because we are God's spokesperson, does not mean that we are exempt from exposure of our sins (should it come to that). We too are expected to clean up our filthy acts of unrighteousness – AND there are no exceptions. Just because we are leaders (or lay Christians) does not mean that we cannot be filled with [or momentarily caught up in] pride or in the illusion of power. And yes, it is only an "illusion", because power is never owned by anyone. If we have any, it is only on loan.

Just like Pilot who 'merely thought' that he was taking Jesus' life – did not he realize that he had no power at all – except that which The Lord allowed? No man had the power to take the life of my Saviour, but He simply chose to lay it down, knowing that through The Father, He could pick it right back up: AND HE DID!

Anyway, moving on...

Dear friends, just in case you wonder who it was that had temporary control of David's mind, I invite you to the passages that I cited in 1 Chronicles. There you will quickly discover who was present and under whose influence David had begun to operate.

You will see exactly who was at the forefront and who was largely to blame for causing even this great king to err and to succumb to pride. Go on...read it. The Scripture starts off by saying...

"AND <u>satan</u> STOOD UP AGAINST ISRAEL AND PROVOKED DAVID TO NUMBER ISRAEL." YES! EVEN DAVID A MAN AFTER GOD'S OWN HEART LET HIS GUARD DOWN AND THE <u>devil</u> CAUSED HIM TO COMMIT A SIN WHICH GREATLY DISPLEASED THE LORD." THIS <u>ONE</u> MISTAKE WAS RESPONSIBLE FOR THE DEATH OF 70,000 MEN.

Count them - 70,000 died because of one man's prideful moment in time. God allowed David's eyes to see The Mighty Angelic Host standing with a drawn sword, ready to continue the slaughter at the command of The Lord. If this anointed king, could be temporarily overtaken by the enemy, then what of you, our leaders or me? Certainly neither we, nor our pastors can claim to be more anointed than David, the root of Jessie; the one through whom Our Lord Jesus would eventually come. It behooves each of us to take an honest and fearless look into our own hearts, and then make an assessment of our lives.

Leaders who claim to be always functioning under the anointing, without ever doing a SELF-EXAMINATION, are often the most vulnerable to satan's attack. Why? Because they never think of themselves as capable of being wrong or out of order – according to them, the fault is always someone else's - that's pride! I pray we each beseech The Lord's mercy.

This is not the time to cover up our faults. Neither is it a time to continue covering up the faults of others. I am not suggesting that we go around looking under each other's spiritual covers to see what sin or what wrong may be lurking beneath, but neither should we continue to be in agreement with things, that we know to be against the will of God.

We can no longer afford to call right wrong and wrong right just because the culprit happens to be our own pastor or our church – or even a friend or relative for that matter. We can no longer afford to lie to ourselves or to others, because God will hold us accountable.

We can no longer deny the truth about our congregations or about ourselves, even if that truth *does* hurt.   Sometimes learning the truth about ourselves and/or about someone or something to which we are attached, may come as a complete shock.

The discovery that they, (or even ourselves) are not what or whom we believed, will certainly deliver a devastating blow to our hearts and our egos. Yet we owe it to *ourselves* to be forthright; but more than to ourselves, we owe it to God. While the truth may hurt us, it will also heal us if we are receptive. If we see it for what it is and are willing to make the necessary corrections and/or adjustments we will certainly receive healing.

Now is the appointed time for The Body to get right! ***FOR JUDGEMENT SHALL SOON BEGIN IN THE HOUSE OF THE LORD!***   God knows how to pull covers. In fact, He does not even have to pull them; He already sees under, over, through and around them. We cannot hide; neither will we escape if we fail to come clean.   ***For goodness sakes, don't let Him have to expose you; it isn't as though He doesn't already know what you are doing!***   Many so-called holy men and women, who claim to be doing the will of The Lord, are going to lift their eyes up in hell. You must know that the gifts come without repentance because *anybody* can play church.

A leader can be very dynamic as he or she dazzles the crowd but at the same time, be in direct route towards the hell fire. What!? Did I say both 'hell' and 'burning fire' in the same breath? Now there's a topic you don't hear much about these days. Prosperity and the acquiring of things have replaced the warnings of hell. It is not very popular to preach about damnation, because preaching the truth is not what most people want – they like being "tickled instead." Well, popular or not somebody has to do it. Brothers and sisters, parents, teachers, leaders, and friends, the saving of our eternal souls depend upon our knowing that what Jesus said long ago still applies even now.

"ONLY THE PURE IN HEART SHALL SEE GOD" (Matthew 5:8).
Even if people purposely choose not to believe in something, their disbelief is in no way the determining factor of the object's nonexistence. We, who are trying to prove a point, may not always have something tangible that we are able to hand over as literal evidence to support our claim. A classic but extremely timely example is that of the wind. Of course, we cannot actually SEE IT! Neither can anyone bottle or bag a sample of it to give away. We can and do however feel it and can certainly attest to the physical effects of its power – for either the good or the bad.

On a cool summer's day, we can certainly enjoy the breeze that it provides. Likewise, we can sail across the ocean using the power of its strength. Yet beloved, we have also witnessed the fiercest of storms as well as the tragically devastating, forever life changing hurricanes, brought on by that same strength. Just because I cannot put a piece of hell into a paper bag and hand it over, does not mean that it is not real or that it ceases to exist. So as it is in the natural so is it also in the spirit. Oh that the masses [for their own eternal sakes] would "ONLY BELIEVE!"

Please study God's Word and find out for yourselves if what YOU are being taught is true or not. Waiting until you die is not the time to plead for mercy. For by then, mercy will have been used up.

Do not be fooled by what you hear; there will be no bargaining with God. The moment that you shut your eyes for the final time, <u>on this side</u>, please know that your fate will have already been eternally sealed. Purgatory you say? What's that??? There is no such place – check your Bible.

People say, "Tomorrow I'll get it right." "I'm young yet; I still have time." Or ether, "I'm too old, what's the use now, I've messed up too much anyway." "Oh, I don't believe in that Jesus freak stuff." Excuse after excuse they give.

May I be frank with you? Here is the deal; the thing is, none of us knows when <u>our</u> time is up. Death can come knocking at any time for any one of us, regardless of our age. Young, old, black, white and everything in between; each of us has an irrevocable appointment date with the "Grim Reaper."

Also for those of you who feel like you have messed up too much to be forgiven. *What?* Are you kidding me? Have you not been paying attention to my story? – Keep reading, there's more (smile). Certainly, you could not have messed up any more than I have! It is never too late no matter your age and no matter how dastardly a deed you may have committed. As long as you are ALIVE, you still have hope.

DON'T SQUANDER IT!

The time for you to investigate is right now. Your eternal life does indeed depend upon you getting this right <u>for your own self.</u> By 'this', I am referring to the whole counsel of God. You need to check HIS BOOK from A-Z - from Genesis to Revelation; find out what you are missing or in what areas you lack and/or have been misled.

Do this for your own self; do not depend upon another to do it for you. If you do not like to read (or if you cannot read very well, or even at all – do not be ashamed), but purchase The Bible on tape. You have no excuse! Moreover, it will do you good to remember, He is not going to accept any – at all.

<u>Don't you at least feel that you are worth the effort, even if no one else thinks you are? Do it for you! You are the only assurance that you have when it comes to knowing if what you have been told, is true or not. Don't leave it up to someone else - not this time!</u>

Remember my brother, my sister; YOUR LIFE really does depend upon YOU finally getting it right.

Selah! Now why don't you pause and meditate on that?

❧The Silencing Of A Servant❧

When a person has a burning desire to serve The Lord, often it will be in the capacity wherein he or she has been uniquely gifted and groomed. Please keep in mind that I am not referring to people who desire a solo in the church choir, but who are unable to carry a tune. Neither am I talking about those who wish to serve in a position for which they are totally unqualified or lacking the divine impartation necessary to do so.

I am referring only to those people who *know* beyond a doubt who they are in God, as well as where they fit in His plan. They do not have to ask anybody, because they already know that God has called them to a particular place and has gifted them to serve in a certain capacity. The people to whom I refer have hidden themselves in The Messiah; with their assignment(s) made clear they are getting into position that they may be about The Father's business.

Shortly after the incident with my pastor, I found myself engaged in a conversation with a female cleric (from a different church). I noticed that almost from the very start of our talk, she began laying down the law – *her own law*. She told me that, "The pulpit is for the pastor" (she and her husband only). She went on to explain what she and her husband expected of the ministers in *their church*. They were required to attend school for a minimum of 2 years, before she and her husband would even, "Consider whether or not they would be allowed to serve."

I don't want to mislead you, but I do believe that this pastor also said that, "If someone *were* allowed to serve in her congregation, she and her husband would be the ones determining which area of ministry the person is best suited." She told me that, "Pastors are not allowing just *'anybody'* to come up in their pulpits to preach." "You've got to be careful what you feed the people," she said. "For that reason pastors are not allowing just *anyone* to speak."

I'm not knocking this, and I understood what she was saying, after all she and her husband *were* the pastors. And yes, I do agree that a leader should be extremely cautious as to whom they allow to address the congregation; I am in full agreement with *that* portion of her statement.

What I did marvel at however, was what she failed to say. It was what she did not say in all of her rambling that caused me to think long and hard about the hearts of many who serve in a leadership capacity. While she certainly made sure to mention <u>all of her and her husband's rules and educational requirements,</u> and also continued with her ranting about how she and her husband would, "Consider whether or not a person would be allowed to serve", never once did she ever mention anything about The Lord. She said nothing regarding those who have been called for service - BY HIM.

She failed to mention that now more than ever, people should be anointed and equipped specifically to carry out the task(s), for which they have been called. She never said anything about the person or about her and/or her husband being led by inspiration of The Holy Ghost, when it comes to the answering of a call or to the choosing of someone for godly service. Whether or not the "Hand of The Lord rests upon an individual", and/or regardless to the fact that the person has a burning desire to serve, did not seem to matter one bit. In fact, these things seemingly were of no significance to her - whatsoever!

<u>Not once, did she even consider what God's plan might be for an individual. She said nothing about seeking His will, but instead she spoke only of her and her husband's expectations and of their selection.</u>

The vast majority of our leaders operate just like this pastor. Serving in ministry seems to be more about what *THEY* want and about whom *THEY* deem fit rather than who God has chosen. Another thing that I could not quite figure out was why she had felt it necessary to lay down her law within the first five minutes of our talk. I mean, almost *immediately* she seemed determined to rattle off her rules and regulations.

This was so unnecessary, especially since I had no intentions of joining her church; neither was I asking any favors of her. Any platform intended for this writer, will be because The Almighty has decided to open the doors Himself or because He has laid it upon the heart of another to open them for me.   Quite simply, I was merely engaging in conversation; I wasn't seeking a speaking invitation or anything.

At that time, I was still trying hard to understand what had happened to me. I wanted to find out if what I had undergone with my own pastor was common amongst other Saints and their leaders. Gee – I guess I got my answer. I was yet foolishly seeking a "spiritual mommy or daddy." I was in pain and I needed help to understand my dilemma. I did not need a book of rules neither did I need any condemnation.

While I am making this point, I ask the pastors one thing. In fact, I plead with you who call yourselves shepherds - could you please <u>*ask God*</u> *to heighten* <u>*your level*</u> *of discernment? IN ADDITION, YOU NEED TO BE SURE THAT YOU KNOW (BEYOND A DOUBT) WHAT* <u>*HE IS SAYING,*</u> *AS OPPOSSED TO ONLY WHAT* <u>*YOU THINK IS BEING SAID.*</u>

And female pastors, you especially, my goodness, what's the matter with you??? Some of you really need help! Not every woman that solicits your advice is trying to take over, nor does every other woman want something from you besides a conversation or some much-needed sisterly advice. I notice that a lot of female clerics are extremely "catty" – MEOW!

It seems as though their guards *automatically* go up. Proceeding to sharpen their claws, they seemingly attempt to ready themselves for a spiritual catfight or bar room brawl. Sometimes they use their obvious positions of authority to gain (in their minds), the upper hand. This they do in an attempt to make sure that the seeker is kept in 'check.' They ascertain that their boundaries are made very clear, within minutes. Often they make their comments in a manner that is less than becoming.

To them I ask - CAN YOU PLEASE CHILL OUT? Not every woman who seeks your advice is coming with an ulterior motive. Everybody isn't after your husband or your man. Please stop being so territorial and so darned paranoid. These are not very becoming traits for any female. They are however, extremely unattractive for a woman, who is supposed to be a vessel, that not only houses but one who is also an expositor of, The Word of God. Can you please stop it?!

What may actually be bothering some of you, is the guilt from the ungodly manner in which you snagged your own husband. Uh oh... Why don't you do us, as well as yourselves a big favor? Go to God and get some help for your insecurities or better yet, go back and seek forgiveness for the role that <u>*you*</u> *played in the breaking up of someone else's marriage.*

I am trying hard, to help you keep your facts in order, so that the next time you start with the name-calling, you will remember to begin with yourself.

As I was saying…

When a person has an earnest desire to serve but is never given the opportunity, he or she may eventually throw in the towel and end up doing nothing at all. Although I hate to say it, but honestly, I believe that this is exactly what many pastors are banking on.

Of course, *they* will never admit to such a thing; but a lot of them would love for those whom *they perceive as a threat,* to just pack up and go away. I know I'm talking right! This is especially true of individuals who tend to ask questions, or of someone who seems eager to learn or to serve. You would think that enthusiasm would be a plus, but depending upon the mindset of the leader, it is very often frowned upon. A leader will deem someone a threat, particularly if that leader suspects that the hand of God is upon an individual.

Instead of mentoring and helping the person, a leader like this may instead choose to sideline or to discourage him or her altogether. Some pastors literally manage to convince themselves, that the person or group has become too eager, this they interpret as the individual "wanting to take over." Clergy like this really frighten me. They are a detriment to The Body of Christ, and are not good for the overall mission of the church; in fact, they have discouraged and derailed many already.

They seem to play some sort of mind game with themselves, as they attempt to justify their unfair judgment/treatment of those who they have purposely held back. Usually they follow-up by passing the word to every leader they know; especially those within their same denominational structure. To add insult to injury, once the person has been neatly tucked into a corner like a good little boy or girl, the cleric then barks out comments about how people are not doing *anything at all* for The Lord. I mean what the hell!?

What do they want from us?! I told you that my pastor did not pray with me; offer to pray for me, guide me or even give me a reference elsewhere. He did nothing accept shoot me down. When we are not allowed to *legitimately* serve in our houses of worship, our feelings will likely vacillate between those of anger, bitterness, jealousy, or depression. On a quest to find out 'why', we often arrive at a place of introspection.

It is at this juncture that we learn to dig really deep – questioning our own motives and purposes. It is here that we are ready to take an honest and fearless look at ourselves and at the quality or lack thereof, in our lives. During our period of soul searching, we come face to face with our past, our present *and* we may even get a glimpse of the possibilities that await us in our future. It is at this point that we are truly ready to let God be God.

Once our cycle of rejection and pain has fully run its painful course, we may feel somewhat "numbed out." As I continued to regularly attend my church, it became increasingly difficult for me to receive anything positive. Rejection and/or abuse victims [or even survivors] are sometimes hard-pressed to 'feel' anything at all, at least for a while that is. At times, I sat there as though I were in a trance. Everything said and done during the service was of little to no consequence. This was definitely not something that I had been accustomed to. I have always loved participating in the worship services and often could not wait to assemble with God's people.

One thing for sure, if in time we do manage to *forgive* those who have wounded us (and we really should and are commanded to); still we do not intend to seek their love, help or approval ever again. Their opinions no longer matter; they as well as their advice are viewed as null and void.

At this point, the church is no longer looked upon as being the *only* arena worthy of our valuable "Christian" service. A brother once shared with me, just a little bit, about why many wounded people prefer to stay in hiding. This brother did not so much want to 'work' in a church setting as I had, but simply desired to be prayed for.

He shared with me just one of his many painful experiences that he encountered amid various Christian congregations. He said that he had attended a gathering, one that he likened unto a "Word of Faith Convention" - very similar to a ministry he had once seen on television. The brother told me that his home, which he shared with his mother at the time, had been lost due to a fire.

"D" as I shall refer to him told me that he asked the preacher for prayer. He said that the minister refused to pray for him, "Because he didn't have enough faith." Wanting to be absolutely sure that I had indeed heard him correctly and that there were no gaps in his story, I inquired again. "Did the pastor ask you some questions in which you failed to answer to his satisfaction, like do you have faith in God? Are you saved? Do you have a relationship with Jesus Christ, etc?

I wanted to know if this young man had said or done anything at all, that would have given the man of God even the slightest inkling, that he was not serious about The Lord. Had he (to his knowledge) somehow provoked or angered the cleric is what I wanted to know, so I really probed.

He assured me that he had not. In fact, he became noticeably agitated upon my deeper inquiry, as though the memories of the event were still fresh in his mind and yet haunted him in some way. He then both sadly and somewhat angrily repeated his story –

"I was a young man standing there in front of the preacher on crutches, explaining to him that me and my mother's house had caught on fire." What did this guy want me to do? "I only asked the guy, this preacher, if he would pray for me and my mother, and he said no." "He said he would not pray for me or for my mother because I didn't have enough faith."

"I was only a little boy, in pain, standing there on my crutches almost in tears." "I mean, what did I do wrong anyway?" (Now sounding like he wanted to cry he said), "I hadn't done anything." "I didn't do nothing wrong." "I did nothing." "I just wanted prayer." "I didn't do nothing to nobody."

As a result, he abandoned the faith for 15 years and became a follower of a different religion. He turned completely away, because one man continued with his summation about his lack of ['enough'] faith, therefore refusing to pray for him at all. Couldn't the pastor have at least prayed for him? If he felt that "D" lacked in the faith department, or even if he had no faith at all, the very least this pastor could have done would have been to pray that he get some – right? *Well couldn't he have?* Jesus did not rebuke His disciples when they asked for a faith increase as we read in Luke 17.

Although The Saviour often commented and marveled at their obvious lack of it, never had He ever sent them away feeling dejected. Never had He wounded them to the degree that they gave up hope and quit following Him altogether. And even though Jesus could not understand how it was that they still did not believe or how they could so easily became fearful, even after witnessing Him perform miracle after miracle; still - never had The Messiah totally discouraged them, neither had He ever refused their requests for prayer. If anything, Jesus was often the person who initiated prayer on their behalf.

He was particularly hard on one Disciple who later turned out to be a mighty Apostle, who by virtue of even his very shadow people received healing. Glory To God! Can somebody please help me say Simon Peter? (Besides Jesus, he is my favorite "fisher of men").

They didn't even have to ask Jesus to pray for them. The Lord was often moved to and made it His business to do so, because that is the kind of Shepherd that He was then and He still is that kind of Shepherd today - as He ever intercedes on our behalf. This gentleman whose story I shared is now a 40-year-old man – no longer a "little boy." He has since recommitted his life to God through Christ. I asked him what was it that brought him back to The Lord. Do you know what he said? Get ready, you pompous pastors, who think it's all about you and your fabulous churches or your long dusty prayers that only bounce from ceiling to wall.

Right in the middle of his pagan religious practices, "D" said that he had an experience with Almighty God. He said that JEHOVAH, The Great I AM came looking for him, and that He let him know how very much HE loved him. He said that The Lord distinguished Himself above the deity that he had started to serve. "D" said that Jehovah loved him back to spiritual health and let him know that he was still His child.

I am happy to report that "D" is once again in the ranks of God's Army. However, he attends church services only on rare occasions. He loves The Lord with all of his heart, but because he had been so deeply wounded, it is extremely difficult for him to give himself over to the tutelage of another man. He *does* however have a thriving relationship with The Lord.

The silencing of this man's voice in Christendom was altogether deafening. For 15 long years, this very educated, multitalented, multilingual man of God, who excels in the study of historical Christian data and who also speaks Aramaic; (the original language of The Messiah), hid himself away in silence, all because of one pastor's vehement and very wrongful accusation concerning his level of faith. "D" would have been a great asset to any ministry. Instead, for 15 years he backed away because a [supposed] "man of God", refused to pray for he and his mother.

Thankfully, he is one of the few who made it back. Although he is on The Lord's side again, I pray also that he will eventually find healing for the hole that has been left in his soul.   Just think about how many we've *already* lost to gangs, drugs, false religions and satanic cults.

All this, due to the vicious assaults, lack of caring and downright neglect and/or abuse that emanates from places that are suppose to be nurturing. As badly as people are hurting, it is sad that the church is often the very last place that many turn for help. Why? Because they do not want to feel further condemned and because they do not trust us.

I am not talking about them feeling guilty because of true Holy Ghost conviction of their sins – because for that, they should feel some sort of guilt. Rather I am talking about the venomous verbal tongue-lashings that are often a sure follow up, even after the person has sincerely poured out his or her heart and has already made public confession of evil doing.

Nobody wants to be kicked further into the ground while they are already down. Nobody wants to [be made] to feel worse than they did before receiving prayer and/or counsel. If they are the ones doing the seeking, than evidentially it is because they are already in pain! They do not need to be verbally assassinated!

We murder people with our big mouths! Why??? Why do church folk always take pleasure in wounding people further? Can we please stop this? I know that God would never approve of our abominable behavior – not at all. I tell you, He is not happy with how we are handling His babes. (He means adult babes too).

Not everyone who has been wounded by church folk or by a pastor, will of *their own accord* depart from the church scene or opt to follow a different religion. But what *does* happen to a person who is unable to serve in the arena to which they have been called? Remember I am not talking about taking over someone else's pulpit, not everyone is called to pulpit ministry. However, I am talking about those who have been called to service, (pulpit or otherwise), but who lack the opportunity or [man made credentials] that they say we need.

What if a person belongs to a very large congregation, where there are say, 20 associate pastors or perhaps 30 other teachers? Such a one can grow extremely weary and become spiritually aloof, as he or she awaits a chance to do what he or she does best - serve. Their turn for teaching or preaching may only come around every few months because there are so many in the rotation.

Sometimes when several people serve in the exact same capacity, a person can find him or herself waiting for nearly two generations [of servants] to die out or to be removed. The individual may have to wait until the pastor and his clones are no longer occupying key positions and then pray that he or she will finally be given an opportunity.

This goes on while so many [other] struggling churches actually have need of such a person or of his/her specific gifts and ministry talents. If a person should change churches, he or she is considered a church hopper, or the same is accused of having left one place, "In order to achieve a name for him or herself elsewhere." The individual will quite often be viewed as a traitor. Even if a person conveys to the current pastor his/her burning desire and need to make a difference, the brother or sister may still be viewed suspiciously.

Should an individual share with leadership the fact that he/she is becoming complacent, while having to wait so long? In most cases, the person's appeal is not likely to matter – the individual is often put off and told to "wait until…" (An until that never, ever comes). Even a valid explanation of one's discomfort, will not always be received with understanding. A member may be sharply rebuked and verbally punished for just *thinking* such things, let alone having the audacity to express them openly to the leader.

Bootleg pastors will always seek to keep sheep "with them", even though that same leader is aware, that the person should be growing, and that such a one is correct in his/her concern about being stagnant and unfruitful.

In a different church, the same person might actually be allowed to serve freely; and while he or she may not have to wait [as long], there yet may be obstacles to overcome. For depending on the type of ministry a person desires to work in, or has been gifted for, as well as the size of the congregation, there may be no outlet for contribution still. At times, a person's gift (in a particular place) may simply not be needed.

Other times, it may not be *wanted,* and sometimes, the gift isn't *needed or wanted.* For example, what if you are a prophet, but your pastor does not want an established prophetic voice in the house? That does not mean that you cannot work in other areas of ministry, but because God has wired your heart towards the prophetic, you are not likely to be satisfied functioning in any other capacity. As a result, you will wrestle with feelings of displacement.

Because you are not in *your element,* those very feelings when verbalized, will usually be viewed by others as your being rebellious and/or uncooperative; they will likely label you as a complainer. What if you are gifted to work with children or teens, but your church will not allow a ministry geared towards that population?

On the other hand, what if your pastor <u>will allow</u> such a ministry, as he or she is open to new ideas, but there simply isn't a <u>need,</u> because the congregation is primarily made up of senior citizens. Yet you have been gifted and do possess a real fiery zeal and passion to serve and/or to teach the youth. What else can you do besides leave?

When people are not given the opportunity to serve in their God ordained capacity, they often become antsy. When I am not allowed to be myself, I turn into a contortionist. Like a pretzel, I feel totally bent out of shape. Consequently, I feel twisted and disjointed because I just don't seem to fit. Discontentment will arise *whenever* a person is deprived of the opportunity, to follow wholeheartedly after that which continues to beckon.

This scenario is like unto attending a university or applying for a job. If a man or woman has a passion for *singing,* why on earth then would he or she become a mortician? If an individual were *all about the vocals,* then certainly he or she would not need nor would the same (for the most part) be interested in a class on, "How to properly embalm a cadaver."

If someone were passionate about the arts, that person would not likely apply for a job in the nursing field; neither would he or she ever seek to become a sanitation worker. An individual can always benefit from learning different things, but eventually the person, (or even you and I), would of a certainty grow weary after a while. What would be the purpose in wasting so much time by engaging in things for which we have no passion, or true inborn ability?

The very talents that we have been given are the things that in turn, will create a longing and will command that we utilize them; this leads to the passion of pursuit. By any means necessary, we <u>must</u> make contact with the God and with the destiny that have connected themselves to us. People may not always know who they are in the beginning, but God does. He has placed things inside each of us that are just waiting to be unleashed.

If the hand of God has touched an individual for a purpose, he or she will have a "bent" towards a certain path. This in turn will [usually] create a burden that is not likely to subside until he or she is walking in *that direction.* We have been eternally and internally programmed to fit perfectly into the scheme of His plan and we will never be 'truly' happy until we are doing exactly what we are supposed to be – everything else will merely pacify for a season.

As co-creators with The Heavenly Father, our contributions are much needed and are very necessary in this world, but we are the ones who must show up; whether or not we report for duty, will be largely our decision (in most cases anyway). When we are not allowed to be who we have been created to be, there persists an agonizing dilemma, which we are hard-pressed to figure out.

On the one hand, we can sit quietly, doing only that which *they* tell us to; while trying hard to fight or to totally ignore that which rages within. We can try hard to turn a deaf ear by not giving expression to the substance and the greatness inside as the constant wooing of The Spirit continues to tug. While on the other hand, we can pursue on our own, that which has been seared deep into our hearts; realizing that if we do, we run the risk of being classified as rebellious.

They accuse us of having "the wrong spirit" and they say we are unruly and that we are not willing to wait on them. In most cases you do know by now, that waiting on *them,* may mean waiting forever right? I have heard pastors who have sternly rebuked The Saints for not doing anything [at all] for The Lord. We are accused of not listening to Him when He speaks a thing, but still with their next breath, these *same* leaders criticize those who *have* stepped out and who *are* doing something.

They say that the person is wrong because he or she did not have permission (from them), which in many cases they had absolutely no intentions of granting in the first place. Just try to figure that one out if you can. I seriously doubt if you will ever be able to. It appears to be a game designed to make sure, that you never win. The goal is for you to remain spiritually defeated and to go crazy while you are.

Some television evangelists and conference leaders are very encouraging – at times. You may hear them say things like, "If you really have a gift then nobody should have to tell you to use it." "You don't have to wait for your (local) pastor in order to use what God has given you." "There are so many needs out there just waiting to be met by you they say, once again fanning the flame of hope."

It is one thing to leave great convention super charged, excited and ready to take action for The Lord. However, after the convention is over, it is quite another to return to our local pastors who continue to snipe at us with unkindness and rude remarks. "Everyone wants to be up front in the pulpit," *they say.* "If you really have a gift, then why not go into the nursing homes or hospitals and lay hands on people?" "That's where the *real* ministry is needed."

"Go out there and spread your gift around", *they* arrogantly grunt. "If you are really anointed, then there is an entire community out there waiting just for you", they smirk. Let us say that their sniping does encourage us; it seems to be exactly what we have been waiting to hear from our "pastor." Even if he did only arrogantly bark it out in a cooperate setting, at least he did tell us that we could go. Besides, we have also heard this at our favorite convention.

By now, we are stoked and very excited. Finally agreement has come. We all know that in the real world however, a group of people or a single individual cannot just go walking into some nursing home or hospital facility claiming to be a minister. Those who would be receptive to the idea and willing to give us a chance would still want to know whom we represent. I dare you to say that you represent "God." How far do you think that would get you?

They want to know, who your pastor is; and to what church you belong. "What credentials do you hold?" "What seminary did you attend?" "Where did you go in order *'to learn'* how to preach etc?" I could say a whole lot here about this being "taught to preach thing" – but I won't. I'll just let you know, that no man can teach you – only God. The Holy Ghost is your greatest teacher.

Anyway…

The pastor will not likely vouch for you, because when he was spouting off, he did not ordain you, license you or even bless you; he was merely pacifying you by making vein comments as he so often does – but nothing of any real substance to back you up should you pursue. If word gets back that you really are "out there", you are likely going to be rebuked. Depending on who you are, they may not be happy with *you* claiming to be a representative or even a member of their congregation.

We have not been given the proper blessing or credentials, so if we present ourselves to an outside facility we may still face rejection and backlash.

So now what? Is our desire to serve left only to smolder into ashes? Should we stuff our feelings and rebuke them away in an attempt to ignore and to disobey God? The very pastors, who accuse us of not doing anything, also attack us for doing what we can. Even if what we are doing, does not interfere with *THEIR* church, nor does it necessitate that we have their credentialing or even that we receive their public blessing, sometimes they still take issue. It is as though we cannot work in the church (to a certain extent) and neither can we work outside of it without experiencing some form of rebuff.

When we cannot stand it any longer, finally we take a chance and decide to obey God anyhow. SOMEBODY SAY ANYHOW! Ding ding ding, a bell goes off. It is ok to pursue what God is telling us because we will do so during our own personal time and in a facility separate from the local church or other public institution.

Finally, we have it. The plan is to stay in our congregation without making waves and without begging and pleading and scraping like a pup - oops, did I just say that? Sorry, I meant to say, the plan is to stay without *asking* them for opportunities to serve. We no longer feel contorted and confused because we are about to function in our capacity. It feels great to know that our lives are finally going to count for something.

The plan is to continue showing up for our various duties (if applicable), but in our own time we will pursue that which we feel The Lord has called us to. We will not have to worry about a public facility that insists we have [what they consider as] "proper credentials", that our pastor has not given to us anyway. This way, we are not being a pain to our leaders; we feel good about ourselves; we are obeying God *and* a genuine ministry need is about to be fulfilled. Everybody will be happy, happy, happy right?

SOMETIMES LADIES AND GENTLEMEN, EVEN THIS CAN GET US INTO BIG TROUBLE!

Don't believe me? Come see.

I once attended a, "Faith Based Initiative Information Exposé." (Just try saying that real fast three times [smile]). Anyway, while there I met and began talking with a fellow sister in Christ. Our conversation took place about a year prior to the encounter with my pastor. At that time, I had no idea that I would even be penning the words to this very book.

I will refer to this young woman as "T". The two of us began discussing and exchanging pertinent information, one with the other. We had attended the same seminar, but had visited different booths throughout, so when we met up, we decided to compare notes in an effort to help one another get the most out of the experience.

As our conversation progressed, "T" told me that she was not a member of any church, but that she was endeavoring to start her own work for The Lord. She then shared with me the series of events, which had led up to her being a Christian who was currently without a home church.

"T" said that she had graduated from seminary a number of years prior. She felt led of The Lord to have a weekly Bible study in her home, and although hesitant, she obeyed God. At the time, she also held membership at a local neighborhood church. She explained to me that her home based Bible study had never interfered with her church duties/activities. She further stated that never had it dawned on her, that her pastor would have a problem with her study, since the meetings were being held during her personal time, and in her own home. Anyway, she said that he "found out about it", (not that she had tried to hide anything). "T" said that she was confronted by him, and that he asked her, "If what he had heard was true – you know, about her having Bible study." She in turn answered in the affirmative; and confirmed that she was indeed hosting a weekly study.

"T" said that he then told her, that she was to "Cease and to desist at once." He told her that she was no longer allowed to continue the study. She explained to me that although she did not feel right about it, still she complied in order to be obedient to her pastor; he was "her leader" after all – she said. "T" went on to share with me that she tried her best to stay compliant, by not restarting the study, while at the same time, ignoring The Spirit's promptings.

She said that she did this, "for a while." However, when she could take it no longer, she felt compelled to be faithful to The Lord's calling. With that, she revived the study group. I am not clear as to how long she managed to host it the second time, before her pastor called her into his office again. Once more upon questioning, she confessed to (having revived the group), and hosting the study. She told him that she "felt led of God to continue the work." She told me that her pastor said nothing at all, but rather without explanation, handed her a letter, (which had already been typed and waiting just for her). It was a letter of, "Membership Termination." After giving her the letter, he then told her, that as of that moment, she was no longer a member of his church. She was told to, "Vacate the premises immediately; and as you are going, do not linger." In other words, she was not to talk to anyone [at all], nor to give explanation, but rather she was to gather up her things and go! (No need to corrupt the minds of the others – just get out).

We exchanged telephone numbers, but to this day, I have not heard from her, nor can I find the number that she gave to me. I have often wondered about her – even before my own ordeal, but she has definitely crossed my mind many times since. I have no idea if whether or not she found a new church home or if in fact, she went ahead with her ministry as planned. I do not know if "T" has given up and completely thrown in the towel concerning her Kingdom Work.

Far worse, I have no way of knowing if like so many others, if whether or not she has given up on God. My prayer is that she will find another church home for the sake of fellowship, but **not for the purpose of mind control**. I pray also that she will go on to do her own awesome work for The Lord as He directs her.

Note: "T" never mentioned if she had solicited members of her church to attend her home studies. Also it is unclear to me as to whether or not she had initially spoken with her pastor, <u>before</u> starting her study the first time; and if he had in fact already told her "No", or if she started it without ever consulting him at all.

I want to be totally fair here, so I will say this. I question whether or not there had been prior consultation with her pastor, for the simple reason that she says he, "Found out about it", which probably means that he got the information from another member – you know how we do.

Some people can't wait to tell everything they know, neither can they stand to see someone else being blessed and/or elevated. You know what they say about those crabs in a barrel don't you? As soon as one starts to climb up, the others reach out with gigantic claws and pull it right back down. People are just like that – ESPECIALLY CHURCH PEOPLE! In fairness to pastors everywhere, I do say the following:

No one should ever solicit membership for a separate work that they are embarking upon. We should never try to persuade congregants to abandon their leadership because we have begun a work of our own. <u>Even if The Lord has approved of what we are doing, member poaching is inappropriate and is totally unacceptable.</u> Never attempt to steal the flock of another! If God has a work for someone to do, that individual will not have to campaign or secretly try to persuade or to convince people to partake in it.

On the other hand, if people find the work appealing, and <u>they [on their own] choose</u> to be a part of it, then that decision must be between them and The Lord, so long as the initiator of the work is not actively influencing them in any way. Each involved party, really ought to be led of The Lord and no one else! If you are a potential leader, you need not worry because God already has followers lined up for your ministry, if you are indeed supposed to have them.

Again, in being fair, "T" in all of her excitement, could have very well mentioned her study to a few members or friends. Perhaps word might have spread through other people. It does not necessarily mean that she was actively encouraging them to attend. If she were doing such a thing, then she should not have been. She did not strike me as a person who had purposely done so, but non-the-less; my point needed to be made perfectly clear here – just in case.

I pray that she does not backslide and proceed to live out the rest of her days as another disconnected servant whose voice has been forever silenced from the ranks. Unfortunately, we may never know - now will we?

❧*Wounded From Within*❧

Have you ever wondered why there are so many "un-churched" people in the world today? It almost seems as though the 'truly' born again elect of God, are increasingly becoming a minority. One would not think so though, not with the thousands of people joining local assemblies each week. Also with the emergence of numerous "Mega churches", we barely even notice the many that have already left by the droves.

I recently observed a congregation on television that has to have at least 20,000 members. Also, I heard a pastor proudly boast that his church had grown to over 30,000. Please understand that in congregations of this magnitude, [or any size for that matter], there are bound to be attendees who have NEVER even been saved [at all], but who merely have their names on the roll. I am not judging by all means, but these are the facts. For every true born again experienced believer, there are equally as many who are only spectators. These people come to church, because *they like the pastor.* Some attend strictly for *networking* purposes - you know, making business and/or personal contacts for future ventures.

Others join for the mere purpose of being part of "*something significant",* while still, there are those who pack the house on a weekly basis, with the hopes of witnessing a spectacular event, such as a 'miracle.' Then of course, there are members whose sole purpose for attending is to find a husband or wife – 'cause' we know that some things never change.

For so many, "church affiliation" has become nothing more than an accessory. They equate [their] attendance and participation with being 'fashionable' and are only making a 'statement' – one that says, "I belong." Being part of a congregation with a grand edifice, wherein they find all of the accoutrements that their carnal and/or sinful flesh can handle, is like attending a weekly "extravaganza" of some kind. As with most of us, holding membership in a "state of the art church", certainly does tickle our fancy. We are especially proud to be "on board" if *our* leader happens to rank amongst the most dynamic or charismatic. Membership under such leadership is considered classy and chic; which seemingly brings a noticeable amount of prestige as one of its many perks – at least that's what people think.

"*That* church, is the spot to be in", a young man once told me, as he described a particular house of worship. He visited this church, after having heard so much about it, and has since officially declared it as "The spot to be in." Depending on the number of people and upon the various aspects of a given ministry, I suppose that charisma *does* have the potential to draw thousands to such a place or "*spot.*"

It is an unfortunate tragedy though, that oftentimes The Lord is not even present in many of these places – but who cares, so long as the music is blaring, the sermons are kept at the "milk level" [nothing too heavy which forces us to change our sinful ways] and the people "feel good all of the time." Who cares whether or not God shows up, so long as we're getting our praise on in our favorite "spot."

Many who have perched themselves upon the pews, actually show up having good intentions, but have no clue as to who Jesus is. Quite often, they are drawn by the allure of the crowd or by the eloquence of the speaker, but they rarely tune in to hear what "God" is saying. They are "turned on" by the message of the messenger and by the electric charge of an anointed atmosphere, but hardly (if ever) are they "tuned in" to The Lord.

Because they do not really know God, it is actually the magnetic roar of the crowd that captivates them and continues to hold their attention. These people actually believe this [the atmospheric charge, to be the same as The hovering, of The Spirit, of The Almighty]. They seek to have their ears tickled but are in no wise receptive to The Lord when He is speaking. How then will they receive Him? How can they know when The Lord is tabernacling amongst them (or not)? Scarcely (if at all), are they even able to recognize His voice, because they have no real relationship with Him.

Those of you who are in the house but are not saved, the only thing that I can offer to you is this; if you don't know Jesus, and have no relationship with Him you need to get to know Him. I pray that for your own eternal soul's sake, you will take the time to learn of Him – and not men! I strongly urge and plead with you to give your life to The Saviour before it is too late! Contrary to what you want to believe, or to what you have been told from the pulpit, from friends or from family members, GRACE DOES NOT LAST ALWAYS!

Believe me; there cometh a morning that you shall not awake on this side of God's goodness. Some of you do not believe anything that The Bible has to say – ok fine; you are grown and that is your prerogative. Nevertheless, think about this; is your non-belief worth the risk?

If hell <u>does</u> exist, would going there to spend <u>your eternity, being tormented</u> be the price that you would be willing to pay for simply not believing or because you have chosen to purposely ignore Christ? Dispense with the lies that you've been told - <u>hell is not a party zone!</u> There will be no partying going on down there – just a whole lot of burning, and weeping and gnashing of teeth!

KEEP OUT! "~~DO NOT ENTER THE HELL FIRE.~~ THIS MEANS YOU!

Following Jesus does not mean that you have no life. Following Him is more than a bunch of man-made rules. Surely, I will get in trouble for this one – but having a personal relationship with Him, is far more important than ever crossing the threshold of a church building! I am not saying that we should not attend church, but neither do we necessarily have to reach His representatives in order to reach Him.

He will grant you direct access, but you MUST respond in the affirmative. He will draw you to Himself and will point you in the right direction - His direction. The question at this late hour remains to be answered is; "Why are you still ignoring Him?"

Before writing Him off altogether because of the "church folk" who let you down, I challenge you to start a fresh new one-on-one relationship with Him. Pick up a Bible and begin devouring it. Start with just you and The Lord. Begin with the New Testament if the old is too hard for now. Let Him be your only guide.

I truly do understand why you may not immediately feel like bothering with "church"; but dear friend, I beg you, not to write Jesus off; He is not to blame for their actions. The choice is simple, and the choice is yours to make. Why not turn your life over to Him immediately? Why not do it today? Really, why not do it right now? YEAH THAT'S IT. SERIOUSLY, I MEAN NOW, AS IN <u>RIGHT NOW</u> - EVEN AT THIS VERY MOMENT!

In fact, put this book down! Did you hear me? I'm very serious. Put down my book because the rest of my story can wait. Your soul is far more important. Get your book marker, put it in-between the page; now – go handle your business with The Lord, then come back and read the rest, because it gets even better (smile). When He comes knocking, do not miss your turn; it could be your only chance for Salvation! He that has an ear, please hear what The Spirit is saying! Making a decision for Christ is that important!

Please take the time to give some serious thought to what I have said. Remember, "Church folk" are not necessarily "truly saved folk." They are not the same as "The Elect." Anybody can attend a local church, but not all of these shall enter into The Kingdom of God, where you will find those who are followers (and doers) of Christ's teaching – for real. Get to know HIM! Let HIM translate you into the dimension of The Kingdom where the air is much clearer.

Now that we have established some of the reasons why people may attend church, I would like to call your attention to another population. These are the people who actually *believe* that they are saved, but in reality, they are not. The difference between the crowd that is merely turned on and amused by the glitz and glamour is that *this* crowd may actually have good intentions upon arrival. Still they are often clueless as to what it takes to obtain a genuine relationship with The Lord. Given the quality of today's preaching, unfortunately, they may not get a clue anytime soon – God help them. Throughout America's pulpits, our theologians seem to be preaching about everything *but* Jesus; still they insist that ALL of their activity is, "All about Him." This remains to be seen, because for the most part, I sure can't tell.

There remains yet one more group to introduce. I call them "The silent majority." These are the people who most leadership would love to dismiss or to ignore altogether. The crooked leaders do their very best to keep them silenced and on the "DL."   Yeah, they want to keep them "down low" where nobody will ever hear their cries or give ear to their stories. They are often kept in isolation and seclusion, so that the wolves will not have to acknowledge the pain that they and their staff have inflicted. Out of sight, out of mind, is how they hope that the story will go. They fool themselves into believing that these people are merely a vanishing few. These are the ones however, who <u>really</u> are saved and who <u>really</u> do have a relationship with Jesus, but who have been battered and mortally wounded from within the ranks of local assemblies.

This crowd does not resemble the unsaved. Neither are they like the saved, but *purposely* un-churched sect. No this group to whom I refer, is not at all like those who are saved but who have no desire to fellowship, *preferring* to remain unconnected and un-churched for life. No! This is not of whom I speak.

The people to whom I now refer remain staunch in the presence of clamor, hype and charisma. They are not at all moved by the passing fads in Christendom but have instead chosen to remain steadfast and faithful to God. They are undaunted by that which surrounds them, as they are "Bound for Mt. Zion." For them, it truly is all about The Kingdom. You see, this crowd *really* does love The Lord and with genuineness of spirit, want nothing more than to serve and to honor their God. Their desire, determination and drive is not assuaged simply because they are unwelcome in a camp full of vipers.

They will not be denied by a majority who wish nothing more than for them to shut up and to go away. They are made out of tougher stuff! Their fire shall not be assuaged just because some theologian has purposely chosen to reject them. They have determined to follow Him "for real" And with their whole heart. Are they perfect? Not hardly! Oh, but this group knows to whom they must go for their perfecting. Dear reader does this sound like you? Do you and Jesus have a good thing going on too? Your worship and outpouring unto The Lord isn't just some Sunday (or Saturday) morning show. Can you and Jesus have church on any given day of the week? Hallelujah!

Are you connected enough to know that He hears your cries and even your silent tears. He cares about you and about your wounded spirit. You know that He is calling you – deep has called, and yeah deep has even echoed an answer back unto deep. **When He calls, you must answer.** What a privilege to be summoned by The King of Kings, but still you find yourself without a church home because you were wounded from within. Those of you, who have left your churches, please know that no matter what *they* tell you, and regardless of the names that *they* call you; remember, GOD **STILL LOVES YOU!**

It may not have been your intentions to leave your church. But neither could you bear to stay and continue feeling angry, unfulfilled and disconnected. The Father knows this too. I am not condoning but neither am I lashing out; for I do understand, exactly how staying in a place [where you are unwanted] can make you feel as though you are dying a slow agonizing death. I know what it feels like, to hear the truth of God screaming on the inside, but your outward announcement of the same continuously go unanswered by human response. I know what it is to speak the truth as an oracle of God, but yet the people surrounding you, deem YOU unqualified to do so.

I understand exactly, how it is that an individual, can feel all alone, even while in the midst of a great gathering. Of a truth, I can identify with feeling isolated because you and God have reached a depth level to where only the True Remnant dare to plunge – as only *they alone actually* can. Try explaining that to mere church folk.

Some of you were (and still are) wounded, to such a degree that you have quit going altogether, while others go only when they feel the urge. You have stopped paying tithes to *that* church and perhaps you have found other means of charitable godly giving. Some of you no longer give to anyone at all. *We* never intended for it to be this way. In fact, we once loved our assemblies very much and could not wait to get to them each week – or even several times a week. However, the majority of our pain continued to stem from the very place that we loved so much and so desperately [once] longed to be part of.

Some in positions of leadership have taken pride in holding their feet upon the necks of God's children. I don't know if they do this out of arrogance, or just because *they feel* (for some reason) as though they can. Perhaps *they feel as though they are the stars,* and the rest of us - well to them, we are nothing more than the lowly ottomans assigned to them, upon which they can rest their crusty feet.

In God's house, there are no stars. We are all equal in His sight. They may have positions of authority, but we each have the position of son-ship in Him. We are the only ones who can forfeit our position, by <u>permanently</u> turning our backs.

I wish to God that pastors in the land would be brave enough to come forward and issue an apology to the masses. Some leaders want to know why their churches have not grown, but have instead undergone a drastic decline in membership. Perhaps someone should inform these so-called shepherds that the decline has been largely due to their own actions.

Others that are growing by leaps and bounds, have not ever crossed into the dimension of unadulterated and pure holiness before The Lord – which without we shall not even see His face. The church seems to be stuck in a "psychological, materialistic, pseudo holy" time warp. We need to position ourselves higher! If you are a pastor who happens to be reading this book, you need to know that a huge percentage of *your constituents* are guilty of running thousands of people away.

If you are such a one, you know exactly what I am talking about! (Then again, perhaps you really do not know). Your crushing mental and verbal assaults have wounded people to the highest degree. It is you who have crushed our spirits and God calls you guilty!

You need to come clean by admitting that you have not really loved the vast majority of people who have been sent to you. They wanted nothing more than to be a help and a blessing to your ministry. You know how to preach about every other abominable thing, but when it comes to YOU PREACHING ABOUT YOU, THEN YOU DO NOT.

Isn't The Kingdom already divided enough? Seriously - do you pastors not know that when you hurt us, you are also hurting yourselves? Do you not realize that your despising of people actually hurts the heart of God? Do you not care? Has your popularity gotten the best of you? Has it caused you to mentally short circuit and now your capacity for compassion has become calloused or seared?

Even if just one person [who you deem] insignificant, is injured or becomes a victim of your wounding, the entire Body is affected. For even the minutest of members (the most overlooked or insignificant) has the potential to cause major damage if injured, provoked, neglected and/or left unattended. Ok, so you don't believe me? Just try ripping off a fingernail and notice how you feel without it. Let me make it even easier, you don't even have to rip the *entire* nail off.

You need only to pull off the portion of a nail that has broken too far down, but is yet attached to a piece of skin. I dare you to remove it and then tell me whether or not you notice/feel the difference. Pull out a piece of your (own natural) hair and see what happens. You will feel the pain if even the shortest piece is plucked or pulled on purpose.

Whenever an injury occurs even in the remotest part of our human body, the rest of the body is also effected. Once the brain receives a signal that something has malfunctioned, it then sends a distress signal of its own. This signal in turn sends messages to various systems throughout the entire body, alerting them that "something has gone wrong somewhere." "Help!" "All blood vessels on deck." "All necessary blood cells man your stations." "Get in position - be ready to coagulate and to stop any possible unnecessary bleeding." "All pain receptors get into place and remain alert." "A breakdown has occurred." "All units of the body stand by; prepare to release your healing powers should it be necessary." ALL HANDS ON DECK! STAND BY FOR FURTHER INSTRUCTIONS FROM ABOVE! (The brain).

THE BEAUTY OF OUR HUMAN BODY IS THAT IT USUALLY SENDS OUT WARNING SIGNS <u>IN ADVANCE, LONG BEFORE THE ACTUAL DAMAGE OR FATAL DESTRUCTION CAN CAUSE "PERMINANT" INJURY.</u>

IT IS MOST UNFORTUNATE, THAT WE OFTEN TEND TO IGNORE THE WARNINGS. SO AS IT IS IN THE NATURAL, AND SO VERY UNFORTUNATE, IS IT ALSO IN THE SPIRIT! Well pastors, There are many in God's Body of Believers who are in agony because of you. The Holy Ghost is therefore sending you a signal – God's signal. Are you even cognizant of this fact or have you been blindsided by your own arrogance? You will give an account for the souls that have been lost on your watch because of your pride and mistreatment.

For The Remnant, it has never been about WANTING to part ways with you. Rather we want no more division in The Body. Haven't there been enough casualties already? We NEED you to admit your errors so that the much needed healing can begin. We need you to accept full responsibility for having participated in the word's buffoonery, which you have in turn brought into the local assemblies. In many instances, YOUR debauchery is largely to blame for the current rift that we are experiencing.

You are the leaders, and of course you never let us forget that. So now what are YOU going to do to help repair the damage? The Holy Ghost is now signaling for you to own up to it and to make every effort to repair the breach! We need you to admit that you were often incorrect with your blanket statements and that you have caused millions not only to leave local assemblies but because of you, many have turned a deaf ear to God's voice. No wonder the laborers are so few. Jesus says that the harvest is ripe but those who were scheduled to work in the vineyard seem to be missing in action. Where are the laborers who have been scheduled for this hour?

I cannot speak for them all, but truly, I do believe that a large percentage of them are somewhere licking their wounds. Some are hiding out in their homes, in gangs and even in false religions as they search for acceptance. Others, who have been halted, are now living in a state of paralyzed spiritual stupor. Preachers you need to face up to what you have done. I adjure you by the mercy of God to acknowledge your own transgressions. Jesus said that truth is the only thing that will make us free – *and us, includes you too.*

Please!? Can we at least hear from some of you who are brave enough to represent your constituents? Are there any of you who will come forward and be courageous enough to openly repent to the masses, so that they, you, and we (as His Body) can go free? Somebody IN LEADERSHIP needs to atone for the mess that we now have in our churches.

If just one of you would have the guts to admit and to apologize for the actions of your fellow theologians, I am convinced that many bruised sheep would come out of hiding, which in turn, will enable them to embark upon a campaign towards spiritual wholeness. Can somebody please admit that you have been responsible for the bastardization of many who have never deserved to wear such a degrading title?

Pastors, I am not talking about you merely standing in your pulpits making some insincere, generic statement like, "If I've hurt anybody, please forgive me." This is what most of you say without a shred of humility and genuineness to back it up. We don't want to see any crocodile tears either - anybody can turn on the water works.

We see you, and we are not amused, neither are we fooled! I am urging you to give a sincere apology, from your heart. If the apology comes from the depths, we will know it and it will be received. You need to use the same amount of blatant brutal force that you so heavily relied upon, as you were grinding your victims to a spiritual pulp. You know exactly whom you have scorned with your flippant comments and venomous verbal assaults. You know when you have been abrasive, indignant and less than kind. If you do not know whom you have wounded, just look around your congregation; notice who may be missing. The Holy Ghost is well able to refresh your memory. If you ask Him, He will surely tell you. I dare you to. The third person of the Godhead has convicted me on many occasions.

He has convicted me to the point where I could not even sleep until I had corrected my wrong doings, especially the ones that He so graciously had no choice but to point out. I remember having to humble myself and apologize to my young daughter. I can recall one time in particular wherein I had to call her at school, ask the administrators to please find her, pull her out of class and get her to the office telephone as quickly as possible, just so that I could ask for her forgiveness. My apology could not wait until later. Absolutely not! God would give me no rest until I had done so. The Holy Spirit commanded me to correct my offensive deed IMMEDIATELY!

I asked her if she would please accept my apology. I then told her that I was sorry, and that I promised to do my best to change. I even told her to signal me, if ever I seem to be heading in the same direction of hurting her feelings or refusing to listen by yelling too loudly or whatever.

PRIDEFUL PASTORS, HAVE YOU ANY IDEA WHAT HAPPENED NEXT?

My Daughter forgave me. Why? BECAUSE I A-S-K-E-D HER TO. *I considered her feelings by acknowledging my own transgressions. I did not skirt around the issue by trying to make believe I did not remember what I had done or said and neither should you. I did not try to down play my own inappropriate behavior in an attempt to make her feel badly by reminding her of what SHE had done in the first place, which may have provoked my anger to the point that I commenced to acting like an idiot.*

Even if she had provoked me, as often she had, still I should have handled MYSELF better. At other times, my own temper would get the best of me. In either case, I should have exhibited more self-control, because after all, she is a child and I should at least be trying to set a decent example for her to follow. I am the adult and I should know better and do better! I told her that I had made a mistake.

I apologized and I asked her for a pardon. I could not let her go through her entire day (with her heart hurting) without first acknowledging my own inappropriate angry reaction and mishandling of the situation. Correction – The Lord would not allow me to go all day without apologizing to her. I also asked God for a pardon. I then asked Him to help me. He did; and then I helped myself by making a change!

Now, I don't know about anybody else, but that's what good old-fashioned, gut wrenching, Holy Ghost conviction makes *me* do EVERY TIME! – Even when 'I' don't want to. Thankfully most of the time I want to keep/make things right, because I do not want The Lord *to have* to finger me. For the most part pastors, you know exactly whom you have offended with your despicable display of verbiage. Some people take offence to everything; I am not talking about them. I am talking about those whom you have purposely scarred so deeply that they have no desire to return to your church or to God.

You may not think so, but many who you have wounded will suffer the effects of your words for a lifetime. "Wolf clerics", your venom was not accidentally spewed. Oh no! Your poison was precisely targeted and unleashed with a vengeance. With accurate precision, you gained a direct hit, as your darts struck the very heart of your intended prey.

You have discouraged highly anointed individuals who wanted nothing more than to sit at your table – they would have gladly settled for the spiritual crumbs that you allowed fall to the ground, but you wouldn't even give them that. You feed people all over the world, but those who are right in your midst are denied your freaking crumbs! What say you concerning this matter? God wants to know! They wished only to be an asset to YOUR ministry, but just like King Saul, YOU were intimidated and YOU wanted nothing to do with them. YOU did nothing but blow them off – and now YOU must atone. When they sought your counsel, you showed no mercy, no compassion and no concern, but only blatant and willful neglect.

You turned a deaf ear! Yes! <u>you</u> did that! You treated them as though they were a mere piece of trash and now they are gone. Woe unto every wolf cleric and hireling! Their blood may be upon your very hands!

Do you remember what I said about the human body, and how it responds to trouble or to danger? When one part is in trouble, it sends a signal to the brain, which in turn sends a series of messages throughout - remember? Well, the interesting and most important feature of our human body is the amazing way in which it <u>rallies together when it needs to.</u> Every section that is called upon, readies itself in preparation to do its individual and/or collective part to dispel the enemy.

Once the signal is released, the rest of the body prepares to pitch in. It commences to operate in, "Stand by repair status", as each system prepares for action and readies itself for duty. Each begins to do whatever it takes to repair the damage, or to expel the invader, offender, intruder or disease. HIS Remnant is being signaled RIGHT NOW! The cooperate Body of Christ, is being sent a major end-time message. He that hath an ear to hear let him hear what The Lord of Hosts is saying right now!

My brothers and sisters, are you now prepared to mimic the same response as our human counterpart? The Body of Christ is in serious trouble. We need each member to be what he or she has been created to be. We need people in place and doing their part to make the necessary repairs. We are calling upon everyone right NOW to convert to stand by status; ready yourselves for damage control duty. Fellow Believers, if you plan on being part of this next move, which could very well be one of the last of our generation, or even as we know it forever, then I strongly suggest you check in regularly with THE LORD for updated instructions.

P.S. Should you decide, for any reason at all, that you are not going to check in, I caution you to beware. For The Lord God knows exactly where to find you if He should have need of you - just ask Gideon (Judges Chapter 6 vs 11).

➷*It Couldn't Happen To Me, Could It?*➶

Whenever we hear of another's painful ordeal, very often our first response is to do our best to 'catch' the person in a lie. We wonder if the individual is in fact *really* telling the truth. Something about human nature makes us prone to investigate. We *look* for holes in a person's story, for no other reason than to pass judgment. This we often do, without ever having full knowledge of the facts. Although we *want* to embrace the victim, thereby believing him or her wholeheartedly, still this will not always be our *initial* response. We may actually find ourselves being very skeptical.

This is especially true, if someone of notoriety has been accused of something ill fated such as the mistreatment of another. Rarely can we bring ourselves to believe that such a thing is true. I don't know if it is that we don't *want* to believe or if rather we are simply not capable of imagining that someone, whom we hold dear can [at times] also, be very cold and calculating. Perhaps deep in our psyches, we simply cannot bring ourselves to accept or to believe the worse about an individual or an institution that we admire or love. "Oh no, not my pastor, not my church, not my child or my family member - please!" "My father did what?" "Impossible!" Just as I already know that not everyone will believe me.

Not so very long ago, I would have made a big deal about the possibility of not being believed. I would have agonized over what people are going to think. Wisdom however, has taught me that things are not always as they appear. No matter what we do in life, we will always have critics, many of whom will NEVER go away. I am no longer concerned with whether or not people believe me. I am the one who lived through the events of my own life; therefore, I ought to know even if my critics do not. Moreover, I also know that God knows the truth, even if others do not.

Knowing that God has been present, every step of the way has comforted me considerably in the matter. As long as I know that I am speaking the truth, and I know that God knows the truth, what others have to say about it [or about me] is no longer a concern.

The perceptions and/or opinions of other people become invalid, as I no longer try to prove anything to anyone. Trying to prove and to defend myself quite honestly, zaps too much of my creative energy. I no longer have time for that – my critics can say and believe what they will! I too was once guilty of sizing people up. Because I knew the personalities of those who had shared their stories with me, I too had sometimes wondered if whether or not the person had done *something wrong.* I wondered what role he or she actually played, which in turn may have led to his or her own demise. What pertinent piece of information had the person [willfully or mistakenly] left out of the story?

Thankfully [as afore mentioned], I wasn't nearly as bad as Job's friends who vehemently "insisted" that he <u>had</u> <u>to</u> have done something wrong. Why would God punish someone who had not sinned they queried? "You must have sinned somehow." "Job you must be hiding <u>something</u>", they accused continuously. Tell us Job – tell us what it is? "What have you done?"

We all know how Job's story ended. He had not done one single thing to mar his integrity. In the end, God not only <u>totally</u> vindicated him, but God also restored everything that he had lost. In fact, God gave him more than he originally had. The Lord even gave Job more children. Why not read the entire book of Job today? Find out for yourself exactly who and/or what was at the root of his suffering and how an even greater blessing was wrought from his affliction. Not that we *want* to go through anything bad; but I am reminded of something that I once heard, **"There is redemption in suffering."** (Thanks Professor Leonard McCoy).

We will not always be able to identify with what others have gone through. We can choose to be sympathetic by trying to 'imagine' their plight, but still we could never fully understand unless we too have walked in their same shoes. There may arise circumstances in our lives that will prove so devastating, that literally, we will want to stick our heads in the sand and remain there. Any number of tragic events could send us running for cover – but often it takes only one. On such an occasion, we might find ourselves seeking shelter from the weather, or from some other element. People have been known to even seek solace from their place of employment.

It is not uncommon to cross paths, with individuals, who have [at one time or another], literally found themselves having to seek refuge 'from other people.' Sometimes we just flat out need a break from everything and everyone.

Never in my wildest imagination, had I ever dreamed of 'literally' *having to* take a break, from my Christian brothers and sisters. Not from those *in "The Kingdom"*, you understand, but from the flakey "church folks" and the "wannabes." Not once had I ever considered that I too, would one day stand in the same shoes, as so many had done before. Not even once had I even dreamed of such a day. Can I get a witness anyone? After my own heartbreaking ordeal, I too found myself wanting to avoid not only church, but also I wanted to stay away from most who *claimed to be Christians.* They do lip service, but like The Lord said – "Their hearts are far from Him." Prior to my temporary paralyzing wound, I had a very difficult time understanding the near violent reactions that I would receive from those in the un-churched population.

Thousands of people have an abiding love for The Saviour, but can muster up little to no respect, for those behind the four walls. It has recently been expressed to me that, "It is hard now a days in some cases to tell the pimps from the pastors." Wow! - I thought, after hearing that statement. I remember being absolutely shocked by a good friend of mine who made a very matter-a-fact declaration. She stood flat-footedly in my office and vehemently declared, "Jonita, I'm sorry, but you could never ever pay me, to ever set foot in another church, ever again!" Again, I say wow!

This she declared after being wounded by her own pastor (long before my own ordeal). Not so long ago, hearing statements such as these, would have left me totally flabbergasted and shocked, to say the least. Not anymore though. I have come to experience for myself, why it is that so many well meaning people feel exactly this way.

One night at school, I listened intently as one of the younger students give her sermon. This young girl by the name of *Ms. Deborah Pierre* attends faithfully with her sister *Rebecca* and cousin *Valerie*. These three young ladies have won my heart and I am honored to sit amongst them each week.

Anyway, Deborah who was only 11 years old at the time, had managed to grasp in only a few short years, what it took me nearly 40 years to realize and then another 2-3 years to digest and to finally accept as fact. For me, having to come to terms with this truth, proved to be extremely painful, because I really did not want to believe it.

In our school, we rotate weekly as we carry out chapel assignments. We have praise and worship (devotional service), prayer, speakers etc. In short, we the students conduct a complete church service each week. This 11-year-old babe stated in her message something that impressed me very much.

It was not only *what* she said that gained my attention as well as my utmost respect, but also I was extremely impressed at her amount of insight as well as her "Holy boldness."

She said, "Some preachers are not in ministry for God but for themselves." She admonished the class to, "Be careful who you listen to, or to what counsel you receive." "The wrong counsel could cause you to lose your mind."

Bingo! How my ears perked up as this babe uttered those confirming but very sobering words. I happen to believe that they came straight from the Throne Room of Jehovah God. Nobody but The Lord had been privy to my situation, concerning the warped counsel and the ill treatment that had just befallen me. Her words were a direct answer from my Father – Bless His Holy Name.

Neither was it a coincidence that I was scheduled to speak the very next week. We usually select sermon topics of our own choosing, but it was to be for this one time only, that the professor had selected them for us. Even then, as I was yet in the midst of penning this very book, my assigned sermon topic was given to me at the precise moment that I walked through the door. I had not even sat down before my professor asked me, if I could speak (the following week) on the subject matter – "God Is Our Refuge." How is that for timing? Confirmation or coincidence; you draw it up.

Anyway, when Ms. Pierre said what she did, I could not help but stand up and listen even more intently. Nobody but Jesus knew what I was going through at the time. That indeed was a "Rhema" if ever I needed one. So significant was what she said, that some might have even missed it. The devil probably distracted several people on purpose, so that her statements would be without any [lasting] impact.

I did hear a few gasps as she rendered her opening comments about some pastors being in ministry for self-glorification rather than for God's. "That's strong," I heard another grimace, as if the little sister's comment had been too harsh or like it wasn't the truth and that she shouldn't be saying it. Her comments may have even angered some – who can tell? However, to them I say, "He that hath ears let them hear him what The Spirit has to say." Amen!

I thank God for "little" Ms. Pierre. She was absolutely right and she at least had the guts to say exactly what I believe The Lord had instructed her to. Jehovah is giving divine unction and wisdom to his babes in this hour. She told the truth and I know that it was The Lord who placed that truth in her heart. Don't worry little sis, I got your back!

She especially hit home when she spoke about their <u>wrong counsel.</u> I really took to heart what she said, just as I had absolutely marveled at the God inspired wisdom of my own 11-year old daughter Kenita, who had said something to me during one of my particularly low points. One day, as I drove her to school, still very much shaken by the incident between my pastor and I, she said something that I shall never, ever forget. While stopped at an intersection, my daughter looked me squarely in the eyes and firmly stated, <u>"Remember mommy, it only takes one distraction, to cause you to lose your dream."</u>

Oh my goodness! How right she was. Again, God had placed His wisdom into the heart of His "little child." Unlike us, [older children], *they* have not been as tainted by the lack of faith or by blatant sinful behavior. For the most part, they are much purer than we are and –

THEY REALLY DO BELIEVE GOD; THEY TAKE HIM AT HIS WORD – FOR REAL! These are they to whom I graciously submit; the children can pray for me anytime.

Without hesitation they say exactly what needs to be said [whether we want to hear it or not]. They allow God to use them, as they speak that which others are either too sinful or are very often too afraid to say. Most of the time, they speak the truth. God can depend on the babes to blurt things right on out – and they usually do! Continuing to focus on the person who wounded me, would only keep me from carrying out my purpose. My constant agonizing and depression over my rejection, was indeed serving to frustrate and overshadow my [God given] dreams and goals, because I could seemingly concentrate on nothing else.

Rejection's paralyzing effects were quickly becoming that which attempted to rob me of my divine destiny. Had I continued to dwell on my pain, (or the inflictor of it), then certainly it would have. This liberating statement by my [then] 11 year old, has served as one of the major golden nuggets that have played a huge role in jolting me out of my complacency.

"Keeping it real", I however must admit that the sobering comments of the youngsters did not keep me from seeking solace from people. Never once had I imagined seeking refuge from the church. Yes, ladies and gentleman, it *did* happen to me, and it could also happen to you. Call me bastard if you want, but if the counsel does not come to me directly from The Lord, then honestly I no longer want to hear it.

There are people who I will not even allow to speak to me about spiritual matters because they are motivated purely by their own thoughts and not by those that emanate from The Mind of Christ. Not everyone has been authorized to speak into my life, for neither the good nor the bad. There are only a few select people that I trust well enough to tell me the truth; even if I am wrong, I need to know that. If I ask them, I know surely that I can rely on them to give me an *honest unbiased answer* – especially my daughter, Lord God!

She has no problem calling me out (in a respectful manner of course, as I am still the mother). Trust me when I tell you, God has given her wisdom which on a number of occasions, she has used to help me.   God has used her to gracefully convict me as well - and quite thoroughly at that, I might add. I do not need someone to tell me only what he or she thinks I want to hear.   Nor will I accept what their 'flesh' may be telling them to feed me. Although I do trust a select few, even their counsel is sifted through the wisdom of The Spirit. God must always have the final say regardless to who is saying what. These days, God has heightened my "Strange fire" detector (The Holy Spirit).

Instilled deep inside is an automatic devil detector that warns me loudly when I am in the presence of people who mean me harm. I know when I am hearing God's counsel as opposed to someone's flesh, because it ALL gets filtered through Him.

We must guard at all costs the precious gifts that are within. We are responsible and will give an account as to the reasons for our failure to use them [to complete assignment(s)]. At times, we do not carry them out because of our own laziness. Sometimes it is procrastination, fear or even down right slothfulness that causes us to miss out.

More often, we allow others to convince us, that we have not *really* heard Him clearly, (or that we have not heard Him at all). When we give up on our dreams, or lose our zeal because of inaccurate twisted counsel, the results will be even more devastating, because God will demand an explanation <u>from us.</u>

Confusion often arises when the counsel we have received from pastors and from other "church folk", appears to conflict with our revealed destiny. If we were completely honest, we would have to admit, that often we never consulted with God. The vast majority of us simply took *them* at their word, because of their position or because they were popular. Sometimes our advisors held no position at all, but for some strange reason, we still held them in such high regards that we value their opinions above our own.

Often when we seek counsel, people do not give us a "Thus Saith The Lord, but rather a thus saith [or thus thinketh] themselves. They counsel us from what <u>they</u> know, feel or think which may or may not be fit for <u>our</u> particular situation. We should always be informed and counseled by the wisdom of God. <u>He is all-knowing, and He has a vested stake in each of His children. His counsel will yield the correct solution for every individual case.</u>

Have you ever known a person (or perhaps even several), who seems to feel as though God is *always* speaking a word to him/her for you? People like this, often try to run your life (control you) by telling you, *what they claim* that God has told them to tell you. Now don't get me wrong, we know that sometimes a person may actually have something legitimate to say, that has indeed been given to them by God. Soooooooooooooo, keeping this in mind, I feel it is my duty to help you out here also. The rule really is quite simple:

The Lord will NEVER speak anything to another person concerning YOUR life, without FIRST speaking to YOU about it. Let me say that one more time. YOU WILL BE <u>THE FIRST</u> TO KNOW! He does however very often confirm His Word through people.   He sometimes uses lay people, pastors, radio/television broadcasts or other means to confirm a thing or to call your attention to something that He has ALREADY placed in YOUR SPIRIT.

Now, depending on the nature of what God is saying, should YOU choose to ignore His prompting [purposely or not], particularly if it is pertaining to a sin that He is "fingering" or to a work that He has commanded you to carry out, or if it has to do with some action that He expects for you to cease doing, then the promptings will likely become more intense. Should you still ignore His "stronger" warnings/promptings, He may be forced to send someone or something your way – God help you.

No telling who or what The Almighty will send; for even a little child or the very elements of nature, can be employed by The Almighty, to carry out His will, or to deliver a sobering message on His behalf. He might decide to assign one of His seasoned "Prophetic Specialists" to pay you a visit or to speak a word. Hummmmmmmmm, "Prophetic Specialist", catchy job title don't you agree? (Smile). Anyway, for those who are particularly obstinate, He may allow a calamity, which heretofore He had been preventing. He does not operate in the same manner with every situation or with each individual, but be assured; HE WILL get your undivided attention, "by any means necessary."

  Also understand this, depending on where you are (in The Lord), you may not always receive an outside confirmation, or even if you do, it may not be immediate. At times like these, you just have to know whether God has indeed spoken or not. By the time you reach a certain dimension, [in The Lord] (if you make it that is), you should be so accustomed to His voice and to so many of His ways [by then], that you should not have to peek around every corner hoping to run into "Confirmation Boulevard" or "Prophesy to Me Alleyway."

  You will not need to visit every prayer line with the hopes that "the prophet" will single you out. By this time, you should be clear that God sends confirmation only if He chooses to, as it is optional and it is up to Him. Certain privileges come only with spiritual maturity and only by spending <u>sufficient time with Him.</u> It may take years to arrive here, so do be patient with yourself as you consistently seek His face and also His heart.

  You must ask Him to reveal Himself and His will in any way that He chooses, as well as in ways, that you desire to know Him. If you want to know Him as Abba Father, then ask Him to reveal Himself to you as that. You must really desire His tutoring. Even if other people think that you have lost your mind, go for it. I tell you that God is real and that He does and will speak to you. If you touch Him [in the spirit], I declare unto you this day, that He shall touch you back.

  <u>*WHY NOT MAKE IT YOUR MINISTRY TO LOVE HIM!*</u> *He who "is love", is also "desirous of love" – our love. We are commanded to love Him you know. Can you?? Will you???*

  Anyway...

  I have already warned you that, it will do you good to avoid people who ALWAYS want to tell you something that they claim God is telling them for your life. Get into the habit of checking with GOD for yourself. If hearing from The Lord and obeying Him, is 'truly' your heart's desire – than be it unto YOU this day according to YOUR faith!

  I tend to ignore what THEY say unless I already know from the very beginning that they are on the right track. If what they say has some validity, then guess what – I <u>consult with God (anyway) before I totally receive it and/or act upon it.</u> Honestly, if I am not sure, I still go to GOD.

There have been a few, who have been correct when bringing me a word. I in turn have graciously received it and did whole-heartedly thank them for being obedient to The Lord – no matter what their counsel. If I KNOW that it comes from The Lord, then I can take it, even if it is a word of correction or rebuke. However, if a person is trying to wound me or is trying to give me some of his or her own fleshly counsel, warped advice or correction, I don't want to hear it. Their counsel will be flat out rejected. Depending upon the pull of the atmosphere [satanic interference], it will be <u>quite sharply rejected and or rebuked.</u> The person may actually be called out – on the spot.

If your motives are pure then you won't have to concern yourself with that. I rely on the leading of The Lord as to how best to deal with each situation. I do not take it very kindly, when people who have little to no proven track record of manifestation, take it upon themselves to come to me claiming to have "A word" or a "God told me to tell you…"statement. I am very observant. If these people can't get their own lives straightened out and are not even sure, if or even when The Lord has indeed spoken [to them or not], how on earth then, could such persons dare to presume, that Jehovah would ever trust them with a message for someone else?

If an individual is trying to attach what he or she is saying, by claiming it to be The Lord's doing, who in reality has not told the person anything of the sort, then God will expose it. Someone can give me a good word, but if it reeks of flesh, I still reject it. I do not need to be flattered; nor do I need to be told all good things about myself. Just tell me the plain, simple truth - that's it. Flattering and lying lips are unappreciated, for ultimately they do not help anyone. I have a serious problem with people like this. I often find them to be way off the mark. I call them – "Prophet Wannabes." I warn you, stay away from me if this is how you operate.

Nobody is "good" all of the time – certainly not me (smile), which is why God convicts me [whenever necessary]. Beloved, you must always <u>be very leery of anyone</u> who refuses to tell you the truth, simply because they want to stay in your good graces. I don't want lies – give me what The Lord is saying. Give me all of it, even if it hurts. If you cannot do that, then keep it to yourself. WARNING: Fellow carriers of The Gospel of Jesus Christ, if The Lord should give you a word, you are expected to deliver <u>'only'</u> that which Jehovah is communicating and not that which you choose to add or to subtract from it.

Be precise – EVEN IF THE PERSON TO WHOM YOU ARE COMMUNICATING SEEMS HUNGRY OR EVEN DESPERATE FOR MORE. SPEAK ONLY WHAT YOU HAVE BEEN GIVEN – THAT'S IT! Sometimes a person may be "fishing" and eager to hear a prophetic (or other God inspired utterance) – but you simply have none for him or her. DO NOT MAKE ANYTHING UP! KEEP YOUR MOUTH SHUT IF GOD HAS NOT SPOKEN! UNDERSTAND?!

If you cannot do that, then it would be to YOUR OWN advantage to refrain from bringing that word. Believe me when I tell you, God is about to introduce a Remnant of Believers - and they do know the difference.

The trap of adhering to bad counsel is especially difficult to loose people from, if they have never been trained to hear God, but only the voice of man. We often seek advice from those we admire and respect. If you are a Christian in a local assembly, it is not uncommon to seek guidance from your pastor or from others in positions of authority – heck it seems very normal indeed.

Getting back to what the young lady in school said – way back there *somewhere* (smile). I too am letting you know in plain English, just as the sister so boldly proclaimed that, **"NOT ALL PASTORS ARE IN MINISTRY FOR GOD!"** Many may have actually started out *for Him* but have since gone astray. Sadder to report is the fact that, many have *never* been in ministry for the right reason to begin with – not ever. Still a huge percentage, only *believe*, that they are doing the will of The Lord by going around spouting off their "strange fire."

If deep down, in the pit of your stomach, you are sensing some type of demonic sickening feeling of dread, right after or even while you are in the midst of speaking to someone, (in person or over the telephone), or if you are in their presence, ESPECIALLY if that person is bringing you a, "Thus Saith The Lord", I would advise you to tread very lightly upon whatever they have to say.

Consider their words carefully as you ponder the communication they bring; for it may not be from The Lord at all. On the other hand, it simply may not be FOR YOU! "Strange fire" is anything that someone attempts to pass off as being from God, when indeed God has not spoken. (More on Strange Fire; See Dad (God) Is That You?).

I can often detect whether or not someone's counsel has been tainted and in fact, whether it has been released as a dart to wound my spirit. The enemy never ceases in his attempt to thwart the plan of God. These wolves in sheep's clothing go around spouting their words of poison, none of which have originated from the heart of God or from the pure mind of Christ.

Ask yourselves, why would The Master purposely try to derail you? Why would He want to keep you from doing a magnificent work for His Kingdom? Especially if He is the initiator of that work, and the set time is at hand for it. Why would He scold you simply for following through? Why would He want you wounded to such a degree that you literally prefer to backslide? Think about it. THAT'S NOT GOD! IT NEVER HAS BEEN!

Why would Jesus tell you to, "Learn of Me", (of Him) only to reprimand you for doing so? Why would the fact that you ask pertinent or relevant questions in an attempt to understand something pertaining to His Word, anger Him or make Him penalize you? Why would He ever get mad at you simply because you desire to excel in the things of God? Why would He ever keep you from acquiring wisdom and knowledge concerning that, which has to do with fulfilling His Holy will? God does not do that!

BEWARE, AS STRANGE FIRE CAN COME FROM ANYONE! Beware of the counsel you receive; do stay clear of the dream killer's arrows.

A word to four very special young ladies:

Thank you ever so much Deborah and Kenita. I love you both, and am indeed forever indebted to you for your words of wisdom, and also for allowing The Lord to use you to rebuke as well as to encourage me. Preach maidservants preach! Sing unto The Lord a new song! Sing unto Him, your song of praise! Dance and Worship in His presence. Bless Ye The Lord!

Valerie, and "Prophetess Rebecca", The Lord wants you to know that He has not forgotten you – and neither have I. Valerie, I saw you at your church, (you did not see me though). It was very refreshing to witness you amongst the young people laying prostrate before The Lord in prayer – it did my heart much good.

Rebecca – stay extremely close to The Lord, for the path that you walk cannot contain everyone. The Prophetic anointing is the hardest to walk out but you can do it if indeed The Lord calls you thereto! You may not understand now, but in time, you shall.

May El-Gebor, (ALMIGHTY GOD THE FATHER) be with each of you as you do your very best to win your generation to Yeshua (The Lord Jesus Christ). In addition, may you always be comforted and led by way of the Paraclete (The Holy Ghost). Each of you have been mightily gifted and also uniquely and "internally wired" to accomplish great things. Don't do like I did; do not allow people to discourage you! Beware of all Humans, and PRAY ALWAYS! I have faith in you and know that none of you shall fall by the wayside – In Jesus Name!

Keep up the good work! For great shall your reward be if you continue on the path of righteousness. You young ladies have touched my heart. I graciously salute each of you and hope to one day pass the baton into your very capable hands - Amen!

Continuing for the readers…

It will take experience to determine if what you have encountered is or is not of God. If you are just starting out, you will get there in time, only if you spend adequate time with Him. When *they* are giving off wicked, grandiose, self-inspired rhetoric, it serves as a crippling force to the many babes who do not know any better. They cannot tell the difference, especially when it keeps coming from a person who *should* have their best interest at heart.

While the babes are eaten alive, those who *can* help seem to be sidelined after having lost their zeal. Thus having been spiritually paralyzed, they sit idly by doing nothing. How many times have you heard pastors telling you how much God desires to bless you and that He has a plan for your life?

How many times do you hear them admonishing you to do what God tells you to do? However, as soon as you begin doing exactly that, you may find yourself in need of counsel. Because they are our spiritual leaders, they seem the likely source to which we should turn. The sad thing however, is that deep down we know that what they are telling us is not at all, like what God has spoken. So now, to whom do we listen?

Had I not experienced such an ordeal [for myself]; I would not believe these occurrences to be commonplace in God's House. Because of my ordeal, I too have felt like giving up on church. Thankfully, I have never given up on God. At times, I may have been angry with Him. Ok! In my lifetime, I have been angry with Him "many times" as I found myself totally baffled as to what in the world He was doing. God knows, at times I have even ignored Him or disobeyed Him [and it cost me; God help me] – but leave Him? Are you kidding??

Like where or to whom could I possibly go? "He alone has the words of eternal life" (Thank you Apostle Peter - John 6:68). He is a "Wonderful Counselor" is He not? He is not the author of such confusion that we are experiencing throughout Christendom today. God realizes that I need His direct line of communication because my life depends upon it. He is my lifeline and He is my source of Spiritual nutrition. Abba Father has become to me what an umbilical cord represents to a growing fetus and its mother. He is my everything; and I am not ashamed to confess to the world that I need Him in order to survive.

Like the sister said, "The wrong counsel can cause you to lose your mind." She was ever so right, because I almost did. Wrong counsel will not only cause you to lose your mind and your dream, but wrong counsel and strange fire may even cost you your very life. Like so many, I too had become thoroughly disgusted and no longer wanted any part of the "church folk" scene. Right in the midst of the church, I almost lost my mind, my faith in people, my desire to serve, as well as my dream.

The things that I encountered were not only spiritually and emotionally devastating, but the blow was quite difficult because my eyes had *suddenly* come open and I did not like what I was *forced* to see. I had a very difficult time, accepting the fact that wounding occurs regularly, in a place that is supposed to be an earthly representation of The Lord's House. Ladies and gentlemen, it did happen to me and it could very easily happen to you too.

Note: Because God is not the author of confusion, you and I must take every precaution to assure that <u>we</u> are not the ones hearing an inaccurate communication. <u>We</u> must also ascertain that <u>we</u> are not acting inappropriately towards our leaders. In our own zeal, we too can sometimes get things wrong; so I warn you to be careful. Take care in making sure that YOU are not the confused one! Be sure that you have been [or are still], hearing from God, no matter what you are attempting to do. <u>A long time ago, The Lord shared with me, the fact that, "He would always have my back, but that I had to be right!"</u>

You dear ones must also be certain that YOU are in the right. You must be positive that YOU are hearing FROM GOD and that YOU are hearing Him CLEARLY AND CORRECTLY. If what THEY say, still conflicts with what God is saying, only then do I advise you to take the exact same stand as Peter and the rest of The Apostles.

"WE OUGHT TO OBEY GOD RATHER THAN MEN."
Acts 5:29

By the way, in this passage The Apostles are not asking a question, as we so often hear it quoted, but rather they are in fact, taking a stand by making a bold and very firm statement. It is a stand that you must take for your selves.

Only you and God can know if whether or not you have truly heard from Him or if your instructions have come from the depths of your flesh, or far worse.

Only you and He can determine if what you are indeed hearing, could in fact be, the taunting demonic residuals, which are often associated with the paralyzing words, of those who have spouted their "strange fire."

Part 2
Fire Straight Ahead!
Enter if you dare!

❧*Warning:*❧

Some people may find portions of this next chapter to be highly offensive. It has been <u>purposely</u> written in this fashion so that you the reader can experience in the scope of a few short minutes, <u>only a sample</u> of what many have had to endure for most of their lives. The intention is not to be vulgar but rather to be informative and give you a dose of reality at its worse.

To the Christians who find the language to be a tad shocking or inappropriate, to you I say - get over it! It has been written this way in order to make a point, not for the purpose of exhibiting foul language. I am not out to prove whether or not, I still remember how to spit profanity. These words represent only a mere fraction of those that have been slung at the many victims to whom I dedicate this chapter. Surely, you have heard this "lingo" at some point in your lives; you have not been saved always!

Once upon a time, you may have even spoken such things. Who besides God, your former [or current] victims and yourself will ever really know what you do behind closed doors? Lord only knows what any of us are capable of. If the truth were told, a lot of us would have to admit, that on occasion, we still utter "a few choice words" and I don't mean in "unknown tongues" either! Neither do I necessary mean curse words. People can be profane without ever saying the ***** words; think about that.

Indeed I could fill an entire book, with the names that I alone have been called, never mind the myriad of insults that have been slung towards others. The victimized set foot in your local assemblies every Sunday [or Saturday], after already having survived a 6-day cycle of physical, mental and/or emotional torture and abuse elsewhere.

Certainly, it must fill your heart with gladness to know, they can count on you to further abuse and mistreat them when they show up at YOUR CHURCH on day number 7.

If merely <u>reading the words</u> "in print", causes YOU to feel angered, outraged or saddened, then YOU can only imagine how the victims on the receiving end of this verbal venom must have felt as the words were vehemently hurled at them. Millions today are walking around damaged because of the verbally and/or physically abusive behavior of other people. Just imagine how YOU would feel, if for YOUR entire life, you found yourself dealing with feelings of self-hatred, distrust, disgust, worthlessness and self-loathing, which had manifested themselves due to <u>someone else's</u> character assassinating, marginalizing, dehumanizing, wounding, crippling communications concerning you; which they bashed you with, every single time that they felt the urge to do so.

I challenge you to take a walk in the shoes of a rejected soul and then ask yourselves "wolf clerics" "bougie church folk", and "conceded co-workers", if whether or not YOU would still be so damned quick to pass judgment on everyone. If you get ticked off at me – great! It is often "the guilty" who get the most upset anyway. If this medicine is a bit strong for you – good! Someone should have given you a dose a long time ago!

I hope my words make you angry enough to take your prideful noses out of the air long enough to stop putting other people down! I hope these words sting you and I hope they bite "THE LIVING HELL" right out of you. I hope they hit you so darn hard that they literally knock some sense into you and make you sick of your own selves. I hope they make you mad enough to change for the better! Mostly, I hope they cause you to remember, that never should you behave so despicably as a human being – especially as a child of God. I pray you repent for every wound that you have ever inflicted and I hope these words serve as a reminder of someone's pain. I pray they cause you to never mistreat another human being ever again!

<u>You did say that you 'wanted' to "deny yourself, to take up your cross and to follow Jesus" did you not? Well then, perhaps carrying YOUR CROSS will require that you take up and put on the shoes of an abuse victim. I dare you to... Let's see how well you walk in their world; that is, if you even have the guts to go down into the gutter!</u>

❧The Making Of A Bastard❧

One night, as I watched Christian television, I saw two of my favorite people on the broadcast. I thought to myself, "Boy this is going to be good tonight." Both were two people whom I admired and have had the privilege of hearing and seeing in person, many times over the years. They were hosting a segment on the show entitled, "The Making of a Bishop." As the program progressed, they began to discuss the importance of being mentored and "properly birthed" into ministry.

They spoke about how this person, a son in the ministry, had respected his mentor's leadership and guidance. They then talked about how he had stayed with his pastor/mentor as an obedient spiritual son throughout the years. Although this son had a following of his own, they commented on how he had never tried in anyway to upstage his leader. They went on to tell the world about how the person that they were elevating to the rank of Bishop, had always been obedient and had never gone against the advice of his "spiritual father." The show was specifically addressing, proper behavior versus improper behavior of the father son or father daughter mentoring relationships.

They said that even when the honoree "could have left" he chose not to. Even as he sensed the timing of God for his departure, still never did he "declare" but instead, [like a good son] he "asked" his mentor/pastor, "What do you think?" This person called of God, humbled himself and submitted himself to his leader, although he knew that God had beckoned.

Honestly, I thought that the entire program, up to that point had been quite touching. It was wonderful to see that *someone* had been blessed to have a mentor that actually had his best interest at heart. It was quite obvious to see that he and his mentor/pastor had a relationship that had blossomed over the years. Seemingly, they had nothing but mutual adoration, respect and kindness one for the other. And so, I watched gleefully as yet another one of God's children received his "spiritual wings." The candidate for Bishop was a member of the male pastor's church. The male pastor did not elaborate too much after making his initial comments.

However, the female host began to emphasize and to again, make her point about how the Bishop Elect had <u>asked his (spiritual) father for permission to pursue his destiny.</u>

She went on and on, and on, and on, about how important it is to have a 'proper' birthing out. At first, her stressing of the point seemed fine and was not a problem. Most of us would love to have a father's blessing, or a mentor's nurturing and approval. She then began talking about how there are so many ministries that are "illegitimate", because they were never "properly birthed out." I watched in anticipation, as I heard them speak on the subject of fatherhood, motherhood and mentorship – because at the time I had also longed for this type of a pastoral/mentoring relationship with my own shepherd.

BUT THEN, she said it! The female said something that caused me to well up with tears of confusion and frustration. You see beloved, it was during this time that God and I had just [for the last time I thought], settled some major issues about the very thing that she was "again" spouting off about. I had finally made up my mind to listen to God, and not to man.

I had already been through a horrific ordeal; was struggling to cope with the fact that my pastor did not want me around; and was left to deal with all of the feelings associated therewith. The Lord etched it upon the tables of my heart to write this book, which addresses where I believe many in The Body are right now, because they too have been gravely injured.

Anyway…

As she continued stressing **her point** about being birthed by a spiritual father, she blurted out something that immediately changed my outlook on Christendom, as well as on how I view many of today's leaders. With my eyes having (already) been opened, I was suddenly and acutely aware, of how we [The Body of Christ] *really* treat one another. What she said, not only changed my view, but it literally gave me the boldness to follow through with my assignment from The Lord.

She said, "God is not making bastards." "The devil is a liar"- she exclaimed. She then went on and on almost in an endless rant about people having a "bastard spirit" and how they want to, "Tell" their leaders what they are going to do and how it is that, they "know that they have been called." She stated that "this was a bastard and a rebellious generation of people." She went on to say that, "God is not into bastards."

I cannot tell you how this horrified me. By the time, she had finally finished with her bellowing, I was bawling like a baby. This was not the first time that I had heard this same very prominent person, who by the way I happen to admire very much, say such things. Whenever a person of prominence makes a statement, usually it will not be long before others decide to jump on the bandwagon as well – trust me. And so, as predicted, that is exactly what they did. True to human nature, people seem almost trained to mimic what they see and/or hear. If a high profile personality initiates or gives credence [or disapproval] to a thing, people are very quick to agree – even if the thing is wrong.

That is why it must not be so with you beloved, but rather <u>you</u> must walk in the integrity and in the truth of The Spirit, and always hear ye The Lord's counsel concerning all matters.

Before finally coming to my senses, her words served to almost devastate me. Hearing The Lord calling, and still without endorsement from my pastor; I had already wrestled with this issue. And now, here was this *same* thing again –here was this bastard talk staring me in the face once more! In an instant, all of the memories of my own wounding came crashing back like a mighty clap of thunder.

I recalled a time shortly after being hurt, as I nearly in tears, endeavored to explain my dilemma to a man of God. I sought his counsel, only to have him retort with - **"You don't want to be a bastard Amen!?** He seemed to be asking a question and making a proclamation at the same time. Of course, I did not **want** to be one, so I reluctantly said – "Amen." Although my mouth said the word, my soul would not agree.

In addition, I thought about what another sister had once shared with me. She said that her former pastor told her that, "God was not into bastard churches." "You know those churches that start up and have no covering." "You know people who are not under anyone at all." "You don't want to be a part of anything like that do you?" (Also called a renegade church).

Eventually I began figuring if other people were saying this, and if in fact two of the most revered people in Christendom felt the same way, then surely, *I* had to be the one that was wrong – *right?* With all this talk about being a bastard and the absolute need for a covering, my doubts began to surface all over again. I could imagine Jesus standing there saying to me the very words that He had uttered to His Disciples – "Oh ye of little faith – why are you doubting *[Me]?*

That which had started out as a clear commission from The Lord soon began to buckle under the pressure of "they say." Because of the things that I continued to hear well-known clerics say, I started experiencing much spiritual torment. At one point, I became so confused that I literally asked The Lord to relieve me of this entire assignment – "That's it!" "Take it away I exclaimed!" Seemingly, I could take no more, and I wanted out of the whole deal. "Forget ministry; I'll just read my Bible, because I can't take this pressure" I told The Lord. "I will enjoy my relationship with you, like I have always done."

"Who needs ministry; I've had enough of people and their babbling; I don't want to be bothered anymore!" "Who needs this aggravation"? [I said between sobs and outbursts]. "What had I done wrong anyway?" "God I told you that I wanted to be a nurse!" *I never asked to be in this position in the first place.* Through my tears and my despair, I cried hard. No! Quite honestly, I wailed! Out of the depths of my heart, literally I wailed! Before all of this, there had been no major torment when it came to hearing His voice and purposing my heart to obey. He established my going as He spoke to my heart, my mind and my spirit, long before I knew any of these people or heard of any Christian broadcast. Why was I <u>now</u> so confused? Why would I have to be considered as "being out of order", or being that blasted "B" word?

God's call and assignment did not go away just because my pastor rejected me. Instead beloved, it became more intense. I wrestled and asked The Lord about the entire matter. In addition, I went back over the, "Whose voice was I hearing thing" again – <u>just to make sure that 'I' had not missed something.</u> Seriously, at one point I started feeling almost like John The Baptist, who when he found himself behind prison walls, began to make his own inquiry. "Hey!" "Hello out there; things are not going as planned." "I'm behind bars and I don't like it back here." "This wasn't part of the deal– *was it?*" "Like are you really *that* Jesus?" "Did I hear you correctly or what?"

My friend, can't you just imagine his mindset as he began to doubt, and then ask the infamous question, "Are you He (The Messiah) or shall I look for another"? I wanted to know, Lord are you sure that YOU want ME to do this? "I agreed to be used for Your service, but this?" "This is *too much* to deal with – help me!" "Are You surely telling me to do this?" Sometimes circumstances and people will cause you to begin doubting a truth that you already know. You will begin doubting the very thing that The Lord has already spoken. That is why you must take care to guard your heart and also your mind.

As fear and doubt set in, I remember making excuses all over again. I told Him how afraid I was, how I didn't want to make a mistake and how I did not want to "drop the ball." "I don't know how to do this; help me to not mess up." "Please Jesus!" "Jesus!?" "Where are you?" "Hello God!" "Hello!" "Please?"

"H-E-L-L-O?" "Help me to please escape this torment!" "Please help me – PLEASE?" "Hello Father – are you even listening?" "It's like you don't even care." "What am I going to do?" "Oh God, I can't do this." "Please come and get me." "Can I sit on your lap and talk?" "I'm so scared!" "You're not even listening to me! (He was). "How can I go up against this system of religiosity?" "Are You going to be with me or what?" "Forget it, I'm not doing it." – "I'm not!" "Really, I'm not."

Dear reader, you do not know how I wrestled and cried, and tossed and turned, and flipped and flopped, all because of the crushing and brutally agonizing weight of this burdensome assignment. Honestly, even now, as I write about it, the tears are welling up at the sheer memory of it all. God however, would not relent; the fix was on and the assignment had been cemented in heaven's stone. "Oh God!" "All right, already; (now crying) I'll do it!" With a sigh and no more fight left in me, I said, "Ok" and "YES LORD!"

When ALL of the doubts and wrestling had FINALLY come to an end, AND I DO MEAN F-I-N-A-L-L-Y, it was forever settled in my spirit that this was something that I <u>had</u> to confront, not because <u>I wanted to but because He told me to.</u> For those who deem this book controversial, and/or feel as though I am out of order for calling leadership into accountability, I invite you to take the matter up with The Lord. Surely not everyone will agree, but God said that the situation needed to be dealt with. The ugliness of this on-going dilemma needed to be brought to the light!

Of course, throughout the book's penning, the kingdom of darkness opposed me vehemently. You can't even imagine the obstacles that arose as I forged ahead to the project's completion. From the very first legitimate "Yes", "Ok Lord, I'll do it"; right up to the final dotted "I" and crossed "T", the battle raged. Even some who were affiliated with the project began to experience an onslaught of attack. Coincidence or satanic interference, you decide.

God is faithful though. He helped me to unravel the pain of my own affliction, and He has always held my hand as I walked through my many lonely valleys. How then could I do anything less than give Him my very best? How could I not comply? Allow me to honor my God for just a moment:

God I praise You and I love You for holding my hand. Thank You for helping me to make it as You burned Your purpose deep into my soul. Together we have walked through some unfamiliar, and uncharted territory (unfamiliar to me anyway) as Thou Oh Lord proceeded to mold me into "Thine Instrument." Thank You for helping me as I cried bitter tears. Thank You for picking me up and carrying me during those times when I wanted so badly to give up. No matter how hard I tried to give in, Thou Oh God would not suffer it to be so.

You have been my guide and The Light that has illuminated my path as You taught me how to walk, guiding me through 38 years of wilderness training and walking through the fire. You have been my rock! You have held my hand as You kept me "hidden" even in the enemy's territory until the set time of my purpose. Even after that, we continued our walk – and we are yet walking! Glory to God! I am honored to have gone through the fire for Your Kingdom. Sometimes the training hurt a whole lot, as the crucible of affliction did its perfect work, burning Your purpose into my soul. But You brought me through it, and this writer sure does love YOU.

Thank you dear reader for your indulgence. But sometimes I need to take a worship or praise break as I, "Look back and wonder how I got over." God had to be "gently firm", with me. Though seemingly an oxymoron, I thoroughly understood. How can something or someone be gentle and firm at the same time? The Lord is as gentle and as meek as a Lamb, yet He is regal and stately like a fierce [Kingly] Lion. In the same manner, a fire baptized believer, can embrace the burning, blazing "Fiery Embers of God", which die not out, while simultaneously playing host, to a rushing supply of active "Living water."

From a human [earthly perspective] this would seem an impossibility to say the least. Yet, both The Fire and The Water are consistently contained in the same reservoir of God's Spirit. The Holy Ghost Fire and The Living Water co-equally and quite peacefully exist without one ever extinguishing the other. If fire is thrown into a body of water [i.e. a lit match or a torch], the fire will go out. Likewise, if a bucket of water is purposely thrown onto a blazing fire, the water will put it out and in time, even the water will evaporate into a mere vapor of nothingness. Yet a true vessel of God can contain within its bosom both elements, with each remaining alive and active. So then, The Lord God can speak both gently *and* firmly, in one simultaneous utterance. God told me -

"If you don't write it, someone else will." (End communication).

I knew that He meant business. If He got someone else to do it, then I would lose something of great value. I was not about to forfeit my own crown by purposely choosing to disobey Him, because I was afraid of *them*. *But also, I would miss my turn in the history book of life. I would have failed to make a difference and my life would not have counted as much as it could have. Beloved I say unto thee, when The Master calls upon you to do something –* **DON'T MISS <u>YOUR</u> TURN!**

Though He spoke to me in a small voice, He did so in such a firm manner, that *I immediately knew* that He was not playing but rather that The Master meant business. He was not kidding at all – and being accustomed to hearing His voice, I knew it. When The Almighty wants to get a word out, He is not ringing His hands due to a shortage of choice vessels. What He wants done is going to be accomplished whether or not *we choose to* cooperate. He has many who are more honorable, more worthy, more consecrated, more dedicated, more faithful and certainly more sanctified than I could ever be. But! He chose me, and for me not to comply would have caused my disqualification for future assignments and/or events. I determined that I would not fail Him – not this time!

Therefore, since I had been privy to so much TV and personal talk about being a "bastard" or about being part of a "bastard church", I thought that those who get such delight in calling other people names might like to hear *our* story for once. Indeed, exactly how is it that a person becomes a bastard, a rebel, a disconnected or "uncovered" Christian, a derailed derelict or a spiritual paralytic in the first place? Allow me to do the honors.

So, on behalf of the world's underdogs, by all means, let me show you exactly why it is that countless numbers of people are now walking down the dusty lonely roads of the outcast, the reject, the overlooked and dare we not forget your favorite, – *the bastard. For once in your arrogant lives, come take a walk in our world for a change…*

Humph, anybody can prophesy."   "I once had a bird that prophesied."   "You're ugly."   "You're stupid!"   "Get away from me!" "What's wrong with you???" "Will you leave me alone?"   "Look at her buck-teeth, ha ha ha."   "He has holes in his sneakers." "No, Mr. Jones, you didn't get this job, either." "Call me next month and we'll see what we can do for you" (<u>Always</u> put off). "You don't have enough experience."   "You need a degree." "You need a <u>higher</u> degree." "You make me sick!" "I'll keep you in mind for next time." (Only next time <u>never ever</u> comes).

"I mean, you can't do nothing right!" "Why can't you do something so simple?" "What the hell is wrong with you anyway?" "What's the use?" "Forget about it, you're no good!" "I don't want her on my team!" "Please don't stand next to me." "And don't sit by me either." "You are such a looser." "I really don't see how anyone puts up with you." "Do you always act this stupid?" "You're crazy." "I said now!!!" "Go away!" "Will you please get away from me?"

"We have 12 doors if you don't like it here." "This is how we do things around here, if you don't like it, then there are plenty other churches that you can go to." "Perhaps we're just a little too slow for you here." "Right, wrong or indifferent, that's just the way it is." "I don't have to ask anybody, because I just had a meeting with myself and that's the way it goes!" "All you guest pastors, stand up nice and tall so that the people can see you, just in case some of them may want to go with you" [to join your church]. "You were qualified but not selected" (Again as usual). "You're fired!" "Get out of my face!" "You whore." "You slut!" "Queer." "Just shut up your stupid mouth!" "What are you doing here?" "I don't want to play with her!" "I don't want to play with him."

"Why is your ugly a*s looking in my direction anyway? "Yuck! I don't want to sit by him." "Do I have to be her friend? "Mommy please don't make me play with her, no one else has to." "Nobody likes her because she's weird." "Did you hear about sister so and so?" "Girl – come here, let me tell you what I heard about their marriage." "You know her husband is cheating on her don't you?" "I heard that the fine brother sitting on the front row lets his wife abuse him." "Can you imagine a man getting the crap beaten out of him by a woman"?

"Are you crazy or just stupid?" "Yeah, he's nothing but a zero anyway; don't even waste your time trying to help him." "You are a retarded test tube baby, born on the wrong day of the week." "I wish you were never born at all." "You stupid little freak!" "I should have aborted your stupid little a*s when I had the chance." "I'm glad you are in your 30's and still feel as though you are nothing more than somebody's little a*s wipe." "I want you to feel like the stupid piece of s**t that [I think] you are." "You are nothing." "You can't sit here." "You can't sit there either." "Excuse me, but you are in my seat." "Excuse me; you are still in my space." "Could you please MOVE – you are always in the way!" "Nobody wants you around!"

*"YOU'RE going to do what?" "Yeah right; you, start a business, please." "In your dreams." "You want to preach The Gospel?" "He chose you – sure He did, you just keep right on believing that dear." "Why would God want to use you of all people?" "You're a looser." "God is not into bastards." "A Proverbs 31 Woman – who you?" "Don't make me laugh." "There she goes again, Ms. 500, trying to give everybody advice." "She thinks she knows every f****n thing about everything!" "Give me a break!" "God does not use women." "You're a moron." "This is my church." "Why can't you be more like the other children?" "You just ain't normal; something's wrong with you." "You know I never loved you. "I never wanted you." "You are no son of mine." "You're not my daughter." "My child is dead." "You make me sick!" "You're just like your father – plain old no good!" "You'll never amount to anything worthwhile."*

*Why can't you be like your sister?" "Are you sure you belong to this family?" "You just don't seem to fit in around here." "You're nothing like the rest of the children; I wish I had never given birth to you." "Really, I wish you were never even born." "I don't think this is the church for you." "You just don't fit; you stick out." "You're different." "Pastor doesn't like you – can't you tell by now?" "Why do you keep coming back anyway?" "Maybe you should do us as well as yourself a favor – just leave." "Give it up." "Sometimes a person is better off dead." "You're not qualified for this job either." "Things just aren't working out." "You need more experience." "You were qualified but not selected." "Why do you want to do this?" "Are you a weirdo or what?" "Why do you want to live way out there anyway? "Why can't you ever do anything, without making a f****n mess?" "Why can't you do anything right?" "WHY WHY WHY WHY WHY?"*

*"Go take a hike." "Black kids are not allowed in my yard." "You need to conform or get out." "You sing too loud." "I don't like you because you don't sing loud enough." "I'm really not sure why I don't like you, but I just don't!" "I'm not really your friend." "Why would I be? – I was just using your stupid a*s to get next to your husband; he's the one I really want." "Look how fat you are." "Who the hell do you think would want to marry your fat a*s anyway?" "That's why you're going to be a miserable b***h all by yourself!" This is a hard church to survive in." "Not everyone can make it in this church." "If you don't like it, there are plenty of other churches around." "If you want to leave, then just go because nobody really cares." "In fact, you won't even be missed." "Wow, you haven't been in church for the last 5 months?" "We hadn't even noticed." "Do you have your back tithes or your dues?" "No!?" "Then get out!"*

"I don't love you any more."   "I absolutely hate you." "In fact, I never loved you, I was only using you and your gullible behind fell for it." "I hate you!" "Get out of here - go away."   "I'm not sensing anything positive [about you] right now." "What did you say your name was again; you're not on my list [of favorites]." "You're not my type." "Everything about you is all wrong." "You sure are ugly!" "Your teeth are crooked!" "You got big rabbit teeth." "You don't even have a father." "You're a bastard." "Your parents didn't even want you." "That's why they gave you away."   "My mother says that your mother is a whore and so are you." "Your parents can't even afford to buy you a pair of sneakers." "Go f**k yourself." "You stupid b***h!" "You ain't s**t b***h! "Screw you and your mother!" "Stupid a*s!" "Oh here she comes again, she thinks she knows everything." "She makes me so sick."   "Your mother is a whore." "I suppose that would make you one too." "Slut!"

"I don't have time for you, because it's all about me now." "I can't afford no mother*****n kids! "You were never planned for." "I got pregnant by your no good daddy, and now I'm stuck with your f****n a*s." "You were an accident; a mistake!" "A freak of nature is what you are." "I never even wanted you, s**t! "What am I going to do with another mouth to feed?" "I can't get ahead because I have to take care of you, all by myself." "Why does this s**t always happen to me? I can't do anything because of you! "I can't wait for you to grow up so that you can get the hell out." "Then maybe I can get on with my own f****n life that your little stupid a*s came along and ruined."

"I can't even keep a man because of your dumb a*s! "I could have made it big, if I weren't stuck having to take care of you."   "Gigolo!" "Bastard!" "Faggot!" "Freak!" "Dyke!" "Homo!" "You little whore!" "Who's your daddy now?" "Oh, I forget you don't have one cause he didn't want you." "I guess that would make you illegitimate!" "Nobody wants to be around you." "Why don't you just go away?" "I'm glad you were raped." "I'm glad you were molested by your own grandfather." "That's why I raped you too, because you were asking for it, you little tramp." "Boy, get out of here and stop your crying, it didn't hurt that much." "I put some Vaseline on before I "did it"! "It felt mighty damn good to me; at least one of us "got off." "Go wash up before your mother gets home." "I said go! – get the hell out of my sight." (After molesting the child). "If you tell anyone about this, I'll kill you; so help me I will." "I'll even kill your stupid a*s mother." (Or father). "What an idiot your mother is, why would she leave you with me in the first place – doesn't she know that I'm sick?"

"Doesn't your dad know that I love to harm little children?" "Oh I forgot, you have no daddy – I'm playing daddy now." "I don't know why you even bother." "Try harder!" "Why do you even try at all?

"We will never accept your kind around here." "Nigger!" "Spic!" "White trash!" "Chink!" "You're not black enough." "You're not white enough." "What the hell are you anyway?" "I know, I'll just call your stupid little a*s stripe; better yet, I'll call you zebra, that's it." "Hell even that sounds too good for you." "I got it! I'll just call you "Spot", like the mixed bread and mutt animal that you are." "You are a mixed nut, a spotted mixed up dog is what you are." "Even God can't figure you out." "God doesn't even want you around." "He doesn't love you." "God would not have made you this way." "He would not have made you all mixed up like that." "You're the devils child." "You're left-handed – only satan's kids use their left hand." "God doesn't even know what the hell you are supposed to be."

"He will never forgive you for what you've done." "God hates people like you." "He all hates faggots and queers." "It should be a crime for anyone to be so ugly." "You should put a paper bag over your face." God made you so ugly – because He hates you! "Why don't you just go away and be by yourself?" "After all of this, if you dare tell anybody that I raped you, rejected you, sodomized you, pimped you, played you, wounded you, abused you, neglected you, failed you, never had time for you, didn't want to hear you, flat out ignored everything about you, bastardized you, and then turned you out like a two-bit whore; right after I robbed you of your childhood, adulthood, spiritual destiny, and even of your innocence as well as your dignity, I will kill you!" "Ya got that dumb bell?" "I WILL KILL YOU!" "So help me, I will f****n kill your stupid little useless behind!" "Is that clear? Tramp?" "Ya hear me – I'll kill you boy!" Stupid idiot! What a looser!

"What's that? Hey, yeah wait a minute; I don't have to kill you, because NOBODY is ever going to believe a word that you say anyway." "It will be your word against mine." "I am always right because nobody would ever take your word over mine, because I'm in charge." I AM THE PASTOR, I AM YOUR MOTHER, AND I AM YOUR FATHER. I AM THE BOSS AND I RUN THE F****N SHOW! I REPRESENT GOD; AND YOU, YOU'RE JUST A BASTARD! YOU ARE NOTHING! YOU ARE NO ONE AT ALL! You have a dead-end job and you ain't s**t!

"I don't have to kill you, why don't you do us all a big favor and just kill your own stupid self?" "There really isn't anything left for you around here anyway." "I've already defeated you in every way possible." "I have destroyed your character, you have no money, you can't get a promotion, you can't be elevated in ministry, because you have no blessing - and now; no one in their right mind will ever believe a trollop like you."

"The congregation you ask? "They are too busy shunning you." "I have single-handedly succeeded in making you look guilty as all hell! AND I am loving it. "You look like a stupid fool in their eyes and even in the eyes of your relatives and friends - AND it was all my doing." "It really was quite easy to carry out."

"My congregation is not exactly the brightest bunch of people to shepherd." "It amazes me that they are ALL so stupid!" "They don't even have a clue that I'm a wolf – dumb a*s sheep." No wonder I can rob them blind – after I spiritually sodomize them of course!" "What's a villain to do without his victims?" "Of course I'll never have to worry about not having any victims to wound, because the people in my church, my home, and my place of business keep providing me with plenty."

This is all too easy; will they ever get a clue? "Hell no!" "I am so convincingly conniving and they are just too damn stupid." "I've got this already sewed up. Game, set and match! I win again! "Like the idiots that they are, my dumb sheep keep right on hanging around and letting me step all over them; I am loving every single minute of it. Check mate!

PREACHERS AND PARENTS DO YOU FINALLY GET IT? IT IS YOU WHO DID NOT WANT US! IT HAS BEEN YOUR PHYSICAL, YOUR VERBAL, YOUR EMOTIONAL A-N-D YOUR PASTORAL ABUSE THAT HAS CAUSED US TO BE DISCONNECTED. WE DID NOT ASK FOR THIS TREATMENT. WE HAVE BEEN THE VICTIMS OF 'YOUR' PERVERSION! WHEN YOU REJECT US, WE GO AWAY.

It is as though you actually expect us to stay around and take your abuse. You have made it perfectly clear by your actions and by your verbal assaults, as to how you really feel about us. Yet it angers you when we refuse to stick around to keep being stepped on.

YOU THEN SAY THAT YOU HOPE TO EVANGELIZE WHAT?! THE WORLD? GIVE ME A BREAK! YOU WANT TO PREACH CHRIST'S LOVE, FIRST TO US, AND THEN YOU WANT TO SPREAD IT ABROAD?

WHAT IN THE HELL COULD YOU POSSIBLY KNOW ABOUT MY SAVIOUR JESUS CHRIST ANYWAY, WHEN YOU ARE THE ONES WHO ARE CONTINUOUSLY AND MERCILESSLY RAPING THE FLOCK TO NO END. YOU ARE THE ONES WHO NEED SOMEONE TO BRING THE 'TRUE' GOSPEL TO YOU! HOW DARE YOU CALL YOUSELFS PASTORS, LEADERS, MOTHERS OR FATHERS OF ANY KIND! GOD HAS ANIMALS THAT BEHAVE BETTER THAN YOU!

One day, as I listened to one of my favorite radio pastor/teachers, I fell silent at the conclusion of his reading. He read a letter which had been sent to a well-known columnist. The letter had been written by a high school student. Here is that letter -

"I don't care what you do with this letter; you don't even have to read it if you don't want to. But I have to write it. A lot of people wonder why anyone my age would want to commit suicide. Most of us have a decent life and it seems like a crazy thing to do. But it doesn't seem so crazy to me. I'm a guy who wishes he didn't have to get up every morning and face the day.

I'm empty, useless and tired of struggling. I feel like I'm in everybody's way and I don't think anybody would give a f**k if I disappeared from the face of the earth. I have no idea why I was born, and I don't fit in any place. I know you can't do anything about all this. But I wanted to explain it to somebody. I wanted to explain what goes through a person's mind before he pulls the trigger or swallows one too many pills.

Signed,
"A non person."

Dear pastors, this is exactly how many people who use to attend your churches have felt. Perhaps most of them have quietly slipped away, totally unnoticed as they simply stopped showing up. The majority of these people will never be missed because YOU could not care less! Pastors most of the time, you are too busy catering to the needs of those who kiss up to you; the ones who have devoted *their* lives to making sure that you are securely perched upon your own pedestal of pride.

I honestly wish I could tell you, that I myself have not felt the same way, as the young man who wrote that letter. There were times when I literally asked God to take my life. I felt as though I would rather be home with Him than to stay down here with such mean, arrogant, ignorant, snotty people. "It's really scary down here." I would say as I cried and pleaded with The Master. "Nobody likes me down here." "The children and adults call me names down here." "My pastor doesn't like me and I don't even know why." "I know that You love me." "Am I violating YOUR Scriptures, by desiring to preach YOUR Gospel?"

"Lord I really need to know, because some preachers say that You would never call a woman, while others say You would." "Some say You won't use me without approval from a man." "Father, what is Your verdict in this matter? "I'm not sure if any of them even know what they really believe, BECAUSE THEY ALL HAVE SOMETHING DIFFERENT TO SAY!" "It's all so hurtful; I'm more confused than ever, and I am tired of fighting to fit in." "I'm just tired of living on the earth realm – can you take me to Heaven, so that I can worship and not cry." "I know I can fit in up there." "Please God can I come?"

"Hey God, do you think that I could get a chance to direct Your Angelic Choir, for at least one song since I never got to do anything down here?" "This way, I would finally know what it feels like to do something meaningful with my life." "I know that I could do a good job, if only someone would give me the right opportunity." I really did not want to die, for I had not yet begun to live; but I also knew that living with The Lord *had* to be a hell of a lot better than this crap!

Had it not been for The Lord, who was on my side, I too could have easily become a dead victim. I could have viewed this rejection from my pastor, as the final straw. Feeling dejected, I could have easily taken it to heart, and just maybe, like so many others, I too would have gone home and blown my brains out! How's that pastor? How would YOU feel knowing that YOUR words of rejection were the final straw that killed me? How would YOU react, if you knew that YOUR arrogance was the very thing that helped someone, make the decision to die? I wonder if you would even care?!

Who wants to live in a world where people are so mean? I could not even be myself. Heck, I wasn't sure if I even knew myself anymore. With so many people criticizing me, I could not help but suffer from complications of low self-esteem. People often tried to compartmentalize me or define me to such a degree, that at one point I had trouble defining my own self. ***Had I ever really known myself at all?*** I often wondered why things had to be this way and if this was how my life would always be. At times, glimmers of hope would shine through. I would regain my confidence, realizing that I too was somebody, and that I could do anything that God said I could.

Times of refreshing would always come after letting out all of my sadness, anger and heartache, as God would restore me to my right frame of mind. By the time God finished counseling me, I would emerge fresh out of the throne room with renewed vigor. Once more, I would set out to discover and to accomplish. After an encounter with God The Father, I would always go my way, like a little kid singing to a constant medley playing within. On the inside, I would be skipping and dancing as I headed back into my Father's gigantic universe. I would start to say, "I think I can do this."

With my confidence and faith now brimming, I could believe in myself once more, because once more my Heavenly Father had believed in me. So, like "The little engine that could", I too would say or think to myself – "I think I can, I think I can, I think I can." No! I would declare - I do not think, but rather I know! I know I can! I can do anything that God tells me to do! Confident of my direction, once again gaining momentum as I approached my destiny, and then…

I would run into another "Amalekite" (an enemy), only to find myself broken and defeated yet again. I wish I could tell you, that these experiences happened _only before_ receiving Christ. Would to God they had ceased the moment that I accepted Jesus or immediately after receiving the baptism of The Holy Ghost. But my friends, I experienced much anguish and confusion over the years as the forces of hell and religiosity continued to rear their ugly heads in an all out attempt to devour my soul. I don't know about you, but this anointed, born again, child of God has struggled immensely. How I use to wish, that I could have had the same testimony, as those who claim to have experienced 'instant' deliverance from all that ailed them. It however became painfully clear, that a quick and easy deliverance, accompanied by a battle-free life, was simply not in the cards.

The easy way out had definitely been omitted from the blueprint of my life. Just like the high school student whose letter you read, there were times that I did not feel like getting out of my bed. I could not help but wonder what arrogance; snobbery and putdowns awaited me each day.

Some of you people, preachers, teachers, co-workers, classmates, peers, mothers, and fathers, are the ones who have made many of our lives a living hell! With your pride, neglect and scornful treatment, YOU are the ones who have caused us to turn our backs. YOU have chased us away. YOU have done this to our youth. YOU have done this to our society, and yes - many of YOU have even done this to the people in our churches. We already know about satan, but YOU are also responsible for many of the walking wounded in our world today, yet YOU refuse to take responsibility for YOUR actions.

If the average person experienced rejection in just a single environment, he or she would likely recover. However, when the same person or group of people experience hostility and/or rejection repeatedly, it becomes very difficult to cope. A lot of us have suffered at the hands of people who have made the conscious decision to abuse their authority. In many cases, people were given the brush off for so long, that they eventually became anesthetized – they got so use to being abused, that they simply laid down, rolled over and played dead. We started believing whatever we were told, when in fact we should have been asking questions. We knew that something was wrong, but yet we said nothing. We remained in places that we knew were no good for us, because we had become fossilized and could not pry ourselves loose.

It may seem a bit farfetched, that one individual [or group of people] could encounter a "cycle of abuse" and/or rejection. But even Scripture can serve as a testimony to people's conditions, as it chronicles how long some have stayed in their misery. The man at the pool of Bethesda was stuck for 38 long years. The people around him had obviously ignored him, as he claimed to have had no one to, "Put him into the water." Perhaps he had given up – as he could not even manage to put himself in. A person (or group) of people can be rejected by parental guides or even by others surrounding him or her. Then, as the person goes through the school system, he or she can again be ridiculed, rejected and buffeted by peers. Later on, say that the same group or individual finds him or her self in the house of The Lord, only to encounter more of the same treatment. If we are abused at the hands of our parents, eventually we become old enough to leave home. Also, the reality of the matter is, we really don't *have* to show up in our churches - we should but we do not HAVE TO.

Anyway...

Let us suppose though, that this same individual frequently experiences rejection at his or her place of employment. If he or she is like the average human being, such a one will likely feel trapped. It is unfortunate, but unless the person is significantly well-off, he or she is forced to remain employed. Now imagine further, that this person possesses a sense of integrity, a vast array of knowledge and a wealth of untapped potential. This *same* individual diligently works on the job for many years. All of the employee's evaluations have *always* been up to par or better. This employee may have even received awards for going beyond the scope of his/her duty's expectations. Let us see what can happen, when this same person (or group) applies for a promotion but is *constantly* turned down and denied the opportunity to advance - in some cases for years!

The employee brushes him or herself off, gets back up and tries for the next opportunity. Nope, didn't get that one either. "I'll get it next time," the individual declares, as he or she encourages him or herself. Next time comes, and still the applicant receives another notice saying, "You were qualified but not selected." *"Well, I really didn't want that one anyway"*, the person reasons. Dear reader, now imagine your own self in these same shoes. The next vacancy announcement is posted. Surely, "I'll get this one, I know I'm qualified," you say. The interview went well and you have submitted a very impressive resume. Leaving absolutely no stone unturned, you also send a "Thank you for the interview" follow up postcard.

In your gut, you just know that you've aced this one. The interview went extremely well; you know that the job is yours for sure, *right?* The interviewer really did seem to like you – honest she did. It has been at least a month now and your excitement continues to mount. Finally! You receive a notice from Human Resources. Your expectation heightens even more, as you anticipate seeing next to your name the words you have been waiting for, but instead...

As you read on, you notice that the dialog is all too familiar. You begin to tear up and your stomach balls up into knots as you read the final devastating words of the paragraph, which by now you know by heart. That old sinking feeling of disappointment sets in, because you already know the bottom line. Preparing to crumple up the paper, you hesitate and decide to read it anyway. Yet again, "You were qualified, but not selected." Because this has gone on for quite some time, by now you may even find yourself slumping into a depression. You feel as though a dagger has pierced your already wounded heart. You even find yourself becoming angry with God.

I once found myself in such a space. I knew that God had to know that I needed more money. Goodness, I mean did He intend for me to work at a dead-end job forever. Like what gives with this loop of non-advancement? Come on already! When this happened to me, I became angry about the condition of my life, and I decided to be mad at God. I did not want to speak to Him! That's it! God and I were officially through with the chitchat! *Certainly, I had no intentions of defecting to the enemy's camp,* but God and I were not going to be speaking for a while.   Yeah, right! How long do you suppose that lasted? I held out for about one day. I ended up speaking to Him before I went to bed that *same* night. Although my severed relationship with deity lasted but a day, the disappointment in other areas continued.

We, like so many other places, also have a union. Unfortunately, their hands seem to be tied when it comes to battling the real hard-core issues. They rank very highly though when it comes to hosting parties, picnics and casino bus rides (for those who attend). Nevertheless, for issues such as challenging and changing many of the unfair promotion practices, they do not seem thoroughly equipped for the task (at least not to my knowledge anyway). I mean, I hear the same complaints that I have heard for years - but still no change. Though some dedicated representatives are doing the best they can, even they can only do so much. A union can go only as far as "the powers that be" will allow them to, as they too must answer to higher-ranking officials.   So, when it comes to implementing and/or changing policies and promotional practices, in order to keep things fair and to better serve the 'employees', who are deserving of "advancement opportunities", they lack the 'real' authority necessary to get the job done.

In addition, I am sad to report, that there have been instances, wherein those who were supposedly representing the masses ("the "little people), were instead found to be conspiring with management. These type representatives have absolutely no intentions of helping, but only tell the disgruntled or discouraged employees enough to pacify them for the moment.   Like most people who have a position, but who lack authority to bring about ANY REAL [SIGNIFICANT] change, they too are great for handing out the same old tired advice – "Well, just keep applying."   "You'll get something eventually", they say.

Yeah, I know I will– *eventually, like when I retire!!!*

People are told to keep putting in for jobs and then admonished to fight when they don't get them.   Some will even suggest that the employee go back to school. With that, a worker may actually explore the option of higher learning. It is my education you agree; surely, that has to be the problem!

Therefore, off you go to get your degree. My word, some of you even went for an advanced degree; you went beyond the call. You go boy! You go girl, with your Baaaaaaaddd self! Eagerly you return with a glint of determination now filling your eyes. It is a breathtaking sight if I do say so myself. You appear confidant as you go about the business of seizing that long overdue promotion. You cannot lose this time because you are "fierce" and you are ready. You are armed and dangerous with your polite mannerism and your degree tucked securely under your belt. Surely, they will *have* to take you seriously. For now, they will have to take notice of your worth. "I *will* get the next job"! This you proclaim with a newfound sense of confidence.

One month later – "Nope didn't get that one." "Oh well, did I *really* want to leave where I am for *that?*" "I *am* rather comfortable here and the new position would have been too stressful anyway", (you psych yourself into believing). "I'll get the next one", you vow. Only this time, you are not even interviewed.   Meanwhile you attend church and hear some exciting and encouraging words. Once more, your joy and your expectation take a flying leap.

You see, at the church service, your pastor called out the word "promotion" and he even asked that the person stand up. And though <u>you</u> were the <u>only one in the entire building,</u> who stood up to cheerfully receive that word, as well as to receive the (anticipated) usual blessing that he <u>always</u> bestows; he did not make the same big deal over you that he always makes over everyone else.
He did not "stretch forth" his hands and pray over you, or bless you, like he always does over everyone else. Neither did he pray for your success like he always does for everyone else.   He refused to rejoice with you over the anticipated blessing like he always does with everyone else. Get the picture? HE DID NONE OF THE THINGS THAT HE <u>ALWAYS</u> DOES OVER, FOR OR WITH EVERYONE ELSE, BECAUSE HE DOES NOT LIKE YOU.

Unshaken by your pastor's lack of enthusiasm, you receive the word with joy, because you know that it *must finally* be your turn. I mean you have only been at your job, "like forever" without much, (if any) advancement. Gee! Lord knows you do *need something.* Therefore, you gleefully apply – again. The reply arrives on a day when you least expect it. There it sits inside your "in-box" – once again lay eyes on that old familiar envelope from Human Resources. As you open it, you are neither excited nor are you anticipating the worse. You are somewhat neutral. In fact, you are surprisingly serene. You open the envelope and casually unfold the paper. As you espy the boxes marked with an "X", immediately your eyes fall upon the words - "You were not qualified because…"

Should you even bother to continue? Does the reason even matter at this point? You read on anyhow. Next, are the words, "You did not meet the specialized experience or requirements." Hummmmm, shaking your head, you chuckle to yourself in disgusted disbelief.

They say that, "You did not [even] meet the requirements", although your skill level <u>far exceeded</u> the requirements that were listed on the vacancy announcement. Explain that one to a sister or brother! Oh well, at least you actually got interviewed this time - not like the usual routine where you may not hear anything but are just left to wonder what the heck happened to your application.

You went back to school, came to work on time and *really* applied yourself, [because you truly *wanted* a change], yet you were denied. Once again, you were passed over; overlooked, rejected, not qualified, did not quite make the cut. Regardless to how you slice the pie, it is plain and simple little darling, you did not get the job - again.

As you fold up another letter of rejection, you begin to sense that something has changed. Something seems strangely different this time. Because you have had so much experience at this, the rejection does not even faze you. It is almost as though you expected it, although not in some sick victim like mentality of expectation. No, you do not enjoy being stepped on or over looked, neither do you look forward to it or draw it to yourself. Still, somehow their decision not to select you, does not catapult you into your usual state of depression or self-defeat mode – not this time. You know that you were not selected, but neither do you seem to care.

The difference this time is that, you have already taken the experiences to your Heavenly Father. After the last time, when you thought that you just could not take the rejection any longer, you put in overtime on your knees. Each time you 'carried' your hurt and your pain to your Heavenly Father, your spiritual muscles got a real good work out. They were being developed right in the midst of your adversity and despair. You didn't even realize the change –until? In fact, you are still unclear as to when your actual transformation took place, but *you know that you have changed.* Your attitude about *everything* is different, because *you* are different.

Beloved friends of God, you must trust and believe that your Heavenly Father **<u>does</u>** have your best interest at heart. He **<u>does</u>** care for you and He **<u>does</u>** have a plan for your life. One day, I finally came to the realization that promotion, whether in or outside of the local church, was not that which would ultimately validate or elevate me.

Moreover, no longer would I allow the lack of the same to devalue me! Certainly, I would have loved a promotion, more money, prestige, recognition, friends, a pastor's blessing you know, the whole nine. But as God began to show me the bigger picture, something clicked in my heart.

My position at work, as well as any that I may have held in church, (including membership) is only temporary. My calling is so much higher. Once God shared with me, who I was to be in Him, being promoted at my job, or receiving a blessing from my pastor was no longer my primary concern. No longer did it matter to me if I received a promotion because in reality, I would be on my way to divine assignment. I would become His employee – "God's Instrument." With this realization, also came immediate liberation.

I began to set my sights on the end product. ***What did I really want to do with my life anyway?*** Was a promotion at my place of employment a part of that for which I had a burning passion? My endeavor was to work for The Lord and to become an Ambassador for His Kingdom. No longer clamoring for promotion or bemoaning the fact that I did not receive one on my job, was the easy part. But because of the continued rhetoric that bombarded the churches as well as the airwaves, things were not as simple in Christendom. *They say* we have become rebellious because after all these years, we have finally decided that we are no longer satisfied with shrinking into nothingness. We refuse to be on the losing end for all of our natural lives.

Let them call you bastards; smile when they call you a rebel. Who cares anymore what they think? This time, we have been running to The Father. They called us bastards, but God says we have a Daddy.

While they say we are not fit for their churches, or worthy of their promotions, God says we are always welcome in His presence. As His children, we have keys to HIS Kingdom. If you do what He tells you to, I can almost guarantee, that you will never ever, put a gun to your head and pull the trigger; neither will you take too many pills, for our Father Jehovah cares for you and He shall sustain you always.

This chapter has been penned in loving memory of the millions of precious children and adults who did not survive the poisonous arrows of abuse, neglect, stigmatization, and/or rejection. It has been especially written on behalf of the victims who could not write it for themselves. It is a memorial unto every single person, who at one time, dared to set foot into a church building or onto the rich soils of a society, only to discover that no one really cared.

No longer able to cope with their pain and with the emotional turmoil often associated with being raped, molested, accosted, victimized, left out, overlooked, labeled an outcast or branded a bastard, they could fight no more. And so, caving in to defeat, they gave up and made the decision, to take their own lives. If earth could speak to the grave, I would personally want them to know, that I love them, I understand, and that I will do my utmost to champion the cause and to carry on the fight for those of us who remain.

May the tears of their sorrows be wiped away and may the restless anguish of their victimized souls finally be granted rest, acceptance and joy. May they finally be free.

❧Too Many Voices❧

I continue to observe much division and unholy sanctioning in The Body of Christ. It isn't hard to understand why so many are taken back, and why others have walked away completely. If what *I* see turns *my* stomach, then I know that *God* who is altogether Holy must be thoroughly disgusted with the institutions that we are trying to pass off as "His."

We cannot even "rightly divide The Word" that we claim to have so much knowledge about, let alone, have we been living it. I further realize that many who truly want to serve The Lord "with their whole heart", have become discouraged because they cannot find anyone who can or who will tell them the absolute truth - without all of the gimmicks.

They are hungry for the counsel of God, but instead the masses continue to be fed only what the <u>theologians think and feel.</u> We are sick of the opinions of men and we want some Word! No more sideshows, please give us the food of The Word! Give us the "Children's bread" – the bread of Heaven that He left on record!!

If a person makes a sincere effort to seek counsel of God's Holy men (and women), who just happen to be divided in *their* counsel, what then is the poor seeker to do? I know that I have been the recipient of counsel that proved to be anything **but** godly. The bombarding barrage of voices can eventually become a wealth of information overload. Voices, voices everywhere, with nothing to offer but endless chatter and warped theology that stems from the depraved minds of men.

The Bible tells us that there is safety in a multitude of counselors. While I believe this to be true, still with great sorrow I must also inform you that *some people* have absolutely no business counseling anyone at all - ever! I must hear from God more than once **before** I pursue or go forth with a thing. On the average, I tend to wait until I have heard Him say the same thing *at least* 3-4 times *before* making a move (depending on the magnitude of what is at stake).

I ALWAYS want [and need] to make sure that *The Lord* is doing the speaking and the leading, regardless of the opinions and counsel of those surrounding me. I am well aware that He also reserves the right to change my course of direction or His plan of action. For this reason, I have never been one to simply plunge ahead forthwith into anything. I often wait, even if it means that I sometimes move too slowly. This may or may not be the best way to go about things, because moving too slowly can be just as costly as rushing ahead. Still, the latter seems to carry far more risks, – I say, wait until you are certain and then act.

When I do finally proceed, it seems as though, the dreaded "it" always rears its ugly head. I can be going along just fine, when suddenly, I manage to come in contact with a carnal Christian or with some cleric or "prophet wannabe", who attempts to befriend me, for the sake of giving me [unsolicited] counsel – oh boy here we go again! They obviously must see me as some spiritual guinea pig or something, because they never fail at attempting to "try out" their "prophetic counseling skills." *They don't know me like that; they had really better ask somebody!*

The subject of church affiliation always comes up. As I tell them where it is that I hold membership, we then go a little deeper. As we speak, the subject of "calling" and/or assignment from The Lord often surfaces. If I do share certain details, seemingly without a moment's hesitation the inquiring individual wants to know, "What does your pastor have to say?" "What does he think about what you want to do?" he or she queries. Once the individual discovers that my pastor has not said anything, one way or the other, the person then gives me the same old song and dance routine about how, "God would not speak to me without first consulting him." Remember, I was yet faithfully attending the place of my wounding, under the leadership of a pastor who hated me.

There I sat, and sat, and continued to sit. All the while The Lord was changing me, purging me, correcting and speaking to me. As He prepared me to go forward, I remained a faithful member but was no longer begging to be "fatherly blessed", nor "motherly mentored" by a mere human being. Even though it was quite difficult [at times], still I regarded the position of my pastor as the shepherd over the flock.

In my heart, I would secretly wish for the opportunity to share with my church family, telling them of the marvelous things that The Lord and I were experiencing together. After all, my church brags about being a family based ministry and I wanted to give my praise reports too. Often my pastor would promote those that "he had raised up." He always spoke so favorably of them, and would talk about how anointed they were. He did not hesitate to promote his son into the ministry as well as various others in whom he had a stake. I am not God, so I dare not say who is or who isn't qualified and/or anointed for what task.

However, I must say that from my observation, many of the people that he *did* elevate seemed to be weak and lacking in real power and communication with God. The majority were either his clones or other members upon whom he could constantly rely, to keep his ego stroked; and from what I saw, they never hesitated, nor had they ever failed at doing exactly that – thoroughly stroking him.

As for me, he said that, "He was all for sending out sons and daughters in the ministry but that some people just did not want to endure the process." He took the liberty to also arrogantly scoff out, "Perhaps they were just a little too slow [for me], but right, wrong or indifferent, that's just the way it is." But, *his son* however, who could not have been much older than 18 at the time, had taken only, "A mere interest in ministry." Did he in fact only have a "casual interest"; or had God called him? Ministry should never be embarked upon based solely on a whim or on some passing fad or interest. Ministry is service, not sampling.

To minister is to engage in The Lord's work. It requires extreme dedication and just like marriage, it should not be entered upon nor taken lightly. We really should know whether or not God has called us, because it does make a difference. Anyone can call himself or herself into ministry! People have even ordained themselves over the Internet, and have called themselves into POSITIONS THAT THEY HAVE "CHOSEN."

Think about it; with just a few short strokes of the computer keys, and a few clicks of the mouse, people can ordain themselves into the office of "A Master Witch" (or Warlock), "A Voodoo High Priestess" or even "A Christian Minister, Bishop, Pastor, Priest or Prophet", all in a matter of minutes, and all on the same website too. AND, they even claim to do all of this in the name of "God." The Devil is a liar! – Which god? Not the God of The Holy Bible! Certainly not in the name of The Lord Jehovah! My goodness has it really come to this??

This is only a suggestion, but if I were you, I would follow whole-heartedly after ministry, ONLY if The Lord has called you to it, and not because some pastor, or congregation or even a long lost or near relative, has pumped you up. You will be dealing with human beings who have real issues and real feelings. These precious souls will either be blessed or broken by your counsel. Do make certain that YOU have heard from God FOR YOURSELF, even if it does take Him a long time to speak to you!

Anyway, only a few months had passed since his apparent "sudden interest" in ministry, before he was sent on a mission's trip, and laying hands on people and praying for them. Not that age has anything at all to do with it (because it certainly does not), but some things take experience in walking with God. AND what about this process that his father, (my pastor) told *me* about. If waiting and "enduring the process", as he had so bluntly and haughtily stated, was to be the prerequisite to higher service in his church, then I would like to know exactly how much waiting time, had he required his son to put in? Let me answer my own question – NONE! What process did *he* "not want to endure" that his father claimed that others did not want to, [but that they had to]? What testing had he gone through for that matter? I do not see him having endured his father's process; neither did he sit through any waiting period.

Here I knew beyond a doubt, that The Lord was calling me to my set time and to my purpose, after already having gone through this long grueling process, and there I sat with my pastor's stinging words ringing in my ears.

I had already gone through <u>God's process,</u> which included man's processing of me as they pushed my face further into the dirt for years. Did you just get that? Ok great. I had not gone through some institutional learning process only, but The Almighty had processed me and now I was on the verge of being <u>birthed</u> by Him. It is not as though I just woke up one morning and said, "Gee, I think I want to be a prophetess today." Rather dear reader, this writer was now on the very cusp of witnessing a 12-year prophecy that had been hovering and was about to come to fruition.

For me, desiring to minister had not been founded upon a whim, or on some mere passing interest. Rather this was the reason for which I had come to this realm. I was born to do this! It is my destiny! Howbeit, I was still willing to be obedient and go through (endure) my pastor's process also, but he never did tell me what he desired or expected of me. Not even once had he ever explained to me what his requirements were or what his process entailed. The only thing that he did do was, very arrogantly give me the brush off. Now I ask you, should I have to abort my purpose because my pastor chose not to mentor me? Again, I will answer my own question. There was no way, that I was going to allow words that lacked validity, to cause me to miss that which God had long ago ordained.

What my pastor really wanted to say, but stopped short of was, "I don't know you, don't care to know you and I really don't want you here." "You don't fit in here, and I'd rather you leave." "You are not going to steal my show" (as if I were trying to steal anything at all). "I can't have that!" "I like the spot light too much to let you preach here."

If the truth were told, that would be very close to what he would have said, if he could have gotten away with it. Is that supposed to be my fault? Am I now to short circuit my own calling? Why aren't the knowledgeable theologians of Christendom preaching against this type of thing? It is a scenario that many find themselves in all too often. Pastoral "isims" occur more frequently than we realize.

Am I still wrong to pursue the call of God? Some say no. Yet others continue to say yes. They tell me that, "No matter what he said, he is still my pastor; he is my covering, and that I would be totally and forever out of God's order, if I failed to listen to him." This is the reason, that so many have chosen to depart from institutional places of religious worship. Some people say that if they have no [bootleg] shepherd, then they are free to fully obey God!

After much deliberation, I decided that the conflicting voices were more than I could stand. The voices of people were literally zapping my spiritual and physical energy. I have forever slammed the door on opinions and am feeling much better already. At the risk of being out of order, (and God knows my heart) I will say this.

God was speaking to me <u>long before</u> I knew my pastor and <u>long before</u> I heard of [supposedly] being at risk for becoming a "spiritual bastard." He has spoken to me and has led me by His Spirit ALWAYS (long before I ever allowed myself to listen to people). To date, I have no evidence to indicate that He has stopped communicating with me – Blessed Be His Holy Name.

He is the same yesterday, today and forever. If He spoke to me [or to anybody else for that matter] on yesterday, He can certainly speak on today and also on tomorrow – regardless to how many tomorrows I live to see. As seasoned and mature Saints of God, if you are use to walking and talking with The Lord, then *you should know* when He is speaking and when He is not. When The Holy Spirit resides in an individual, He will always lead you (if you want to be lead).

"When The Spirit of Truth comes, He will lead you and guide you into all truth." (John 16:13), better yet why not read the entire Chapter of John 16? There is not a man in hell and neither in the realm of the earth, who can take His place when it comes to guiding you and teaching you. So why are you as a seasoned believer continuing to allow others to fill your mind with so much garbage? Are you not being lead by The Holy Spirit or what??

When I realized that I would be one of the few in *that church* whose gift(s) would **never** be embraced, I had yet another talk with my Father. I also knew that I would have to give an account for my own self. He is not going to ask my pastor why I did not complete *my* assignment(s). Nor will God ask your pastor or anyone else why it is that **YOU HAVE FAILED TO OBEY HIM. WHY HAVN'T YOU DONE WHAT 'HE' TOLD YOU TO DO?** Everyone must give an account for the things that they have or have not done. There are no excuses that could possibly be acceptable, and neither will any be allowed.

As a believer in Christ, [if you do not fall away], your Salvation is secure. The Bible does however speak of rewards, as well as the loss of them. Every work shall be tried in the fire, to see what remains, 1st Corinthians 3 (Read the entire Chapter). I for one intend to go for the Gold! No wood, hay or straw for me if you please. The day is approaching, wherein many who think they have it together, will stand before King Jesus to be judged for their works, and will be in for a rude awakening. Though many things have been said and done, they have not necessarily been done with good intentions, with purity of motive, or by persons whose feet are planted upon a sure foundation. All of our works will be tossed into the fire of *His Holiness.*

Beloved of God you cannot be rewarded on a big bunch of nothing, but you will certainly be judged by it. If you have not occupied, but have instead left your work undone you will be held accountable. Please give the matter some serious thought.

There will be tears and loss of reward. I don't know how anyone else feels about the matter, but I certainly can't afford many more losses. I have had far too many on this side of grace.

On 1/18/04, while spending the night at the home of my parents, I found myself tossing and turning all through the night saying, "Just leave me alone." "Leave me alone." I blurted this out as I saw myself in a "night vision", sitting on the floor, in the dining room of my own home, with a camel colored cloak, draped over my head. Desperately trying to drawn out the voices of religiosity that had taunted and confused me, and were making a serious effort to suffocate me, I saw myself praying, as I rocked back and forth, being comforted under the wings of Jehovah. My God covered me, as I sat under His protective shelter, shutting out the world. The Lord has since instructed that I have such a cloak made - and I have. It is a physical reminder of this night vision. I pull it out whenever I need to feel the arms of The Most High wrapped around me. It is my blanket of security; symbolic of the span of His wings as they spread, shelter and engulf me, all the while protecting me from the voices of people.

At that time, I found myself wanting only to be wrapped up in Jesus. I wanted all outside interference to vacate the parameters of my mind. Indeed, I wanted the shrill, piercing and tainted voices of the fake theologians and their clones to shut up and to go away! No more voices if you please. No more carnal or psycho laden babble with manmade rules and opinions ringing in my ears. I wanted only to talk to and to hear from The Lord. It was during this same time when, as I previously shared with you, that I began uttering words I thought impossible. It was at this time that I came to the place of wanting nothing more to do with deceivers who only claimed to love God and His people.

I did not say that I wanted to turn my back on HIM, nor on those who are "the pure in heart", but I needed a break, from the "so called" false network of believers and their conflicting voices of counsel. I found myself no longer wanting to return to the local church, because I felt better at home. At least I am not rejected in my own house; neither would I be subjecting myself to a constant state of theologically based emotional confusion. I can't be a reject or be made to feel like an outcast in my own home, I reasoned.

Wow! It *had* happened to me. This was coming from someone who had grown up in church. But you know what? Even I found myself saying that I did not want to return. Why didn't I want to go back, to a place that I loved so dearly? It was because of the way in which I had been treated. Moreover, it was because of the outright defaming of God's Word that *they* so love to twist to their own advantage!

I had been hurt too many times, had witnessed too much and had given ear to too many voices and lying lips; and so I no longer wanted to be bothered. In addition, I would continuously hear the same complaints from other well-meaning Christians. Not *everyone* who has a nightmarish "my pastor" or "my church" story, has brought these things on themselves. Sin and/or rebellion could in no way, be the only cause for so many finding themselves on the road to spiritual illegitimacy.

WE 'ALL' CAN'T BE WRONG! CERTAINLY, NOT EVERY SINGLE ONE OF US COULD HAVE BEEN OUT OF ORDER. IN NO WAY COULD SO MANY, AT DIFFERENT TIMES, FROM THE SAME CHURCH, OR FROM DIFFERENT CONGREGATIONS OR EVEN DIFFERENT STATES, ALL BE IN POSSESSION OF THE SAME BASTARD SPIRIT. CERTAINLY NOT 'ALL OF US' COULD HAVE BEEN BELIGERANT TO OUR LEADERS OR DESIRIOUS OF THE SPOT LIGHT AND/OR IN A STATE OF REBELLION AS 'THEY' CLAIM. IMPOSSIBLE!

Reservations and all, still I attended church. I determined that I would stick things out but that I would also pursue whatever The Lord had for me, despite my lack of pastoral blessing.

The thought of standing before The Lord with my works undone; made my decision that much easier. I would rather be out of order with my pastor and ask for The Lord's forgiveness, than to face God with a big fat zero in my works column.   Expect the voices, realize that you will be misunderstood and in many instances even hated.   Know that if you pursue, the critics will blast you. Their voices will accuse you of not being submissive to leadership – God only knows what else they will try to pin on you. The voices inquire, "Who is your covering?" "Who has authorized you to do what you do?" "To whom are you accountable?" It took me to nearly lose my spiritual sanity, before being able to say with boldness and to proclaim to the world as well as to the church, that God is my authority.

I AM WITH HIM! GOD HAS CREATED ME. GOD HAS EQUIPPED, CALLED, ORDAINED, QUALIFIED AND AUTHORIZED ME TO DO WHATEVER HE HAS OR WILL ASSIGN TO MY HANDS. IF ANYONE HAS A PROBLEM WITH ME OR WITH ANYTHING THAT I DO, THEN I STRONGLY SUGGEST FOR THAT PERSON OR GROUP OF PEOPLE TO SPEAK WITH HIM! I DID NOT STUTTER, NEITHR DID I LEAVE ANYTHING OUT.   IF ANYONE HAPPENS TO BE LOOKING FOR THE LATEST GOSSIP, THEN BY ALL MEANS, PLEASE FEEL FREE TO GOSSIP ABOUT THAT!

Long before I knew what a covering was, God was already covering me. He has always blanketed me with Himself and with The Blood of His Son. This girl had been wrapped up, tied up, tangled up and covered, long before frail humans ever began voicing their opinions. To what extent did people of Biblical times have to plow through this jargon? Imagine, when The Lord spoke to Holy men AND WOMAN of old, what would have become of them had they succumbed to the rhetoric that many in leadership are slinging today. I am not suggesting for anyone to take some blind leap of faith, only to get out there and be beaten up or eaten alive by the wolves or by satan and his imps.

This is not a word for baby Christians; it is for those who are seasoned, mature, anointed *and* called by God for a particular task. What if Moses had checked with Jethro, his father-in-law, or with some of the other surrounding elders, whose opinions might have differed one from the other? Suppose that in their counsel, they would have prohibited him from pursuing that, which he had clearly heard The Lord speak?

Moses never would have confronted Pharaoh. When Moses received the mandate from God to go down into Egypt, he was living with his father-in-law, Jethro Priest of Midian. However, when God called him, he *told Jethro and the others* of *God's instructions to 'him.'* His father-in-law in turn, told him to go in peace. Had Jethro not wished him well, do you think that Moses would not have gone anyway? I don't read in the Scriptures where Moses was actively seeking *permission,* but rather, out of common courtesy, he was asking his father-in-law to bid him favor or blessing for his journey.

He was seeking more of a "God be with you" [my son] type blessing from the elders. How confusing it would have been, had Jethro tried to convince him not to go or if he would have tried to make Moses think that God had not really spoken. What would have happened had Jethro advised or admonished Moses to wait until [much] later, when God was telling him to "Go now"? **Saints, sometimes you just have to know and then go.** Jethro did not tell him to sit, and sit, and sit. He never tried to make Moses feel like an outcast because he HAD to leave. God Himself had commissioned Moses, as he gazed upon a bush whose fire refused to burn out. From that moment on, Moses' mission was clear. He had no choice but to obey God; his father in-law's place was to help him (if he chose to).

Later in Moses life, Jethro had the opportunity to do exactly that. He gave Moses some great advice, on how to judge matters amongst the people, [more efficiently], in order that he might preserve himself, and not wear away so easily (Exodus 18:14-23). His advice was heeded. In this instance, both parties knew their rightful place. Never is there an appropriate time, for *anyone* to hinder another, from carrying out that which The Lord has commanded. What about Noah and Abraham? Who in the world were there coverings? From whom did they seek permission as to whether or not they should build an ark, or abruptly uproot family and self? From whom did they seek permission to obey God? The Lord did not even tell Abraham exactly where he was going, but still he trusted that God would guide him, and He did.

The Amplified Bible says, that Abraham (<u>Abram</u> at the time), "Urged on [driven forward] by faith, ventured out, not knowing or even giving thought as to where it was that he was going" (Hebrews Chapter 11 verse 8 Amplified). God spoke and Abraham went. In fact, the Entire 11th Chapter is filled with God speaking, and His servants simply obeying. Oh my goodness; poor Noah, surely they railed as he went about the business of building the massive boat. Certainly, they criticized and considered him as one who had gone mad. Build an ark! For what? It had never rained before. "What was rain?"

Just think of the jeers and insults he must have endured. Without fail, the voices of doom spoke harshly as they scoffed and mocked. "In no way could *this* be from The Lord" – they said. Notwithstanding, The Bible declares of Noah, in II Peter 2:5 to have been, "A preacher of righteousness."   One Bible commentator describes him as, "The only preacher who never won a single convert." Yet Noah *was* in the direct will of God. Whether or not the people chose to listen and/or to obey was not Noah's issue. Had they listened, then they would have been saved too. The fact that they refused to do so would not be laid to his charge. ***Noah's [only] assignments were to preach and to build; not to convince people that he was telling the truth – Amen.***

Therefore, for the entire 100 years, that it took to complete the ark, he warned people of the wrath to come. At 500 years old, God instructs him to build an ark, (Genesis 5:32 [we find his age]), (Genesis 6:14 [the command to build]); and at 600 years old he, along with his family boards the massive boat, (Genesis 7:11) AND THEN, Jehovah "shut them in." (Genesis 7:16). No place in The Word of God, do we read of Noah asking anybody else anything as he built and prepared to enter. He did not concern himself with what other people thought; for The Lord was his covering and He backed Noah up. Noah and his family, were the only people in all of civilization, who were spared of the judgment.

I already know that the critics and the voices will say that Abraham and Noah were in "The Old Testament." You know how folks love to conveniently "pick and choose" what is and what isn't relevant for our times– depending on the point *they* are trying to make or attempting to debunk. I don't worry too much about critics these days. I have already mentioned these people, but just in case you did not hear their names the first time around, listen up; here they are again. I have just seven words for the critical voices:

"The Disciples, John The Baptist and Paul." They took their orders from The Lord and not from the religious leaders of their day. While they too were surrounded by voices of scholarly men, the only thing Jesus had to do was speak two of His most famous words -"FOLLOW ME." It was not a question, but it was a command.   "Follow me" - they could have chosen not to, but it would have been their loss. However, without having a conference with anyone, they dropped their nets, preached in the wilderness or fled to Arabia. They did not seek opinions, but they heeded the commands of "Follow Me" and "Go ye." Their obedience and willingness to follow The Lord, not only changed their destiny, but also the lives of everyone with whom they made contact. No one would ever be the same again.

I am sure that some of you will argue by saying that these were called, *before* the first "official" church had been established (in the book of Acts). You will probably argue that God has since set up leaders over the church – yeah, yeah, I know, I know. Would you please give me a break? For the last time, will you wake up and realize that there have <u>always</u> been religious leaders who have <u>always</u> stood in direct opposition to those who had been called of The Lord. This is not something new. While I am not in agreement with rising up in revolt against leadership, sill it must be clearly noted that God has always spoken to those whom He has called. God is eternal; (El-Olam) He is *still* speaking and calling people today.

Yet the critics retort, saying that God <u>had</u> to speak directly to the people because "church order" had not been established; and that coverings had not been placed, neither had the "five-fold" (Apostles, Prophets, Evangelists, Pastors and Teachers) been set in order. Maybe not, but have we not already seen the example of Eli the priest, and Samuel the child? Was not Eli what we consider, as being Samuel's covering? But… you are not yet convinced.

Okay, ok, so let us examine some of our coverings. Remember in The Old Testament, how Israel simply *had* to have a King like everyone else? They were not satisfied with Jehovah being their leader; oh no instead, they insisted on having a fleshly king, one that they could *see and smell like - everyone else.* They wanted a man with "skin on" who was biased and subject to the same evils and passions as they were. This is what they wanted to rule over them, instead of The Lord. Well, Jehovah complied with their wishes, and they got Saul. We all know exactly how that ended up don't we - in a mess. Remember people, you asked for this!

Never had it been God's original design for His people to be guided by a man, but only by Himself, through His Spirit, which [by the way] should be residing in <u>every</u> Believer, even now. It is He who is our ultimate guide, not a human being. The people are rejecting Him today, just as Israel did then – they are rejecting God by following men! Read the entire book of I Samuel – then tell me what you think of having a king, instead of having God.

So many today are claiming to be apostles, prophets, evangelists, pastors and teachers. We have so much covering - everywhere. Hummmm, well let's see now; if we are so thoroughly covered by all of these *people*, why then are so many of our local congregations in a mess? Why is it that so many people are hurting and are more confused than ever? Why are they leaving with broken hearts and wounded spirits? Why do we have so many theatrics but little or no power?

The hookers hang out on your steps, but refuse to go in – why is that? With five churches on one city block, tell me why are the addicts still strung out? If our "coverings" are really covering and nurturing us, why then have not more Saints been thoroughly empowered and equipped for service? They need to be "out there" engaging in the work of The Lord!

Why are we so spiritually impotent and inept? Tell me pastors because inquiring minds want to know. Explain it to us, because many of us truly need to understand.

Our supposed coverings have turned the house of God into nothing more than a freak show, designed to dazzle the crowds and to satisfy their own greed; and we dare not forget their sexual lusts, which have also been satisfied at the expense of unsuspecting followers – especially women who are either "silly", lonely or extremely gullible. Many leaders have presented themselves as covering to others but have not shielded or protected them. Instead, many of these so-called coverings have raped the very life out of them on all accounts. The masses have been damaged physically, spiritually, emotionally and financially.

Some church denominations are bombarded with *nothing but coverings.* There are so many layers of ecclesiastical leadership, that there appears to be little to no room at all for the Lordship of Jesus Christ. We have bishops and cardinals, pastors and priests and any other position that a person can think of, to round out the liturgical hierarchal parade; yet the clerics as well as the people continue to swim in a cesspool of sin, while countless others throughout Christendom vacillate between lethargy and charismatic pandemonium.

People are being "jump started" and "grand-fathered" into positions. They are making up titles, as well as bestowing the same upon themselves. They are appointing themselves to the offices of Apostle, Prophet, Evangelist, Pastor and Teacher – Lord knows what else. I have already told you how in the name of "god", people are ordaining themselves – as witches and as Christian leaders at the same time; so I guess, what the hell.

The handing down a five-fold ministry office has become almost like handing down a family business. Clergy are now bestowing upon the people, gifts as *they* will. Never mind whether or not the person is qualified; and forget about him or her being anointed. Who cares, so long as he or she is a relative, or is someone who is willing to play the game. We have formed the habit of placing people into offices or positions because they are related to us or because "we like them."

We give titles because they are our children, spouses, relatives, parents, or friends. Sometimes persons are granted positions based solely upon what they can potentially do for their leader (a future investment). And of course, we know that those who 'give the most' will be rewarded with a position of prominence. We automatically assume that people want a position - and most do. I suppose they feel a sense of importance, or that they will receive a certain amount of prestige based on their newly granted status. It seems as though pastors no longer bother to check in with The Holy Spirit to see if these people are even qualified to lead. Have they been anointed for the task?

Are they up front only because someone likes them or because they give the most money? Like in the days of old – people right now, are <u>doing that which is right in their own eyes.</u> I have told you already, not to meddle in places that you do not belong. The five-fold is not for any human being to appoint. Jehovah gives these gifts to the churches, not the pastor. Pastors, you are not qualified to appoint someone as a prophet – confirm, perhaps, but appoint, never.

It would do all leaders good to check out 1st Corinthians 12:28 to find out who it is that places these gifts into the church. It would not hurt for you to also pay Ephesians 4:11 a visit, so that you can stop fooling yourselves. God runs the show not you! Some clerics appoint people to positions, based on them claiming to "know" the individual(s). I really do hate to burst bubbles here, but how well could they possibly *know somebody* anyway? The pastor sees most people a few times a week at best. Just how well can he or she really know them? Anybody can put on a "church face" or run the church game. A person does not even have to be saved (for real), but can fool nearly an entire congregation. Anybody can pretend! You must know that even satan goes to church; at least I hope you know this by now.

When it comes to preaching and/or having a deep knowledge and understanding of The Word, there are crack addicts and sinners who can run circles around some Christians. Many of them know more about The Word than we do. I know it is the truth, because I've met a few. For that matter, how well does a congregation really know its cleric? We don't know what he or she does apart from seeing him or her behind the pulpit or around the church. A discerning person can usually smell a rat, and herein lies the crux of the problem. Most pastors do not want people around who possess a high level of discernment, especially if they appear to be a little too knowledgeable. Neither do they want people in their congregations who *truly* carry a prophetic anointing. Not even married couples can claim to know EVERY SINGLE THING ABOUT ONE ANOTHER.

Imagine sleeping in the same bed with a husband or wife for years, without ever "really" knowing him or her AT ALL! Can you say, living with someone who has been on the "D L", (in any sense of the word) only to have your spouse find out, years or perhaps even decades later, that he or she had never been as advertised? Uh oh!

Well, being that seeing is believing, let's see now, exactly how well does a congregation know its "covering" cleric? We won't have to go deep or look very far. Let us check out a few examples, shall we? How well do you suppose the unsuspecting altar boys knew their priests? You know, those very same "fathers" who prayed for them and then sodomized them. Yeah, you know, like the "covering" minister who hands out the bread and wine for Holy Communion, but right after service, he or she uses those *same "holy hands"* to unzip his pants, or lift up her dress, as he/she prepares to pounce upon and steal the innocence of somebody's little boy or little girl! Oh, my goodness and dare we not forget the prophets who claim to send people "A word from God" – *for a small fee of course.* Did I say fee? I don't know what came over me; I meant to say "seed." Seed, you know – send a seed, for a word!

How are our clerics providing a covering when in fact many of them are the ones who are hurting and swindling us? "Wolf clerics", the inquiries of the babes have gone up to The Father, and God shall soon demand that you answer Him! How many parents without even realizing it, and for years at a time, have literally turned their little-ones over to perverts each week?

Come on "fathers" and "preachers", I don't hear you calling us bastards now! Why can't you preach more about your own filthy issues and hidden agendas instead of beating us to death with your lopsided theology? I am not saying that all churches have these type problems; but I am saying that people should at least be aware that these things are happening somewhere and that God is tired of it! The entire Body is suffering because of the "wolves", the "perverted" and the "ignorant" and we are fed up!

Not every wounded person has been "physically" molested or victimized, but thousands upon thousands have been stripped of their dignity and of their ability to think for themselves. The outcry of a "bastard", a reject or a rebellious individual is not always one that stems from a desire to take over. Please do not confuse us with David's son Absalom, who literally resented his father and therefore desired to boot him out of his own [earthly] kingdom. He formed a conspiracy against David in an attempt to overthrow him.

In absolutely no way am I condoning or even suggesting conspiracy or ambush against any leader; so don't get it twisted.

I personally would have no interest in even attempting to "take" members from my pastor's church anyway. In addition, you must understand that a congregation will often possess the same characteristics or spirit as its leader. If the top reeks of arrogance, stubbornness, pride, witchcraft, control tactics, intimidation, sexual perversion, thievery, drunkenness, fornication, malice, slandering, indecency – or *whatever,* then likely so will the majority of the people who sit under that leader. By the way, did I hit your church's impediment or chief ruling demonic principality yet? Why in the name of God would I even *want* a following like that? Personally, I really don't need nor do I want the added stress of trying to re-evangelize people who are supposed to be regenerated already.

My desire [If The Lord allows] is to build a "ministry house" for those who the world and the church have deemed as misfits. I regard these people as my family, largely because I too am a misfit. I have absolutely no desire or intentions of building a ministry with all types of arrogance, hypocrisy and stupidity running ramped. No thanks! I will take a mobile tent or an "RV" any day! Besides I already told you, I am not called to be a *Pastor* (at least I hope not - God help me); I function in a different office entirely, and I am quite happy being who I am. My fiancé on the other hand, is more the loving, kind **'sweetie-pie pastor' (shepherding type), while I am "the mean one."** Although he does wield a pretty sharp (spiritual) sword himself, still he is more the gentler sort than I, (well at least sometimes he is anyway [smile]).

But honestly, lately we actually seem to interchange positions and personalities at times – wow! I mean, I can be sweet *sometimes,* gee. While I do have my very, very, very compassionate evangelistic moments, I also have an extremely low tolerance level for foolishness, hypocrisy, falsity and stupidity, for which I do not apologize. That's just the way *my mold* has been cut. If The Lord should ever call me to co-shepherd, it will be under the leadership of my soon to be husband. Right now, my business is to do *only what I am told.* I have been charged to fulfill my own purpose and not anyone else's.

Most people, who appear problematic, are often hurting on a deep level. The problem is that church folk are rarely concerned enough, to find out what is going on in the life of an individual; except of course, when they want to pry for the sake of gossiping or being nosey. Despite their tough exterior, wounded people just want to belong. They want to fit in. They want to be given a fair chance and not be judged, based on someone else's skewed opinion of them. You really do not know a person, until you know a person.

Unlike Absalom, NOT ALL OF US WANT YOUR STUFF! Pastors, we don't want your empire; but we do want what God has set aside <u>for us.</u>

Many of the un-churched have said to Jesus, "Just leave me alone, stop dogging me Lord." "I no longer want to be bothered." This they say to The Master, because "the voices" have brought them way down. I heard a preacher recently say that, "Just as The Word can (and should) be rightly divided, it can also be wrongly divided too." There are so many teaching (or attempting to teach) God's Word, who are themselves ignorant *of that very word – and in a lot of cases, they are clueless when it comes to knowing Him.*

In addition, several are attempting to teach from realms for which they have not first suffered or gained a <u>personal</u> eternal perspective. They are not necessarily familiar with the revelatory knowledge or with the responsibility that comes with that knowledge, yet they endeavor to impart it to others. At best, they can only mimic that which they have picked up along the way. They simply repeat a thing that they have heard from someone else, *who does have legal access.* They are imitators and not the genuine article. As a result, the wannabe expositors (sometimes without realizing it) cause great conflict and confuse the masses. They literally are doing more harm than good.

Dearest clergy, you really ought to "stay within the scope of your own realm," until *YOU* receive clear instruction and/or revelatory knowledge from The Lord for yourselves. Stay until God releases *you* to share *that word.* He is not going to do that, until *you* pastor, are the first to grasp hold to the truth, that comes with the responsibility of having received that same word. Stop trying to preach the same message that you heard someone else preach, just because it 'sounded good' when he or she did it. Can you stick with what God has given to you? Do not tread where you have no authority, no business and no legal "God granted" access, because you will not fit well in the atmosphere.

Warning: The stratosphere is no place for wolves, imposters and "carnal church folk!!"

I pray that no leader has it in his or her heart, to lead another astray *on purpose.* Unfortunately, some preachers are not rightly dividing anything, and some don't know how. It is a travesty, but instead of preaching The Gospel according to Jesus, they preach their own Gospel. It is imperative that every Christian study for him or her self. The Bible instructs us in II Timothy 3:15 to, "Study to shew (show) thyself approved <u>unto God</u> a workman that needeth not to be ashamed rightly dividing The Word of truth."

I pray those of you who have been responsible for the bastardization of God's babies will feel guilty enough to repent. You need to acknowledge the pain you have caused others through your words and your actions. I pray you come to understand how it feels to be rejected, criticized, oppressed and held back – it isn't right; but this is what you have done to countless others. Perhaps experiencing the same thing first hand will be the only way for you to understand the devastation that you have caused. For one moment, I hope you experience enough guilt to repent of your evil, conceit, arrogance and pomp. Repent of that which you have unleashed, which in turn has caused the physical and spiritual deaths of so many. I pray that The Holy Ghost convicts you so badly that you will never again even "think" about carrying out such deeds. God will not hold you guiltless of hurting His little ones. Jesus took great care in how He handled children.

Woe unto every unrighteous pastor! Did not Jesus say that it would be better to tie a millstone around your neck, than to offend even one of these? I know that He was referring to the small children that The Disciples were trying to keep away from Him. (I am quite aware of this fact so do not correct me). Still I am a big kid, and am running for my life. I hide under the protective covering of my Heavenly Father. My Father sees your envy and disdain towards me. He can see through your facade, right into that deranged mind and stony heart of yours. He knows that in your sick private thoughts, you have allowed yourself to become altogether perverted, and that you think ill of me. He is even aware of how the very sight of me sitting in your congregation makes you sick. I could easily say that you also make me sick! But, if I said that or if I behaved as badly as you have treated me, I would be no better or no stronger than you.

The anger of a rebel is very often, nothing more than a protective coating. Let me share with you what is deep in the heart of most rebels. Simply put, we want to be loved. We want to be valued by you. We do not like it when you to merely tolerate us, because we want to be genuinely accepted.

The only thing that we have ever wanted, was for you to love us! We wanted you to include us in the festivities, but you refused. You did not think we were good enough!

The hostility that you may notice in our actions or hear in our speech is very often a cry for help. If you do not love us and if you don't want us around, we at least need you to help us understand why – we need closure. What is so sad is the fact that many of you leaders don't even recognize when we are hurting. Why didn't you accept us? We heard you calling us bastards, and we heard you speaking all manner of ill against us, but still we did not understand.

We never understood why it was that you refused to be our fathers or mothers in the first place.

Some of you say that you are parents, but you are only willing to nurture and to mentor those who are exactly like you. You always make time for those who present no challenge. You promote only people that you can control and others who are exactly like you.

Whenever your degrading voices have screamed bastard, reject and no good; His kind, loving voice bid us to "Come."

Don't be angry with us for doing exactly that; we are going! For we are on our way to be cared for and instructed. You have only yourselves to blame, as your devastating voices have done their perfect work; they have led back to The Father.

– And truly we thank you!!!

❧Whom Are "You" Calling A Bastard?❧

Whom are you calling a bastard anyway? I am just as legitimate as you. God, who allows me to call Him Father, does not have bastards in His family. He has adopted all who dare to call on and believe in The Lord Jesus Christ. As a result, we have been granted rights as His children. We have been given the right as well as the privilege to call Him, ABBA FATHER (Galatians Chapter 4).

<u>Those who have humbly submitted to His chastening have never been in danger of bastardization.</u> That means, we are so much a part of The Father's plan that we are even as the apple of His very eye. <u>Our position is jeopardized only if we choose to permanently walk away from Him.</u> Had we defected to the enemy's camp, then perhaps THEY would be on to something. Besides our own disobedience, we have no reason to fear. Take heart little flock, for your adoption has already been made eternally secure. <u>We are never farther away from God than we ourselves choose to be.</u>

When we do not adhere to His chastening, or to His correction it is then that we are in danger of becoming bastards instead of sons [and daughters]. Why? Because what we are in essence saying and acting out is the fact that we really do not want to endure God's correction or adhere to His way of doing things. We are saying and acting as though we have no (Heavenly) Father and neither do we want one. But also, we are making a statement that says, He does not know better than we do. We shove His desire to father us right back into His face. If this is the attitude of <u>our</u> hearts, then Jehovah is more than able to oblige us, by letting us have it our way.

One of the prevailing problems throughout the ranks of Christendom is that so many leaders are trying to take on God's role as it pertains to chastising. They see themselves as fathers, which I suppose to some degree is a good thing, because many of us would value a father's input if we had one. But often they do not realize what their role is, as well as what it is not.

I've already shared with you, many of the comments I heard during my own soul-searching ordeal. "God is not into bastards." "God does not have bastard churches." "If you pursue the call of God without your pastor's permission, you will be a bastard." "Women are not supposed to teach a man – ever." I have heard it personally; I have heard it blasted on the airwaves. In addition, I have also heard a word of concern, from other people who are very confused and are worried about their own impending doom to spiritual illegitimacy. Listening to someone else's opinion and ill-fated rendering of The Word can kill you. Wrong counsel has the potential to demolish. Because of such, I almost voluntarily aborted my own destiny. I said "almost" but thanks be to God I reconsidered and He gave me a "do over."

You know something though; I can't even stay angry with *them*. As much as pastors try, they are still only human after all. They have been set in a place of authority and leadership, but sometimes because of their own ignorance and insecurities (which they often refuse to acknowledge), they accidentally (and sometimes willfully), lead us straight into a ditch. Some have been so blinded by their own success that they absolutely refuse to move over, or to pass the baton when the time comes to do so. God shall soon do a new thing, but unfortunately, the old thing does not want to budge. Like modern day Pharaohs their hearts have become altogether hardened. This new order does not necessarily want to move pastors out of the way, but rather we are trying to find *our* way.

We wish only to take *our* rightful place in God's army, along side of them. If anybody is to be *moved*, God will initiate the orchestration of that movement. Believe me when I tell you; Jehovah has absolutely no problem overthrowing any Pharaoh, who may be trying to prevent a worldwide spiritual Exodus. Sometimes the book deals, record contracts and big bright lights can blind even the most humble and sincere leader. It is easy to become accustomed to all of the attention, the roar of the crowd, and the adoration of people; I do understand. When they are at their most pride-filled moments, they speak things that have the propensity to damage or to even destroy those who are listening, and who may not know better. I am certain that most of them do not even realize the harm that they have done already. An even sadder fact is that, many do realize, but they simply do not care.

Leaders like these specialize in spitting out words of fire that burn. Unlike Holy Fire, their combustible chatter does not penetrate to the depths of a person's spirit, for the express purpose of bringing such a one to repentance. Neither does their fire burn out the dregs and dross for purification's sake.

No! Instead, they hurl out accusations and wounding words of grandeur like finely sharpened arrows that have the ability to destroy those with whom they make contact. As a result, many babes are now fearful and afraid. Thousands have dropped out of the ranks all together. They have been particularly taken back, by the blunt cutthroat manner in which leadership venom has been relentlessly executed. Some pastors have a knack for unleashing poisonous sludge without ever thinking twice about it. Pastors may have their picks and favorites, and while they *should* possess wisdom and insight, still they do not see as God sees. God sees motives, ability, and potential. In a word - He sees everything. He can see directly into the heart of every individual on this earth – man cannot do that. How then can clerics therefore assume that people are disrespecting or disregarding authoritative figures just for rebellion's sake. How can pastoral hierarchy make snap judgments and thereby render so many as illegitimate?

In many cases, they are totally oblivious to the facts; but neither do they really want to know, because they simply do not care. How do they know if someone has acted in a belligerent manner?   Since they like to discern everything, why can't they see that people might just be trying to obey the will of God?   How do they not know if whether, it is actually a leader who has run amuck and not the sheep at all? Leaders are not always blameless; it would do us all good to remember this. It is not always the sheep who are at fault, you know. Remember, it wasn't David's fault either!

Men and women [of God] have been brought to tears, as well as to a place of bitter public repentance, because The Lord <u>had</u> to deal with <u>them</u> [openly].

Pastors, who try to play the role of "Father God", are not really in a position to discipline or to correct anyone except their own biological children, and even that is temporary, because children grow up and eventually become responsible for themselves. While our pastors are supposed to, "Watch for our souls"; certainly, they cannot save them. They are not the ones to whom we must give our final account.

They however, <u>will</u> give an account for their neglect of us. Besides keeping an eye on the offering, I really don't know how much watching out they are doing anyway.   They never seem to miss an opportunity to verbally assault people, who they feel are not giving to their satisfaction.   Who (besides GOD) could ever pronounce <u>anyone</u> as illegitimate? We need not fear man, but only God.   Even Jesus said, "Fear not them which kill the body, but are not able to kill the soul: but rather fear Him which is able to destroy both body and soul in hell (Matt 10:28). It is Him we ought to fear and it is Him we are to follow. It is The Lord's opinion of us that should be etched in our minds. He alone gives life, and he alone grants everything that we need to accomplish His will.

Some theologians seem to find it difficult to remember from whence they have come. Dear pastors, not so very long ago a lot of you were standing in the same exact shoes that we are in right now. Someone to whom you were accountable may have considered you a bastard also. Did your pastors *always* recognize your calling? Did he or she *always* affirm the gifts that were inside of you? Did he or she encourage you to go forward?

Listen up female pastors, what about this? Are you bastards because of the many male clerics, who to this very day, are vehemently opposed to <u>you</u> even being in ministry? They believe that *you* are out of *your* league.   Even in 2005, many of your male counterparts feel that *you* have no place behind the pulpit. I cannot tell you of the countless materials that I have read by men (and even other women) who are in total opposition to women preaching. Some are so against it that they flat out tell you, that your <u>only</u> roles should be those pertaining to childbearing, babysitting and cooking.

How about it my smug female clerics with your unwarranted statements of ill repute? Do you also consider your own selves to be bastards by virtue of your gender, or because you desire to do a work for The Lord, which consists of a lot more than cooking and changing dirty diapers? It is downright bewildering to understand, how you can treat <u>us</u> so badly, when so many men, are saying the same exact things about you. Instead of you helping us, you are busy helping them to destroy those, who <u>just like you</u>, are only trying to walk in their purpose. What is up with that nonsense? I'm trying very hard to understand it all. Can somebody help me out here please?

Have you been sentenced to live out the rest of your years, in the land of bastardizm, rebellion, and sin because of your gender?   Had they condemned and scoffed about your calling into ministry, would it have made a difference to you? No! Because you say, that you received a word, from The Lord. So, how is it that you now, want to vaporize and zap the spirit out of us, for doing the same things that you did?

Why are you trying to disrupt our destiny and dispute our legal right of spiritual passage, by constantly referring to us as devils and as bastards? Ladies of the cloth, why are you so brazen in your acclamations as you boldly exclaim that, "The devil is a liar", when it comes to <u>us</u> hearing from God, as if you are the only ones who are supposed to hear Him? That would make you no better than your male counterparts who wish to place a chokehold and an apron on you.

Besides, we already know that "the devil" is a liar, but you are also liars, if you think, even for one moment, that you are in any way, more legitimate or any better, than the rest of us.

With all do respect Madam Cleric (and Clergy Sir); you are no more a son or daughter than I am. You are no better than any other person whom you have accosted with your verbal rubbish - and that's a fact! Recall the things that you encountered as you released your book or CD for the very first time. Think about how your very own [then] pastor and fellow congregants treated you. No! Not the pastor who <u>FINALLY</u> affirmed you and made you feel accepted, but rather think about the one under whom you served at the time. How were you treated? When you received a call from The Lord, or when God gave you an invention, a song, a dance, a book, or anything at all, what were the people's reactions and how did they receive you? How did they react to the things that you set out to accomplish?

Some of you have been spewing your attacks for so long; that you now want to make believe that you can't remember. Nevertheless, you will remember it this day – The Holy Ghost commands you to bring it up right now!!!

Think about what the *"they people"* in your life have said to you. How did it make you feel? How crushed were you? Were you told "Not yet"; "Get [back] to the end of the line" [once more]? Were you admonished to, "Go to the back of the class, and to stay there" – like maybe until… forever? I know that you had to await the timing of God.

However, I am confident, that when that time came, had anyone called you a bastard or had they tried to stop you, your spirit would have been crushed, just like those who <u>you</u> are crushing right now. I am positive had anyone, including your pastor, told you that you were never going to be anything at all, or that God had no place for you in ministry, or if he/she had compared you to "a bird", you would have done exactly what we are doing right now. You would have ignored the voices and continued to pursue that which you *knew* to be the will of God.

It is all too easy *now,* to say what you would have done *then.* Perhaps you do not want to remember, because now you are popular. There are too many people calling your name and taking your picture. Oh my, so many conferences to attend, so many autographs to sign, but so little time to remember, because your limousine awaits. Jehovah can visit you in your sleep – He has no problem making you remember every single detail! Pastors, the bottom line is this, God has led you by way of your own Red Sea in order to propel you to the various locations wherein you find yourselves right now.

I know that many of you preaching at this hour were not always confirmed or affirmed by your own leaders. If the truth were really told, a lot of you this day would have no choice but to admit, that you were not even called by God for the work that you are now doing, but rather that He has allowed you to do it anyhow.

Although you were never called, the lack thereof has not stopped your performance behind the pulpit. In addition, sadly, I must say, for an entire host of you, it is exactly that – a mere performance. You now have the audacity to wound others. You dare to do this in the name of Christ? You have some nerve!

However, to those of you whom The Lord *has* called and you know it, I beg you to never forget that it was He who has birthed you and not a mortal man. I pray that you make every effort to remember from whence you have come and how far you may still have to go. Instead of chalking everyone else up as bastards or as unworthy, why not help somebody up the ladder? Why not be honest enough to share with the masses the perils of your own journey? Why not explain to them, how it was that at one time, you also struggled with your own [then] leaders? Let us in. Share with us about how you felt when your supposed spiritual fathers refused to validate you– but God! [stepped in]. Help us! Tell us about how, even for you, it has not always been easy. Tell us how in the face of it all, you [just like us], continued to trust in The Lord - tell us; help us to understand. Your stories will help the millions of babies that God is scouting out and rounding up. For goodness sakes, can you please tell them the truth? You really should you know!

Stop condemning everyone who indeed may have a pressing assignment. Can you please stop condemning people for only trying to obey God?

Is this not the exact same thing that you also did? (If in fact, you were actually obeying God to begin with). From where the masses sit, it is very difficult to tell from whom you really received your mandate, because a lot of you reek of nothing but yourselves (or some other person). We can scarcely see any trace of HIM in you at all.

What may in fact be at the root of your dilemma is that you are not accustomed to a generation of Believers, who are insistent upon fully obeying God rather than obeying you. They probably did not teach this as you were coming up. Instead, they taught you to be people dependant, just as they once were (or still are). I know, because it is the same thing that THEY also taught me! And look what a mess that caused – BUT GOD! The difference for me is that today I am free. I am free to be who I am in The Messiah. Your constraints no longer bind or cause confliction.

Maybe you are feeling a bit uncomfortable because you have called your own selves into the ministry. It does not mean that we are doing the same thing. Could you actually be experiencing your own sense of guilt, which in turn now makes you want to tear us apart? We are supposed to be on the same side remember? We are family, and I find it quite strange, and hard to believe – no, frankly, I find it very disappointing that no one has bothered to come to our defense.

While everybody jumped on the bastard bandwagon, not even one person emerged on the scene, with enough strength, dignity or gumption, to tell the "bastards" how much they are still loved by Jehovah. Nobody bothered to tell the rejected that they still have a Father in God, even if their pastors or biological fathers did not want them.

The clerics never tell you what The Bible says in Deuteronomy 23:2, wherein The Scripture states that, "A Bastard shall not enter into the congregation even to the 10th generation." Now I know if we were still under "The Law", there probably would not be one pulpit or pew that could 'legally' [in the spiritual sense], qualify for occupancy. Nearly every church in existence would have to permanently shut down. How many families' bloodlines do you suppose would be found untainted if traced back for 10 consecutive generations? God did not want anyone who was considered "illegal" to occupy an office of such high regard, as The Levitical Priesthood. The Lineage of the priests needed to remain pure - always. So awful was the stigma of "illegitimacy", that scholars say God implemented this law, in order to deter ANY illicit and unsanctioned sexual activity as well as the intermingling of His Holy people Israel, with the heathen nations surrounding them.

In order for the lineage to remain pure throughout, there could be no births out of wedlock. There could not exist *in the entire bloodline any* unauthorized offspring, *for any reason whatsoever.* These would include births resulting from incest, rape, molestation and the like. It would include every child born because of pre-marital sex, as well as adultery. Now preachers, you tell me, just how many churches do you suppose could remain open? How many men would legally qualify to be in ministry? How many families today do you suppose would qualify to enter in and to occupy? Just how many, if traced for the span of 10 consecutive generations, would be without at least one person, who would be legally classified as a "bastard"? Remember, there only needed to be one in the entire bloodline. One lustful act of temptation, one unsanctioned/unauthorized relationship is all that it takes to produce just one illegitimate child. Some people would not have to look far at all to find such a one. As painful as it may be to admit, there are those who would only have to look at themselves.

You see, *they are (or were) the family secrete. They were/are he or she who was best kept tucked away – they are the bastard or the 'illegal' or 'illegitimate' family member. They were the "love child", born out of an affair that nobody wants to talk about. In many cases 'the rest of the siblings' (and betrayed spouse) didn't even know about or them or would try to 'explain them away' even if they did.*

<u>For all our sakes, we can be thankful that we are not under this law</u>, for grace has made the difference. Bless His Name! So then, are the physically and spiritually bastardized souls to be doomed forever? Of course not! Because of God's great love for us, even the illegitimate can rightfully call Him Father.

In the Old Testament God speaks much about widows, orphans, strangers, and the fatherless. Orphans are fatherless because in most cases their parents are dead. But people can also be orphaned if they were given away, totally abandoned or put up for adoption, even with their parents still living.

You already know that men and women who were left unwanted or unclaimed, (not vouched for) by their fathers, are 'legally' called bastards. Many of these forgotten people, for the most part, do not even know who their fathers are. Droves of people have been conceived without the sanctity of a legitimate marital union. A reject is one who is unwanted because his or her parents or very often society in general, has turned its back and has sent such an individual away.

As I see it, orphans, bastards, rejects and outcasts have pretty much the same needs. Regardless of their individual circumstances or dynamics involved, they have all been displaced. Although many may have lacked earthly parental care, these same precious souls can yet receive heavenly care. God Himself will adopt all who make their way to Him by way of His Son. Because of God's love and Jesus' shed blood, even bastards, orphans, rejects, rebels and outcasts can be met with a warm Fatherly welcome and a loving embrace.

Clerics, for your own sakes, I would advise you to revisit what God has to say about those who are fatherless. I warn you to tread carefully. Never call me a bastard again, lest Jehovah, my Heavenly Father, rise to the occasion on my behalf. If He does, I assure you, it will not be a pleasant outcome.

&Like It Or Not, Ishmael Was Also A Son&

As I grew up, I would often hear pastors say things like, "Don't settle for an Ishmael", or "Because Abraham and Sarah did not wait on The Lord, they produced an Ishmael." Even well meaning Christians would say things like, "The devil will always send you an Ishmael before God sends you your Isaac." "Ishmael did nothing but cause trouble" - they'd say.

Anyone with even a minimal amount of Biblical knowledge will likely be familiar with the story of Abraham and Sarah. Surely, by now most of you have heard the details as well as the circumstances surrounding the birth of their promised child named Isaac. God promised them that they would have an heir, a son who would be born of their own bodies. To medical science, this would be impossibility, because both Abraham and Sarah were well beyond childbearing age. Nevertheless, for those of us who serve The Almighty God, we know that there is nothing too hard for The Lord.

And so, Jehovah made a promise that they would have a son. In fact, He even told them what they were to name him. The unborn child named Isaac was the destined son of promise, with whom The Lord Himself would establish His very own covenant. Like many humans do, we often get impatient and in a hurry. It is easy for us to be excited at even the very thought, that God would make us a promise. For we know that unlike man, God who is faithful and cannot lie, keeps all of His promises. Can I get a witness anybody?

Even with this knowledge, still we tend to become anxious. We wonder *if maybe, just this one time only,* whether or not God is *really* going to come through – *for us.* We have seen Him do marvelous things for others, but will He indeed come through on *our* behalf? What if something goes wrong? Although we don't want to, still sometimes we simply can't help wondering if whether or not He will forget about us. We become anxious and start worrying. He seems to be taking just a little too long, to make good on that which He said He would do.

If too much time goes by, we may find ourselves really beginning to grow weary. At times like these, our very solid "knowing" will often turn into a "shaky maybe" or an, "I wonder if…"

Sometimes brothers and sisters just like Abraham and Sarah we also try to, "Help God out" (Thanks Bishop Weeks). We often try to hurry the process along by taking *some* sort of action. This is exactly what the beloved patriarch and his wife did. I have lived long enough to realize that people in "Bible Days" were no different than you and I are today – they were ordinary people, just like us. God used them to do extraordinary things, just like He can, and will do with us – if we obey Him.

Nearly 25 years had come and gone, since the moment of The Lord's initial promise to Abraham, until the time that He finally made good on what He had spoken. We say finally, because in our frail human minds, 25 years seems like an eternity; but to Almighty God, years are but a few short seconds. Bless His Holy Name!

However, before the child of promise was conceived, the couple had grown weary, and indeed, they *did* proceed to help God. A lot of you probably already know the story. Nevertheless, for the benefit of those who may not or for people who are new to the faith, allow me to review. Sarah being barren and well beyond childbearing age, grew impatient as she waited upon The Lord. She began thinking that maybe, just maybe, The Lord had intended for her to have this child, by some other means – like through her slave named Hagar. Sarah then requested that her husband have intercourse with Hagar in the hopes that conception would take place. Anyway, the couple proceeded with the plan that they had concocted. Through Hagar, Sarah would have her son; as Abraham *did* lay with Hagar, and soon Ishmael was born.

Abraham and Hagar were not married, so technically Ishmael would be a "bastard" in the physical sense I suppose. However though, due to the customs of their time, Ishmael (and other's born in like manner), may have been exempt from bastard status. For example, "Hurrian law provided that a barren wife might authorize her husband to obtain children by her personal slave. The slave would be raised to the status of a secondary wife, and would no longer be under the direct authority of the barren wife. The children, however, would be born "on the knees" of the barren wife (See Genesis 30:3). It would be as though they had come from her very own womb; and the offspring would legally belong to her." (Children's Ministry Resource Bible Commentary pg. 21)

Let me forewarn you, this is not is customary *in the Christian faith* for our times. I don't want to hear anything about today's **Christian men** using this passage as an example or as an excuse to justify having sex outside of his marriage. I am sure you get the point. Amen somebody? One thing that I do know is this; if in fact God did not want Ishmael here, he would never have been born.

I will not go into every single detail; you can read the rest of the story for yourselves in Genesis 16 and 17. You will discover that with Isaac and Ishmael as well as Hagar and Sarah, all living together, friction and strife were the order of the day in the Abrahamic household. As you read on, you will also discover the final incident, which prompted Sarah to have Ishmael and his mother Hagar sent away. The point that I really want to make is this. It has been said by many a theologians that because of The Patriarch's impatience, these two nations have been at war ever since. Whether or not this is or isn't the exact [or the only] cause of their constant feuding, I wish only to call your attention to one point, and it is this. People say that Abraham produced "An Ishmael" as if Ishmael were a piece of rubbish or as though he were someone of little to no significance or value.

While I understand *in principal* why they say what they do, still a little sensitivity is in order. Pastors should be extremely careful and tread very lightly when they make comments concerning these two nations, as well as when they make comments about people in general. **What they say may sound just fine, if you are not an "Ishmael."** What the theologians <u>are trying</u> to emphasize is that, when we are impatient and when we do not wait on The Lord to do things His way, we may end up with something or with someone that may not be in our very best interest. We may inherit something, which totally pales in comparison to the thing, the job, the spouse, the ministry, or even to the life that God had originally prepared especially for us. The situations that we get ourselves into may not be best for us and as a result, we may end up with more trouble on our hands than we could have possibly imagined.

A person can end up with something born of the flesh and not out of a right committed relationship or set of circumstances. Many women (particularly in their younger years) who found themselves desirous of marriage, went rushing ahead of God. In many instances, they did not consult with Him at all. In addition, even when they had, and His reply happened to have been, "No!" or "Wait!"; they *made as if* they hadn't heard what they know they did. Unfortunately, they ended up with a raving lunatic instead of a loving, nurturing husband (or wife). Who's been there? Me! Me! Throw your hands up if this has happened to you. The message is clear; we should <u>always</u> wait on The Lord, no matter how long He takes to fulfill His promise(s). According to The Bible, Jehovah stated that His Covenant "Would indeed be established with Isaac." However, in saying this, it did not mean that *The Lord was implying* that Ishmael was unimportant or that he was any less loved. Many people in our world have found themselves in Ishmael's same shoes, and are daily forced to walk therein.

Perhaps they were not the loved daughters or the "promised sons." So what now is to be their portion? If you have never stood in the shoes of such a one, then you could not possibly know what it feels like to be an Ishmael! When Ishmael and his mother were sent away, God also said to Abraham that He (God) had heard him (Abraham's prayer/request) concerning the child.

God knew that Abraham loved his son Ishmael. The fact that Sarah was not his (biological) birth mother did not make him any less of a son to Abraham. For his seed had made a deposit, regardless to whose womb served as the incubator – Abraham's blood is that which ran through Ishmael's veins. When Hagar initially ran away of her own volition, The Lord became so concerned that He sent His angel after her. For God gave Ishmael his name even before his birth (as He often would name people). The Angel of The Lord told Hagar, what she was to call him, as well as what would become of him.

She was then told to return to Sarah and to submit herself. However when the <u>set time</u> for the transference of the covenant came, at the urging of Sarah, it indeed was a time for Ishmael and for his mother to be sent away. As Hagar and Ishmael Journeyed, Jehovah provided the water that it took to sustain both she and the lad at a time wherein she had seemingly come to the end of her rope. Ishmael could not die yet, for God had already promised Abraham [and Hagar] that, "He would make of him a great nation." The Lord God promised to, "Make Ishmael fruitful" and to, "Multiply him exceedingly." "12 Princes would be born of him." These were the words of The Lord God Jehovah, who never ever reneges on a promise. Bless His Holy Name!

Now, for all of the people, who still feel as though Ishmael was "a terrible mistake", and that he symbolized "nothing but trouble", (because he was to be a "wild man" and had been "born of the flesh"). I want you to realize that if God did not want him to come forth, He could have spoken from the heavens, and prevented the entire conception. He could have closed up the womb of the Egyptian slave girl. The Lord could have even taken the life of Ishmael immediately after his birth.

Unlike the adulterous affair of David and Bathsheba, that resulted in the birth of a child, which The Lord God did not suffer to live, He instead spared the life of Ishmael. Jehovah could have easily destroyed him, whether in or outside of his mother's womb; but He blessed him instead - AND abundantly at that.

While it is true that Abraham and Sarah made a grave error in going ahead of God, yet Jehovah blessed the child. He blessed him because of His covenant and relationship with Abraham his father, whom He had promised would become, "The father of many nations."   But also, The Lord spared Ishmael, simply because He had a plan for Ishmael's life. I suspect that Abraham's position as, "The Friend of God", as well as his prayers, may have also played a part in The Lord's decision. Abraham's intercession and concern for Ishmael makes this story even more endearing. You see he could have been just like so many other men [who call themselves fathers].

Abraham, like many other men, could have chosen not to care at all. To begin with, Ishmael was the son of a bondwoman – a mere slave girl. By the time, she and the lad were sent away, Isaac the son of promise had already been born.   Abraham was very wealthy, and he really had nothing to lose. He even had The Lord God on his side, who had already blessed him abundantly with material things and also with favor. It really would have been quite easy for him to simply turn his back, never showing a bit of concern for Ishmael's welfare. However, Abraham, Ishmael's dad, cared enough that he took the time to pray for him. Abraham beseeched The Lord on Ishmael's behalf. The Lord heard him and He abundantly blessed the offspring of the Egyptian slave and the Hebrew patriarch!

Jehovah blessed the illegitimate one; the son of a bondwoman!

__AND, at the end of Abraham's life, The Bible clearly states that both Isaac and Ishmael, "Abraham's two sons" buried their father together.__ Whether or not people accept it, the fact was then, and remains, even to this very day; Ishmael and Isaac were brothers. They were of the same father and were blessed by the same God.   Therefore, so shall their decedents forever share that same common bond. Why indeed must the feuding continue? Why must they allow others to "divide and conquer" them – (or make them conquer their own selves through bloodshed). Why must they constantly be at odds with one another)?   The Lord loved Ishmael and He also loved Isaac. Each had the protection, love and blessing of their earthly father as well as the protection love and blessing of their Heavenly Father.

No matter how we see it, and even if we choose never to see or to embrace the truth, the fact still remains that these two boys were brothers and that Abraham was the father of them BOTH. ABRAHAM WAS THE FATHER OF MANY NATIONS AND WE CANNOT CHANGE THAT, NOR SHOULD WE WANT TO AND NEITHER SHOULD WE EVEN BE TRYING TO! THIS WAS GOD'S DOING, NOT OURS!

You may be asking yourselves, "How much indeed did The Lord really love Ishmael"? Well, you need only to think of him each time you pull up to a gas station, or whenever you fill your furnace with heating oil. That my friend should give you a ripe indication as to how much Ishmael was loved and provided for by The Lord Jehovah.

Be extremely careful when slinging your insults. For those of you who have not figured it out yet, there is a new breed of Ishmaels in town. They have come forth to represent the sons and daughters who have been sent away by man but who have yet been embraced and mightily blessed, of The Lord. We are they who may never receive validation from our earthly nor spiritual fathers, but our Heavenly Father has divinely kissed each of our faces and has called us His very own. And even though nobody [else] may want us around or feel as though we deserve to be here, allow me to inform you, that we are still divinely blessed by YAHWEH (YHWH).

I must further inform you, that Jehovah loves all Isaacs and all Ishmaels. You, who have stamped us as unworthy, need to know that God is just as concerned about us, as He is about you. He has enough power and He owns enough land to give us our inheritance also. He has room for all of His children, even the ones that *you* have sent away. Thousands of babies are born each day. The fact that many of them are not wanted nor loved by human beings, does not mean that God loves them any less.

News flash: The fact that they are not welcome does not prevent them from being born. They are going to show up whether people like, and/or accept them or not. They have just as much right to be here as everyone else. Please be informed that we are also here and we are not going anywhere. Whether or not you have been preparing for our arrival, is not our affair, but it is yours to deal with. May you be further informed that, with or without your blessing, we will be taking our rightful place and position in His plan.

You may as well get use to seeing our faces, because we are here; and we shall not be moved. We are not going away; but we will be here for as long as God wants us to be.

❧Stuck In The Middle❧

Once *we finally* realize that we *are* valuable human beings, it is then that we attempt to live our lives as emotionally healthy individuals. We have had a change of heart as well as a paradigm shift. Suddenly we see things in a completely new light and from a much healthier perspective. Our self-esteem has been awakened and we realize that we *are* worth the effort after all; if not to anyone else, then certainly to ourselves. We owe it to our own selves to advance in the areas of our professional, personal and [for some of us] even in our spiritual lives. It is our turn to be all that we can, and we will not be denied.

We have had a startling realization that we too want more out of life. We have been blessed with great potential and we are capable of doing marvelous things indeed. At least now, we actually *believe* that we are here, because The Creator has seen fit for it to be so. Many of us have been endowed with creative abilities. Could it be that we also have a song to sing or a story to tell? Who says that we cannot write a book or perhaps even a screenplay? Our imagination and potential says that for us, "The sky is the limit." It is as though our eyes have come open for the very first time. Suddenly aware, we must cope with the reality of knowing, that we have been "stuck", for a very long time. As a result of our slumber, we have missed out on much that life has to offer.

Revelation often comes at a moment in which we least expect. It is as though a switch is suddenly flipped to the "on" position, and our power becomes instantly illuminated and begins to radiate, allowing us to see everything more clearly. For light has been shed – and now thank God, finally we can see. As we search for answers about one thing, we may actually discover a veil being lifted concerning another. Suddenly we make a connection between the two that heretofore we had never noticed.

One day as I engaged in conversation with a client, we were briefly discussing the ordeal of my pastoral situation. We were also comparing the hiring and promotional practices of various companies and organizations throughout several cities and states. The client and I discussed in general how similar many institutions are when it comes to their policies and procedures. Like any place of business, there will always be people in charge, who are at the top and who are paid the highest wages. Looking from the outside, it appears as though their futures are secure. They seem to have no major financial concerns.

For the most part, these people strut around wielding their power as they run things and attempt to keep the rest of us "in check." If they themselves are not at the very top, then quite often they are not far from it. In the same institutions are people whose place appears to be at the very bottom. These are the people who most high-ranking officials classify as employees, "Who seem to be going nowhere." These people are often treated with near disregard by the haughty upper crust. I say <u>near disregard,</u> because if the higher ups did not on occasion absolutely *have* to interact with the lowly, many would not speak to them at all. The majority of higher-ranking officials tend to view those at the bottom as lazy, apathetic employees who lack ambition and motivation. As a result, they are often treated in a condescending and degrading manor. They are considered valuable, only if the institution as a whole finds itself in a crisis. You know how it goes, whenever trouble strikes, it is then that the "nobodies" are suddenly invited to participate. It is when trouble strikes that, "Everybody is needed; and suddenly, everyone is part of the team." Once the crisis is over though, the commoners are ordered back into the dungeon where they belong. They are immediately reminded of their status in the organization – back to the bottom they must go.

I have seen people who have been content to abide in their dead end jobs for 30 years or more, before finally retiring. In all those years, many had never made even the slightest attempt to advance. Upper management tends to view such people as lacking and lazy. As a result, they usually play out through their actions, the opinions that they have already formed in their minds about an individual or a group.

Prejudice (of any kind) is not easily concealed. Regardless to how hard people try to hide it, (or think that they are hiding it), their true feelings will manifest in one way or another.

People at the bottom are often treated with little to no respect. Higher ranking officials, tend to judge others based solely on their positions. Never even looking beyond a person's *employed status,* they fail to realize that a huge percentage of the very people who are looked down upon, and who are although laden with menial job titles, more often than not, actually possess a great wealth of knowledge and/or creative ability. How many times have you heard people referring to others as, "He's just a…"(Fill in the blank) Or, "Oh she's not important – she's just a…" The "just a" title often refers to a menial position of some sort (menial or unimportant according to the haughty folks). People who hold positions such as file clerks, secretaries, maintenance personnel or fast food attendants (as well as a host of others), are often seen as a "he's/she's just a." In our society people who hold certain positions are viewed as being "just a" – nobody. They are deemed as unimportant and unknowledgeable, by virtue of nothing more but by the position they occupy.

WHEN WILL WE STOP JUDGING OTHERS FROM THE OUTSIDE AND REALIZE THAT - ***PEOPLE ARE NOT THEIR POSITIONS!*** I, AS A HUMAN BEING, AM NOT <u>WHAT</u> I DO FOR A LIVING! FURTHERMORE, <u>GIVEN</u> <u>THE</u> <u>RIGHT</u> <u>ENVIORNMENT</u> <u>AND</u> <u>THE</u> <u>SAME</u> <u>OPPORTUNITY</u>, I COULD RUN CIRCLES AROUND MOST OF THE PEOPLE WHO TRY TO OPPRESS ME – YES! BELIEVE THAT!!

It is not uncommon to discover that some vagabonds, who have graced city streets, have turned out to be millionaires in disguise. Never measure a person's value or worth merely by the task that he or she carries out, or by that which can only be seen through the natural eye. Don't be fooled. Remember, Jesus humbled Himself and came in the form of a servant, BY CHOICE but He was still a king! Although not everyone *wants* to be where he or she is, still [for some reason] a great many seem complacently satisfied; which of course plays right into the hands of the haughty executives, who take pride in seeing that those beneath them stay exactly there – at the bottom. Likewise, in every organization there exists another group that is seemingly stuck or "sandwiched" directly in the middle. While they receive somewhat more respect than their lower counterparts do, still they are unable to excel.

Even if people in the middle desire to advance, they often encounter those ahead of them, who will (for whatever reason) vehemently try to block their success. I don't know why people do this. Some people simply cannot stand to see others get ahead. They are constantly on the look out for the "up and coming", for the express purpose of extending a foot. Those in the middle are called lazy if they appear not to be trying hard enough, yet they are pushed backwards if the upper crust notices them trying [too] hard.

Sometimes a person will get a break, and with solid determination, he or she manages to push on. In rare instances, a mid-level employee is fortunate enough to gain the attention, respect and even the assistance of a much higher-ranking official. But, in no wise will this stop the haters who are just waiting to scoff and fault-find. Sometimes their plots of discouragement work all too well, thus sending the newcomer right back down the ladder. The middle person cannot help but aspire to be like those on top, while simultaneously trying desperately not to slip to the very bottom.

They refuse to take a step backwards, but they appear unable to move forward. Hence, "stuck in the middle" is very often, where they find themselves. Often the majority, this group accounts for the highest number of workforce laborers, yet they are at the mercy of *everyone*. Can I get a witness anybody? The higher ups keep them from excelling; as those at the bottom, perceive them to be an enemy or threat – consequently both parties despise the middle population.

Although the stuck party is not at the very top, he or she is still higher than those at the [very] bottom. Such an individual (or group) is targeted as the one to hate, which makes the middle ground a very lonely place to be. It is particularly frustrating if such a one, seemingly has no apparent means of escape. It is here, where many are literally forced into playing the game of "too much" or "not enough." They lack the necessary influence, experience or connections needed to successfully ascend towards the big boys and girls; but also, he or she possesses entirely too much drive, ambition, potential and motivation to keep settling for so much less. We have all heard this line – "You don't have enough experience." Alternatively, you will them say - "You have too much experience." Give me a break; if a person has *no* job at all, then surely the individual would be happy to have *something;* even if he or she is overly qualified.

Unfortunately, someone in this predicament, desperately needing employment, is instead rejected on both ends. He/she may go on without promotion or remain totally unemployed for a long time to come (depending on the situation). Regardless to how it plays out, no matter the scenario, the word for such a one is - S-T-U-C-K! Staying stuck is not confined to the business setting. Politics and circumstances have literally forced society to take even more notice, of this "tri" level way of existence. Even if a person in the middle happens to make society's version of a decent salary, the individual may still be unable to live free of financial worry. People in this group often see their circumstances as an inescapable reality each month as their bills are due.

Like millions in the middle, I too have found my own self in need of assistance. The few times that I have applied for help, i.e. home heating or home evaluation programs, I have always been turned down. Being refused the same services, that other people receive free of charge and on a regular basis, has given me no choice but to examine my own situation. For the most part, I have always received a flat out– "No!" "No we can't help you." "You don't qualify." "Your income far exceeds the limit of our program's allowance." Give me a break! As prices continue to skyrocket, I have become acutely aware of the dilemma of being in the middle and stuck! Juggling finances as attempts are made to make ends meet each month can be quite a challenge. I wish I could tell you something different, but it has been my own personal experiences that have deemed it necessary for me to examine and to acknowledge this truth. We live in a "land of plenty", except for many people, the "plenteous part", seems always to pass them by. I am a child of God, and still I struggle. Thank goodness, that The Lord has always provided. Nevertheless, if you will permit me to be perfectly frank, I would have to admit that there have been times, when the provision has come just before the stroke of midnight - if you know what I mean.

This may not be what some leaders would want me to share, but can I just keep it real please? I am sick of the pretence! Although unfortunate, but for the vast majority, struggling has been their *only* reality.

I never said that God did not provide, but often *our situations* have been a lot bleaker than those who were constantly barking out commands, about how we (not them), but about how *we should be giving.* They always condemn us when it comes to not giving enough, but offer little to nothing else - like telling us how it is *that we are supposed to pay our own bills. Their bills, on the other hand are paid (and on time) – believe that! I know all about faith and I do have faith in God. But life (and having faith) can be a lot more difficult for those who have less than what they need [to meet expenses], than for those who have more than enough!* With the exorbitant salaries that a lot of *them* receive, perhaps *they are* exempt from these problems, unlike the rest of us. I mean if a person is fortunate enough to be the recipient of hefty love offerings on a regular basis, in conjunction with that which can be skimmed from the collection plates, then I suppose that *they would not* have any major financial concerns. *They can rest easy when it comes to paying their bill, providing for their families and then some.* If I received as much as some of them, I would not have to worry either. Likewise, if I had a convenient till at my disposal, in which I could dip my hand, as often as I pleased, (at the expense of others who cannot even afford food to eat, because I am the leader and can do that), then I too would be living the leisurely life of Riley. And the church said – I know that's right! I had better leave this alone, because then I would be forced to write an entirely different book.

And no, I'm not "hating!" I'm simply saying, what I'm saying and nothing more. When I attended college, I couldn't get financial aid. There were no handouts for *me.* I had to pay my own tuition semester by semester *and then, take out a loan.* Those were my only options. I never qualify for any of the services that those in a lower income level are afforded, such as free food, dental care, home weatherization services and the like. I need help too! - And neither does it necessarily have to be monetary. There are many service-based programs that could be of great benefit, yet for those in the middle, these programs are off limits. We seem to have the hardest way to go. Very often, we must budget extremely carefully. *I for one would love to pay all of my bills on time each month.* I would love to do this without worrying about what I would do if something were to suddenly break down. I wish the dreaded checkbook balancing were not *always* an issue. Each year everything goes up, with the exception of my paycheck of course. Well, that isn't exactly the truth; I stand corrected. My salary *does* go up, but often by a measly 2.8%. If I'm real lucky, I may even get a whopping 4% (gee).

WHATEVER IT IS, IT DOES NOT HELP VERY MUCH, BECAUSE <u>ALL</u> OF MY OTHER BILLS ALSO INCREASE; <u>AND THEY DO SO AT A MUCH GREATER RATE</u> THAN THE "COST OF LIVING" RAISE THAT SHOULD BE HELPING TO DEFRAY THESE EXORBITANT INCREASES. THIS RAISE IS DESIGNED TO [HELP] RECTIFY THE SITUATION, BUT THE ALLOTTED AMOUNT IS SIMPLY NOT IN ACCORD WITH OUR CHANGING TIMES. WE NEED A LOT MORE TO LIVE ON THAN OUR PAY RASES HANDLE. HAVE YOU SEEN THE PRICE OF GAS LATELY? WHO CAN EVEN AFFORD TO DRIVE AT ALL – LET ALONE HANDLE A LENGTHY DAILY COMMUTE?? A RAISE WILL ONLY HELP THE MASSES CATCH UP, IF NOTHING ELSE GOES UP; AND WE ALL KNOW THAT ISN'T LIKELY TO HAPPEN.

Don't get me wrong, while I am very grateful to have my job; and I don't want to sound as though I am unappreciative or like I'm "complaining", but *I am* speaking the truth. I do not have the luxury of escaping to a secluded hilltop hideaway. Nor do I have the option of selling my assets; such as a yacht, or one of my many homes or extra automobiles, should things get too financially devastating. I am too busy trying to pay for the one home and for the one automobile that I do have. I don't know about you beloved, but with the acceptation of one time only, I have <u>never</u> had the pleasure of benefiting from any one of the thousands of free programs, that are (supposed to be) designed to aid those in need; many of which by the way, are paid for and kept afloat because of MY tax dollars.

I am forced to pay my taxes so that <u>everyone else</u> can get these services for free. Some people receive them for a lifetime; while I cannot even qualify for temporary assistance should I need it. Again, can somebody out there help me, "cause" I just don't seem to understand? Maybe I have an impediment of some sort that just does not allow me to "get it" – because I don't.

I would love to understand how decisions are made, when it comes to the distribution of funds to these programs. I mean, who determines how much goes where, why and for how long? Like can we rotate or something? I mean, like are the people making these decisions serious or what? Do I have to be sleeping on a park bench before I qualify for SOMETHING? While I am not looking for a "hand out", it would sure help if on occasion, I could also receive a helping hand should I have need of one! How does sending a spaceship into Mars, benefit those of us who are in need right here on earth? I do understand that many of the programs are designed for the purpose of research and experimental endeavors.

Still, I cannot see how the goings on in outer space, can possibly compare to people starving to death and sleeping in the gutters on this realm. We cannot even afford decent health care (without going broke trying to pay for it). Neither can we afford decent housing, and forget about extensive dental work. Unless you are fortunate enough to make it onto a reality show doing makeovers, you can forget about having a "Hollywood smile."

People are living on city streets in abject poverty, while the authorities, are more concerned with the living conditions of another planet. Moreover, there seemingly is no problem [or lack of funding], when it comes to providing for everyone around the globe, but yet the needs of the people in *our own country* [constantly] go unmet. What is *that* all about?! There does not seem to be a voice crying out for those who are stuck. I don't mind sending aid out, but can we also leave some in? AND if there is some here, can the middle folks get some of it too?? I mean like, can there at least be a FAIR ROTATION of the funds?

To add insult to injury, it is as though our leaders actually become confused, bewildered and even angry if the masses verbalize their frustrations, (*as if they are speaking something that isn't the truth*). It almost seems as though they actually enjoy seeing us stuck, and in a perpetual state of lack. People who do voice their opinions are often scolded and labeled as troublemakers. Or they are asked, "Why don't you just find something else?" Get another job making more money instead of complaining", the haughty ill-informed, financially secure crowd scoffs. Sure, we could do that – yeah, right! That may be easy to *say*, but have you seen the unemployment rate? In addition, the majority of people that I know have at one time or another had serious issues with their credit for a variety of reasons.

Most companies now run credit checks when people apply for jobs, apartments and the like. Even if the position for which a person applies has absolutely nothing to do with the handling of money, his or her credit score will still [very often] be the determining factor as to whether or not he/she is hired. An individual with unresolved credit issues will even have difficulty finding somewhere to live! How then shall such a one ever begin to pull him or her self up by the bootstraps, if *no one* is willing to give the person a chance. Unless God supernaturally opens a door, it seems as though some people, are almost guaranteed to remain stuck – wow! Moreover, with so many jobs being geared towards the 'technologically sophisticated', many who do seek advancement will likely remain stuck, unless they can afford the costly investment of pursuing higher education, to acquire the necessary skill.

***Seeing, [and or keeping] people in a "stuck status", somehow
seems to make the higher ups feel superior. From their viewpoint, the
masses [seem to] serve best if they are kept in the lowly positions of
begging and groveling.***

By now, I'm sure you must be wondering, what in the world does *any of
this* have to do with the church or with bastardism? I'm glad you asked. In every
house of worship, there *also* exists three levels of people. So as it is in the
natural so is it also in the spirit. First off, are the *newly* converted folk. These
precious souls arrive on the scene with great expectations. They are optimistic
and anticipate finding happiness, acceptance and a sense of belonging, as they
bond with their new church family. Enter in are these bright-eyed, bushy-tailed
newcomers, who just love "everybody, everybody, everybody. With their eyes
aglow, they see their pastor as one who can do absolutely no wrong. While
these are newly converted followers of Jesus and the Christian faith, others have
already formed a relationship with Him, but are new only to a particular
congregation.

Remember the client to whom I was speaking (way back there, about
10 pages ago [smile])? Well, he told me that if I looked closely, I would be able
to see the same bureaucracy and unfair practices of the business arena, also
operating throughout the church. To me, his comment was like a light suddenly
being turned on. I know this may not be rocket science, *but* the client's
statement helped me to make a serious connection. Of a truth and much to my
chagrin, he had hit the nail right on the head. In an instant, this writer had
become acutely aware, and was able to verify his every word. Indeed, the same
worldly, non-ethical practices are alive and well in the House of God. Heretofore
there had been no illumination of this very painful fact; but suddenly I began to
see with clarity.

Dear reader, *your* church may not be an exception. Perhaps you
already knew this and are saying "duhhhhhhh so what!" "What church *hasn't
been unethical in its wheeling and dealings*?" This may not be enlightening to
you, but for me, it was shocking and very informative to say the least. It really
did take me back, because frankly, I had never thought of comparing the two.
My place of employment was not *supposed* to be anything like the church; at
least *I* didn't think so anyway.

The very mention of the two, in the same breath, seemed somewhat of
an anathema. One was *secular,* the other *sacred.* One worldly, with an
"anything goes", cut throat mentality, while the other was set apart and sanctified
unto The Lord. In my eyes, there were no comparisons to be made, as they
were worlds apart. What could they possibly have in common?

Quite honestly, I had never thought of them as being similar. To do so, would have forced me to acknowledge the entity, that we call *"church"*, as being nothing more than an institution, where people assemble to conduct *"business" as usual,* and not *necessarily* the business of winning souls. Never had I thought to compare political practices with spirituality; not the secular with the sanctified, this was simply unheard of – I thought. Perhaps I am simply behind the times or something; I don't know.

Sure, I have heard of pastors who were guilty of swindling congregations, but I thought that those were <u>only the bad ones.</u> Never had I considered shady politics and worldly methods as being commonplace in "God's House." For in my mind, the two simply were never supposed to mix. However, having had a sudden epiphany, I could at long last see <u>everything</u> for what it was. For the first time, this startling realization forced me to acknowledge the painful truth. Indeed, the same hype and cutthroat activity "out there" does in fact, run ramped throughout Christendom – may God help us all. The client was absolutely right, (Thanks Mr. C.S.).

Some lessons will never stick save *you* experience them first hand, and that I did. Though we listen to other people's stories, there is nothing like experiencing something for one's self. I *had* to see, feel, walk and taste the gut wrenching emotions of church let down, pastoral neglect and church politicking, first hand. Once you learn and come through a lesson of significance, (and though this may sound a bit strange), you actually gain an appreciation for *the pain* that it took to take you through. A person can only appreciate such a lesson after emerging from his/her own "place of pain."

Never again would you ever want to repeat those very hurtful lessons, but what you have learned has been of such great value, that you would not trade the experience for anything in the world. It is similar to when a mother gives birth. Bringing a child into the world, can be extremely painful, but once the birthing process is over, the mother happily emerges with a wonderful new baby to care for. Love, is a force that one "learns to respect." It can either take you higher, or it can break you all the way down. You are not giving it *respect* because of the devastating affects that it can have on you (if you have ever experienced abuse), but rather we must give it credit for being so darn powerful. Love, just like wisdom, commands that we sit up and take notice. There is an unexplainable power behind its force, as well as a force behind its power.

I once read a book called, "Something More." In one passage, the author stated that, "Even bad men bring good gifts." Wow! This can be rephrased to say, "Even bad men, women, pastors or any negative person and/or experience that you will ever encounter, [or that takes a serious toll on you], has the ability to bring "a good gift" – a valuable life changing lesson. There were certain things that I had to go through, in order to come through, so that I would be able to help others. Even though, you and I may not like many of the things that have befallen us, certainly we will be stronger, if we are wise enough to glean from the valuable lessons they have left [or will leave] behind.

Had I known then, about some of the trials, associated with my *"making"* [no doubt], I too would have been just like Jonah, and would have ran for cover in the opposite direction. Likewise, many of you would have said, "Absolutely no way!" "I'm not joining *that* church!" "I'm not staying on *that* job and neither am I staying in *this* marriage." "Please Lord don't make me do it!" How far do you think we would have gotten, before God would have created something to apprehend us, and bring us right back? I knew going in that I would not be there (in that church) forever. The Lord told me prior to joining that, "This was not going to be my last stop." In other words, I was just passing through. I am reminded in The Book of John, where it is said of Jesus that, "He (Jesus) 'must needs' go through Samaria."

Likewise, The Father in His infinite wisdom had ordained it, that I "must needed" to go through what I did; because somewhere down the road, my experience would serve as a testimony and as a confirming word to others, who would someday, find themselves "going through" the same exact thing. As we grow, we are to become helpers one to another. When my pastor rejected me, and darn near came out and said, *"Why don't you just leave"*, I didn't quite know how to accept him anymore.

Okay, he did not *exactly* "tell me to leave"; what he actually said was - "Perhaps we're just a little too slow for you here, but right wrong or indifferent (humph!), that's just the way it is (humph!). This he said to me, as arrogantly and as cocky as he pleased, as he thoroughly proceeded to give me the brush off! I mean, he might as well had asked me or told me to leave. What else was I suppose to think after the things that he *did* say? As a result, I was hurt, wounded and traumatized, but yet - I stayed stuck! Some would think as the saying goes, that I was "Stuck on stupid." Looking back, I suppose I was. Perhaps I did not leave, for fear of encountering more of the same [treatment] somewhere else. Besides, I did not know where to go, but neither had I felt it time to leave.

If it were my decision, "alone", then maybe, I would have simply walked out or done things a lot differently – I don't know. In no way do I wish to give the entire church a bad rap. I have been very fortunate in that, I did manage to meet a few Saints there. Unfortunately, the people who were the most arrogant also occupied the key positions. I don't know what it is about people and "a title" or them having even the slightest bit of authority that makes them so crazy.

If they cannot even handle an office, in their local assemblies, without prideful exhortation of themselves, why in the world, would God ever trust them with Kingdom Keys? I found most of the leadership there to be down right snobbish; many of them not even realizing how very much they were lacking in the Spirit and lacking as human beings. The majority of them did not display even the simplest of curtsies – like saying "hello" or "good morning." The most pitiful thing [I think], is the fact that they cannot even see their own lack.

Much like the church of Laodicea, in many ways they too are miserable, bind, poor, necked and wretched, having need of much – only they do not think so. However, to a trained "spiritual eye", their apparent lack is easily detected. As long as they have preachers who continue to tell them, *only what they want to hear,* they will never discover how blind they actually are. Save The Lord opens their eyes, their spiritual growth will remain stunted. Sadder than being blind, is to be blind and not know it. Far worse is a person or entire congregation, having knowledge of his/her or their own wretchedness, but not caring. Just when you thought it could get no worse, it does.

The greatest atrocity of all, is the fact that many [who are blind], don't even want to know that they are – they do not care to know the truth. Facing the truth, forces people to either make changes and/or adjustments, or to continue in their rut. Change takes a whole lot of work. For this reason, many individuals/congregations prefer to bask in the ear tickling gatherings that most leaders willing provide.

As long as members continue to have their ears tickled, they will continue to be blind and to function in ignorance. Thousands of congregations may be in danger of missing the greatest movement of God yet. Sadly, so many members with good intentions will be led straight into a ditch. We are seeing a fulfillment of many Scriptures. Check out II Timothy 3:1-9 to see if the characteristics of *your church* are similar to what you read in this passage.

Dear reader you should also check out [or revisit] II Timothy 4:2-4. There you will discover exactly what most people are in search of today. This passage is applicable to both Christians and sinners alike.

They have itching ears that want to be tickled with entertainment, half-truths and prophetic utterances of grandeur, illusion and those that are filled with promises of material gain. *They want only to hear of good things to come.* Blind congregations will welcome you with open arms, so long as your speech is filled with good soothing words that overflow with promises of physical and materialistic blessings. Hearing prophesies like this, affords them their much sought after "flesh praise."

They don't have a clue that they are under a seriously "strong delusion." This is where we are ladies and gentlemen, and it is not a pretty sight. We will likely encounter hellions in the majority of gatherings [congregations or places of business], because they <u>are</u> mixed in amongst the wheat everywhere. Jesus said that they would be, so we really shouldn't be that surprised. However, it stings far worse, when the hellion is our very own leader. It is especially difficult when that person (leader) is not only blind, but also when the person refuses to admit that he or she is the primary reason for the congregation's demise.

Lord knows I had plenty reasons to "shake the dust" and to keep going. Do not think for one moment, that the situation with my pastor had been the *only* negative experience there. I am not a week minded individual. Neither am I so fussy that the least little thing disturbs me. There were at least six prior incidents which stand out in my mind, that were very hurtful to either my daughter or to myself. I am so thankful that children have lots of resilience, and that they are able to "bounce back" relatively quick. If I were a weaker individual, perhaps any of these incidents could have discouraged me from ever desiring to set foot in another church. They could have even caused me to totally give up on Jesus. But thanks be to God, you have to do a lot more than that, to break me. Besides, it isn't Jesus' fault that people act the way they do.

Each wounding could have sent me on a tailspin with my head tucked between my legs. I know it may seem as though, I am a glutton for punishment, but I stayed there and still took it in stride.   Somewhere along the line, I had been brainwashed into believing that I *had* to take *whatever* they dished out, all in the name of "Christ."

Note: Turning the other cheek does not constitute allowing one's self to be a doormat or constantly giving one's self over to be abused and/or neglected.

With regard to one of the incidents involving my daughter, I simply told her not to worry about it (just as my mom had told me), because be it The Lord's will, He would open a door for her - and He has. She wanted *so badly* to sing in the youth choir – I mean she longed to do so. Upon making inquiry to the choir leader, I was told that my daughter was too young (9 years old at the time), **but that same leader had a child in the choir; who by the way just happened to be the same age as my own.**

As usual, the old double standard was in operation. The leadership and *their* "pets" bent the rules to their liking, in order to accommodate whomever *they* pleased, while we commoners had no choice but to take whatever was dished out, if we expected to remain there that is. In fact, my daughter *who could actually sing,* would have turned "10" (the required age), within two months. Upon expressing this to the leader, I again was flatly told "No! "She's not old enough." This incident broke *my* heart, because it broke the heart of my child. The fact that she heavily involved herself in her grammar school's gospel choir, served to cushion the crushing blow. Also at my parent's church she could participate whenever they had a program involving children. Their pastor and congregation have always welcomed us with open arms.

Although God did open doors for her to sing, the fact remained that she wanted to sing in her own church home, but was unable to do so. She later joined the children's praise dance team there, but her passion was in the song. Unfortunately, her voice would never be heard in *that* congregation. With all of the other incidents, still I stayed stuck. I suppose that I was trying to prove I could take it and could remain humble. I stayed stuck because I did not want to be seen as one who is "easily offended" as one sister had accused me of being. Sure, we are all sensitive at times. Some people are even ultra sensitive and leave a place at the very first negative offence. Ladies and gentleman let me assure you that this however, is not my style. I can take a licking with the best of them, and keep right on ticking.

Often I will brush off and in fact overlook many things *before* making a drastic move. While I too have my issues, I would be less than honest if I told you that *everything* had always my fault, because it certainly was not. Not every negative encounter has been because of something that my daughter or I had provoked. How could she be at fault, for only wanting to sing at her home church? We did however manage to overlook this too, and we stayed. We eventually did have our breaking point and our date of deliverance was set. How much cheek turning is one person expected to do in the same place anyway? I can take an awful lot, but I am not Jesus.

I previously shared with you that I am in school. My church had a school too but The Lord did not lead me there. He placed it upon my heart to attend a different one, [even *before* the incident with my pastor]. I did not go right away, but I did begin about 3months later (which just happened to be a couple months after the incident).   Look at God's timing – wow!

And though I did not leave my church, I would at least not have to see my pastor as much because I would be in class on the same night of our mid week services. Some of you may be wondering if whether or not *at that point,* I informed him, that I would be attending class and therefore, would not be in service. I don't know if it was right or not, but I did not tell him, because I saw no reason to. God was the one who had led me to the school in the first place. In addition, if you will recall, by that time, my pastor had already arrogantly informed me that if his church were too slow for me well... Apparently, God already knew what was to come down the pike, as He knows everything.

I had already gotten the message quite clearly, that I did not matter to my pastor anyway. If he did not know who I was, and if he had indirectly implied that, it would not matter if I left, then why would it matter to him if I were pursuing my Doctorates Degree? By that time, my recovery from people pleasing and "wolf cleric bondage" had already started to take affect. Why should I stay stuck, and continue to hope and beg like a puppy, waiting for him to drop me some stale spiritual biscuit? No! I don't need anybody's spiritual handouts, nor do I need to be laden with anybody's religious hand-me-downs when it comes to what God is speaking to me, for me.

I don't have to beg God, so why in the world would you even think that I am going to beg a man? Begging at any time is bad enough, but begging a man and seeking his approval after God has already spoken, (which is what I use to do), is beneath me and it should also be beneath you. You do not need anybody's broken off, half eaten crackers of affirmation. There will be no more begging and wagging of my tail as I await some lame pat on the head from a man who made it QUITE CLEAR, THAT HE WANTED ABSOLUTELY NOTHING TO DO WITH ME!

At that point, even if someone had taken issue with my decision, I could no longer have afforded to care. My destiny was calling, and dog-gone-it, I intended to be there to answer for myself. God had always spoken to me; certainly, He would not lead me wrong, – not now, and not ever. Before my total deliverance, there would be many occasions in church when I would watch and listen gleefully as I observed various others giving their testimonies.

I use to envision myself also standing before my church family, giving my praise report as they smiled and cheered *me* on. Because they prided themselves as being a "family" orientated church, I was excited to be a family member. I suppose however, that certain people were excluded from that privilege though. To stay there, the best that such an overlooked individual as myself, could have possibly hoped for, would have been to occupy the position as the family's black sheep. I did not bother to write a letter or phone him regarding my attending Bible College to account for my whereabouts. I decided that I would not keep trying to submit to someone who had on more than one occasion made it painfully clear to me that he had no interest in my growth as a person or as a child of The King and especially not as one of his daughters in ministry.

I am pleased to report that I am being blessed at school. I am glad that I was obedient to God and that I decided not to stay stuck any longer. Some of you are festering sore in the same old spot that you have been in for years, simply because you are too afraid to move. Waiting for approval from a boss, a pastor or some other fleshly being, to finally recognize your value or to approve of you, has served only to further humiliate you, leaving you at an emotionally crippling standstill. Others of you are in organizations, just waiting for someone to either leave, die or to be sat down, so that you can finally advance.

I hate to tell you this, but in many cases, elevation is <u>never</u> going to come from the place wherein you currently find yourselves. Some of you are <u>never</u> going to get ahead on your current jobs, <u>nor will you ever</u> be used at your churches. Some of you will even remain stuck <u>forever,</u> unless you stop being afraid to move, when The Master calls your name.

Beloved, sister or brother, please know that just as there was a balm in Gilead, I want you to know, that The Lord God Almighty, has a door open somewhere that continues to wait for you alone, to show up and to stand before it. The door is not waiting for just any old person to insert a key.

Do you not know child of God, that YOU ARE THE KEY! Has God given you the command? For whom or what are you waiting? Go! Stand! – And it shall open unto you!

Perhaps you are not looking hard enough; maybe you should search inside your soul; go back and seek The Lord again. I too had been stuck for years, waiting, waiting and still waiting for approval, for validation and for crumbs. I waited for church folk, for employers, and for life to pat me on the head and/or to place a loving arm around my shoulders, and to tell me that I was worth it. I wanted them to take me in, and to help me work out my potential.

However, everyone failed me. The worse thing though is that I stayed stuck; therefore, <u>I allowed them to do it - to fail me that is.</u> Through my own lack of action, the harsh reality really is that I failed myself! Pastors are often busy catering to the newly converted, cajoling with those who they feel have the potential to bring them more riches, or rubbing elbows with their kiss up members. People who are willing to jump through all of the sexual, political, and bureaucratic hoops, will usually do quite well for themselves in any arena, as they claw and/or sleep their way to the top. As for the rest of us, we are accustomed to seeing leaders do that which they do all too well – THEY IGNORE US! I [eventually] decided to not stay stuck any longer. I have decided to obey Him only. You too may need to untie the noose of people from around your neck, so that you can receive clear instruction from The Lord without interference.

When you drop your constant need to depend on those who have already dropped you, only then will you be able to see and hear Him. Only then will the frequency become clearer and only then will you be in a position to obey Him with reckless abandonment, without first having to shovel through a pile of opinions. From this point on, refuse to allow yourself or any other person or organization to keep you stuck and boxed in. Life is too short and it will be over before you know it. You will not get those years back, and trust me when I tell you, you will miss them. You may live to regret your many wasted seasons – take it from me, because I know all too well.

Beloved, like fine cream, it is time for you to rise to the top!

ℰ Calling All
Mephibosheths ℰ

Many people in The Body of Christ today, are just like Mephibosheth. In case you have never heard of him, or are not that familiar with his story, you can read all about him in II Samuel Chapters 4 and 9. He is also mentioned in II Samuel 16:1 and 16:4. Mephibosheth was the son of Jonathan, who was the son of Saul. Saul as you already know had been appointed as the very first king over Israel.

Remember, God's people were not like the heathen nations surrounding them. They had Jehovah God as their leader. But for some reason, as is common to human nature, they wanted to be *just like everyone else,* and so God gave them their wish. Samuel tried talking some sense into the people, but it was to no avail – Jehovah said, "They are not rejecting you [Samuel], but they are rejecting Me." Therefore, Saul made history, by becoming the very first *flesh and blood* king to rule over God's people, which heretofore had been the responsibility of Jehovah alone.

Ironically, Saul's relentless pursuits and assassination attempts on David's life had never stopped Jonathan and him from forming the deepest of bonds and becoming best friends. For even Jonathan must have known that God had spoken, and that He had already selected David as the next king. By virtue of his lineage, Jonathan "should have" been next, but clearly God had another plan. Notwithstanding, never once does The Bible speak of Jonathan ever disputing Jehovah's appointment of David as the next king. He did not question God, and neither did he despise David, because of GOD'S decision.

Moreover, The Bible says that, "The soul of Jonathan was knit with the soul of David and that Jonathan loved him as his own soul." (They were very best friends – like brothers). Unfortunately, this is another Sacred Passage that has been drastically misused, as man yet again attempts to justify his own lusts and wicked deeds.

This Passage is often cited by gay clerics, in an attempt to pacify individuals (or couples) in their congregations, who have "CHOSEN" to adopt an "alternate" lifestyle. David and Jonathan were not gay! I wish they would stop twisting The Holy Writ in an attempt to justify their SIN! There was nothing gay about David and/or Jonathan at all!

STOP MANGLING THE WORD OF THE LORD JUST BECAUSE YOU HAVE CHOSEN TO CONTINUE IN YOUR UNGODLY AND UNNATURAL LIFESTYLE. THIS GOES FOR EACH OF US! GOD IS NOT THE SKEWED ONE, WE ARE! MOREOVER, I AM NOT ONLY ADDRESSING THOSE WHO HAVE MADE THE CHOICE TO EMBRACE THE GAY, OR OTHER ALTERNATIVE WAYS OF LIVING; I AM SPEAKING TO EVERYONE WHO CLAIMS TO BE A CHRISTIAN – GAY OR NOT.

AND I AM ADDRESSING ANYONE WHO TWISTS THE BIBLE. WE NEED TO UNDERSTAND, FOR THE LAST TIME, THAT REGARDLESS TO WHAT WE CALL IT, AND NO MATTER WHO ELSE MAY BE TOLERABLE OF IT, OR MAKES THE DECISION TO LEGALIZE IT, GOD DOES NOT CONDONE IT!

GOD DOES NOT CALL IT A LIFESTYLE AT ALL; HE CALLS IT SIN! ALTHOUGH HE LOVES THE PERSON, STILL HE CALLS THAT WAY OF LIVING, ABOMINABLE! IT IS IN THE OLD TESTAMENT AS WELL AS THE NEW – WE CANNOT MISS IT, IF WE REALLY WANT TO SEE IT! AS FAR AS ME (OR ANYONE ELSE) JUDGING OR CONDEMING ANYBODY, NOBODY HAS TO DO THAT, FOR EVERYONE INCLUDING MYSELF, SHALL EITHER SAVE OR CONDEM THEMSELVES, BASED SOLELY UPON THE CHOICES THAT THEY THEMSELVES MAKE!

IF WE ARE ASHAMED OF ANYTHING THAT WE ARE DOING, (BECAUSE DEEP DOWN WE KNOW THAT IT IS "WRONG", "UNNATURAL", "UNHEALTHY" OR "UNSCRIPTURAL"), THEN JUST MAYBE YOU, THEY AND I OUGHT TO STOP DOING IT! PERHAPS WE, (BOTH HETERO AND HOMOS), SHOULD LOOK MORE CLOSELY AT OUR OWN FILTHY WAY OF LIVING INSTEAD OF ARGUING THAT THE BIBLE IS OUTDATED, SIMPLY BECAUSE IT WILL NOT CONDONE OUR [PARTICULAR] SIN – YA THINK?!

STOP TELLING LIES ON GOD AND PLEASE STOP TRYING TO MAKE EVERYONE ELSE FEEL GUILTY, JUST BECAUSE THEY DO NOT AGREE WITH YOUR "ALTERNATIVE" WAY OF LIVING!

ANYWAY...

David had now ascended to the throne, just as Jehovah God had long ago ordained it. One day David wondered whether or not there remained any decedents in Saul's family, to whom he could show kindness. Having no prior knowledge of Jonathan's son, he was told about Mephibosheth.

Once upon a time, when Mephibosheth was only 5 years old, he had become permanently crippled. An accident occurred as he and his nurse named Ziba, were forced to run for their lives, upon hearing the news that both Saul and Jonathan were dead. Fearing that their enemies would soon be in hot pursuit, Ziba fled with Mephibosheth. In a hasty attempt to escape, somehow Ziba accidentally dropped him. The Bible does not tell us if Mephibosheth was also "trampled upon" before escaping altogether. We only know that because of "the drop", he suffered a permanent injury. The Bible describes him as being, "Lame of his feet." (Not lame "on" but "of"; [he had little to no use of his feet]).

In the world today, are millions of people who have been physically, spiritually, and/or emotionally "dropped." Not only have they been dropped, but many have been kicked, stepped on and spat upon too. By the way reader, who was it that dropped you? Are you still an emotional cripple because of someone's abusive treatment? Are you yet paralyzed from their venomous words of put downs and attack? Who was it that let you so far down, that you, just like Mephibosheth, have chosen to dwell in Lo-debar? *(Most often spelled as Lodebar; no "dash" in between).*

Was there an accident that left you lame and unable to physically maneuver, and now you are unable to care for your family as you once did? Who in the world was it my brother or sister? Who was it that dropped you? Who was it that left you with a limp? Perhaps you once faithfully attended a church or belonged to some other organization, but now you are in hiding. Were you set on your course, happily thriving, and on the road to your destiny, when a "wolf cleric" appeared out of nowhere, and successfully managed to wound and/or to discourage you? How far down were you dropped, and tell me Mephibosheth, just how low did you go as a result? Did the "church folk" wound you? Mephibosheth, I am now speaking to you! God is calling you. He is calling for all Mephibosheths to come forward.

Lame [cripple] or not this man was still a prince; he was a royal heir. He may have been alone, in hiding, and suffering from low self-esteem, but the blood of kings and princes flowed through his veins. Mephibosheth's current living quarters may have been in Lodebar, (a place of no pasture), but his destiny would soon summon him to the palace of the king! Oh God! David, God's earthly anointed king, invited this physically challenged prince to become part of his very own family. No more would Mephibosheth have to hide out, never again would he have to dine all alone. For now, he could begin his very own journey of healing. Not ever again, would he feel compelled to refer to himself, as nothing more than a "dead dog." From now on, he would be able to dine with The King - forever.

Each night in the palace, as the king's kids took their seats, no one dared to eat a morsel. For they all sat quietly, awaiting the sound of thumping crutches and dragging feet. Everyone waited patiently, for Prince Mephibosheth to round the corner; for soon he would make his way into the dining hall, and take his very own seat at the royal table.

Like Mephibosheth so many of you have stayed hidden. To this very day, thousands, perhaps even millions of you are in hiding. You still hang out in the land of the dead, occupying your own little "Lodebar." I know you feel that it hurts too much to show your face outside. For this reason, you stay put, and at times, you even deprive yourselves of God's great love. Parents that did not want to be bothered and spiritual leaders who wished we would just disappear as well as peers who refused to believe that we could do it; these were the culprits who wounded us. They pushed us away! They stepped on us! They laughed at us! They called us names and made fun of our physical limitations!

They neglected to fulfill their roles as our caretakers! They left us no provision! Many of them wished we had never been born at all! They simply wrote us off! Yes my brothers and sisters; they dropped us real hard! For these reasons, we have continued to hide. We have chosen to stay away from the crowds and in many cases, even from The Christ of The Cross. We have purposely hidden from God and Lord knows we have hidden ourselves from the phony people who claim to represent Him.

The same young man whose story I shared with you earlier concerning his supposed lack of faith, also told me that he too had stayed in hiding [for a very long time], because his wounds were far too painful to reveal. He too dwelled "way down there"; in a land, we call "Lodebar." "D" as I referred to him, had been wounded so many times, both in and outside of the church. He told me how it was, that The Lord had come looking for him, and how Jehovah rescued him and brought him back to Himself. Although his name has since been written down in Glory, he is still very skeptical of most Christians. He shared with me, how it was that he would stay away from people. Like Mephibosheth, he too preferred to stay in isolation and obscurity. This is what he had to say:

"I would shield myself from people during my time of humiliation." "The life of a bastard is when one shields himself from society and lives a life of falsehood. Not for hurting others but for the purpose of not hurting himself, because of what others might think if he were to reveal his true self. This is called the essence of living a lie."

Like this brother, many of us have lived nearly an entire lifetime under the guise of falsehood. Before we reveal our genuine selves to the world, it seems as though we find ourselves in a perpetual state of misery. We torture ourselves over whether or not *they* will accept us; whether or not we will be thought of as being "good enough." Like little abused children, we are afraid of being found. To us, "being found", means making ourselves available, to be made fun of all over again. It means that our wounds will be open once more - Oh God. "Will *they* love me as I really am or must my pretense continue?" "Is it safe to come out and show my face, without them laughing at me?" "Will *they* hurt me once more, making me sorry that I dared to peek beyond my fortress of protection?

Because people are so darn cruel, they cause many to shrink right back into their Lodebar. If they are not rescued, they will likely die in the land of nothingness. Anyone can end up there; and if we are not careful, there we will remain, unproductive and all alone. I too was trying to hide. In my case however, *I really did not want to*. Nevertheless, I did anyway; I hid because I did not want to be hurt or to be made fun of or totally dismissed all over again. The closer I came to inching towards my purpose, the more the enemy would slay me to a grinding silence. Let me tell you of an incident that happened one night as I attended a service at the same church wherein I received my deepest spiritual wound to date. This incident occurred approximately one year *before* the final meeting with my pastor. At this point, I had not even let on to anyone (there) that God had been preparing me to take my rightful place in His army.

Anyway,...here is what happened one night, during a prayer meeting:

I was excited to be numbered amongst The Saints. It was the first shut in that I had ever attended in *that* church. Shut-ins seemed to be a thing of the past. Therefore, indeed, I was very excited that our church had decided to have one. I suppose that I am somewhat of "an old soul" because I came with expectancy and with the hope that the power of God would move in a mighty way as The Saints prayed. After about 2 hours into the service, The Lord began speaking to me. He was urging me go forward and pray. Of course I responded with my usual – "Uh Oh. "Oh God I'm scared." Because I had been very accustomed to His promptings, I knew beyond a doubt that He wanted me to do *something*. As usual, I tried to ignore The Fire welling up, down on the inside – hoping that if I ignored His promptings long enough, He would call upon someone else.

You think I would know better by now…

I knew His voice, but still I tried to psych myself into making believe that maybe, *just maybe I had heard Him wrong* <u>*this time.*</u> *I hesitated, wanting to make sure that He really did want 'me' to do this, because 'I' was scared to death. I tried to fake myself out, but I already knew that He had spoken.* As always and true to His nature, God would not take "No" for an answer, neither did the "Who me?; I'm scared" routine go over very well. God was quite specific in what He wanted and whom He intended to reach.   He wanted me to offer up a prayer specifically for the "broken."   I was to call them out, and offer up a prayer as I called on the Name of The Lord. Though not "exactly" sure of what I would say or do, I knew that God would put His words into my mouth once I made a move. He had said,

"I WANT YOU TO GO UP THERE AND OFFER UP A PRAYER FOR MEPHIBOSHETH."

For *me* this was extremely out of character because I am not one who likes praying publicly. I would rather pray when I can be alone with God, because I can really get down to the heart of my issues.   I do not have to pretend with Him. I can be very ugly (crying, nose running, slimy things coming out of it; can somebody say, *iiiiiiiillllllllll, disgusting! and YUCK!* - You get the idea. I can let it all hang out when God and I are alone. Well actually, The "Angelic Host" sees me too but they are quite accustomed to me and my antics by now (smile).

Anyway, I continued in my hesitation because I really do not like a lot of attention but more than that, I really was afraid to go forward. I came to the prayer meeting for support and to be present in the number. I wanted to be in "the atmosphere of prayer." My only intensions had been to participate from my seat or from a prostrate position "on the floor."   Alas, The Lord continued prodding, and I just couldn't take it any longer, because The Fire of His Spirit seemed to burn me right out of my seat. It felt like The Holy Spirit, literally grabbed me by the scruff of my neck and yanked me up; I had no choice but to get up there – oh God.

Shaking in my boots, I went forward. Somehow, I managed to make it to the front row – hesitating, wobbly knees and all. I bent down and gently asked the prayer leader, "Can anybody pray?" (Throughout the entire evening there had been only a few people praying). I figured that *the same people* did all of the praying simply because no one else *wanted* to. Perhaps they were like me, and wished only to bask in the atmosphere. I figured that the floor was open to everyone.   After all, they had announced the meeting several times and with each announcement, they had literally urged people to come out and participate, so…

Upon inquiry, as to whether or not I (or anyone) could pray, I was told by the prayer leader, – "No, uhhhhh, only us five can pray"; meaning she and the four people sitting on the front row next to her. "Only us 5 who come out on Tuesday's for regular prayer meetings can pray," she said. She then told me that they each had something for which to pray. There were five of them; and all five had a different [specific] thing that she/he was to pray for.

Once again, in direct obedience to The Lord (in that church), I found myself crushed. I did not even want to pray. God had insisted that I do so. I was simply trying to be obedient so that He would stop "burning" me! Direct obedience to Him had once more allowed a mere mortal to dash my spirit. After that, I became choked up with tears. All of my insides were hurting and I became very despondent. I was hurt, angry and bewildered because GOD HAD BURNED THE BURDEN OF MEPIBOSHETH DEEP INTO MY SOUL.   THERE WAS NO MISTAKE; I KNOW THAT I HEARD HIM CORRECTLY – I JUST KNOW I DID...; WELL, I DID!!!

I became more confused than ever, but I also knew that it was not me and I knew that it was not God's fault either. My anger had not really surfaced until later on, because at first, I was still trying to figure out what had happened. All I could remember saying to myself was, "God, I can't even pray in church!" "Not even in a prayer meeting am I allowed to do anything in this church." "My prayers are not even welcomed here." I had gone there with my pillow and everything because my original plan was to spend the entire night with The Saints in prayer.

When I could no longer hide my tears or my frustration, I become very turned off and quite numb, so I left. For a while, I really tried hard to stuff down those feelings and to overlook how I felt, but I simply could not do it. My heart was bruised, I needed to cry, and I wanted to be alone. I know that I sound like a big baby, but I don't care. That was my reality at the moment; and that was how I felt.

I WAS HURTING, BECAUSE I WAS TRYING TO OBEY GOD, BUT THEY WOULD NOT LET ME!

Also, if THEY knew from the very beginning, (which they did), that THEY were going to be THE ONLY ONES doing the praying or that THEY had specific things for which to pray, then THEY should not have announced that this meeting was going to be an open prayer meeting for EVERYONE. WHY DID THEY MAKE IT A POINT, OF URGING OTHERS TO COME OUT, FOR A NIGHT OF PRAYER, IF THEY WERE GOING TO BE THE ONLY ONES ALLOWED TO DO ALL OF THE PRAYING, ALL NIGHT LONG?

THEY DID NOT NEED THE REST OF US; THEY COULD HAVE MET AMOUNGST THEMSELVES IN ORDER TO RENDER UP THEIR SAME, OLD, DEAD, TIRED PRAYERS! THE FIVE OF THEM COULD HAVE "SHUT THEMSELVES IN" – WITHOUT US! THEY HAD AN AGENDA, BUT WHAT ABOUT WHAT GOD WANTED? WHILE IT MAY BE ORDERLY TO HAVE A PROGRAM WITH AN AGENDA, THERE STILL SHOULD BE ROOM FOR EXCEPTIONS. CLEARLY, THERE WAS NOTHING WRONG WITH THEM HAVING A LIST OF THINGS FOR WHICH TO PRAY, BUT THEY FORGOT THE MOST IMPORTANT PART OF THE LIST. THEY FORGOT TO LEAVE ROOM FOR GOD!

THEY FORGOT TO CONSIDER THAT PERHAPS HE HAD AN AGENDA OF HIS OWN AND THAT <u>HE</u> [TOO] JUST MIGHT HAVE SOMETHING TO SAY!!!

At the time, I was to spend the weekend at my parents' home in order to be closer to the church, because I live quite a distance from there. Because I had told my mother, that I would be spending the entire night in service, she was very surprised to see me back so early. I explained to her what had happened and then I went to bed. As I exited the room, my mother was shaking her head in disbelief, and told me, "not to worry myself to death" [about it], because she knows how I am. She knew that I would take it to heart, and would become quite bothered by the entire ordeal – she was right, I did. I take things very seriously when it comes to my assignments on God's agenda, because I am responsible and will be held accountable for what He gives to me.

This happened on a Friday night and it could have ruined my entire weekend. By Saturday evening, I found myself watching a televised ministry program. At the end of the broadcast, I decided to dial the telephone number on the screen. I was fortunate enough to actually get the senior pastor of the church. I did not want a biased opinion, so I started out by simply "asking him" how was it that *he conducted prayer meetings (or shut inns) at his church?* I wanted to know if everyone was allowed to participate, or did he [also] have a specific or restricted agenda or what? He told me that anyone that The Spirit of God leads to pray was welcomed to do so. In fact, what he actually said was, "Who so ever wills to come, could come." "We don't hold anyone back who is led of The Lord", he said. *Only then* did I explain to him in full detail my encounter of the previous evening. He said he had never heard of anything like that, but went on to assure me that prayer meetings were not conducted *that way* at his church. "I guess every place is different", he politely stated as he chuckled slightly.

I did ask a few other people, including my parents as to how their prayer meetings were conducted. I thought back to my former church of 16 years and how it was that they conducted corporate prayer services and/or shut-ins. My mind's journey even took me back to age five. My thoughts soared gently as I favorably remembered my earlier childhood church experiences.

I thought about the churches that I attended with my grandparents [on both my mother and father's side of the family]. As a youngster, I would always attend church down south in Georgia or either in my birthplace of Brooklyn NY – Yay Brooklyn! In an instant, my mind filled with memories of The Second Morning Star Missionary Baptist Church – a little country Baptist church in Georgia, and of the huge Washington Temple Church of God In Christ in Brooklyn New York. In each instance, it was the same. There were no closed agendas when it came to prayer meetings. The floor would be open to whoever "The Lord would lead" to pray; be they member, visitor, Saint, friend, stranger, maybe even enemies – all were allowed to pray or to be prayed for. At least I felt a little better, because it wasn't just me - I wasn't crazy after all.

The next morning, which was Sunday, I started not to even go to church. I am not ashamed to admit it either. I was still hurting, I had gotten depressed and I did not feel like being bothered. I felt this way because I knew [in my heart], that it was God who had told me – excuse me; it was He who had literally "burned me forward" to begin with. I mean, it wasn't as if I were begging Him to let me pray at the meeting – I already told you that I was afraid, and also that I prefer praying alone. Although I am not exactly sure why, but this time I hadn't gotten angry with Him. However, I was still very bothered by the entire matter. Despite my feelings, I went to church anyway. I sang in the choir as usual. And because I sang in the choir, it afforded me a front row seat and a close up view of the speaker. Prior to my arrival, I had no way of knowing that we would be having a guest speaker that morning. Dearest reader, would you care to guess what this man preached about?

HE PREACHED ABOUT MEPHIBOSHETH!

He preached about the very thing that The Lord wanted me to pray about just two nights earlier. I felt so vindicated. As the man of God read The Scripture and gave his topic, I darn near fell off my chair. What I *really* wanted to do was to run around the church, shouting to the top of my lungs – "See!" "I told you!" "I knew God wanted me to do that." "See?" Why doesn't anyone ever believe me? "No one ever listens to me!" The Lord will *always* have His way. This pastor preached the exact same thing that God wanted me to pray about.

Not only were the people who ran the prayer meeting present, but also so many more. There were many that The Lord wanted to reach - and He did. I wish I could have had the privilege to fulfill the assignment, but it was not my fault that *they* would not let me pray; surely, He will not lay it to my charge. I am guiltless concerning the matter. In obedience, I went forward, attempting to carry out that which He had commanded of me - and He knows that. I tried to be obedient, but I had to adhere to the rules, and comply with the authorities running the service. Their rules stated that THEY alone could pray and so, only THEY did; but God still came through as He always does. ***HE WILL ALWAYS HAVE THE FINAL SAY!***

The one thing, in the entire matter, that I found a bit strange though, was the fact that the prayer leaders hadn't had a clue. These same people, who claimed this to be their job as they were the "prayer warriors" and the "intercessors of the house," had not even discerned The Spirit and the agenda of The Lord, Hummmmm. Makes you wonder right? They probably couldn't hear Him, because they had come to prayer, with only their [own] agenda in mind. Oops! - how could I have forgotten?

Why was it that not even one of them had discerned The Lord's heart? Why could they not see that ***HE wished*** to reach today's Mephibosheths? There obviously had been a need for this word amongst them, as God would have a guest preacher to come forth with a powerful message only two days later, about the very same population of people whom He loved. God wanted to reach these very precious people who had been dropped and who were now broken. Intercessory prayer is not even "the main" ministry in which I function, yet God gave *me* the concern that was on *His* heart. He burned the burden of Mephibosheth deep into my soul. He placed this task upon the shoulders of the same person, whom they had taken such great delight in treating like a reject. Why did I bother to share this story with you? I wanted YOU to finally realize dear one of The Most High that YOU are not crazy and that YOU are not merely hearing things.

You are hearing God (if you truly know His voice), far more than you realize. There are times when you will be, directly in the center of God's will, but yet you will encounter grave opposition from those who hold an office or position of authority. It is sometimes hard to view these powers as enemies because they are after all, fellow Christians. Beloved let me tell you, I have discovered that they can be the most deadly of all. Sometimes they try to block your path, because they think [for whatever reason], that they are the only ones who are supposed to hear from God.

They believe themselves alone to be the only ones capable of knowing His voice. What ever gave them that impression truly boggles my mind. They can sometimes hinder you temporarily, but rest assured, God already knows and He will not blame you. Encounters such as these may be unavoidable at times. Always remember, the absence of conflict does not necessarily mean that you are in the will of God. Likewise, neither is intense opposition a ripe indication that you are outside of His will. Remember, Jesus was in the perfect will of The Father at every point of His earthly life, but He was misunderstood, and vehemently opposed by the majority of those in authority. In fact, the leadership gave Him the most trouble. Be encouraged my friends. God will always have the final say concerning your life.

When we speak of spiritual warfare as it appears in Ephesians, Chapter 6, which lets us know, that one of the forces we wrestle with, is "Spiritual wickedness in high places." We often attribute that ONLY to satanic beings "out there somewhere." Sometimes though, the high places will be those in our very own churches. Some wicked principalities will set up shop almost anywhere. These evil imps come into the building and proceed to operate through people. They don't just stay "out there." Sometimes pastors who have become like modern day Pharaohs are pleased to keep us constantly grinding at the brick pits, as they attempt to achieve some level of stardom. Ministry is not show business; it is servant-hood. I am not interested in taking over anybody's star dressing room.

My only ambition is to do my part of the assignment on God's calendar of events – I am intent on doing my best to follow His agenda and not a man's.

The forces of hell are often at work in our clerics. We in turn label *them* as the enemy, when in reality it is satan who has beguiled them. Because we know that God will eventually bring down every wicked and high place, and every thing or anyone that dares to exalt itself against His knowledge, for this reason, we really ought to feel very sorry for them. We really should feel much pity for those so-called shepherds, whose only power seems to stem from their oppression of the flock (or of people in general). Many of them don't have a clue that satan is operating through them. Nevertheless, even this shall soon be revealed. Take heart my broken friends, just as there was, "A Balm in Gilead", there is also one coming to a city near you. Behold, He's coming even straight to your doorstep. Will you let Him in when He knocks?

Thus Saith The Lord unto all present day Mephibosheths:

"There is to be no more feeling sorry for yourselves. It is because you have failed to heed the voice of "Your True Deliverer; My Son that has caused many of you to remain in bondage. It is time to go forward, but you must first come out of hiding. Come out from under your rocks. Come out of your very own land of Lodebar, which you have conveniently carved out for yourselves; the same has become even your habitation.

Hide your face from Me no more. Instead, I Jehovah want you to dwell within the parameters of the secrete place of My love. Get thee up hither. Your damaged emotions and lame feet are to no longer keep you hiding from Me (Saith The Lord), for I made you. I know all about your feet and your hands and your face. Even more, I know your heart.

I know every inch of your body. I know the inner workings of your very being [your soul]. Even before you knew you, I knew you. In fact, I still know more about you than you do! I know the depths of your skin's surface. I have seen every beauty mark, and also that which is marred by imperfection. Neither beauty nor deformity are as important as character. I know everything about you and yet I love you. Know ye not that you also are a possessor of royal blood; it is The Blood of My Son. You belong to My family – I acknowledge you as My very own.

Come out of hiding; for I even I The Lord God Jehovah YHWH (Yahweh) have need of you. Come out limping if you must, but find your way to me. Come even with your wounded hands, but come. Yes Mephibosheth there awaits a healing balm prepared especially by Me to heal even your deepest of cuts. Come that I may pour the oil of Myself therein, that you may be soothed under the nurturing power of My love. Come take your place. There is room for you in My family. Allow Me to nurture you; let Me feed you again.

Let Me love you back to health. Come so that you can get on with your life as well as with My business. Come because I have work for you to do. Come because there are people who are waiting especially for you. Come because there are others who really need you now. You can afford to hide no longer; The Kingdom now calls for you. Come because I [Jehovah THE LORD] say so. Come because I have need of you. Tarry ye no longer.

[But] come right NOW! (End communication).

❧Dad (God), Is That YOU?❧

Once we ascertain that yes, it is indeed The Father who has called for us, no longer should we concern ourselves with what everyone else thinks. Don't be too hard on yourself if you do not get this right away. "People-pleasing" can be extremely difficult to overcome. Every now and then, you may even find yourself slipping backwards, as you once again go "validation hunting." However, if you are anything like me, it should not take you long to remember, that it was your "people dependency" which nearly led to your (spiritual and/or emotional demise in the first place.

Because we have been brainwashed for so long, it may be extremely difficult to stop the tape from playing. In our mind, we seem to continuously rewind and play back the same old chart topper. We constantly revisit that ancient 'come hither; dance with me" ditty entitled, "Did you check with people lately?" Even if we know in our hearts, that what we are hearing from others, could in no way possibly be the will of God, still for *some strange* reason, we tend to listen [to them] anyway.

We were often the minority, because for most of our lives, everyone surrounding us has always agreed with *them*. *This in turn, made it even easier to believe that we were totally out of touch.* Finally, it was not until, as the saying goes, that I "got sick and tired, of being sick and tired." Not until then, did I become liberated for good – what about you?

Not until a few years ago, did I begin a process, which solidified that which I have always known since my earliest existence. That is - I need no man's approval to do what God is saying – regardless to what *they* teach. It has taken *this long* to break free of their shackles. It has taken me all these years, to realize that many of them have done nothing but lie to me – and would then blame me, if I called them on their lies, or if I chose not to feed into them at all.

Dear reader, it took me nearly 40 years, before I got tired [of hurting] enough to do something about it. I have finally put *their* tape to rest; I stopped it from playing altogether. Finally, I have enough courage to stand alone in order to confront that which haunts me and to do *something* about my pain. I pray that my courage (through God), will in turn challenge and inspire others to do something about theirs.

Am I a rebel just because THEY say so? I ask you, is it rebellious for someone to be more concerned with what God says than with what man thinks? Is it a bastard spirit that makes people fight back because they are tired of being abused, stepped on and treated like a piece of trash? Is it rebellion, for a person to want to make something out of his or her life? Is a crime to desire to fit into something other than the status quo compartment that everyone else seems hell bent on keeping gifted and anointed individuals in? Is it rebellious to simply demand some respect?

Is it a rebellious or un-teachable spirit that provokes a man or woman – or even a child to take a fearless look into The Word of The Lord (for him/her self) and realize that he or she shall give an account for works unfulfilled? Is it a bastard spirit that makes me want to see the church, stand up and be the church, instead of becoming identical to the world, thereby confusing everybody? Is it rebellion or an un-teachable spirit that makes one yearn to hear The Word of God, preached with accurate precision, from under the unction and convicting power of The Holy Ghost, rather than from the contents of men's flesh? Tell me preacher, is it rebellion or being a bastard that makes people want to have a better life?

Does it make people belligerent and worthy of bastard and/or reject status, simply because they refuse to lay down and die as you trample upon them? Is it so wrong for others to desire a better life for <u>their children,</u> like the one you have already acquired for your own? Are hurting people troublemakers simply because they vocalize their concerns and even their anger, because every door of opportunity seems to shut in their faces? You tell me, are people like me rebellious, just because we would like to enjoy, some of the same fruits of <u>this life</u> that you are enjoying right now? Tell me, is it a bastard spirit that makes me want to put a smile on the face of a fellow outcast?

Should I be labeled a bastard, for only wanting to be somebody, or for trying to make something decent out of my [wretched] self, by doing something meaningful with the talents and/or gifts that have been bestowed upon me? Is it a bastard spirit that causes me to yearn for more than mediocrity, or for desiring to have something worthy of hading down to those who are coming behind me? Why must I be classified as rebellious or branded a troublemaker, for doing nothing more than striving to make "The impossible dream", possible indeed?

Somebody answer me!

I want to know – does a bastard spirit, make people choose to obey God, as He apprehends their soul and commands them to make a difference? I ask, why must anyone be a bastard for wanting to do good? Must a person be reduced to illegitimate status, just because such a one longs to be free, to be whom God said he or she could be? What does it mean to be made free? For this girl, free means being <u>authentically me,</u> - strictly "J.G."

If these things qualify me as a rebellious bastard, or as a rejected soul who is unworthy of your time, your love and your respect, then I stand guilty as charged! You will not have to kick me out of your church; I will gladly leave on my own. You will not have to revoke my "Religious Membership Affiliation Card"; because I have already cut mine up! Who needs your church or your cards when I already have keys to my Father's Kingdom?

For years, I did everything in the manner in which *they* claimed I had to. I tithed, I came to nearly every service, and I gave and gave and gave. I respected/honored my pastor and was faithful to my posts - I did so only to find myself paralyzed and non-productive. Like many of you, I also went to my pastor and to various other leaders, only to have my feelings bruised and trampled on. After so many years of being rejected and kicked aside, should people even have to wonder why I no longer care what *anyone thinks?*

Very early in life, I found myself plagued with thoughts of dying at age 38. I never understood why; but for many years, this was something that really bothered me. When I turned 37, I dreaded the possibility of having only one year left to live, (because I had not done anything of significance with my life up to that point). I told a deacon at my former church, (the one of 16 years), about my fear of "38."

He in turn shared this information with the "Church Mother." She then, told him to tell me that, she did not believe this to be the age of my *physical death,* but rather this would be the age wherein The Lord would begin to do a work in me. Bless His Holy Name! It would be *the beginning* of my sanctification and of a process that would prepare me for that, which He intended for me to carry out further down the line. Little did I know that during this process, I would come to know Him in a much deeper way. He would reveal Himself as Jehovah M'Kaddesh. I had this same conversation about my dying so young, with a nurse named Gwen. She said, "Dying does not always necessarily have to mean physical death." "Sometimes it means dying in the spiritual sense."

As I relentlessly pursued a career in the nursing field, I could not understand for the life of me, why my schedule never seemed to work out the way I needed it to. I had to work around my job schedule, but I also needed to be home by a certain hour each night. The times in which I could attend school, seemed never to coincide with what the college had to offer.

No matter how I tried, I simply could not work out a schedule that fit my time constraints. Although I had taken all of the preliminary courses, seemingly I could not make it to the most important classes – the ones necessary for the degree. As I spoke with Gwen, I remember blurting out in frustration these very words; I said, "The devil sure is trying hard to block me, for some reason, cause I just can't get the classes that I need." "I don't understand it", I said. Totally, on cue, without even a moment's hesitation, she immediately replied with a question.

"Jonita, have you ever thought that maybe, just maybe, it isn't that the devil is trying to block you, (this time) but rather, it may be that God, is trying to get your attention? Wow! Never before had I though about *Him* being concerned with my choice of career, since it was an honorable one. I wanted to be a nurse, but it had not occurred to me that God might have had a problem with it. Maybe I thought that He had no interest in this sort of thing - duhhhh.

I suppose that I just wasn't thinking at the time. Because nursing involved helping people, it had never dawned on me that He would object to "my choice." Hummmm sound familiar? I wanted to be in His perfect will, but had never asked Him about the *nursing.* All I know, is that I wanted to work in a capacity, which would allow me to help others; so I never thought that it would be an issue, because I would be helping the sick after all – right?

Shortly after that, I attended a Praise Power Convention. The theme that year was, "Dying to Live Again." One could take this to mean that an individual is, "hoping really hard", as in he or she simply cannot wait, and is very anxious to live and to get on with life, (perhaps after having overcome a crisis or a traumatic event of some sort). Alternatively, it could mean dying on a spiritual level. This death would entail the putting off the old man, by the stripping of one's self, (or having God strip anything of His choosing off and/or out of a person's life), so that such a one could follow Him with his or her whole heart.

For someone desirous of surrendering to the will of God for real, this death would be symbolic of the individual giving up his or her "wants", and trusting fully in the plan of The Lord. To me, the dying process meant, asking God what it was that He wanted for my life, and then allowing Him to lead me in that direction.

Shortly after this experience, I began to inquire of The Lord as to what *He* wanted me to do. Soon, He began to move upon my heart, which in turn led to a complete change in my college course curriculum. Thankfully for me, *this part* of the transition was a lot easier than the trials that later followed. Achieving a "Yes Lord" from me was easy, (at least most of the time anyway), for I had always been taught to tell HIM Yes!

I can recall a few times however, when a "Yes Lord" has caused me great agony. It is extremely difficult to give up something or someone that you do not want to let go of, right ladies? I know that women know what I mean. Sometimes, a relationship that we think we just have to have, may not be good for us - you know the deal. Ok, – I'll include the men too. I suppose it can be just as difficult for guys to let go of something or someone. It can be equally, hard staying in a place, a job, a marriage or any situation, when your insides are longing to leave, as is sometimes the case.

Anyway…

I really did not have much to offer Him, except my big mouth and a very messy life, which of course I now realize, has worked out perfectly, as it was part of HIS plan all along (smile). In no way do I wish to imply to people who may not understand this that I became some sort of robot or spiritual zombie. God has given me much freedom of choice, but the final say will be His.

What I have discovered though, is that I actually liked changing from the pursuit of nursing, to a pursuit of Him. Had I not obeyed, it does not mean that my life would have been better or [so much] worse, but very different indeed. We are each co-creators with God, and things work out best when we cooperate with Him. It wasn't until a few years ago that I came to embrace my true purpose and reason for being. I am still very much on my own personal journey of discovery. I am learning that there are many more facets to discover about God, as well as about myself. I am re-learning and changing a lot of the things (and the people), that I allow into my heart and into my psyche.

If we are not careful, we will discover that even the positive things we allow into our lives, can set us up for total failure. If we fail to tread cautiously, we too can become prideful and arrogant, which in turn can lead to our demise. Receiving complements and flattering remarks are fine, as they can be a great boost to our ego, and to our self-esteem.

Compliments however, are more rewarding, when we are actually trying to walk worthy of them. We are even more gratified, when it is God who happens to be proud of us and when it is Him giving us a pat on the back. People may sometimes mean well, but if we are not careful, we might just find ourselves off track and in a ditch.

Just as a compliment can make us "feel good", so also can negativity cloud our better judgment, lead to a cycle of confusion and ultimately cause us to disqualify our own selves. Confusion and the like, brought on by others, can actually cause us to leave our "spiritual baby" behind, or far worse, we may miscarry before ever reaching the birthing process.

My brothers and sisters, beware of all things, of all advice and of all opportunities. Not all things that "appear" good to your eyes or ears have been sent from God. Test them; always allow God's voice to have preeminence over all others – including your own.

Every piece of advice that you get, should be put through a spiritual metal detector. The Holy Ghost is awesome in this regard. Since He is the one [with your cooperation], who will lead and guide you into all truth, He is always happy to assist in dispelling the "strange fires" that seek to devour your dreams, and even your soul.

Strange fire does not come to you from The Lord; and neither should it ever be offered to Him. Strange fire can be classified as ANYTHING that fails to be carried out in a manner in which God has already instructed.

STRANGE FIRE CAN BE CLASSIFIED AS ANYTHING THAT:

(a) Has not come from God – at all. Although something may *sound spiritual,* it doesn't mean that it has come from God, especially if what is being communicated goes totally against His word. Never should you ever forget that satan speaks to people too. Your enemy, who is also spirit, happens to be a great imitator and master deceiver; he would love nothing more than to see you stumble or die!

(b) Is not something that God is speaking specifically for your life. For example, someone may offer you advice or try to persuade you to do a thing, other than that which, God has [ALREADY] spoken directly to you. Even if what the other person says does not go against The Revealed Word of The Lord, still it could be considered strange fire.

Their counsel may in fact sound quite wonderful, but if it is not something [that you know] God has ALREADY ordained *specifically for your life,* then it should be avoided, because it may have been sent by the enemy to serve as a distraction or as a temporary [or permanent] smoke screen. *Losing your focus at anytime, can throw you way off, but especially at this hour, it can be deadly! Always check with The Lord – FIRST!*

(c)   Enlists the use of ungodly methods, in an attempt to bring about acceptable, godly results. It is when we do anything (for Him) in a manner other than that which He has already prescribed.   If we are following Jehovah, then we must be willing to do things in the way that He instructs us to. *Any deviation* will be as foreign to Him.   *How can we stray from His authorized method of going about things, and still expect to receive His nod of approval?*   Uzza, (sometimes spelled Uzzah), in II Samuel 6:6-7, reached out his hand to lay hold of "The Ark", in an attempt to prevent it from falling, as it was being transported to, "The City of David" (Jerusalem). Although having "good intensions", Uzza, being a Levite, and having been well versed in "The Law" as well as in the instructions on the caring and transporting of "The Ark of The Covenant" (which represented God's Holy Presence), already knew that it was to be carried with 'staves', extending through the 'rings', which were to be borne upon the shoulders of the priests – not with the use of an ox and/or cart! There would have never been an occasion for the "new ox-cart" to have stumbled, had the ark been properly transported to begin with. Still Uzza's "good intensions" (to keep it from falling, by touching it), cost him his life.
Carry out God's instructions only! Our filthy hands are not fit to touch He who is Thrice Holy! Neither does He like it when we fail to follow His very specific set of instructions.

  (d)   "Purposely" mixes the secular with the sanctified, which we then attempt to pass off as being HOLY!   I may as well go ahead and finish getting into trouble. Take some of our praise and worship music for example; we want to "bump and grind" to the same melody that we use to do our "holy jig" (shout or dance). We want to "get our freak on", and still "lift up our hands in the sanctuary", *to the same exact tune* – by just changing the lyrics. Some say that there is no problem with this because it is *only music.* I too can appreciate a good tune or a love song – because I absolutely love great singing, and tasteful music. I mean, I am not made of stone you know. I have danced and partied with the best of them! But NEVER do I ever believe in mixing the secular with the sanctified. No way! The two of them together – absolutely not! ARE YOU FOR REAL??? Church is not the place to "get your groove on!" For where then shall we draw the line? *FELLOW CHRISTIANS LISTEN UP. Here I offer you a litmus test for your time of praise and worship.*

I don't care what else you've been told, or who else condones it, but if the music that you use for worshiping 'The Lord', in any way, makes you want to "wiggle, jiggle, bounce, do the electric slide, bump, grind, shake it up, smack it, flip it, rub it down, drop it like it's hot, or jump around like an a*s, an absolute idiot or buffoon, then chances are, you have entered into a dangerous zone with your so called "praise and worship" or HOLY [Gospel] experience.

If someone can explain to me, how it is that God is being reverenced, glorified and worshiped while we are "dropping it" and getting our "freaky-praise on", then perhaps I would understand – but I don't. Again, a little explanation here would be appreciated.

Still it really does not matter what I think, because I am not God. However, we are told by *Him* to, "Touch not the unclean thing" and to be "separate" and to "come out from amongst them." How then do we justify and attempt to explain away our "mixing", in the face of a Holy GOD – AND THEN, classify it as being praise and worship unto Him? How do we deem this mixture as being something pure or Holy? We cannot. Enough said! STRANGE FIRE! God does not take it lightly when He is offered a thing dripping with the smell of strange fire and sinful flesh; so why should we offer it and/or wallow in it?

Nadab and Abihu, priests of The Lord had determined *for whatever reason,* that they would gather fire for their censors for the evening sacrifice. Some scholars feel as though the two might have been drinking at the time, and were therefore smitten because of their wrongful handling of the [holy] instruments, in their intoxicated [sinful] state.

Others argue that the two acted presumptuously, in that the retrieving of the fire and/or the offering of incense had not been the task assigned to "them", but rather it was the responsibility of another (perhaps someone higher in rank). Still some have concluded that the two simply did not follow instructions; they gathered their fire (for God) from an unauthorized location.

Regardless of the [true] reason, the outcome was the same – it proved fatal. They filled their censers with fire and added to this the "Holy" incense to be offered before The Lord's presence. This one careless (or prideful) act cost them their lives (Leviticus 10:1).

After the two offered *"their fire"*, The Bible says that, *"Another fire [then] came out from The Lord and devoured them."* The Fire of a Holy God burned the two of them to a crisp! Never are we to mingle that which is Holy, with something that is not, AND THEN, throw it into the face of God, *as though He is obligated to* accept it. Like a bad chemical reaction, God's anger was kindled by their polluted fiery concoction. Remember boys and girls, bleach and ammonia simply do not mix! Do not try this at home or at your local church.

Once more, understand that even 'the slightest' deviation at this hour, could cost you your anointing, your physical life and/or your eternal soul.

Sometimes a person will tell us a thing, and for some reason, it makes us squirm and we become somewhat, (or perhaps even very) uneasy. You know what I mean? Although we cannot quite put our finger on what is making us uncomfortable, but for some unexplainable reason, we are taken back, alarmed, or our senses are totally on edge.

Strange fire does not necessarily have to be something that goes against Scripture, for often it will not. Fire to light the incense for the altar was indeed a very necessary part of the sacrifice or worship experience. In this respect, Nadab and Abihu had not done anything contrary to The Word of The Lord.

People may not necessarily tell us to do something 'wrong', if they do, then you had better run for the hills. What they tell you may not be out of line with The Bible at all, but you sense that *something* is gravely wrong. That feeling could very well be God's way of signaling *you* to beware of what you have just heard, because that communication is as strange fire [for your particular situation, calling or assignment]. Other people do not know everything that God has planned for your life – I have already told you about Peter and Jesus. The Messiah *had to* rebuke him. The devil was trying to use Peter to interrupt God's plan.

Likewise, people may tell you that you should build a "church", when in fact, The Lord has [already instructed YOU] to build Him an orphanage. Perhaps He has told you to accomplish something [for Him] that has absolutely nothing to do with "pulpit" ministry. On the other hand, perhaps *He has* called you to the pulpit, but others want you to remain an usher. Strange fire remember, does not automatically or necessary equate to something being sinful or ungodly in nature.

You may not even identify the person's command, request, suggestion, activity or advice as being strange fire, because what they are communicating is very ethical and actually does line up with Biblical principles.

A fellow Christian may even tell you that God has told them something to tell you. Brothers and sisters please do not be fooled. Yet again, I will repeat something that I have already said (as I have done a lot throughout this book, because it is that important ([smile]).   **Like I said, *satan also speaks, and people do listen.***

If deep inside, you experience a gnawing, disturbing, downright uneasy, (at times almost ominous) dreadful feeling, as you converse with someone or as you enter (or leave) a room, or even as you are on the telephone or embarking upon a project, I'm telling you, you had better think long and hard before proceeding. I admonish you to tread very carefully, regardless to the source of that communication.

Whenever I encounter anything that may be trying to thwart God's plan for my life, The Holy Spirit will make His presence known even more, by signaling to me that what I have heard needs to be tossed to the trash. You may feel as though your entire body (or certain parts thereof) seem to be reacting – that's because it literally is. For me the feeling resembles that of dread, sort of like a churning, deep down in the pit of my stomach.   Unless you have experienced this for yourself, it really is difficult for me to explain or for you to perhaps understand (sorry).

Many things that I experience are not always easy to explain. Like my grandmother use to say about her unexplainable experiences - "I just know what I know." Some things, my brothers and sisters, you just have to know. I have faith in you, that in time you will, if you do not already. Strange fire can leave us confused, dazed, bewildered, struggling to regain clarity, baffled and completely drained. This is especially true if the communication has come from a source that we trust, such as a pastor. Very often, we feel guilty for even questioning his/her advice. *Yet we know that something just isn't right.*

Although strange fire will cause The Holy Spirit to rise up in an attempt to obliterate what you have heard (so that it will not have an opportunity to penetrate your spirit or cause you to waste precious time), still He needs and expects your cooperation. We are the ones who must, "Cast down everything that exalts itself against the knowledge of God", (II Corinthians 10:4). We my friend, must take an active role in extinguishing the strange fires of our lives by using our weapons of war.

Strange fire will not always be direct. Sometimes, it will be <u>so</u> <u>subtle,</u> that you may not even recognize when you are being hit with it. <u>You have to be well trained to detect certain forms of it.</u>

As I was about ¾ of the way, with the completion of this book [assignment], I had a conversation, with a fellow Believer, who I met at a Christian bookstore. We decided to exchange numbers so that we could finish our conversation. At first, we talked about "Christianity" in general, but then we began to speak about things of "the prophetic."

Like a well-trained K9, my ears "perked up" as they always do, whenever anything about the prophetic ministry is being discussed.

At some point during the conversation, I mentioned to her that I was in the midst of writing a book. I gave her no specific details, (no title and no subject matter), for I was yet "feeling out" her spirit. For a while, the conversation progressed nicely – and mainly uneventful, with the exception of me still "feeling" (for somewhere in the back of my mind, I could sense that something was <u>suitably strange</u>).

For about ten minutes or so, we spoke about other things – something other than my book. When suddenly and very unexpectedly, she began telling me in a matter-of-fact manner that, "If God was the one who had instructed me to write it, then He also would have told my pastor about it." "Oh boy, here we go again"; another "prophet wannabe" I thought.

Anyway, I'm fair, so I listened patiently and very carefully.

Dear children, please make a mental note to yourselves: When speaking to people, <u>always "feel out"</u> before you <u>"blurt out."</u> Learn how to keep your mouth shut until further notice from "the gut." Be mindful when telling your plans or your dreams to ANYBODY! NOT EVERYONE IS YOUR FRIEND – NOT EVEN THOSE PEOPLE AND OR RELATIVES WHO PRETEND TO BE! SO BE CAREFUL AND REMAIN WATCHFULL ALWAYS!

Anyway, this person suggested that I get permission from my pastor to write the book. Now keep in mind dear friend, that I had almost finished writing it ALREADY. She said that he would give me the confirmation that I needed as well as his blessing for it, if the book were truly from The Lord.

She then told me, how she had received an idea from The Lord about having prayer, "several times a week in her home." Upon speaking with her pastor, he agreed to the prayer meetings, but he only agreed to once per week, and not to several times, as she claimed, The Lord had told her. This is the example she used, in an attempt to convince *me,* as to how God, her pastor and she were all in agreement, with what [she felt] God had given her to do. She said that her pastor's approval was a sign of God's approval and confirmation. Therefore, said she that her idea for prayer, really had come from The Lord.

My brother, my sister, as I've already stated, it is always desirous, to have a leader to whom you can go, but it simply is not the pattern for everything that you do, neither is this the pattern for everyone; for not all leaders will have your back. Sometimes you might just find yourself under a leader who will "never" embrace you [or your ideas/assignments], even if they have been birthed from above and your leader knows it. Some leaders will not embrace what you have to offer, simply because they are intimidated by what they see in you, or quite simply, because they don't want to. They may never give you the blessing, merely because they do not like you! Please let this sink in; I beg you.

TRUST ME WHEN I TELL YOU THAT, MANY OF THEM STILL WILL NOT ENDORSE YOU, EVEN IF GOD HAS ALREADY SPOKEN TO THEM! JUST AS WE <u>PURPOUSLY</u> DISOBEY HIM WHENEVER WE SIN, SO ALSO DO SOME IN LEADERSHIP <u>PURPOSULY</u> DISOBEY THE LORD'S INSTRUCTIONS CONCERNING A PERSON OR GROUP! SO, WHY NOT LET THE LORD BE YOUR GUIDE TO BEGIN WITH?

<u>*Although my book was nearly 'complete', she told me to speak with my pastor (in order to obtain his permission and his blessing). Keep in mind brothers and sisters, after my last devastating encounter with him, which left me thoroughly dazed and depressed, The Lord had ALREADY TOLD ME that, "There were to be no more meetings" [with my pastor]. Now dear reader, I ask you, to whom do you suppose I listened?*</u>

I had to go with what God had already spoken [to me], long before she and I had ever connected. Had I known her for years, still I would have done the exact same thing. I would have ignored her advice! This sister's counsel became as "strange fire", because it did not line up with what God had already spoken. Because The Lord had not spoken to ME PERSONALLY about changing direction – I did not.

I cannot caution you enough to be extremely careful, as you are actively engaging in that which you know to be The Lord's will, when somebody, (whether friend or stranger), suddenly attempts to give you advice, or to "bring you a word", even as you are in the midst of the assignment. Do not heed it, unless YOU have heard GOD tell YOU to shift gears, because there has been a change in HIS plan.

Beware that satan will send new people, or he may even dig up a former acquaintance. A person (or even several) people from your past, may suddenly resurface – so be very careful! Do not fall for the bait; this has been conjured up to serve as a distraction.

Your adversary, who wants you to fail, and who even wants you dead, will use anybody! Even in the subtlest of forms shall they appear. Be warned; and be careful. You my brothers and sisters, who are in the midst of an assignment, must especially stay on top of your game, because believe me, your adversary certainly stays on top of his; he will use ANYBODY to mess you up – believe that!

If you fail to reach those to whom to you have been assigned; if you fail to deliver the message that God has given to you, how then will the next group of assignees know what to do? Do not fail! Stay focused! Shut your mouth! And keep moving! Do not return that phone call – you hear me?! Don't go with that man, or that woman!

I recommend that everyone visit (or re-visit) The Old Testament. There you will find in the book of 1 Kings 13:1-34, a story about a "Young man of God" (A young prophet), who was sent by God into a place, to deliver a word of judgment to King Jeroboam. His job was to deliver the message, and to keep moving.

He was given clear, precise instructions FROM GOD, BEFORE ever entering the town. Anyway, the king did not like the message that was given, and tried to lay hold of the prophet. Upon doing so, the king's hand dried up (withered/shrank). He besought the young man to, "Intreat The Face of The Lord", that his hand might be restored. The prophet did, and it was.

The king having been humbled, asked the prophet to come to his home in order to "refresh himself" (by dining, drinking and resting). The king also wanted to reward him for the restoration of his hand. Flatly refusing the king's offer of food, drink, or reward, the young prophet went about his business - he left. So far so good.

The young man now on his way, having **_ALREADY BEEN TOLD BY_ _GOD_**, that he was not to eat or drink **_AT ALL_** while in that town, and furthermore that he was to exit the town by a different route than the one he had used to enter. After he left the king, and went on his way, he took a break and sat under an oak tree – big mistake! In that same town was an older prophet, who by this time, had gotten wind of the events, and made it his business to track down the young man and invite him to his home. The younger prophet refused, telling the older that The Lord had straightway charged him, that he should not do so.

Listen up reader this part is for YOU:

The older prophet then told the young man that it would be ok for him to come with him, because he too was also a prophet, just like himself and that an angel had visited him and told him, that he was to bring him (the young prophet) back to his home. Verse 18 clearly states that – THE OLDER PROPHET LIED TO HIM! He lied, on purpose in the name of The Lord, and the young man believing him, went home with him. Deadly mistake! There at the old prophet's home, the younger prophet ate, and he drank.

Howbeit, right in the midst of his meal, The Word of The Lord came (for real this time), into the mouth of the very prophet (the older guy) who had deceived him in the first place. God said that inasmuch as the young prophet disobeyed THE [ORIGINAL] WORD OF THE LORD, **_SPOKEN DIRECTLY TO HIM_** – INSTRUCTING THAT HE WAS NOT TO EAT NOR DRINK IN THAT TOWN, AT ALL; HIS CARCASE WOULD NEVER MAKE IT TO THE GRAVE TO BE BURRIED WITH HIS FATHERS.

As the young man went his way, he was killed by a lion. He lost his life, because he disobeyed THE LORD. He allowed himself to be fooled by the older prophet who lied to him. That we may know, this was indeed **_the judgment of God,_** his carcase remained in tact– (under normal circumstances, a lion would have eaten the carcase too, but The Lord suffered the beast to kill him only and not to rip his remains into shreds or to completely devour his body and bones). Word quickly spread abroad, and everyone was told that "This was [the carcase of] the man of God, who disobeyed God!" At first glance, it seems as though the older prophet should have died, because he lied. To us it doesn't seem fair; there however is an urgent lesson for all to learn.

The moral of this story boys and girls is: – LISTEN ONLY TO GOD! IF THERE IS A CHANGE IN PLANS, HE WILL TELL YOU HIMSELF! He that hath an ear to hear [The Spirit of God] had better certainly take heed!

Not so very long ago, a conversation such as the one that I told you about with the person from the bookstore would have been enough to take me on a whole new journey of torture. Why? Because again, I would have gone crazy not wanting to be wrong in God's sight by not consulting my pastor. I would have began doubting myself, wondering as to whether or not I were truly hearing from The Lord. "What if this?" "What if that?" This would have led to yet another round of cruel mental anguish.

I would have believed that this person absolutely had to be right and that once again; it was I who just had to be wrong. Thank God, for my deliverance from that crap! Had I not already overcame it by the time of my encounter with the "wannabe" from the store, then you my brother or sister probably would not be reading this book right now.

This point cannot be stressed enough; the key is to be certain that you first, know when The Spirit of God is speaking to you! Once you are certain that The Creator is on your side, then I say go for it! It will be up to you to muster up the confidence to politely [or to very sharply if need be], dispel and rebuke ALL unsolicited opinions and/or advice.

The subtlest of suggestions can originate from the annals of strange fire. Even these have been conjured up for your destruction and/or for the aborting of your purpose – KILL IT ALL! REMEMBER THE AMALIKITES! LET NO RESIDUAL OF THE STRANGE COMMUNICATION RAMAIN IN YOUR MIND!

If you have truly been baptized by Fire, then The Holy Spirit resides on the inside, and will always warn you of possible dream killers. "DANGER, DANGER, DANGER, do not listen to that!" "Ignore at all costs!" "Limit your conversation with him or with her." "Do not entertain those thoughts!" "For your destiny's sake, do not take to heart what you have just heard!" "That's not me! I repeat that counsel was not from The Father – DO YOU HEAR ME?"

The Holy Spirit warns me, and proceeds to flush out the intruding words. He turns on the fountain, nestled deep within my belly's reservoir. Jesus said, "He that believeth on Me (Jesus), as The Scripture hath said, out of his belly shall flow rivers of living water." (John 7:38). The living waters of The Lord are much mightier than the forces of hell. His Words of truth are the living waters. They are capable of forcing up and out, every poisonous "word dart" that proceeds from the enemy. He does expect your cooperation of course. You will eventually come to the place wherein you will have the courage to stand up, come against and say "no" to the strange fires that come your way.

Deprogramming your mind from the opinions of people is extremely crucial for your survival. For me, it is a matter of life and death. My spirit had been vexed to the very core, but Jesus the lover of my soul rescued me. He keeps a thorough watch over me, now more than ever – especially over my mind. He is the only one able to keep me from falling and to present me faultless before the presence of His glory with exceeding joy. (Jude 24-25).

Early in life, I figured that if I pleased people, I would fit right in - you know, I wanted *everyone* to like me. I thought that if I stayed in my place, and *colored between the lines,* that I would be well spoken of and that I would have many friends. I did all of that, but still they rejected me. Even if they did not verbally deem me an outcast, their subtle (and even not so subtle) ways and actions were sufficient to do the job.

I am relearning who I am, as well as whose I am. No longer do I doubt my inner gut when The Spirit speaks to me. The Blood of The Lord Jesus Christ covers me. I may never be wanted or accepted in the circle of people, but I can guarantee you, that I have a VIP membership in His court. So many people are plagued with memories of fathers (or mothers), who never affirmed them but who instead only served as a constant source of criticism. If our natural fathers were any indication as to what we could expect from those who are supposed to nurture us, it is a wonder that we ever desired a [spiritual] father at all. Nevertheless, we did only to receive more pain.

Women without fathers have often turned to prostitution, drugs and the like. The world is filled with grown men (and women), who have children of their own, but who are yet craving a safe, valid touch from the one they call dad. A good father lovingly brings life, sustenance and hope to his awaiting family. There was a time in my life that I came face to face with my own [then] reality; realizing that just about every male figure, in whom I had ever trusted, had in some way or another failed me. They had let me down real hard! At first glance, this discovery nearly devastated me.

However, I later uncovered something more. I found out that *my Heavenly Father* would never toss me aside. He would never make empty promises; He would never use me, lie to me or treat me with disdain or total disregard. He would never give me a way, or turn His back on me. Never would He ever neglect or reject me. I realized that He would not make fun of me, nor would He ever leave me. I have made it my occupational duty, to fervently cling to one man only, "The Man Christ Jesus."

Following Jesus and understanding the things of The Father are not always easy. Jesus admonished us to "take up our cross."   Cross carrying is hard work. This is serious, business and only the committed need apply. If along the way, you feel hurt because of life's circumstances, just know that He is right there. We have a comforter who promises to be with us every step of the way. You have me; I will be praying for you.

You will also have at your disposal your very own private coaching team. For peering just over the banister of heaven is a great cloud filled with witnesses, who are always urging you to go forward – imagine having a 24-hour cheering section. "You can do it!" "Accept The Lord now (while you still have a chance). "Learn of The Father just as we did." By faith, can't you just hear them!

Come on what do you have to lose? You have already been through enough. Won't you come and be adopted by my Dad? If you are already one of His children, have you ever even thanked Him for taking you in? If you haven't, then why not take a moment to do it right now? I will even do it with you.

Father we just thank You for loving us enough to even *want* to be our Dad, because many of us are deserving of nothing but Your wrath. And so we thank You Lord God for being merciful and for loving us too much to leave us in the hands of parents who hated us; under the coverings of "wolf clerics" who tried to bite us; or even to ourselves as we became our own worse enemy, when we seemingly could take no more. And in Jesus' Name, we say thank You Father God from the bottom of our hearts.

He is, as my daughter would say - the bomb!   I pray that you will also discover this for yourself. No matter how old you are you too can crawl up into His lap and tell Him all of the little girl and little boy secrets that you could never share with anyone else – including your own fathers. You will never find a closer friend, a better counselor, consultant, or confident than The Lord. I found Him to be a mighty refuge.

I found in Him everything that I ever needed. If you trust Him and talk to Him (even when you sin); I believe that you will also discover Him to be exactly what you have been looking for- a true Father and friend. My brother, my sister, If you really want to know who it is that may be calling *your name,* and who it is that might be trying to get *your attention,* simply ask the question, "Dad is that you?"

Remember my friend, wait and then carefully listen for **HIS reply.**

Note: When quoting Scripture, all spelling is as it appears in The Holy Writ. These are not errors. For example, instead of "entreat", you will see "intreat". Instead of "carcass", (like in the dictionary), you will see "carcase."

❧Oops, Wrong Fold❧

Struggling to fit in, has been something with which I have contended, since my earliest existence. I would even have to fight <u>before</u> legally making it into the earth realm. Looking back, it seems as though a force, sent directly from hell, has *always been intent on trying to make me its causality – in one way or another.* For even the drawing of my very first "post womb" breath, would not be possible, without me first having to engage in serious warfare. It seems as though, I was expected to *"first"* overcome [in the spirit], the very thing that threatened to snuff out my voice (before it would ever be heard) in the natural. I literally had to fight, for the right to exist on this realm. This same thing, [which would follow me for much of my life], would eventually try to keep me from fulfilling the will of God. It was as though I would have to conquer it, *before it conquered me, or before I actually faced it in the natural. Very strange the business of spiritual warfare – but it is ever so real!* "God must have something awfully big for me to do, cause the devil sure is trying hard to stop me", I would often think and say as I grew up.

Little did I realize, that many years later, while on the verge of tears, I would find myself once more uttering the very words that seemed to become my mantra. "God must have something awfully big for me to do, because the devil sure is trying hard to stop me", I blurted out in-between sobs, as I spoke to a friend. As you already know, sometimes God may be trying to get our attention. However, dear friends you must realize and <u>always</u> remember that your adversary rarely takes a break – if indeed he takes one at all! It is his mission to do everything possible to keep us from fulfilling our purpose and to prevent us from becoming all that we have been created to be. "Darn it if something hasn't always tried to block my path." So as it is in the natural, so is it also in the spirit. Brothers and sisters you have got to fight just to be free! Moreover, you may have to fight, in order to live! My mom has told me the story, of how she encountered some major complications during childbirth. Stricken with a life-threatening illness, the doctors *had* no choice but to literally ask my father to choose which of us, they should 'try' to save.

Would it be mom or me? According to the physicians, neither of us had but a slim chance of making it through the birthing process alive. My mother said the doctors asked my biological father, (now deceased) which of us should be saved, *if it were even possible to save one at all.* Of course, my dad chose my mother. I mean after all, I cannot really blame him because I had not even been born yet, but my mother, well she was already here. Like most couples, I suppose he figured that they could always try again. Pop, I "ain't" mad at you, and I do understand. If I were married, I pray that my husband would make the same decision. Not that I would *want* my unborn child to die, but honestly, most of us would probably hope that our spouse would also opt to try again.

In those days, mom said that she prayed a lot. At that time, "prayer cloths" were all the rage throughout Christendom. Mom often tuned in to people like Reverend Ike and Oral Roberts, who were both very popular in her day. I do in fact recall seeing the "red" prayer cloths that she obtained from one of them. Anyway, she said that she prayed and held on to her prayer cloth as a "point of contact." While I am on this subject, please allow me to say a few brief words about the whole "point of contact" element.

We know that "the cloth" in and of itself is powerless, as it is only a piece of material. It is the power of The Living God, however, that provides the healing, but somehow it seems to help, if we have something tangible upon which to cling. From the body of The Apostle Paul, the sick were brought handkerchiefs or aprons. In turn, sickness departed from them, and the evil spirits went out of them. God wrought this great miracle through His manservant. God used the Apostle Paul, but – "the virtue" came from above. Read all about it in – Acts 19:11-12. I feel the need to clarify this for people who are younger in the faith or in age, as well as for the many who have been taught or who have "assumed incorrectly." Some may believe (for whatever reason), that the actual healing comes from an inanimate object or from a man. Because there are so many crazy things being taught out there, I felt compelled to make it plain.

As mom prayed to The Lord, she promised Him that if He would bring her *and* her baby through the ordeal alive, she would serve Him for life, and would bring her child up in the things of The Lord, to the best of her ability. Well, as you can see dear reader, *I* at least managed to survive the life-threatening ordeal; and am alive and well. I am here and able to tell my own story. Unfortunately, the outcome for my mother was not quite as successful. She may have gotten the worst part of the deal; for you see she has had the task of having to listen to my big mouth and to put up with all of my "talking and dreaming" for all of these years (smile).

Got ya! Besides her bouts with "Arthritis", mom is doing just fine.

Well, since The Lord did not permit satan to kill me at birth, he would continue to harass me throughout much of my life. The one thing besides Jesus that I use to desire was to be liked by people. I wanted lots friends. You know, like many of us, we want to be loved and to be well spoken of. Although I have never relentlessly pursued the spotlight or endeavored to become overwhelmingly popular, I did however, *want to* fit in or to at least be an integral 'functioning' part of something significant. I also wanted to do my part in working for the cause of Christ. I wanted my life to count for *something.* I wanted it to have meaning and purpose. While I did have *a few* friends, still much more of my younger life was subjected to rejection and pain – for quite early in my life, the opinions of people had managed to oppress me – just like satan had always planned it.

Growing up, I constantly seemed to attract opposition and/or unwanted attention. For some reason I simply did not fit and people never seemed to let me forget that very painful fact. Don't get me wrong, no matter who we are, sometimes we will encounter people who will not like us, *for whatever reason.* At times, even our very presence is enough to irritate them. The worse part about not being liked is that often we do not understand why we are hated so much. This can be extremely devastating, if fitting in and forming friendships rank high on our list.

In fact, to this very day, [for the most part], I still do not fit. The difference now though is; I am ok with it. I have since learned to embrace my calling as well as my differences, and am quite comfortable with being me. To be down right blunt about it – I no longer care about fitting in, because I've got to be who I am and not a carbon copy of what others view as being acceptable. It took a very long time, but finally I realized, that I had never fit in, because frankly, I wasn't supposed to. God had designed me this way from the beginning. I have been born to blaze a trail and not to follow in the footsteps of the majority. For my differences, today I can now say - Thank You Lord!

For those of you, who now walk this same path, I want you to know that I realize how difficult it can be, to feel displaced. But it is even more difficult to feel that way, in an organization that is supposed to be an earthly representation of The Lord's House. I mean, it is bad enough when you are not welcomed or respected in other areas – but in the church too? My longing to belong only pushed me deeper into the arms of my Heavenly Father. In the midst of my pain, is where The Lord began to share with me, how He also had been a reject.

Sometimes we may read something, or simply skim over it, but about nine years ago, The Lord began to burn this into my soul. He really comforted me, by explaining, in great detail, how He too had been rejected. He let me know that it was ok not to fit with people, so long as I fit with Him. This same precious pearl, I now hand to you. I urge you to strive to fit with Him – and not with them! We are told in The Book of Isaiah concerning The Lord Jesus that, "He hath no form or comeliness (beauty, grace or majesty), and when we shall see Him; there is no beauty that we should desire Him." In every day language, the people of Jesus' day considered Him to be "ugly" or "plain"; there was nothing at all about Him that would make you even want to look twice – he was ordinary (I'm sorry Jesus).

Perhaps the prophet was speaking prophetically, in that it would be the world's sins that The Saviour would later take upon Himself, which would indeed render Him unattractive and marred to the natural eye. He was destined to become a bloody mess, hanging on a rugged cross that should have instead held me (and you!) as its captive.

He paid the price, which was legally ours to pay. With His skin ripped to shreds, and with The Red Blood streaming down, He hung there with the blackness of our wickedness upon His sinless righteousness. With this, I suppose that He had become very ugly indeed. He laid down His own life and allowed Himself to become an awful sight upon which to gaze because the destiny of a sinful world lay in the balance.

Again Jesus, I am so sorry for whatever part I have personally played in sentencing you to that cruel death, (God I am so sorry).

If this were not only the foreseeing of the prophet, but if indeed Jesus had been *physically* unattractive as well, then He too literally had no choice, but to understand exactly how it feels to be picked on because of some external flaw or feature. His experiencing of the world's cruelty would make Him an even more touchable Saviour and King. This is why I love Him so much. *He truly does understand me.* The Bible says of Jesus that, He "was despised and rejected." "He was a man of sorrow and acquainted with grief." He was an outcast; He was just like me! He knows what it feels like to possess great value and yet lack affirmation, opportunity and respect. He knows exactly how it is that *we* feel when we desire to fit or long to be accepted, but instead we are turned away.

The Word of God also tells me that my Saviour came to His own people and they received Him not (John 1:11). Even at His birth, The Messiah would have to settle for being born in a manger, used to house the animals. In Matthew 8:20 and Luke 9:58, Jesus Himself lets us know that, "Even the foxes have holes, and the birds of the air have nests; but The Son of Man hath not where [has no where] to lay His head." He lets us know that if we follow Him, we *must* prepare for some discomfort along the way. Even He had been unwelcome on more occasions than imaginable. He *can* unequivocally identify with all who possess gifting and ability but are not able to utilize them in the places wherein they find themselves.

At times, The Lord Jesus could not even perform miracles in His own town because of the people's unbelief. They did not accept Him, nor had they any faith in Him. In fact, it was His own people that eventually voted to have Him crucified, for they believed not who He was. Imagine, He who had breathed life into creation, had been rejected and would be killed by them. The same people, into whose nostrils He had exhaled, [descendants of the first man Adam], were now using that very breath to scream for His crucifixion at Golgotha, [the place that we call Calvary] - Lord God!

From my earliest recollection of childhood memories and even to this very day, there has <u>always</u> been something inside of me, which causes me to identify with and to vehemently route for the success of the underdog. It is as though I see those who do not fit, as being part of my extended family. I have always been drawn to and have always felt the deepest connection with the rejected, with the left out and with the outcast. Whether or not the victim happened to be a 'real life' or fictional character, was of no real significance. What was important is that I had someone with whom I could identify. As I witnessed their struggles, and applauded their triumphs, my heart would break as well as cheer. I would get a glimmer of hope, just knowing that someone who had been a reject, had also risen victoriously. I figured that if they could overcome the pain of it all, then so could I.

Thanks to Hans Christian Anderson, there exists a tale of one "little ducky" whose story shall remain immortal. His life has served as a pillar of hope to a myriad of others who have their very own ugly duckling stories to tell. A person will not always display a noticeable physical defect. Some people choose not to like another individual "just because." In the words of the late Reverend James Cleveland, "Some people don't like you – cause they just don't like you." "Not that you've ever done anything to them, but they just don't like you." Others have felt the backlash of people's cruelty and hostility because of skin color, race, religion, weight, economical status or perhaps, because they actually *did* sport an obvious physical and/or emotional defect of some sort.

No wonder even The Lord Jehovah repented in His heart, as He wished He had never made man. It hurt Him to the very core to know that, "Every imagination of the thoughts of man's heart was only evil continuously." (Genesis 6:5-6). It saddens me to know, that even in *our* congregations, people have been the brunt of cruel pranks and jokes, because of some physical characteristic, over which they have absolutely no control. In our world, there exists individuals who feel exactly like, "Rudolf The Red Nosed Reindeer." They have been made fun of, purposely excluded and left totally out of life's reindeer games. They are taunted just because something about *them* or about their appearance does not measure up to what *society views as normal.*

These people are faithful in serving, and also in giving, *but* due to their noticeable external differences, they still do not fit the mold and are quite often, viciously scorned. They are stamped REJECT! Very often, they feel compelled to hang their heads in shame. Oh sure, they may feel good as long as the music is pumping and the preacher is ranting, so perhaps *you* cannot tell. They put on a "great face", but how are they 'really' feeling deep inside? It *seems* unlikely, but even churches that claim to be so full of love, love, and more love, are not guiltless of maligning individuals who are not as they expect them to be. Even those that advertise themselves as being "family friendly", where *everyone* is supposed to be welcomed and where *everyone* is supposed to be loved; even in churches like these, there exists a high percentage of the neglected and the lonely.

To people in my church, on my job or in society, I am a mere nothing – a nobody. Maybe I am a "zero" just like a boy named Cliff, whose painful story I shared with you in the beginning of this book. I suppose they see me as nobody at all; only a huge pile of flesh with nothing to offer. I see how they look at me, and I have felt the effects of their ill treatment. I bet though if someone like Billy Graham were to become my mentor, my pastor would sit up and take notice. Let me record an album or suddenly become famous, surely then symbols of dollar bills would replace the piercing glares of disdain that now fills his eyes. Surely then, I would gain some respect from people. If I possessed great wealth, everyone would see me as a candidate, worthy of their precious time. Surely then, I would have no shortage of mentors or lack of advancement opportunities. Instead of my pastor, tossing me aside, surely then he would embrace me as his own.

For thousands of people acceptance has been something for which they have long sought; but to this day, it remains only a dream. Even if such a one should depart, the local assembly may still attack. Although the individual [or group] had been totally ignored while laboring amongst them, neither had he/she ever been given an ounce of respect (nor common courtesy in some cases); yet the person is stigmatized for leaving.

It matters not whether he or she departs peacefully, more often than not, there will remain a trail of dusty gossip swirling in the air. Should a brother or sister leave a congregation, he or she is then placed on the pastor's hit list. God forbid anyone should inquire about the brother or sister, <u>after the pastor has shot him or her down with negative comments.</u>

Some congregations can be so brainwashed, that they literally rebuke another person, for simply *asking* about an estranged member. "He has some nerve, leaving our fine, wonderful establishment." "What does she think she will find 'out there' that she can't get from us?" "We have one of the largest congregations in the area – why would anyone *want* to leave?" "Our pastor is the best." "They must have a serious problem!" "Who do they think they are anyway? Humph!" Even a member, who at one time may have received the pastor's public praise and adoration, can suddenly find him or herself on the black list. It is bad enough to be 'totally ignored' and unrecognized; but it has got to be especially painful for a person, who had once been part of the pastor's elite pet club, and who at one time, found him or herself being well spoken of, to suddenly find that he or she has been reduced to bastard or reject status. It must be darned painful for a person to realize that he or she has been booted out of the club and demoted to the same rank as the common folk. Ouch! Now that has to hurt! I don't know what's worse. Is it more difficult to stand, *after one has tasted the morsels of favoritism,* served from the table of "fleshly" delight, only to suddenly be put out? On the other hand, on the other hand, is it worse to have never tasted of the delicious delicacies at all?

Because of an individual's departure as well as the crafty, divisive words of the leader, very often a congregation's opinion of a person is swayed. The poor soul then becomes as one who is deserving of congregational shunning. At the giving of the shepherd's command, the once faithful brother or sister has been reduced to a rebellious foe.

Dear reader, I ask you, is it not better for a person to depart *in peace,* rather than to hang around and harbor ill feelings, or to be forever slighted? How does *anyone* in the congregation even know the *'real'* details that led up the person's departure? When an individual (or group) leaves an establishment, those who are left behind, only hear one side of the story. If a member, and the pastor (or another leader) has a falling out, and the bruised individual leaves, (or in some cases is asked or told to vacate), the congregation remains totally oblivious as to what <u>really</u> might have gone down. They are left with fragments of details and at best, can only make assumptions. You know what they say, that a person makes of him or herself as well as of others, whenever one dares to <u>assume</u> don't you? They make an "a*s" out of "u" and "me", while satan makes one out of us all!

Don't you dare do it! It is ugly to hold a brother or sister in contempt based solely upon something you've heard.

More than one person has shared with me, how that upon leaving their assemblies, there was the initiation of an immediate gag order concerning them. The members of their former congregations were told, (in some cases ordered) to have nothing more to do with the departed person (or group). The pastors would tell the leaders; in turn, the leaders of the various auxiliaries would inform the rest of the people, letting everyone know, that their one time brother or sister, had now entered into "sin and rebellion."

Should a current member run into a former parishioner on the street, the order would still be in affect. Even if a former member happened to be a relative, the member, "in good standing", would be prohibited from having any dealings with the traitor. The order would remain effective until the departed sister or brother, makes the decision to come to his/her senses. Until then (if ever), the person would be given the silent treatment or cold shoulder. Regardless of relationship, be it friend or family; any known violation of the gag order, would place the member in good standing, in direct danger of also being "shunned." *What the hell!?* Church, what in the world is up with this foolishness?! Do we as Christians honestly believe that this is how Jesus would handle such matters? We are in worse shape than I thought, if in our hearts we truly believe, that this is how we are *supposed* to treat one another.

There is one thing, that I want you all to get straight and it is this, PASTORS TELL LIES TOO! I did not say that they made mistakes in telling the congregation things; I said that sometimes they outright lie in order to make themselves look good! They are flesh just like the rest of us and they often foul up too.

Clerics have been known to blatantly twist the truth, by *intentionally* omitting parts of a story; consequently, the congregation remains ignorant as to the real events of a matter. They are left clueless, as to what actually transpired. Many brainwashed, controlled congregations have had their minds seared. Often they are the last to know it, and in many instances, they are not even capable of discerning truth from error. I understand that pastors will sometimes enhance their sermons as they paint vivid pictures into the imaginations of the listeners; which is often harmless. However, the danger occurs, when embellishment takes a completely new spin, and is used to purposely add harmful lies.

The problem arises when there is an omitting of truth or the covering up of blatant evildoings. The unsuspecting listeners often take everything at face value, based solely on a person's position.

How do we know what <u>really</u> went on? How can we be so sure that our accused brother or sister is actually the guilty party?

We have this notion that leaders are perfect individuals who are incapable of doing wrong. By wrong, I am not referring to them making mistakes or having weaknesses for which they are actively seeking deliverance, because each of us has *some* struggle. Moreover, if we do not admit to such – we are liars and there is no truth in us. What I am talking about though, is when pastors purposely set out to target those in the congregation. I have already told you about Saul and David. Most congregations believe their leaders to be exempt from slandering, and so, the flock tends to automatically take sides, as many therein proceed to talk about that, which they know absolutely nothing about. What they really need to do, is to shut their mouths and go somewhere and pray! I urge you to reserve your quick rendering of judgment, because you do not necessarily know the entire [truthful] story.

If you *must* know what *really* happened, then why not ask The Lord? Let Him decide whether or not He feels it is any of your business. Be warned though, the shoes in which you stand today, may not be the same ones in which you will be standing on tomorrow. For on tomorrow, YOU too could very well be, in the same shoes as today's victims. You may suddenly find yourself on the outside looking in, realizing that you have been kicked out of the clique.

Don't you dare turn your back on, or permanently dismiss a brother or sister based purely on speculation or on the strength of a rumor. You do not know the whole of a matter – but God does. How do you know, if whether or not it was simply within the timing of God for the individual to move on? Why would any <u>righteous leader</u> or congregation be offended in that?_Why does a person always have to be blackballed or described as being in rebellion for doing nothing more than trying to follow Gods lead? Sometimes He does lead people out of places. This is supposed to be God's business and not everyone else's. We have been created in <u>God's image</u> and have been chosen to do <u>His will,</u> not the will of a pastor who refuses to let us - get it?

Although some people will be born in, raised up in and eventually die in the same old spot; be it in a particular church, town, city, home or other; this simply is not the plan for everyone.

The destinies of some people will take them over the four walls and into another place entirely. Remember the emphasis on the importance of growing and not remaining stagnant? God will at times, ordain that a person remain in a place for only a season.

Just as He leads us <u>to</u>, sometimes He leads us <u>from</u>. Just as He sends us <u>in</u>, there are times when He will demand us to come <u>out</u>!

There are times however, due to traumatic or unbearable circumstances, that a person may [finally] decide to leave on his or her own. An individual can arrive at a place in life wherein he or she realizes that; *any place* has to be better than his/her current surroundings. It is not until *we* get tired of hurting, that *we* finally begin to seek answers. It is not until *we* as individuals realize that it hurts too much to stay put, that *we* finally find the courage to do *something* about our pain. When *we* just cannot take it any longer, because <u>we need</u> to stop hurting, we may stop coming around altogether. Little do we know, nor do we even realize, that this decision may actually be the defining moment of our very lives.

You see, my brothers and sisters, one day we may <u>accidentally discover</u>, that we are nothing at all like those, with whom we have always surrounded ourselves. Often it is by The Master's design, that we literally, find ourselves stumbling into destiny.

I hope that you, dear reader are familiar with the all time classic story of "The Ugly Duckling." Venture with me as we explore the life of *my* little feathered friend, whose personal destiny, left him no choice but to leave his familiar surroundings.

One fine day a mother duck decided to take her children out into the world. As they journeyed, the little ducks passed by several creatures. Mother duck instructed her babies to have manners and to always be polite. She told them to give a curtsy to the, "Big haughty-looking duck with the red ribbon around her leg." Mother duck explained to her babies that she was a very important person; she was a "Spanish Grandee." The little ducks were to curtsy politely as they made their way. They obeyed momma duck and did exactly as told. When the Spanish Grandee however, caught a glimpse of the poor ugly duckling, she bit him on the neck. In his defense, momma duck told her not to bother him. "You leave him alone!" she commanded." "He may not be as pretty as some, but he has a sweet disposition, and he *is* the best swimmer of the lot." "Besides, he'll look better when he grows up." "He won't seem so big and awkward then." (Gee thanks momma duck! – I think).

Taunting, teasing and rejection were something that the little duck would have to get use to. Not only did the Grandee bite him, but *all* of the other creatures in the yard made fun of him too. The ducks pushed him, the chickens teased him, the turkeys bit him; even the girl in charge of feeding the animals kicked him. His own brothers and sisters were mean to him. He felt awful; He was isolated and ever so lonely. The little duckling had in a very short time, become the object *everyone's* ridicule and scorn. One day while hopelessly discouraged, he concluded that he *could not* stand it any longer, and with that, he flew away. Like many of us, I imagine that he came to his conclusion after carefully considering the matter. "Would anyone even care if I were no longer around? "Probably not", he reasoned within himself, and with that, he left. After fleeing his surroundings, the little duckling soon discovered that other people and other animals could be just as cruel as the ones he had left behind. He was still mocked and teased by nearly **everyone** he encountered. One cold winter's day, the little duckling found himself frozen in the center of a solid ice block, which sat directly in the middle of a pond. He had hidden himself behind a bush, as he attempted to escape the dangers of hunting season.

Unfortunately, he did not realize how long he had stayed in that same spot, and now, he was stuck! Somebody please hear God right now!

After a very long time a farmer came along; feeling sorry for the little duckling, he decided to take him to his house. All warmed up now, and inside the kind farmer's home, the children wanted to play with him, but the duck became flustered; for he was not accustomed to *anybody actually wanting* to play with him. He immediately became anxious and afraid, which in turn, made his already awkward movements, even worse.   Like so many who have been abused, abandoned or rejected, he had never been the center of *good* attention. Most people (and even animals), who have been abused, are only use to being sought after, in order to be made fun of, or either for the express purpose of becoming the object of another's vicious prank or cruel joke.

Because the only purpose, that they have ever served, has been to be a recipient of ridicule and pain, many abuse victims (and survivors) may not even know how *to receive* kindness. "Good attention" was an entirely new concept for the duckling. Not only was he awkward *looking*, but also his movements were less than graceful. He probably did not know *how* to play; besides we all know how little children can be with animals.   In their excitement, they probably frightened the poor duck half to death. At that precise moment, the farmer's wife happened to be doing some baking in the kitchen. As the children tried to play with him, the duckling became all the more awkward and unbalanced.   He eventually landed in a tub of butter.

The children continuing with their futile attempts to capture him, while at the same time the duckling was attempting to recover from the butter incident, made things even worse. The duck still being off balance fell again - this time landing in a barrel of flour. He must have looked an awful mess, as he fluttered aimlessly around the kitchen, trying to regain his composure. As if *that* were not bad enough, in her agitation, the farmer's wife shooed him away, forcing him to make a hasty escape. Out the door he went in a flash, with a trail of flour and butter following close behind.

In a matter of minutes, he was homeless again, and once more, he set out on his lonely journey. Since the time of the duckling's departure from his home of origin, to the time of the butter and flour incidents, right up to his present set of circumstances, there had been a change in season. The duck had endured an entire winter virtually alone, and still had no place that he could call home. So far, he had not fit anywhere – Lord God! This is so familiar. As he journeyed, he saw these incredibly beautiful white birds. "Oh how graceful they are", he thought as he marveled to himself. He was amazed at how they flew with such grace and precision. Oh God how he loooooooonged to meet them.

He found himself completely taken back by their beauty – they were breathtaking. Not only that, but for <u>some</u> <u>strange</u> <u>reason,</u> he felt connected to them. Though he had never met them, still for reasons that he did not understand, nor could he even begin to explain, he found himself intensely drawn to those elegant creatures of flight and grace.

One day, as he [again] was feeling incredibly down on himself, he made another decision. Unbeknownst to him, *this one* however, would change the course of his entire life. Oh God! Can somebody help me say turning point! He determined in his heart that he would go over and meet those beautiful birds. There was *something* about them that *made* him just *have* to meet them. *He simply HAD to – Oh God!*

There is a mighty big difference in someone <u>wanting</u> to do a thing, as opposed to him or her <u>having</u> to. For some of us, ministry has never been optional. Being "marked" by The Almighty has been our portion. We were created for a purpose; we have been commanded to accomplish a thing, and we will <u>never</u> be able to do anything else, no matter how hard we try, and regardless to how violently we may oppose the plan – we simply <u>must</u> comply. Frankly, we would have to admit (or we will eventually discover), that we could never be content doing anything else anyway. Though other things may pacify for the moment or even for several seasons, our soul refuses to be totally satisfied. Never will it be content, until we have become who or what we were destined to be.

And so it was for our friend, who had made up his mind that he would inquire about those lovely creatures, even if it cost him his life. He purposed in his heart that he would go and meet them. He reasoned within himself as he concluded that, "It would be far better to be plucked to death, bitten or rejected by these lovely birds, than to be beaten by the hens, pushed around by the maiden who feeds the poultry or to starve to death each winter."

Yes! The duckling's mind was made up; "this is it", he thought. He was afraid as to how they would receive him – *for he expected to be rejected. Ridicule and rejection had after all, been the only things that he had known since birth.* Undaunted by fear, and driven forward by faith, determined to meet them, the duck set out on his intentions.   I believe that as he inched his way towards them, doubt and fear began to set in. I *know* that he had second thoughts about going – I am positive of it. As fear began to overshadow determination, he hesitated. I tell you that his story is similar to my own. This is "soooo" familiar! This is much the same way that I felt, as I attempted to speak with my pastor, about the call that relentlessly beckoned my soul's walk towards the divine. Come on here church!! Beloved of God can you praise Him here with me right now? Open your mouth and shout it to the top of your lungs with a jubilant voice - Ohhhhhhhhhhh God! I AM APPROACHING MY DESTINY!

The duck procrastinated. During this time of hesitation, he must have had an instant replay of every painful event that had ever befallen him during the span, of his young life. Surely he recalled how even his very own family had mocked him – and then, he took a step forward. He recalled the time when hunters tried to shoot him; and took yet another step. He even found himself comparing the color of his feathers, which were not at all like those of his family's.

Their feathers had been soft and yellow. In addition, *they and their feathers* were physically much smaller. Not only were his *feathers* darker, and his stature larger, but also his movements were very awkward in comparison. This time, he took a great big 'giant' step, maybe even two. He recalled how he had been shooed away by the farmer's wife – and with that, he took yet another. Oh my, he even remembered the time that he came across a different group of hunters with dogs. Not knowing whether to rejoice because his life had been spared or whether to feel far worse, because of the reason it had been, the duck shuttered at the very thought of this scary but extremely painful memory. You see dear child of God, there came a day in the midst of that dreadful hunting season, as he sat frozen in an ice block, that a massive hound dog came by, took one look at him, and become terrified. "Imagine that", the duck thought to himself, "My very ugliness is even more than a hunting dog can stand."

The dog thinking the duckling was too ugly to attack, supposing him to be a "strange creature" of some sort, and maybe not even a duck at all. The dog could not figure out what he was - refusing to bite him, the massive hound ran away instead.

Deep in his heart rang the silent but very loud beckoning of his inner most being. Everything within him yearned, as he with all his might longed to move forward; but half way there, he had become stuck. "Ok", he determined – "I *must* meet those beautiful birds." "I've got to go all the way, even if they hurt me!" "Even if I am rejected and even if I die!" To the duckling, those beautiful creatures represented every thing that he was not, nor could ever hope to be. This thought alone, propelled him another five giant steps forward, for grace sake. I suppose he also recalled the time that he had been permitted to stay on trial, at a farm for one week. The owner's <u>sole</u> interest in him had been only for the hopes of achieving some sort of financial gain. She wanted to see if the little duckling could lay eggs, or "do any thing cleaver." While there, he found himself being teased, mocked and tormented – yet again. He was ridiculed this time, only because he had no obvious talent that he could flaunt, like the rest.

By now, finally the duckling had made up in his mind that he was going to meet those beautiful birds, even if it killed him. For to live in a state of perpetual rejection hurts far worse he concluded. In spite of the probable consequences of being pecked and bitten to death, he yet pressed his way forward towards the unfamiliar – towards "the divine."

That is exactly what destiny does. It pulls you; it gnaws at everything inside of you. It causes your insides and even your very bowels to yearn for that which you know you've been created to accomplish. You cannot get away from it, neither can you ignore it. Even if <u>you want</u> to turn around, <u>your divine purpose</u> refuses to sanction such a request. It will not take no for an answer as it ever tugs at your heartstrings and even at your soul. It bellows; it woos and it ever summons you unto itself. Often it is into the blistering darkness of the unknown you must walk. Destiny commands you to keep moving towards that which demands your presence –"keep going!" "You have an audience awaiting your arrival!" "Keep moving forward until you make contact." "Don't stop!" it commands.

Better to be killed by them he supposed, than to be pushed around by everyone else for a lifetime. Not knowing what would become of him, he continued his journey. His heart raced even at the very thought of being rejected and wounded once again; *still he was willing to die should they decide to kill him.*

I can imagine the little duck breathing deeply, and then, releasing a loud gulp. Everything within him now beginning to cry out and race feverishly – exactly as my insides had done on that faithful day. Go ahead and take a breath my brother, my sister, this is your hour! Hallelujah!   With one "final deeeeeeeeeeeep breath", a thunderously pounding, pulsating heartbeat, and with a leap of faith, he moved forward, into their midst, and made his presence known. The little duckling flew into the water, and swam towards those beautiful, beautiful birds. "Kill me", said the poor duckling, and with that, he bent his head down to the surface and waited to be pecked to death.

When the beautiful birds espied the stranger, they rushed over to meet him with outstretched wings. With his head still hanging down, he noticed something. He began to see - What's this? It was - naaaawwwwwooooooo, it couldn't be!   Not lifting his head for a moment, but instead looking deeper into the water, paying strict attention to what he saw atop the glistening surface – he was in awe. He intently studied the image that stared back at him. With a huge gasp, and with utter amazement, he found himself speechless, for his eyes were locked on the pond below. Shocked and bewildered, he could barely believe his eyes.

What he saw was his very own reflection! In just one season, he had completely changed. No longer was he the awkward looking, grayish-black, ugly creature he had been born only one short year ago. He was beautiful. In fact – oh my goodness; he was as lovely as those creatures to whom he had been drawn, since first laying eyes on them.

They immediately embraced him. Reader did you hear what I just said? They immediately embraced him – they recognized him; they understood him! They saw him for who and for what he was; they were able to discern him. Not only was he "like them", but he was one of them. He was not an ugly duckling after all, but he too was a beautiful swan. He had always been one, but had never known it - apparently neither had anyone else with whom he had made contact.

Because he was different, nobody had ever taken the time to get to know him; neither could they discern his 'true' identity. Not only had his family of origin been unable to detect him, but neither had they cared anything about him. Never once, had they taken the time to care; neither had they ever bothered to look for him after he left. Well, as it turns out, he had never been one of them at all. (I just said a mouth full right there). What might The Lord be saying to you right now dear friend? Has He been trying to show you something that you refuse to see? Has He already told you something? Are you where you belong?

He that hath an ear let him hear what The Lord is speaking!

> *Our little duckling friend had always been a beautiful swan in the making, only he had never known it. Surely now, he had to be bubbling over with joy. He could scarcely believe that the reflection his eyes beheld was his very own. "A swan?" "Me?" "You mean I'm too am one of them – I am a swan?" "You mean I have never been a duck at all?" "All this time, everyone treated me like a duck." "In fact they treated me as if I were a very, very, ugly horrible creature; they persecuted me for being unattractive, and now you say that I am beautiful?"*

> *"The entire time that I longed to meet those beautiful birds, someone also wanted to meet me." "I have been one of them all along, but I never knew it." AND - "No one had ever bothered to tell me that I would not be awkward always." "Never had anyone taken the time to give me an identity; instead they stamped me 'unworthy'. "The few, who did try, [to identify me] were always wrong." "I was destined to be beautiful, and to accomplish great things but I did not know it." "They never told me that I wasn't ugly; I believed every bad thing that they said about me." "For not even once had anyone ever told me the truth." "Wow!"*

And with that ladies and gentleman, I believe that our little friend, shed several tears. There is something about discovering who you 'really' are that should make you extremely joyful, but never "puffed up." When The Lord God places His hand upon an individual, it should never make the person haughty or proud. When He places upon you and I, the "Mantle" of His choosing, and thereby decides to use us in His program, it is a humbling experience. Once more, in our huge world, another light has been 'turned on' by The Almighty - and that light my friend, my brother or my sister, happens to be you!

> *Ever so often, He allows us to see, what He has known all along. When was the last time you saw yourself? Come on...take a closer look. Go ahead and pick up that mirror. This may very well be the set time, on The Lord's calendar, for you to connect with destiny. This may be the very day wherein you discover something beautiful. For this, child of God, could be the actual moment when you discover YOURSELF!*

An entire year had passed since the duckling departed from his home. He had not even seen himself in all that time. As the springtime emerged, so had he. Our little guy was no longer an ugly, awkward looking duckling; but had transformed into a creature of sophistication and had become altogether lovely. The other swans swam around him and stroked him with their beaks.

Even the old swans bowed their heads to him. A family that had come to visit the pond made mention of "the new one." The children exclaimed that he was the most beautiful of all. The story says that –

"He felt quite ashamed, and hid his head under his wing; for he was so happy, and yet not at all proud. He had been persecuted and despised for his ugliness and now, he had heard them say that <u>he was the most beautiful</u> of all the birds. Even the elder-tree bent down its bows into the water before him, and the sun shone warm and bright. Then he rustled his feathers, curved his slender neck and cried joyfully, from the depths of his heart. "I never dreamed of such happiness as this while I was an ugly duckling", he said. "To be born in a duck's nest in a farmyard, is of no consequence to a bird, if it is hatched from a swan's egg. How he felt glad at having suffered sorrow, because it enabled him to enjoy so much better all of the pleasure and happiness around him; for the great swans swam around him, and stroked his neck with their beaks as a welcome – for finally destiny had led him home.

"Weeping may endure for a night, but joy comes in the morning (Psalm 30:5). Thanks to Hans Christian Anderson, my little friend's story will be told until the end of time, as we know it. Just as the duckling was, so are many of you right now, in the wrong folds. So many of us are in congregations that mean us no good. They do not have *our* best interest at heart and in many cases neither are they concerned about Kingdom business! And though we are unproductive, unloved and uncared for - yet we stay. We know that where we are, is no good [neither is it emotionally or spiritually healthy] for us, but for some reason we seem, determined to stay put. "At least we are still in church" – we reason. For what point is it to be "present", if we are living in a perpetual state of misery? What use is it to be "in the number" when we are dying on the inside? Many of us are not growing because we continue to surround ourselves with people who are unable to discern us, and/or to introduce us, to "our authentic selves."

Some put downs and/or abusive treatment, [that we receive], is blatant and obvious, while other 'blows' (just like the strange fire), is quite subtle, but equally effective at ruining our lives.   STILL, WE INSIST ON HANGING AROUND.   WE CONSTANTLY SURROUND OURSELVES WITH PEOPLE WHO DO NOTHING BUT TEAR US DOWN. BUT WHY?   Why do we stay? Why do we continue to allow them to hurt us? We are not like them; we have never been. We stay around people who care nothing about us, simply for the sake of *belonging somewhere.* But, do we? Do we really 'belong' [there?].

Are we supposed to be where we are right now – at this hour? What is The Lord saying to you? What has He already told you to do, that you have refused to take action on? Are you constantly making excuses? Are you fearful or are you just frozen and stuck?

If something or someone appears to be different, very often that difference, causes it to be the object of society's ridicule and scorn. The person or object is looked upon as valueless, or possessing nothing of beauty, simply because <u>those surrounding it are unable to see it, for the masterpiece that it truly is.</u> Ironically, it is very often, the scorned individual or object that possesses far more worth [far more value, far more anointing, far more integrity, talent and grace, than those who are intent on doing the scoffing. Whether in ministry, (or in general), it is not necessarily a matter of someone being better or being more valuable, but it is a known fact that human nature tends to reject, fear, envy or devalue anything or anyone that they see as being "different."

<u>Not only is a masterpiece or valuable antique often stuffed into a corner or tucked, away in a dark closet [by those with an untrained eye], but it is often hatred or totally avoided. It takes a 'true master' to identify a masterpiece (or to recognize one in the making). There is a grave difference between "an ordinary concert violin" and a "Stradivarius." Just ask any master violinist. Can you tell the difference? Are you worthy to receive enlightenment concerning the things of The Spirit? Brothers and sisters, they do not hate us because of anything that we have done. No! The reality of the matter is that they have detected a deficiency within themselves. It is their own fallacy that renders them unable to recognize you.</u>

We have given them no reason to fear us, and we wish them no harm; yet because of their [own] prejudices and insecurities, they may never give us a fair chance. Sunday after Sunday, *THEY* preach about how important each of us are. They tell us how The Lord has a plan for each of our lives. Some of us have already espied part of God's plan for our lives, but we are discouraged from coming forward, because whenever we do, we are met with a 'scolding hostility', for simply wanting to grow or to comply with the plan. Based upon their actions, I know that many pastors cannot possibly believe even half of the things that they preach about. They tell you to follow The Lord's plan, but as soon as you do…well we all know what happens next.

We find ourselves grounded, because we continue to walk with and to be entertained by chickens, buzzards, and turkeys, when in fact it has always been by God's design that we soar with majestic eagles.

Why do we to allow *them* keep us at ground level when God has called us to fly high into dimensions and even into stratospheres? I'll tell you why; it is because we have not looked to our Father for the revelation of who we are *in Him.* We have instead digested the words of others and we have gnawed on the opinions of jealous people, who only possess ground level mentality. This we did without sticking to the "original" blue print for our own lives – the one that God graciously allowed us to glimpse so very long ago. Perhaps we thought that He had forgotten us, and so we believed *their words* instead - and they hurt us.

Because many of <u>them</u> don't know who <u>they</u> are, they don't want you to know who you are. Moreover, <u>if you do happen to know, they seem to hate you even more.</u> Just like satan, they do their best, to <u>kill</u> your dreams, to <u>steal</u> your joy and to <u>destroy</u> your confidence, [and faith] in what God has spoken. Most of them cannot discern you, because they are not high enough (in the spirit) to even see you. Moreover, even when they can, often they lack the common sense and the spiritual depth to realize that they, themselves are the ones who are in need of deliverance. SOMETIMES THEY HATE YOU, BECAUSE SECRETLY, THEY WISH THEY WERE YOU! Did you hear what I just said?

Females especially, are abundantly atrocious when it comes to dishing the hate. Rather than pay a fellow sister a complement, they would prefer to tear her down. How pathetically sad! They only dislike you, because deep down, they dislike [or hate] themselves. It is much easier for them to make you feel badly about yourself. This they do my friend, because they are too proud or too blind to ask for help. Do you not know that hatred, arrogance and pride (or ill treatment towards others) is often nothing more than insecurity in disguise?

It is essential that you not give them that kind of power over you. Never should you ever allow ANYONE AT ALL, to force you into a place of self loathing or low self-esteem. Insecure people get their kicks, by making you feel bad. Or shall we say by "trying" to make you feel bad, because their tactics will only work if YOU let them.

We have been *made* to feel useless. All of the best jobs were always taken. We stopped holding the glass to our own faces. We believed *them* as we beheld and gave glory to *their* accomplishments, much to the detriment and neglect of our own. This we did until, the day that the light finally came on. I pray that you will prepare yourselves for the day that *something* happens in your own life.

I pray you will realize, that even though you may not be welcomed in your church, valued at your place of business or appreciated by your family, always, always, always remember that you are welcomed and are accepted in The Beloved. You are welcomed, you are loved and you have a home with like kind. You are neither ugly nor awkward. Glory to God!

The day that I decided to ask The Father, what He thought of me was the beginning of my turning point – it was the last day that I ever asked anyone else what they thought, and neither did I care. Blessed Be His Holy Name!

People may be in the wrong place because they have wondered there on their own. Like sheep, we do sometimes go astray. Nevertheless, even during our stay in the wrong fold, we can acquire much wisdom. Even while we are there, God is working [on our behalf]; we can catch glimpses of Him, if only we would look a little harder. Sometimes people are led into destiny by way of the wrong fold. If it is by The Father's design that you stay there for a season, then you need not worry, because He knows exactly where you are, and what it will take to bring you out.

For a long time after my pastor rejected me, I tried to stay and be a part of the program. It was not until I could no longer pretend that I simply *had* to make some sort of change. Up to that point, I had gone along with the program in order to avoid sticking out and being further rejected. I tried to stuff down, that which The Lord was calling me unto. Like when the duckling found himself absolutely *having* to meet those swans, I too had been drawn and compelled to acknowledge and to finally embrace, the very thing that has always embraced me.

It has been there since my soul's existence. It was been there long before I ever knew my own name.   So many people try hard, to be things that they are not. They must continue in their charades as they lie to others and even to themselves, as they constantly try to fit in.   I am so glad that I'm free! I use to be a liar also. Just like them, I too was guilty of pretending. God accused me of denying myself, as in who He had made me to be. To His accusation; I pled "guilty as charged", and I then asked for mercy.

Instead of pretending to be something that I was not, I instead kept trying to stuff down who and what I was, thereby denying the very destiny that had called my name so long ago. Because of other people, I found myself struggling to keep it (the gift) tucked away. I would not allow the true me to shine through. I stuffed it, because whenever I would try to make, even the slightest attempt to reveal my true self, I would always be sorry that I had. Those who *were* able to discern me, usually did their very best to discourage me, because they hated me and they hated the gift that had been placed inside of me.

When the 'burden of pretending' not to be bound to the prophetic became harder than acknowledging it, (by fighting past the opposition), I too felt like running away. Like the ugly duckling, I also *had* to [eventually] make a move. Although I did not immediately depart physically, in my heart as well as in my mind, I had already moved on.

One day, someone confronted me, and told me that I was operating in "false humility." "What do you mean?" - I inquired. The person told me that God would not be pleased with me not being who I am. The person further stated that God would not be happy with me continuing to "play down" that which He had placed inside of me. "Because it had pleased The Master to make me in such a manner that He Himself had been pleased." The person said that I should never attempt to hide who I am, no matter what people have to say. To pretend not to be me, would be to deny the God who made me. In essence, I would be insulting 'His' handiwork and would be slapping 'Him' in 'His' face. (Also, I would be deeming my own self as inferior). Wow!!

I HAVE NO CHOICE BUT TO BE WHO I AM. THE PAIN OF PRETENDING HAD NEARLY DESTROYED ME. THE FEAR OF [MORE] REJECTION FROM OTHER PEOPLE, HAD CAUSED ME TO BE UNTRUE TO GOD AS WELL AS TO MYSELF. NO WONDER I HAD BECOME SO MISERABLE.

So here I am; like me or not, believe me or not, hate me or not - it no longer matters, neither does it change who or what I am; neither does anyone's opinion of me alter God's plan for my life one bit. I am one of God's finest creations. I am "God's Instrument", [one of them anyway], and I am quite proud of it! I have been "fearfully and wonderfully made" by Him. Sisters and brothers, many of you are also pretending, while others of you have not yet discovered your identity. Some of you are still wearing the stickers that people have placed upon you. Be they family members, friends or foes – you are still digesting their words. As a result, you have failed to discover, what God has already said (and what He wants to say). He is not going to compete with everyone else's words.

Take it from me, no longer should you continue hiding or living in a state of pretense. Allow your God ordained self to shine through, for it pleased The Father to cut His fabric in such a way to make yet another design; a design called YOU! And we know that our God does not make junk! There has been no mistake in fashioning you exactly as you are – you are a "Designer's original." Talk about strutting you stuff on the "red carpet"; honey, you are a fashion statement and your Father is the greatest designer of all times! Now let me see you walk! That's it – do your thing!

Lastly, it is in no wise unusual for a person to discover his or her identity while in the midst of great affliction. In fact, it is there that God often chooses to introduce us to our purpose and to ourselves. Nearly 20 years ago, when I got married, (Wow! It has been long).

Anyway...

There came a time, in the midst of my emotionally abusive marriage, that I one day found myself in the valley of decision. I stayed in the abusive situation mainly because I did not want church folks to know that my marriage was failing. It is unfortunate, but I have found fellow Christians, to be down right notorious when it comes to viciously talking about one another. And those who know I'm right about it said– Amen!

My now "ex husband" and I were amongst a series of young couples who had gotten married around the same time. I know it sounds silly *now*, but I did not want to be the *first* of those couples to be heading towards the divorce court. Anyway, as I neared an emotional breaking point, my hair started falling out, my skin started looking bad and the bathroom at work had become one of my dearest friends. Almost daily, I found myself slipping into a stall, for the purpose of having a good cry. I would emerge after my crying spell, facing the world; and pretending as though everything were perfectly ok. On the way home however, I would engage in another crying fit. The very thought of entering into my apartment totally depressed me.

At one point, I even contemplated suicide (just so that I could live with Jesus). For at the time, and before I knew better, it seemed to be the only way out of my misery. This I hid from the world, (with the exception of a mere few, who I would call at random, and would proceed to pester them to death. By the way, thanks for listening and for toiling with me – Kenny H., Amy M., and Derek B. For a long time, I denied my sanity, and it wasn't too long before I started to deny myself. Somehow, I had allowed the tape that played in my head, to convince me that I was no longer worth it. Honestly speaking, I had become too weak to fight back.

A co-worker said something that was so simple but yet deeply profound. I suppose that he must have observed the changes in my personality over the years, and also my weight loss, as well as my pitiful emotional condition. As I neared the zone of an emotional crisis he said, "Jo, you need to make a decision." "You really need to do something." He further stated, "If you don't make a decision soon, eventually one will be made for you." I have never forgotten those words, spoken to me so long ago.

Whenever I seem to be at a fork in the road, I still recall them to this day. "Make a decision" – "For if you do not, one will be made for you." Those are classic words – they are eternal! Thank you Maurice S.

A divinely orchestrated set if circumstances will be called upon to propel you, forcefully if need be, into the next lesson connected to your divine assignment. Your destiny will have no choice but to rescue you, especially if you have been chosen for a "specific" purpose. There be many who are called; but only few who are chosen. Blessed be His Holy Name Forever. Some of us have absolutely no choice in the matter; we are going to follow the plan of The Almighty, even if He must create the very circumstance, [or use the thing that satan has attempted to destroy us with], for the express purpose of capturing us, in order to rescue us from ourselves.

Can somebody please say Jonah and "the great fish?"

In other words because of your destiny's sake, because of the assignment that has been placed upon your life, as well as for the sakes of those, who are awaiting your anticipated arrival, the heavenly realm will be forced to help you out should it come to that.

Boy was Maurice ever right about a decision being made for me. I wish I could tell you that I made it on my own. I wish I had had the guts to walk away. The fact of the matter is, *my abusive husband left me.* When I stopped pleading with The Lord to, "Fix me," or to "Fix him," or to "Work it out Jesus"; "Please keep us together Lord. Oh ladies, you know how we do it! You know exactly how desperate we can be, as we plead with The Sovereign One of the universe, to keep us in a "mess" simply because we do not want to be alone, or because we don't want others to talk about us or about our marriage.

"News flash" – THEY ARE ALREADY TALKING ABOUT YOU ANYWAY! HELLO?????????? THEY CAN'T STAND YOU NOW – SO WHY SHOULD THEIR GOSSIP MATTER TO YOU?? DON'T ALLOW WHAT THEY SAY (OR DO NOT SAY) TO KEEP YOU IN BONDAGE! DON'T BE ASHAMED OF YOUR FAILED MARRIAGE – IT NEARLY KILLED YOU REMEMBER?? WOULD YOU RATHER BE TALKED ABOUT OR DEAD???

Oh God, I can still remember. I was half out of my mind – but yet I wanted Him to - "Please fix it Jesus." "Keep my marriage together." "Please don't let him leave me Lord." I begged and cried, and then cried and begged some more. Oh you know I did – and so did many of you. How pitifully pathetic I must have sounded at that time.

I am both sick and saddened as I think back on my then state of mind. Oh but today, I am free! Go on and admit the truth, it will make you free too! Not even your bad memories can hold you hostage once you are truly free! What were we asking Him to keep together anyway? A sexless abusive marriage? What? A spouse who raped you or who thoroughly bashed your brains in? Were you being supplied good finances – although your spouse was cheating on you with every man/or woman that he or she could find.

Did you stay for the sake of the children or for the family property - even though your husband or wife was addicted to drugs, and never contributed to the household nor to the bettering of your lives as a family. What was it that you were so afraid of losing? What was it, that you were pleading and begging The Lord to keep you in? I can tell you from experience, that the only real item of value, worth holding onto is yourself! If you do have children, you will be unable to help (or literally save their lives) if you are not ok.

When I finally asked Him to, "Have Thine own way Lord." I remember saying these exact words – "Whatever it takes Lord; even if it takes death." "I don't care what you have to do." "Please help me." Honest to God, at that time, with the condition that my mind was in, [the majority of the time], I would not have cared if I had died, or if The Lord's decision would have been to "smite" my husband from off the face of this earth. My emotional turmoil was just *that* fierce, and I did not care how it was, that The Almighty would see fit to put it to rest. All I know, is that I wanted the torture to stop.

When I asked Him to intervene and to do so as He in His sovereignty saw fit, I got serious, and I didn't care what it took. I had no pride and I no longer cared what the "church folk" were going to think, say or do, because it was I who had endured a living hell. It was I who yet dwelt in agony at the time, AND it was I who needed somebody to rescue me, because evidently I lacked what it took to rescue myself. Therefore, I turned my husband, my abusive marriage and myself completely over to The Lord. God in His Sovereignty was merciful. He decided, that enough had been enough.

Within two weeks, it was all over. I remember being on the telephone with a [mutual friend of my husband and me] from church. My husband came home, walking through the door, with hell already in him; hell that he brought in from "out there." Without saying a "kind word", he came in and proceeded to rant and rave, (without me first having said anything to him other than, "Hi"). He came home, cursed me out, and then, he left. Guess what? It was the best thing that he could have ever done for me.

When the pain of remaining in your abusive surroundings becomes too much for you to bear, you will make a decision. If per chance you are taking just a little too long or perhaps like me, (in those days), you are simply unable to make the life saving decision for yourself, no need to worry. When you just cannot seem to do it, there will come a time when your destiny will necessitate that you be driven out or kicked out. The Spirit of The Lord will force you to move, unless He moves the other person [or thing] out of the way first.

From your churches and/or abusive relationships, some of you may need to venture out. Others of you will HAVE to, because you will have no choice in the matter. A portion of you will be PUT out, I am certain of it. Brothers and sisters, if you are put out [first], count it as joy, because you have literally been done a favor – you've been granted "A get out of jail card." Flee from your abuser!

You may not go willingly, but you will go. I pray that unlike me (years ago), that when you come face to face with your pivotal point, or hour of visitation, I hope that you will have the guts to make the proper decision – a decision that might just save your life (and/or that of your child/children if you have any). Nevertheless, if you cannot, be exceedingly glad that the decision you are unable [or unwilling] to make for yourself, has been [or will be] made for you.

I WARN YOU THOUGH, DO NOT FIGHT THE DECISION!

In your new home, new job, new church or wherever your journey leads, you will face more challenges, as there will <u>always</u> be lessons to learn. However beloved, such is life. If you allow Jesus, The Good Shepherd, to be your guide, you will survive them just as you have survived the others.

Now there is at Jerusalem by the sheep market a pool, which is called in the Hebrew tongue Bethesda, having five porches. In these lay a great multitude of impotent folk, of blind, halt, withered, waiting for the moving of the water.

For an angel went down at a certain season into the pool, and troubled the water: whosoever then first after the troubling of the water stepped in was made whole of whatsoever disease he had.

And a certain man was there, which had an infirmity thirty and eight years. When Jesus saw him lie, and knew that he had been now a long time in that case, he saith unto him, Wilt thou be made whole? The impotent man answered him, Sir, I have no man, when the water is troubled, to put me into the pool: but while I am coming, another steppeth down before me.

Jesus saith unto him, Rise, take up thy bed, and walk. And immediately the man was made whole, and took up his bed, and walked: and on the same day was the sabbath.

                                                      John 5:2-9

There has been a special "troubling of the water" just for you. Crawl if you must! The Angel of YHWH stands guard as He waits to personally escort you into the pool. Have no fear as you make your pilgrimage onward and upward. Courage to you for the journey.

Let me be the first to congratulate you my brothers and my sisters – because for many of you, your season has just - *"Changed."*

May the blessings of The Lord Jesus Christ go with you as you travel.

Remember children,
"There ain't no danger in the water…"

⮞A Massive Altar Call⮜

Anyone with a true connection to The Spirit of God has got to know that something is brewing. There is soon to come upon this realm something that Christendom has not witnessed heretofore. Even people, who cannot clearly articulate what they are sensing, still know that *something* is on its way. The very elements of nature are groaning, because even creation can attest to the fact, that God's most prized possession has run amuck. For the time is even upon us wherein God shall make all things new; He shall shortly pluck up and pull down. Those who are under the umbrella of His righteousness are well aware, that for far too long the church has been under attack. It is time to take back that which we have allowed to be trampled under foot.

It is not unusual to hear Saints say things like, "We're going to take back what the devil has stolen from us." Why is it though, that we never hear them speak about taking back, the things that they have freely given to him? What role have the people of God played in the madness that we are witnessing right now?

The Bible let's us know that the devil is a robber, a thief and a liar. We already know that his mission is to steal to kill and to destroy. Unless you are a [total] "babe", every "believer" ought to know the enemy's modes operandi. I mean really, his agenda and ways of going about things, should be quite clear to you by now.

<u>Brothers and sisters, there are some things, that we have willingly handed over to our adversary, and now God is calling for His people to take responsibility for their own actions.</u> It is not satan who makes us commit gross sins; he does not cause us to fornicate, or to become drunkards, sluggards, molesters and the like. While the devil does know what each of our likings and passions are, and while he can indeed set the tone for our demise, still we are the ones who are ultimately responsible for the choices we make. The choice has always been ours, and God has always told us to "choose life." Do you want to be blessed or cursed? You and I my fellow Christians have <u>always</u> had a say in the matter.

It is our fault, that we have allowed that which is sacred, to be taken for granted and handed over to the dogs. The enemy has led us around like puppets on a string. It is he who has ruled over us, instead of him fleeing at *our* command; and now God is angry, as the world laughs us to scorn. They don't believe in Jehovah and they certainly do not believe anything that *we* have to say. Moreover, brothers and sisters, when we think about it, why should they believe us? We are a people who are divided even amongst our own selves. We have become like a house [or people], which Jesus says will never stand. Division amongst The Saints shall no longer be tolerated. Bless His Holy Name Forever!

<u>Right now, I am addressing only those who are saved. This means every person who claims to call upon The Name of Jesus Christ. God said, it is time to clean house right now! It is time to take back The Kingdom of God, by taking a stand for God.</u>

If you are cowardly or a bit timid, and/or fearful, God can still work with you, as long as you are willing to cooperate with Him. You will first need to regain your composure and your strength. My suggestion is that you have a real heart to heart talk with God during your time of prayer. You should ask Him to give you the courage and the strength to stand in the midst of adversity.

<u>If you should find that you are not serious about God's business, then for Christ sake, and for the sake of us all, get out of the way. If you mean The Kingdom no good then you need to move before His Mighty Hand removes you. If you are a "church folk" or "church member" that too is all right, but be ye forewarned, that you are standing in the way of God's Kingdom Kids and they are fast approaching. We will come through; and if you refuse to move over, be duly informed that you are placing your own selves in a direct path to be mowed down!</u>

"Church folk" are interested in the latest styles, gossip and fads. They have a "fleshier" point of view, and they have been trained to see and to obey men only. They are saved because they "believe", but because they have never gotten a glimpse of the *True Master* they operate from a much lower estate. Church folk are often carnal and very superficial. They can't possibly see, nor can they even hear what Kingdom people can. Therefore, they simply are not capable of walking on [spiritual] water. They are not the best people to have in the heat of a battle - that's for sure.

This is not the time to be on the front line with mere church folk. At this critical hour, you had better link up with those who have been stamped, "Kingdom Certified" and "YHWH approved." Bless His Holy Name Forever – Hallelujah!

You need to link up with people who have been inspected, and who have been found to have their spiritual ears sharply tuned and their gaze *eternally* focused; as "true iron" must begin to sharpen iron. For The Bible declares that The True Worshippers are coming, these are they who make up the heart of God's Kingdom. The mark of The Saviour has been eternally stamped upon their hearts. Jehovah requires that we worship Him in Spirit and in Truth; if you have no in-depth revelatory knowledge about *that truth* – then access for you will be denied.

Jesus says of Himself that, "He is <u>The</u> way, <u>The</u> truth and <u>The</u> life." He is not, "A" way, or one of many ways, but <u>FOR THE CHRISTIAN BELIEVER, JESUS IS "THE ONLY WAY."</u>

Who wants to be stuck at a mere surface level when there are realms, dimensions, and even stratospheres to explore? Knowing that you are saved is great, but my brothers and sisters, how you have cheated yourselves for all of these years, by stopping only there. Know ye not that after receiving Salvation, there is yet much more to be gained/learned. It would do you good to search out the deeper things of God. Our churches are in turmoil because of the division that exists in the house of The Lord.

Many of our churches are more in harmony with worldly events than they are with The Word of God. While God certainly does love the world, as in "God so loved the world", in order that He might 'save it', (John 3:16), surely He never intended for the world to take up residence in the church! At one time, the line of demarcation was clearly drawn for all the world to see. Now, we can hardly tell where the boundaries between Saint and sinners lie. We can scarcely tell if we are shaking the hand of a brother or sister in Christ, or if indeed we are locking grips with a tare in disguise.

Our churches and our leaders are in crisis. We have reached a pivotal point, and we must now begin to pool our spiritual resources. *God's people are suffering, because God's people are not doing their jobs* – Did you just hear what I said? It is bad enough when the sinners want out, but when seasoned Saints want no more to do with the church, then dear children we are standing before the face of impending disaster.

From the surface level (which is where many in the ranks appear to be), to them, everything seems to be just fine, in order, and quite ok. For with prosperity and falsities being taught at an all time high, we can scarcely detect that we are in major trouble with The Lord. Again, like the Laodicean church, many of our leaders and many of us do not even realize that they and we are miserable and wretched. We are a sad case indeed. The only problem is that, **<u>WE</u> DO NOT THINK SO.**

Nevertheless, fear not Elect Children; for I believe that Our Father is about to make a mighty blast of HIS trumpet. He is again going to make a clear distinction. Whenever there is a division or a line drawn in the sand, pertaining to spiritual matters, we immediately think of sinner vs Saint. While that division is <u>always applicable,</u> this time the sinners are not the target upon which His Holy gaze is fixed. I speak not of sinner vs. Saint this time. We <u>already know</u> that sinners are exactly what they claim to be - they are sinners. They are doing their own thing and for the most part, they do not intend to ever submit to the will of The Lord; or at the very least, they have not done so yet. If they have not given their lives to Christ, then <u>according to The Bible,</u> they are not saved, and are therefore, still referred to as SINNERS!

If you are of another religion, or have no dealings with the Word of God as in <u>The Bible</u>, then I am not addressing you at this moment; you must make your own decision for eternity. Right now, I am speaking only to the people who claim, to have received Salvation, through The Blood of Jesus Christ. If you plan to stand on the side of the 'sheep' and not the 'goats', then you had better get your act together! He that hath an ear to hear, what THE HOLY GHOST is saying, had better 'sho-nuff' listen up!

Those of you with even an inkling of foresight have to know that God is about to come through here. He is about to pay His church a mighty visit. The Sword is about to make His way into many of our congregations, to see if whether or not those who claim to be operating in His Name, are really doing so. In the beginning was The Word and The Word was with God, and The Word was God (John 1:1) – The Sword is The Word and The Word is Jesus. He is alive and well and He is about to come through. Make way for The King of Righteousness! All Hail King Jesus! He is coming to see why it is that we have everything in our churches EXCEPT HIM!

He is going to perform a mighty separation. It must be done, because we have played church just a little too long. While we were busy 'playing', satan was viciously destroying. The devil was doing his job, and we were not. As we were hurting and destroying one another's character, and busily gathering riches that doth corrupt; satan was busy making fools out of us all. It is imperative that a distinction be made, for how else shall He find that which is without spot or wrinkle, as judgment is imminent. The church of God must be swept clean, for the babies have got to know, that He alone is God, and that He indeed means exactly what He says.

The time for the purification of our hearts and of His temples of worship, is right now. Cleansing in "the house!" shall be the next order of business. How will He find a church without spot or wrinkle if there be not first a cleansing, and/or a division? This same shall usher in a changing of the guards, as God will do a new thing in Zion. Ye who are now in the deserts and the wilderness hear me! Purify your hearts, tune your instruments. You, who are with the "special spiritual forces", sharpen ye your sickles and prepare to reap!

Everyone, make hasten themselves and be ready to stand before God – prepare yourselves for Holy inspection. The Lord will remove many who are now holding your positions. The time has come for us to weep as well as to rejoice – Bless His Holy Name Forever And Ever!! As we anticipate revival, we do not know exactly who or what to expect, but without a doubt, we know that something or that someone is on the way.

Gross indulgence in sinful activity, has <u>always</u> forced God to make a drastic move in order to bring about change. Jehovah is no stranger to The Remnant and neither is The Remnant strange to Him. He has often made personal visitations to the earth realm and HE can very well do it again if He wants to! He came down to check out the blatant <u>unrepentant</u> sinful activity of Sodom and Gomorrah did He not? He came down from the portals of Glory to witness close up, and in person the erection of the Tower of Babel.

Do not think for one moment, that a theophany (a visible manifestation of invisible spirit), could not very well be the next order of business. For how do we, as mere humans know, if whether or not one is already scheduled, and is in the making? For God who is Invisible Spirit, has absolutely no problem making Himself visible to a sinful world, for He can take on any form that He darn well pleases. We are warned to be careful when entertaining foreigners, and strangers – for The Bible says, "Some have entertained angels unawares." (Hebrews 13:2).

Could He have already visited YOUR CHURCH, or YOUR HOME, without you even knowing it? He that hath an ear let him hear what The Spirit is saying. God has no choice but to do something drastic, He must. For Him not to, would be to make mockery of who He is and of His very essence - for He hath declared Himself Holy! Moreover, brothers and sisters, God will not be mocked.

Egregious sinful activity, blatant downright disrespect, disloyalty, disunity and disharmony has taken up residence in The Body of Christ, and in the household of The Lord, and there must come a swift Sword. There are thousands of leaders in Christendom today who will themselves never make it into The Kingdom. Although they continue to preach their hearts out, still they have conformed to the will of the world as they please their flesh instead of making it a priority, to please a "Thrice Holy God."

THEY ARE PREACHING ABOUT ANYTHING AND EVERYTHING, EXCEPT THE WORD OF THE LORD! CAN SOMBODY PLEASE GET BACK TO PREACHING JESUS? CAN SOMEBODY OUT THERE PLEASE MAKE THE MAIN THING, THE MAIN THING?

Prosperity and psychotherapy have their places, but can somebody behind the sacred desk, please preach about *HIM?* Some pastors have made an absolute mockery of the pulpit. In many instances, churches have been turned into everything but a [true] house of praise and prayer. They have turned the platform into a sideshow spectacle. Churches have venues that are more like comedy hours, freak shows and fashion extravaganzas than they are about the sharing and the preaching of The Living Word of Almighty God.

We can hardly find a church wherein the <u>unadulterated</u> <u>Gospel</u> <u>of</u> <u>Jesus</u> <u>Christ</u> *is being preached with power, precise accuracy and with the kind of dogmatic authority that sends demons running for their lives. Where are the true and mighty oracles of God? The wimps and the compromisers can stay home! Instead of fleeing from us, satan and his crew have taken up residence and have also come to witness the events. As one brother shared with me, after his experience at a particular church, "It's like, I almost felt like breaking out my bag of popcorn and peanuts, as I watched the show", he said.*

Everyone seems to be talking revival, shift and transformation. Well, as I have stated already; revivals are not for sinners only as *we* suppose. True revival begins whenever "the church" (or anything else for that matter), is *brought back to life* – after it has died, or because it has fallen too far from its original state and/or purpose. Whenever something ceases to function, as it ought, and needs to be resuscitated; in a word, it needs to be - revived! (Thanks Professor Flemming). Yeah, I know that it does not *look* dead; but God said it has become altogether filthy and dead whenever sin continues to run ramped, in the midst of that which is *supposed* to be clean and set apart. Look around; see for your selves. Are or are not our local assemblies in trouble? Do a lot them reek with the fragrance of sin or not? Such atrocity shall not be permitted to thrive much longer. When last I checked The Book, it still said that the wages of sin is death! (Romans 6:23A).

If Christians continue to corporately (or individually) not only wallow in, but also literally bask and relish, with excitement and joy, in practices that bring forth no real repentance and/or deliverance, but serve mainly as entertainment, disguised as a "sin alternative", then The Lord God shall smite us even in the very midst of them.

Having a Christian alternative is fine, if The Word of God is being imparted and if deliverance is being wrought thereby. (Deliverance and the preaching of The Gospel should be the main objective). God is not asking leaders to provide youth (and adults), with 'another atmosphere' that merely feeds 'the [Christian] flesh' – the devil is a liar! Do not forget about the "strange fire" that I warned you of earlier – there is NEVER to be a mixture when it comes to the things of God and the things of satan.

There cannot be, "in The Name of Jesus" – venues that allow you to "get your shout on" as you worship God, only to walk a few feet down the hall, and "get your grove on" [with the secular folk] – all under the guise of 'church' [and entertainment]. GOD SAY'S STRANGE FIRE! STRANGE FIRE!! STRANGE FIRE!!!

If we are merely heaping up the same dung from which we were once delivered, by slapping a 'Christian' label on it, while attempting to pass the same off as ministry, then The Lord shall surely wipe us out. He shall kill us, in the midst! For we are like dogs who have returned to our vomit – only this time, it is "Christian vomit."

We are given over to religious falsities that do absolutely nothing to feed The Spirit man. People of God, it seems as though we have become altogether pleased to wallow in the shallow, and the muck - and God is not happy! The Lord shall smite us if we do not turn things around. He means business and He is not playing! We have turned a deaf ear for far too long and He has stood up!

Circumstances will sometimes dictate the necessity for the total revamping or making additions and/or corrections to something that had been previously established. When The Lord speaks of "Doing a new thing", and/or of "Raising up shepherds after His own heart" (to properly attend to the needs of His people), it is because there has been a serious breakdown somewhere.

God speaks of raising up prophets who will speak ONLY THAT WHICH HE COMMANDS. No more lying, we have had quite enough of the prophetic charades and so has God!

Your days of false prophesying and lying to the people, shall soon come to an abrupt end! Sorcerers, soothsayers and false prophets have given the gift of prophecy as well as the authentic prophetic office a bad name – it is enough!

Revival is for the purpose of returning something to life or to consciousness. It imparts new health, new vigor, and a right spirit.

We cannot revive sinners because they have never died to themselves. A sinner has not yet ever tasted of, the new life in Christ. To them, what we speak is a bunch of foolishness. Revival can however begin with the true children of God, which in turn, can and should ignite a spark, in even the vilest sinner.

As the unsaved witness the true worshippers, and the children of The Most High catching on fire [for real], then they will be drawn to HIM. They will come running to the lover of their soul. The people will be drawn back to The Lord, and not to men.   Today's church is nothing in comparison to churches of old when miracles were commonplace. The former churches may not have had the flesh pleasing accoutrements that we now do, but they had gumption and they had power.

THEY WERE ENDUED WITH REAL HOLY GHOST POWER AND NOT WITH THE HOCUS POCUS CRAP THAT SO MANY TODAY ARE PROCLAIMING AS BEING 'POWER FROM ON HIGH.' NEITHER WERE THEY TRYING TO IMMITATE SOMEONE ELSE, BUT THEY WERE THE GENUINE ARTICLE.   THEY WERE AUTHENTIC, FIRE BAPTIZED BELIEVERS, WHO NOT ONLY KNEW THE LORD, BUT THEY HAD A HEALTHY REVERENTIAL FEAR AND RESPECT FOR HIM!   HEAR ME IMPOSTORS AND MODERN DAY "SONS OF SCEVA" EVERYWHERE:

THE LORD REBUKE YOU!!!

(Sons of Sceva – Acts 19: 13-14) The entire chapter is a great read!

Though the older churches were not laden with dramatic skits, comedy hours and psychological babbling sessions, true deliverance took place in the pews, at the altar and even behind the pulpit. I don't know about anyone else, but I want to witness the dynamite explosive action of "Dunimas Power." I want to experience for myself, how walking in someone's shadow can bring forth healing, such as was the case with Peter. That's the kind of anointing/power that I want on my life, but if not, at the very least, I would like to stand in the presence or sit under the teaching of someone else, who has been 'endued' FOR REAL.

Before I die, I'D LIKE TO SEE A DISPLY OF THIS KIND OF HOLY GHOST POWER IN OUR CHURCHES – WHAT ABOUT YOU?

Assemblies of old may not have had coffee houses, art galleries and exhibitions; but they had love, one for another. They did not have built-in shopping centers, movie theaters or malls brimming with state of the art equipment; but they did have the power to rehabilitate the most hardened sinner. The church floors were not always decked out with plush carpeting; in fact, many had no carpeting at all. Neither did the windows have stained glass or elegant appeal; oh but my brothers and sisters, their reverence for God could be felt the moment one stood in the doorway.

Never did they appeal to the flesh of the sinner in order to "entice" or to convert him, her or them. Rather they made their appeal to God, with faith in the knowledge, that <u>His Power</u> would transform them and thereby usher them in. God is going to do a massive sweep. His Holy Firepower is more than capable of removing everything or everyone that refuses to bow down. Every person that refuses to change will be removed or destroyed. Every candlestick and every church must be set in right order.

You must know that God will never be out done. He certainly will not put up with being mocked, by His own creation. He would not be God, if He allowed us to continue as is or if He permitted man rule over Him! The time is at hand for both judgment and revival. Some will be forced to turn themselves over to God, as they know that they are not right – at all. They also know that they have absolutely no business behind anyone's pulpit, because they have blatantly and continuously refused to heed His instructions and His warnings, time after time – they know who they are.

Many in the land are preaching their own version of The Gospel. Theirs is a false Gospel, filled with hypocrisy and ardent lies. This they pass off to the gullible sheep and to the babes who do not know any better. The Lord God calls you out right now, blasphemer. Come out with your hands up in repentance to God, while you can still walk out on your own two feet!
Do not let the finger of The Lord, have no choice but to point you out, or worse, please do not let Him have to lay you out! God said it is now time for you to come out! For your own sakes, do not lie when The Ghost fingers you, as He pricks your heart, but rather agree with Him and admit the truth about your wretched self.

You may live to regret it if you don't; that is if He lets you live at all! He that hath an ear to hear let him hear! I beg you not to be like Ananias and Sapphira, who were smitten dead on the spot because of one unnecessary little lie – ONE THAT THEY CHOSE TO TELL. (Acts 5:1-11).

If the Holy Spirit operated today, as He did in those days, then God help us everyone! Just how many tall tales do you suppose would continue to emanate from the pulpit? How many of our hearts and thoughts, would be pure enough to pass examination? Woe unto us all! God help us each to fall upon our faces in PURE repentance – And I do mean, ALL OF US!

PREACHERS, SAINTS, YOU AND ME! For we have each been individually guilty of something at one time or another. AND WE AS HIS BODY, ARE GUILTY RIGHT NOW! WE AS A WHOLE NEED TO REPENT! THIS IS A MASSIVE ALTAR CALL – I CALL UPON THE SAINTS OUR TIME! I CHALLENGE YOU IN THE NAME OF THE LORD TO COME CLEAN. THE APPEAL HAS GONE FORTH AND THE INVITATION HAS BEEN SENT. WHO WILL ACCEPT THE CALL TO REPENTANCE? WHOSOEVER WILL, LET US NOW PRAY.

Lord God,

For every lie that we have ever told - Guilty! God have mercy on us. For every person that we have wounded and damaged - Guilty! Please be merciful unto us oh Lord. May we repent of having turned others away from even wanting to hear The Gospel of Jesus Christ, and from wanting to You oh Lord to be their God – we are Guilty!

Because of our abominable acts and our foul language, somebody on today is not counted among the redeemed – God please forgive all of your people; for we are all GUILTY!

May we as Your people fall flat on our faces even now. For every act of lust, and for our sexual perversions, and even for our fornicating and refusal to control our sinful passions; we are - Guilty! For not bringing our flesh and our lusts under subjection, You have recorded evidence against us. The Court on High calls us out. Your Honor, Your Majesty, we plead – GUILTY! GUILTY! GUILTY! GUILTY! GUILTY! God help us. For our greed, and for the rape and robbery of innocent people, and for neglecting our responsibilities – Guilty! God help us.

For our gossiping and lying lips, we are GUILTY AS CHARGED! God help us. For our labeling and slandering of one another both Saint and sinner alike – Very GUILTY! God please help us and have mercy upon us. For not being good stewards with our time, with our finances, with our talents, with our bodies and even with our lives – WE PLEAD GUILTY! Please, please Father help us. Please don't leave us. Please don't leave me!

For watching television all the day long, for sleeping and/or engaging in illicit activity when we should have been praying – WE STAND BEFORE YOU GUILTY AS CHARGED! For failing to teach Your "babies", those who You told me were so many in number, and who now need to be "rounded up", because Your Blood Brought Believers have failed You in so many ways. WE STAND GUILTY!

WE HAVE OFFENDED YOU! WE HAVE BROUGHT <u>FLESH PLEASING ACTIVITIES</u> INTO <u>YOUR HOLY SANTUARY</u> AND HAVE PROCEEDED TO CALL THEM "MINISTRY." LORD, WE HAVE OFFERED YOU STRANGE FIRE. We knew better but yet, we did these things anyway. FOR FAILING TO BE THE HOLY ORACLES THAT WE SHOULD BE, LORD WE ARE GUILTY! GUILTY! GUILTY! GUILTY! GUILTY! GUILTY! GUILTY!

Father would You please have MERCY, MERCY, MERCY, MERCY, MERCY! Would You wash us again? Would You cleanse your people once more? Father please send Your Holy Fire to burn us pure – through and through. Many tried to speak out about the wrong doings in your sanctuaries Lord, but were sharply rebuked and silenced by leadership. Thus we stayed put and went along with the majority, although the majority was wrong, and we knew it.

For fear of further scolding (from men), and for not having the guts to stand alone, we did absolutely nothing – and now God, we stand guilty of both the sins of "omission" and "commission"; and Lord we repent. Father would You please have mercy on us all for failing both You and the babies? Would You grant us Your grace again?

Like Sampson Lord, would You please "permit our hair to grow just one more time?" Would You grant us the grace and the strength to get it right? We beseech Your mercy. Let this be the completion of our "guilty pleasures" and let our "genuine repentance" signify a new error for YOUR CHURCH and a new beginning in You.

We ask Thee to anoint us with fresh oil, dispensed from Thine own hand. If YOU touch us we shall be touched! (no man touching us this time). Revive us Lord and WE WILL do your will! We pray in the Name of Christ Jesus, our High Priest, Mediator, Saviour, Lord, King and Judge. And those who mean it from their hearts said – Amen! Amen! and Amen!

I pray that we each assemble ourselves at the foot of God's altar that we might seek His divine and gracious mercy. It is "extremely urgent" that we <u>right now</u> begin to "strip ourselves" (so that He will not have to) of everything and of every persona that does not resemble Him. We must strip off that which is diabolical and despicable. We are a mess, and have become altogether disgusting to look upon. It is time to be naked and bare before our God; it is time to come clean.

Surely, some of you feel as though you have no reason to bow down. Even now, you are too darned proud to get right. Many of you will not do so, because you may be wondering who I think I am to tell you these things. I AM NOTHING! In my own estimation, I am a total mess AND I STINK JUST LIKE YOU! I have however, been apprehended and am an instrument – "God's Instrument", to use as He sees fit. I am no better than you are, but I belong to Him. For those of you who <u>want</u> to get right with God, I beg you to do it even now, do not delay.

For thus speaketh The Spirit of The Lord unto His People:

"It is time to weep! For you have made My house into a madhouse. It has become something altogether abhorrent and detestable. The children cannot eat of My bread because you are serving up your own concoction. Because of your filthiness, they know not of Me.

Where is The Living Bread, even The Bread of Heaven that I left on record? What have you done with My Son? He is The Bread of heaven and forever living. My children are hungry; they are even starving at very the gates, but you have turned your backs and have denied them. Some are even dead already because you have ignored them.

You have refused to take them in. You would not befriend the backslider. You would not provide for the widow. You would not take in the orphan whom I love. Revival I say! Know that revival shall start in My household the same as My judgment and even My wrath.

Get down lest I take you down [Says He]. Harvest you say, you want harvest? Get bathed, then will come the harvest. If you want revival, then YOU must die. YOUR FLESH MUST NOT COME BEFORE ME ANY LONGER! Get [thee] down I say! I AM come to see about My children. I come to see about those who have cried unto Me. I come! I come! and I come! But YOU recognize Me not. (End communication).

The Lord must have His way in and outside of our churches, and then will sinners be drawn unto Him. We must lift HIM up – not prosperity, not ourselves, not the latest trend. Like the song of old says, "If we [the Christians] would **"lift Jesus up",** then all men will be drawn unto Him."

The Spirit of God never pointed men to Himself, neither did The Son ever point to Himself. The Son sought not His own glory, but He pointed both Saint and sinner to The Father – Him it is we are to glorify, Him it is we are to praise and Him it is we must obey.

There is not a man on earth, neither does there exist one in the realm of the heavens who is deserving of God's glory. Neither shall Jehovah permit such a one to remain alive, if he or she expects to receive such. All glory, all honor and all praises go to God! He that hath an ear to hear let them hear what The Spirit is saying.

To Thee Oh Lord, Your Remnant ascribes glory and majesty! BLESSED BE YOUR HOLY NAME FOREVER MORE!

How dare we point to ourselves? How dare preachers set themselves up as God? Who do we think we are anyway – calling our own selves deity? How dare we expect sinners to come into the house when we are exuding such a vile odor; we absolutely stink! Why on earth would anyone want to be like us in the first place?

We, the people of God have become a foul stench in His nostrils. In our current state of lukewarmness, we are abominable; we are like a filthy, dirty detestable wretch, and worthy to be vomited out of His Holiness. We offer Him idols! We deserve hell – every single one of us. We make Him absolutely sick with our list of depravity. In the hospital, you've seen an "IV drip" – well, we seen to be lavishly feasting on a "Sin drip." We keep ingesting more and more and more and more! We are a contemptible mass of flesh!

Our churches are oozing with OUR sexual perversions, pride, arrogance, greed, lust, lying tongues, adulterous escapades, whore-mongering, blasphemy, idolatry, false accusing, slandering, leaving out the beggar, robbers of the children's bread, oppressing the widow, pastors impregnating members, raping the flock, sodomizing men, fathers molesting their own daughters (and sons), taking God's offering for filthy gain, acceptance and tolerance (without demanding genuine repentance) of an increasing display of those who engage in alternative lifestyle behaviors, by allowing infiltration and the taking up of residence in the sanctuary to make mockery of The Word of The Lord, with crooks and whores ruling the pulpit.

WE ALL STINK! YET WE THINK THAT WE ARE BLESSED?? WE REEK! WE HAVE BEGUN BLENDING WITH THE WORLD – AND WE HAVE BECOME QUITE COMFORTABLE IN DOING SO. WE, THE SO CALLED PROFESSING PEOPLE OF GOD, ARE UNABLE TO SMELL OUR OWN PUTRID FLESH. WE ARE AN ABOMINATION, BUT WE THINK THAT WE ARE BLESSED OF THE LORD. WAKE UP PEOPLE OF GOD! ASSEMBLE YOURSELVES TOGETHER! GET THEE HENCE TO THE FOOT OF THE ALTAR AND FALL UPON YOUR FACES! GOD IS NOT FINISHED WITH US YET!

YHWH SAYS, DIE! IT IS TIME TO BE IGNITED BY THE FLAME OF MY SPIRIT WHEREIN I WILL CAUSE EVERYTHING THAT IS NOT LIKE ME TO BE BURNED UP.

MY FIRE POWER SHALL BURN OUT THE UNCLEANNESS, THE IMPURITIES AND THE FILTH. YOU MAKE A MOCKERY OF THE SACRIFICE, WHICH WAS PAID, ON YOUR BEHALF WHEN YOU CONTINUE TO LAVISH IN YOUR SIN. YOU RENDER THE LAMB'S BLOOD TO BE OF ILL EFFECT. MY SON'S BLOOD IS NOT SICK; YOU ARE THE SICK ONES. YOU ARE THE ONES WHO YET NEED A PHYSICIAN. IN ALL THIS TIME, ARE YE NOT YET HEALED OF YOUR INFERMITY? DID NOT I PROVIDE THE REMEDY? [ALREADY] ARE YOU NOT YET CLEANSED? NO WONDER SINNERS BELIEVE THEY CAN COME TO MY HOUSE, AND DO AS THEY PLEASE.

SINFUL MEN BELIEVE THAT THEY CAN TAKE THE BLOOD OF MY SON'S COVERING AND USE IT AS A WELCOMING MAT TO WALLOW IN MUCK. THEY EXPECT THAT I SHALL TURN A DEAF EAR AND A BLIND EYE ALWAYS.

KNOW THEY NOT THAT I SEE AND THAT I HEAR ALL THINGS? KNOW THEY NOT THAT I SHALL IN MY WRATH UTTERLY CONSUME THEM? DOES NOT THE SINNER KNOW THAT I INDEED AM A HOLY GOD AND THAT I SHALL INDEED THOROUGHLY CUT THEM OFF? NO! HOW CAN THEY REALIZE THAT THEY ARE DOOMED FOR HELL? THEY DON'T KNOW BECAUSE YOU WON'T TELL THEM.   THEY OF A CERTAINTY BELIEVE THAT THEY CAN COME TO MY SON [JESUS], AND YET CONTINUE TO LIVE AS THEY PLEASE, BECAUSE THAT IS EXACTLY WHAT MY PEOPLE ARE DOING. THEY DISHONOR ME!

THOSE WHO SAY OF THEMSELEVES THAT THEY ARE MY SERVANTS; EVEN THEY HAVE BECOME ALTOGETHER FILTHY AND COMFORTABLE WITH THEIR EVIL DEEDS. THEY THINK I AM NOT HERE. THEY THINK THAT I DO NOT SEE IN THE DARK. THEY BELIEVE THAT I SHALL STAY MY HAND [FROM JUDGING] ALWAYS. MANY SAY IN THEIR HEARTS THAT I HAVE DONE NOTHING YET. THEY BELIEVE THAT I HAVE TURNED A BLIND EYE TO THE DEBOUTCHARY PLAGUING THE LAND. THEY SAY THAT – "THE [GREAT] "I AM" SEES US NOT."

THE PRETENDERS SHALL ALSO BE CUT OFF! I AM THE LORD; I CHANGE NOT MY RIGHTIOUSNESS FOR ANY MAN, NEITHER FOR ANY MANNER OF PEOPLE! [I STILL AM, THAT I AM!]. YE SHALL ALL DIE BY THE VERY WORDS YOU PREACH IF YOU DO NOT REPENT! APOSTASY SHALL NOT LIVE IN MY HOUSE. SIN SHALL NOT REIGN UNDER MY VERY EYE.

I SHALL EXAMINE THAT WHICH YE SAY AND SEE EVEN IF YOU LIVE THAT WHICH YE NOW DO PREACH TO OTHERS. DIE PREACHERS DIE! DIE SAINTS DIE! DIE HYPOCRITS AND THIEVES! LEST I RAISE MY HAND [AND BREAK OUT] AGAINST THEE! [YOUR FLESH MUST DIE!]. IT IS TIME FOR THE CHURCH TO LAMENT SO THAT SINNERS WILL WANT TO COME TO MY HOUSE [SAITH GOD] OR ELSE I WILL PERSONALLY REMOVE YOU.

<u>I WILL NOT REMOVE THEM, NOT WITHOUT FIRST GIVING THEM A CHANCE TO HEAR THE TRUE GOSPEL.   THEY TOO MUST MAKE A DECISION [ABOUT MY SON] BUT THEY MUST FIRST HEAR A TRUE WORD FROM MY HEART AND NOT THOSE FROM YOUR LIPS OF WHOREDOMS, WHICH DO SPEAK MISCHIF AND FOLLY.</u>

I SHALL REMOVE YOU BECAUSE YOU, MY PEOPLE HAVE BECOME MORE LIKE THEM, INSTEAD OF THEM BECOMING TRANSFORMED BY YOUR TESTIMONY. YOU ARE FAILING IN YOUR ASSIGNEMENT TO MIRROR THE IMAGE OF MY SON.

BECAUSE YOU KNOW ME, IT IS EXPECTED OF YOU TO SET STRAIGHT THE EXAMPLE. IS IT NOT MY PEOPLE WHO ARE CALLED TO HUMBLE THEMSELVES, SEEK MY FACE AND MAKE A COMPLETE TURN FROM THEIR WICKEDNESS? THE SINNERS ARE NOT ALTOGETHER RESPONSIBLE FOR THIS CALAMITY, YOU ARE! DID I NOT PROMISE TO HEAL THE LAND? DID I NOT PROMISE TO HEAR YOU EVEN BEFORE YOU CALL? I PROMISED TO HEAR YOU WHEN YOU PRAY.

WHY IS IT THAT YE HAVE CEASED WITH YOUR EARNEST PRAYERS? WHY IS IT THAT MORE OF YOU ARE NOT CLEANSED IN ALL THIS TIME? KNOW YE NOT THAT MANY HAVE EVEN TASTED PHYSICAL DEATH BECAUSE OF YOUR DISOBEDIENCE AND VILE CONDUCT? YOU KNEW BETTER THAN THEY.

THEIR BLOOD SCREAMS FOR JUSTICE! IF YOU DO NOT REPENT, YOU SHALL BE CAST DOWN AND CUT OFF FOREVER, FOR JUDGMENT IS EVEN NEIGH. I KNOW HOW TO CREATE ANEW; THOSE WHO WILL CONVERT THE SINNERS UNTO RIGHTIOUSNESS. THEY KNOW HOW TO CALL BACK THE BACKSLIDER, THE WHOREMONGER, THE ADDICTED, THE AFFLITED AND THE LEPER.

THEY KNOW HOW TO RETRIEVE WITHOUT LOSS. THEY HAVE BEEN TRAINED TO GO EVEN INTO THEIR TERRITORY AND TO COMPELL THEM WITHOUT BECOMING AS THEY ARE. [HIS REMNANT OF END TIME SERVANTS WILL NOT BE WEAKLINGS].

MY ARMY KNOWS [RIGHT WELL] HOW TO BEFRIEND THE SINNER AND YET NOT BECOMETH AS SUCH WHO COMMITTETH SIN. THEY SHALL CALL BACK ALL WHOM I LOVE. THOSE WHOM YOU HAVE TRAMPLED UNDER FOOT ARE STILL MY CHILDREN.

THEY TOO HAVE THE RIGHT TO RECEIVE THE PROTECTION OF MY SON'S BLOOD. [SHOULD THEY ACCEPT HIM AS SAVIOUR AND LORD]. IT IS TIME FOR REPENTANCE, IT IS TIME, AND IT IS TIME (End of communication).

When the church re-awakens, only then will it be able to minister with fresh fire, Holy power, and with a yoke destroying anointing. Not until <u>we are the first</u> in line to get right should we ever expect to reap a true harvest.

It is time to make <u>TRUE CONFESSION before The Lord.</u> He is calling for every preacher everywhere to examine him or her self to see if they be truly in the faith or not. What are your motives for being in ministry? Pastors, you had better think long and hard about it before answering.

Remember, He already knows; and again, it would do you good to remember Ananias and Sapphira! Make restitution whenever and wherever possible.

I pray you make a special effort to repent; even if <u>YOU do not feel that YOU need to.</u> My advice to YOU, is that YOU do it anyway. For YOU PASTORS are no better than the rest of us! Please don't let the hand of The Lord have no choice but to publicly break you.

The space has been given for each of us to judge ourselves. Hear ye the word of God. My heart breaks for each of us. GOD IS NOT PLAYING, AS THERE ARE SO MANY TO ROUND UP; He told me so. So many babes, God help us. God commands that an apology be issued from the pulpits for whatever part our pastors and our fathers have played in the destruction of His children.

God says you had better do it! Where and if at all possible you must make every effort to pray for those who YOU KNOW have been slighted and hated without a cause for which you are responsible – check The Book.

EACH LEADER, AND MNISTER OF THE GOSPEL OF JESUS CHRIST, MUST MAKE EVERY EFFORT TO GET RIGHT WITH GOD RIGHT NOW. IF YOU VALUE YOUR LIFE AS WELL AS THE ROLE THAT HE ALLOWS YOU TO PLAY IN H-I-S MINISTRY, YOU HAD BETTER COME CLEAN!

As I told you before, you may be the founder, but it still belongs to Him! All of it! Preachers and fellow laborers it is time for those who have a mandate from God to step up to the plate and to preach The "Good News" everywhere, as too many are perishing because we are not in place.

We must preach the <u>unadulterated Gospel</u> of Our Lord and Saviour Jesus Christ. You are to preach that which you like, and even that which you do not.

Now is the designated time to come up higher. NO MORE SCALED AND WATER DOWNED VERSIONS! PREACH "THE TRUTH" OR SHUT UP! PREACH THE TRUTH AND LET GOD DO THE REST!

You have been hereby warned and are charged to preach the whole counsel. There is to be no more picking and choosing. Upon graduation from a realm, you are held captive by and are thus responsible for that knowledge.

It then becomes your duty to submit to that which you now know as being absolute truth. Position on the front line is not about you calling attention to yourselves; it is not about your comfort.

This is not about you excusing yourselves from your own sins, neither is about your exoneration from judgment. Leaders, you especially will give an account.

The Remnant and the Worshippers do not care who <u>you</u> are. They want to know if there is any word from The Lord. They want to know more about HIM whom their hearts adore.

They don't want to always hear about you and your material riches and exaggerated stories about your fabulous lifestyle!! They are eager to learn of Him – the one who loved them enough to save them.

They want to hear more about He who has 'their back.' We need you to preach about Him and Him crucified, resurrected, watching over us and soon to return and Judge and King!

For now unto the wounded I speak:

Children, The Lord does not pardon us, just because we have been someone's victim. We too must run and embrace the altar of God. Those of us who were wounded must come clean and repent, as we are not guiltless.

Out of our hurt and because of our pain, we have talked about our pastors/leaders. Some have even caused strife and division in ministries and in various congregations.

Out of your anguish, you of a truth have in fact trashed <u>ALL</u> of God's people because of the ones who have done you evil. Others of you (including myself) have stopped attending church on "a regular basis" and have instead opted to stay at home, or to attend only on occasions. A large percentage of you have stopped going altogether, and have absolutely no intentions of ever looking back. I am hoping that we will each reconsider our positions and that we will be led by The Lord and not by our bruised or damaged emotions (if that has indeed been the case).

I know that I did not want to be bothered, because I did not even want to see the faces of those who had hurt me so deeply. Each time I saw him (or them); my feelings of anger, depression and contempt would arise. I started coming only when I served on duty in the back, because I felt too hurt, numb and angry to be in the sanctuary, where I would have to see my pastor's face. Every time I saw him, my mind would flash back to my piercing, gut wrenching painful encounter.

I openly repent of ALL that I did as well as of ALL that I failed to do. I repent for not handling my hurt in a more mature manner. At times, I chose the cowardly way out (on purpose). I chose to stay home and not face my pastor, not out of fear of him, but rather because of my anger towards him as well as my pain because of him.

I could not shake my bad attitude, that had stemmed from being rejected by him. Deep down, I was hurting in the worse way and did not think it appropriate to sit in church, fold my arms and totally "disconnect" from everything going on in the service. At the time, I simply could not face him without becoming critical or angry, (or without tearing up) – and so, I stayed home.

I do not know if this was "always" how I should have handled things [staying away that is], but I publicly repent and ask for Your forgiveness God, for each time that I missed YOUR mark; and I know there have been many.

Should You require that I return to that particular pastor, Lord, you know my heart, and You know that I will. Swiftly I shall go; at Your command should You will it so. I sincerely wish nothing but to get on with Your business as Your Instrument, doing things Your way. This is the desire of my heart.

To My God, to my brothers and sisters and even to my former pastor – once again: I publicly and openly acknowledge and confess my own ungodly ways of handling my hurt – please forgive me.

Dear children, dear readers, dear brothers and sisters, everything that I preach, pray, or write about must first begin with me. I gave open accounts of my own life, and shortcomings, as you have already read.

I am a servant of The Most High; I share your pain, but I too must partake in the same judgment and punishment if I fail to repent. Right or wrong, I [choose to] acknowledge any part that I have purposely played – or any that I may have played without even realizing it. There is nothing wrong with asking The Lord to search us, because He does a much more thorough job of it then we could ever do.

Like Job who prayed for his children in advance; I too pray for forgiveness "just in case" He finds something other than the things that I already know condemn me as guilty! For that matter, may I have the guts to look deep within and to (genuinely) forgive EVERYBODY who has ever meant me harm and even those who have literally carried out deeds of evil against me. It is not my desire to feel anger, pain, resentment, jealousy, nor hatred towards anyone, including my enemies – (any longer).

I know who they are and so does God. It is The Lord's job to bring vengeance and to punish. He shall deal with them according to how He sees fit. Children, let The Lord have His way – Bless His Name.

Dear reader, and precious Saints of God, I want you to know, that I publicly lay my own self upon the altar of God and cry out for mercy. May He continue to change me, from the inside out.

May His Holy Fire purify my soul. Even the very bowels of my insides may He purge completely – I pray! Like Peter, I want you to not only my feet, "but my head and also my hands." Cleanse me Lord; until You burn up every drop and even the very residue of hurt and/or bitterness that I may yet harbor towards those who have hurt me, wounded me or done me evil – help me to love them; even if You have to MAKE me.

May He burn up every lingering and/or besetting secrete or revealed sin in my life. May He give me an utter hatred for the same – In Jesus Name. Purify me <u>again</u> Lord; and then use me, until You use me up!

Beloved Remnant of God, I beseech your prayers, as likewise, I shall be praying for you. In this critical hour, we need one another.

Can God trust you to present your [own] self at the foot of His altar without Him having to drag you there? (Or on the other hand, smite you for not showing up as the trumpet blasted to gather the assembly). I for one certainly plan to get in a hurry; I am running to the altar! See you soon.

Even after all of this, I am certain that there will be those, who insist on calling us bastards (or whatever other name they choose). They will continue to say that we are still out of order. Children, just remember what I've told you: If you have given your life to The Lord Jesus Christ as I have, then you already have a Father.

<u>You are sons and daughters already. He loves each of us – and He has no bastards in His family! Do not allow them to fool you any longer. I don't care who they are or what they preach – God loves you!</u>

Because of our own ignorance and because of our pain, we did not always do everything as we should have, but Jehovah still loves us. May His Holy Name Be Blessed Forever and Ever More! Do not view yourselves as unworthy.

Hold up your head, but remember, never in pride or arrogance! Rather, hold it up in the confidence of knowing that you are in right standings as you walk with The Father. If they insist on calling you bastards, let them. So what!? Who cares what they think? Don't even waste your time thinking about what they say. Don't always try to defend yourselves; fight only the battles that He instructs you to.

You need not trouble yourself on this, because He's got your back. Besides, having to 'constantly' fight or be on the defensive, zaps entirely too much [creative] energy. That same effort you put forth when you attempt to 'justify', 'fight' or 'defend', can be better utilized on more valuable undertakings.

Besides, many of them, shall soon be removed from the parameter of your life anyway. For the most part, they will be nothing more than a memory (to be used as part of your testimony), and so will their accusations. Should the world call you a reject, know that I will proudly wear that title with you.

Many consider me as such, but I no longer care! Why should you? If that is how they choose to see us, then so be it. God has a way of taking those who are first and putting them to the back of the line or removing them out of your life altogether. Likewise, those who are last shall soon be front and center. I stand with you as a fellow maidservant and do affirm you as my family. I am proud to have you as my sisters and as my brothers – and I love you.

P.S. If the circumstances of your <u>physical birth,</u> dictate that the world can legally label you as "bastard" or as "illegitimate", never should you ever forget, that in the midst of "The Secrete Place", Our Father has already provided, especially for us, a "High Holy Ground", located just under, "The Elevated Shelter of The Eternal Rock of Ages."

It is a place of solace that has become the hangout of nearly every physically and/or spiritually fatherless child, outcast or rejected soul. We who frequently gather there, refer to <u>our special place</u> as –

"A BASTARD'S REFUGE."

Come running to the mercy seat. Where Jesus, is calling; for He said His grace shall cover thee.

His blood yet, flows freely, and it will provide your healing. Come running to the mercy seat.

(Taken from a song called "Mercy Seat").

❧*Finally, Before I Go*❧

I feel like the young high school student, whose letter we read (See: The making of a Bastard), when he stated that, "He did not care whether or not his letter was ever read, but that he *had* to write it." Likewise, this author feels much the same way. I don't care if millions of people read my book or not. I am not writing it to become an overnight success or for the sake of popularity. Well, wait a minute now, a *little revenue from sales* couldn't hurt. Lord knows I could use the money (smile). Seriously, though, the penning of this book did not originate from something that *I* had purposed to write about. Instead, it was at The Lord's command that this work came into existence.

He helped me to realize, for the last time, that I am nobody's spiritual bastard. He then compelled me to spread the word, so that others would also know that they are not alone in their soul's struggle. There needed to be a clarification as to what Scripture says, as well as what it does not say. In addition, people needed to know that there are others who do totally identify with their plight. Like you, I am a live, breathing "human being", who has experienced many of the same feelings of worthlessness, hopelessness, disgust, anger, rage sadness, rejection and neglect. Remember, *even those who claim to be saved* can deeply wound you, thereby placing you in grave spiritual and/or emotional danger. Always remember - ***EVEN SAVED FOLK CAN BE TOXIC!***

I needed my own daughter to know that above all others, God's voice is the only one that she should believe and take as her final authority. His is the only one worth listening to as though her life depends on it, because it literally does. My desire is to leave a better legacy, than one built upon a foundation of emotional pain and religious depravity. I wanted to accomplish something worthwhile, not only for my child, but for God. I wanted Him to be the most proud of me. I wanted others to know, but I especially needed for the children who have no voice, nor earthly mother or father, to come into the knowledge, and to realize that God loves them, and that He has them on His mind, even if no one else does. We have taken the word 'bastard' and have literally unleashed it upon countless souls who never deserved it. Millions, who due to no fault of their own, have been forced to bear such a disgraceful identifying label. The children did not sentence themselves to bastardizm, through any actions of their own. It has never been their fault that they have been thrown into the bastard pile. Why must they pay the price when dad walks away?

I take pride being the voice of the bastard, reject, orphan and outcast because they seemingly have no voice and they need to be heard also! My prayer is that The Almighty will raise up more, who will lend their voices, money, songs, talents, abilities and ministries to aid in helping this misunderstood and vehemently ostracized population. As a mother and as a child of God, I needed for my daughter and for my God to know that I <u>could</u> accomplish something worthwhile. They needed to know that, <u>their</u> <u>faith</u> <u>in</u> <u>me</u> <u>has</u> <u>not</u> <u>been</u> <u>in</u> <u>vein.</u>

My child needed to know that she too could make it through life's difficulties. She can do mighty exploits for The Lord and for His Kingdom. When I close my eyes in death, I want the words of this book to live on in the hearts of those who the world and now even the church, have left for dead.

Children, YOU CAN DO IT! YOU CAN DO IT! And yes, even YOU CAN DO IT! No matter who you are, you can do whatever The Lord has called you to do and never ever should you forget it! Regardless of their position, status or title, never allow people to convince you otherwise. I am saddened, because I must include many Christians as well as the "wannabes" to the list of those to watch out for. Do take great care in watching and guarding your heart from them especially.

When the haters come, (and surely they will be nipping at your heel), you will already be prepared with an airtight rebuttal. God wants you to know that you do not have to leave this earth with your heavenly inspired ministry, book, song, dance, poem, business, dream or invention still inside of you. The Lord will provide the platform and you will not have to beg anybody. No longer should you hide your head in the sand. He will avenge you of your every enemy. He knows just how to make them your footstool.

I once heard a pastor describing the use of a footstool. He went on to say that, a footstool is something that has been designed to, "Give a person a leg up." Its sole purpose is to give someone 'a boost.' In so doing, the person standing on top [of it] is able to step up just a little higher. Having gained elevation, he or she is afforded an expanded view of everything surrounding him or her. So as it is in the natural, so is it also in the spirit.

Were it not for our enemies, friends, relatives, co-workers and others who tried to sabotage our progress, the majority of us would have never discovered our value. We would not have had the courage to fight back and to move forward.

Were it not for them, never would we have discovered, what we mean to ourselves. Next to Jesus, we never would have become our own best friend. In many instances our greatest pain, has become the very stepping-stone, or footstool that we so desperately needed.

Our rejection has actually served a great purpose – because it has propelled us into destiny. While waiting on God, you can learn to turn every pain into a triumphant victory. Waiting can be the hardest part. It is particularly difficult to wait, when it seems as though everyone you know, is either on the verge of passing, or have already surpassed you.

If you are not careful, jealousy will set in. A critical spirit can creep in before you realize it. Oh, I know that you don't mean to be jealous or critical, but you wish that *you* were getting the promotion. You had hoped that *you* would be the one planning the wedding or having the baby – by now.

You wish that you had written even one of the many songs, books, or screenplays that you have always dreamed about but had never acted upon. They kept saying that neither you nor your ideas were any good - and you believed them. Nothing you did was good enough; they'd say. You nearly gave up on yourself, because of their put-downs, jeers, accusations and insults. This you did because of the many voices of strange fire. I know how difficult it is to recover from [any form] of abuse, it is extremely hard to trust again. It is more painful when the culprit, is someone that we trusted and *wanted* to believe in.

I know it was hard for me to receive my pastor's preaching of The Word after he hurt me so deeply. Although The Word of God is true, the fact that *he* was the one preaching it totally repelled me. I was immediately turned off because of the horrible way in which he had treated me. I did not see how in the world, I could sit through a Sunday service, listening to him be so phony. I admit it, and I am so guilty – God help me.

Held by pain's grip, I would often find myself being critical, as I sat throughout the service. I would think to myself, "Yeah, he has a lot of nerve taking about, 'What to do when someone rejects you' (and he's rejecting me)." "He can give such great advice about how to handle rejection, yet here he is doing the same exact thing to me, that he's giving the advice about." "What a hypocrite!" I'd think to myself. As the congregation enthusiastically applauded his speech, I on the other hand, would all the while, wonder what they would think of their dear pastor, if they **really** knew him.

My pain proceeded to blind me, *until one night,* when I was feeling so bad, that his message literally blessed me – real good. Like a puppet on a string, God used the very pastor who had wounded me so badly, to release a dynamic, soul steering sermon, on how to overcome the pain of rejection. As much as I hate to admit this, I must give him his "props." The man really did preach that night – and quite well at that. His advice actually helped me a great deal. In fact, it helped me so much, that I literally used it on him – and now I am free! Wow! What a mighty God I serve! He made the enemy bless me! My pastor never even realized that he was being used as a pawn in God's hand.

He was being used that very night to help *me* out. I know that it was God who **made him** preach about rejection, because he literally made a comment to that affect. My pastor said that *he* had planned to preach something else, but that *"for some reason"* he could not get away from *this* topic – *"Thanks God", I thought to myself. Touché!*

But before this delivering message, I would sit there, secretly hoping for him to be broken by God, so that he could experience exactly what he had put me through. I had hoped that God would bring to his remembrance everything that he had said to me, so that he could be made to experience the same pain that he and others have inflicted to the masses for years. I wanted him to pay for my pain because at the time, I was hurting just that deeply and I wanted him to feel some of it too. I wanted him to mess up!

On the verge of being 'driven' by my pain and anger, hoping for his exposure, and/or for him to foul up in some way had become my near obsession. Until...

Ever notice that there always seems to be an "UNTIL" moment? Anyway... this went on *until* one night, right in the middle of service, I felt The Holy Spirit say to me that, "If I didn't pray for my pastor (at least try to <u>really</u> mean it when I asked God to <u>bless</u> him), then I would miss my own blessing."

Bless him?! Pray for him? "For what???!" "Why?" **(because Scripture commands us, to pray for our leaders – even the bad ones; even those who hurt us).** Ahhhhhhhhhhhhhhwwwwww Maaaaannnn! (You do know that I <u>felt like</u> saying something else right along there, do you not? However, I dared not to (smile). Gooooooh! Sighing, pouting and whining like a baby by now, I gasped! Whyyyyyyyyyy *meeeee??* Come on already God! With the sucking of my teeth and an aggravated, disgusted sigh! I said, "All right, fine already! Sheeeeesh!" "You win God" – as if He could or would ever lose to me (smile). "Ah Lord God." "You won't have to say it again Lord – I got it."

With one final round of wrestling, The Almighty did at least allow me, to throw one more 'tizzy fit', which involved a teeth sucking episode, and a frowning escapade, before finally...

Breathing yet another sigh – this time it was one of relief. Why relief you ask? Because once more, I had heard **His Voice.** Fingered by God! – I had no choice but to comply, even if it would be a struggle to do so. I guess my [valid] excuse for remaining angry with my pastor was now over. It was time to put the pain away, and to move on! God made it apparent [to me], that if I continued to purposely dislike him or if I continued harboring anger against him (even if I only thought or even if I had legitimate reasons to be angry or hurt), that I would be in danger of short-circuiting *my* blessing. *I would risk missing my own hour of [The Lord's] visitation.*

I told you that The Lord calls me out too. He has my number; and believe me when I tell you, He knows exactly how to dial it, even so – Blessed Be His Holy Name! He is quite aware of the areas wherein I need deliverance. Sometimes our blessings are held up because of <u>our own unwillingness</u> to forgive, even if we are the ones who have been victimized or violated. Notice, I did not say that the problem, is in our inability to forgive. Sometimes we are able to, but we just don't want to.

Can I get a witness?

At other times, we indeed may be *willing,* but due to the depth of our pain, we are yet unable to. We simply cannot let our abusers off the hook. Staying angry (we think) somehow makes *us* feel better. Forgiving our enemies or our predator(s) is a very difficult task, but alas, it is expected of us, if we in turn expect to be forgiven by God. I know it can be difficult, because I was once exactly were you are right now. I know first hand, and can totally identify with the heartache that you have suffered. Also, because I am one of you, I can as well share with you from my own experience some of the things that it took for me to break free. Ready?

To get a <u>real</u> breakthrough, you may have to begin at the very first step. You must <u>at least have the desire to forgive</u> – start there. I had to go to my Heavenly Father in <u>complete honesty.</u>

My secrete place became my car, my bathroom at home, my hallway, my dining room floor, my living room floor, even the adjoining bathroom in my job's office. Wherever I happened to be, when my ill feelings resurfaced, would be the place wherein I would stop whatever I was doing, and would run for cover – I *had* to seek The Lord. I became desperate; and it mattered not where I happened to be, so long as I could spend a few minutes alone with God.

Sometimes I would just cry, because I did not want to be rejected again. I still could not figure out exactly what I had done and why all this had befallen in the first place. With agony gripping my insides, I cried unto The Lord as I begged to be free. With hot bitter tears of anguish and confusion, I poured out my heart in a desperate attempt to escape the pain that held me as its hostage. ***Talking helps – and believe me, I talked a lot.*** I guess you can tell by the length of this book, that I like to talk [and write] (smile). Anyway, I would have probably aggravated God to death if that were possible. I figured that even The Angelic Host must have gotten tired of me. I imagine that on several occasions, even they must have exclaimed with a disgusted sigh, "Oh god, here she comes again Lord." At times, I felt as though my entire body was tangled in knots.

I had to pour out the feelings of hurt and ill will that I had towards him. I literally had to admit <u>EVERYTHING</u>; I had to take total responsibility for my own actions, and my own feelings - and so will you. Remember, the circumstances or reasons leading up to your wounding and/or rejection don't really matter <u>at this point of the journey. You are seeking deliverance so that YOU can go on. AT THIS JUNCTURE, WE NO LONGER FOCUS ON THOSE WHO HURT US, BUT RATHER ON HOW TO OBTAIN 'OUR' HEALING.</u> Because of your hurt, you also have said and/or done some things – and that is the part, that The Lord is after. What was YOUR reaction? He already knows what happened to you. He knows what <u>they did</u>, but what <u>did you</u> say or do in response to the pain that they caused you? He already knows anyway, so you might as well come clean. I told God that, "I did not like my pastor very much anymore." I told Him that, "I liked the church, but I was still mad at the pastor and that I no longer wanted to hear anything that he had to say."

I know I sound like a big baby, but this is exactly how I felt at the time. You do want me to tell the truth don't you? Well, at that time, this happened to have been my reality. It is because I can openly admit to these things, that I am free right now! Bless God.

Anyway, I told The Lord that if I were not going to be released from that church (that pastor), then He (God), would have to help me, to be able to receive from my pastor. I then started attending the evening services, because we often had guest speakers. This way, I would still be in church, continue my membership, but would not have to see his face for too long. I suppose I could tolerate him being behind the podium long enough to introduce the guest. I attended a few times when he preached as well – but not many.

Unfortunately, I didn't always get it right, in that I should have attended more regularly when my pastor preached, and not only when a guest was scheduled to. At the time, I just couldn't because the hurt and the anger would still surface. Thankfully, The Lord was merciful. I suppose He pitied me, because in my heart I really wanted deliverance. I wanted to forgive, and for my own sake, I really needed to. It is also for the sake of your own soul and your own blessing my brother or sister that you will also have to. At the very least you must be, "willing, to be made willing." God can help you "will to forgive" even if you don't want to.

I thank God for His amazing grace during my time of struggle. I know that avoiding my pastor, did not necessarily mean that I had been delivered. For each time that I saw his face or heard his voice, immediately I would be reminded of his flagrant "word wounds" because they never failed to resurface.

As time went by, The Lord began to help me. In the midst of my tears and my prayers, I admitted to God and to myself, that I wasn't feeling as much anger as I was hurt. It was the sting of his excruciating rejection, that made me hurt. I HAD TO TALK. I know people got tired of listening (just like you are probably sick and tired of reading by now), but I did not care, I had to get it out.

I talked to my fiancée; I talked to my mother, I even talked to my child. I WAS A TOTAL MESS. Look, I even talked to myself, ok??? However, I also knew that God was listening to every thing that I said, each time. Therefore, I poured it out! I served it up truthfully and completely. I literally let God have it! It became very necessary for me to expel the poisonous thoughts and feelings, as soon as they surfaced. I could not afford to open any "attachment" sent by the enemy [concerning my pastor] as he would have loved for me to have reverted back to wrong thinking.

Remember the abusive marriage that I mentioned? Remember the suicidal and other unhealthy thoughts that God had delivered me of? Well, the enemy would have taken great pleasure in causing me to un-do all of that hard work. Now, here it was many years later, and once more, the battle raged within. But this time, I knew what to do.

By the way, there are yet a few more people whose ears, I know I burned over the years as I fought my way through various situations. Thanks for listening Carmen, Debra, Adrian, Amy, and Shirley, I don't know what other people do when they are wounded. Some may turn to drugs, sex or alcohol, but I usually talk or write.

I called ministry hotlines clear across the country for prayer, affirmation and advice. I frequented the Internet looking for articles based on my situation. "What to do when your pastor wounds you?" or "Wounded people in God's house." "Where do wounded sheep go?" "Who is my real covering anyway?"

On and on my search continued. Most of the time I found people who could totally identify with my pain. Often The Lord would lead me directly to someone that had recently been through the same (or a similar) set of circumstances, and therefore he or she could "minister" from a fresh first hand perspective, just as I am now doing for you. The person(s) were capable of pouring "fresh oil" into my gaping, wounds. Some people found my ordeal to be a bit foreign. It was difficult for them to even fathom the idea, that <u>any</u> pastor could be so cruel. They would offer words of encouragement and then proceed to pray for me.

On occasion, I would encounter someone, who would either say something mean, or make a comment that did not make much sense. Like one lady from my church said to me, (and I quote), "Maybe he don't see 'notin' *(nothing)* cause you ain't got 'notin'; you've got to show him." Was she saying that I had no anointing and had therefore, not really been called of God; hence, the pastor could not see anything of value in me? Or, was she saying that I had 'nothing' tangible, like an up and running ministry, audiotape, book or CD, to "physically" present (in order to "show him") or what?

How exactly was I supposed to 'show him' anyway? Remember, they have always told us that God shows them. I had already been bashed with the, "God speaks to them first about those He's calling" routine, remember? Should I have wrenched the microphone out of his hand on a Sunday morning and proceeded to preach my little heart out? Was I supposed to try to convince his devoted congregation that their loving shepherd had been biased towards me? Again – SHOW HIM HOW???

In my searching, I was told by yet another pastor that, "God was not into bastards." He then reminded me about how I should not want to be one. In addition, he stated that, "If I were 'out there' without informing my pastor, that a bastard is exactly what I would be." However, brothers and sisters, with his very next breath, the man made me an offer. He said – "You could bring your ministry under my ministry." "I could license you, but I must know what it is that you are doing at all times."

First of all, I had no "official" ministry to "bring under him." Secondly, as painful as my situation was at the time, do you think that I took this guy's offer to be licensed? Here's my chance right, *I'll show my pastor;* he'll be sorry! There I was in agony, from having been tossed aside, and here this person was offering me a chance – a license at that. My big break had finally come right? WRONG AGAIN!! I still could not move. Why not you query?

BECAUSE <u>GOD</u> HAD NOT SAID THAT I COULD. MY FATHER HAD NOT AUTHORIZED ME TO GO WITH THAT PASTOR EVEN AT THE OFFER OF A LICENSE. NOT EVERY DOOR IS A DOOR OF OPPORTUNITY SENT BY GOD! NEITHER IS EVERY OPEN DOOR A CUE, FROM GOD, THAT THE TIME HAS COME TO LEAVE WHERE WE ARE, <u>EVEN IF WHERE WE ARE HAPPENS TO BE "A PLACE OF PAIN." YOU HAVE TO KNOW WHEN GOD IS SPEAKING AS WELL AS WHEN HE IS NOT, BECAUSE IT WILL SAVE YOUR LIFE!</u>

Sometimes an opportunity indeed, may actually be God's way of escape, but not always. Be led by The Spirit of God and not by YOUR feelings and/or your emotions. I knew in my heart that <u>this pastor</u> was not God's choice. To me he seemed to be only another opportunist. At that time, I did desire ordination for formal recognition's sake, so that I could function (or be ready to function) freely in ministry, <u>without</u> fearing the application and the hanging on of a bastard tag. Still I wasn't desperate enough to go along with someone who had not been sent by God. By now, I had already allowed people to cloud my better judgment for far too long and for too many times. This time, I followed <u>MY OWN GUT!</u> The Holy Spirit never leads me wrong – but I am the one who must do the listening as well as the following!

Poor judgment and "snap decisions" are daily occurrences in the lives of people everywhere. Existing in our world are beautiful women and men who allow themselves to get involved with others who may not mean them a bit of good. These precious souls stay trapped in harmful and unfruitful relationships and/or situations even to their own detriment. This they do, because they have no one else or because they feel lonely and have therefore concluded that, "Being involved with *anyone* has got to be better than having no one at all", - the devil is a liar!

The Lord rebuke you right now, for even thinking such a thing! (This line of thinking is often attributed to low self-esteem. You are worth much more than that! In fact, you are worth a whole lot more! You are a class-act. Far better it is to wait, than to rush into something for which you will be much sorrier for later on.

I had to decline *that* pastor's offer for licensing, because I knew, he was not the one. This was not part of God's agenda for me, and I have absolutely no regrets concerning the matter. Even without a man's formal ordination ceremony; I am still anointed to do whatever He wants ME to do, and I know this. I have already told you that The Master ordained and bestowed upon me <u>His own credentials</u> a long time ago. A position in a man's building, was not something that I simply *had* to have.

I don't need anybody's licensing to do what God has already commissioned me to do! Many people are granted a license, or are ordained by man; but they have never, ever been ordained, equipped, approved or appointed by God, so what's the difference? A paper without God's approval still equals NOTHING! A license is something that they can take away, as soon as a person leaves their ministry or no longer fulfills a need in the organization. Why settle for that which can be rescinded as soon as they feel like flexing their human muscles? Once you are no longer worthy of their penmanship on paper, signifying that they approve of you, then zap, they take the paper back, and in an instant, your flesh granted privilege to preach The Gospel is g-o-n-e – gone. You are henceforth licensed no more!

Although some pastors will happily grant you license to preach, but if you are eventually led elsewhere, (even if God is doing the leading), *they* take it personally. Even when an individual leaves on good terms, the license in most cases is rendered invalid. The deal is, you are licensed to "stay put" forever. In addition, if you dare preach a "truth" that they are not ready or willing to acknowledge or to accept, you will likely be called to meet with them and your privilege to preach may be revoked. At the very least, you will probably be placed on trial or probation. You will always have *their standards* looming overhead, and by gosh you had better live - excuse me; I mean, you had better preach by them, whether or not you are preaching and/or obeying God's standards. You had better keep up with the ear tickling and the "milk pouring" or you will be out! Never mind that God may be telling you to preach a certain thing. You must line up and jump through *their* hoops or else. No thanks! Who needs licensing accompanied by "a man muzzle?"

Church licensing, as we know it, has become similar to the governing policies of driving privileges. If a person leaves one state, and moves to a different one, he or she must acquire another license in the new state. Likewise, practicing medicine in one state may differ from practicing in another. In order to drive or to practice medicine in a place other than the location, of the original license granting, a person may have to start all over again.

He or she will likely have to sit through another grueling examination, or several sets of tests, in order to acquire *the exact same* privileges that he/she already had somewhere else. Ok, so now what if after all these years, the person fails the <u>written</u> portion of the driving test; does that mean that such a one actually lacks the ability to <u>drive</u> an automobile? **Some people simply do not test well.** While I am all for the transferring of paper work, I still cannot understand why an individual is required to start totally from scratch, especially if he or she has already been practicing medicine or driving a vehicle for years. *Doesn't that time and experience count for anything at all?*

I am not sure I understand why so many churches have adopted this <u>same</u> method of license granting. If a person has been licensed to preach, and later leaves the issuing congregation, I do not think they should be stripped of <u>all</u> ministerial or preaching privileges.   Are they not still vessels called by God, regardless of their physical location? I thought that 'called meant called' and that 'chosen meant chosen' no matter what state or which church a person finds him or her self in. God does not have limitations like this, so why do we?

"Orientation", on the other hand, is necessary for obvious reasons, as no two places are exactly alike. But, I cannot quite understand, why it is that a person would no longer, be allowed to retain the same license, for the preaching of, **the same Gospel, that never changes.**

Wouldn't the person still be anointed and called, regardless to which (Christian) church initially issued the "man made" piece of paper? Why must a person be made to begin all over, on the same level as someone who has no experience at all? The same thing applies to the "New Member Classes" that many churches have incorporated.   Again, while a person may be new to a congregation or assembly, and as such, he or she *should* receive orientation; sill the person is not totally new to the ranks of Christendom.

While some things may be necessary for beginners, how many times does the same seasoned Saint have to be taught, "In the beginning God...?" (Genesis 1:1). Let's face it; some things remain basic regardless of location.

No matter where a person lives, one thing is for certain, a vehicle will never move, unless the individual behind the wheel first puts it into "drive" and then steps on the gas. Likewise for the most part, regardless of the country or state, a bandage is a bandage, is a bandage, is a bandage! How many times does the *same person* need to learn how to apply one?

While I am not against formal licensing and/or ordination, still I think that we make far too much of the entire matter. This is especially my conviction, after having been privy to so many atrocities that have already resulted, due to the licensing and/or ordaining of so many scoundrels, who should have never been granted those privileges in the first place. Far too many bootleg preachers possess paper, (some may even have great book knowledge), but not much else – no real anointing, and no approval from on high. The call of God does not vanish because someone lacks a piece of paper. Neither does the anointing diminish from a person's life, just because a leader decides to revoke his/her license. For that matter, the granting of a license does not increase the anointing by one iota.

People have either been called and/or appointed by God, or they have not been - plain and simple. In reality, a paper means nothing more than having easy access to "the club." If God has not commissioned an individual to do or to be a particular thing or to hold a certain office, then I don't care who else confirms him or her; the individual is still not qualified (in God's sight), to operate in that position. However, even if they do manage to operate, still they will never be as effective as someone whom He has chosen. It does not matter who chooses not to condone, license or accept such a one. It matters not how long a person is overlooked, he or she will be exactly what God has ordained. No one can stay His hand in the matter. Nobody is duly qualified to stand in any office unless God says so.

Back to what I started to say, several paragraphs ago (smile). During my ordeal, there came a time when I felt like a stranger in my own church. My church was somewhat large, but even with all of the people, I still felt very lonely. I remember a co-worker, asking me, "Why don't you just find yourself another church?" By now, the person no doubt, had gotten tired of hearing my woes. Go where? "Where am I going to go?" I replied." God had not yet released me to leave!

It is hard to explain to people why I stayed in a place that became so uncomfortable. It is hard for people who have never had to walk *this way*, to actually understand that *I had* to wait on The Lord. God did not do this, in terms of me having to suffer. No, this was not about, "Suffering for the cause of Christ." However, I could not leave until certain lessons had been thoroughly comprehended. How else could I possibly be in a position to minister or to share these things with you right now, had I not already gone through them? I am not making this stuff up. Also, I am sorry to inform you that even when God *does* have His hand upon the life of an individual, sometimes the pit must be his or her portion for a season. Can somebody say "Joseph?"

There are times and reasons of God's own choosing (that we will never understand), when He simply will not allow us to run away. For 15 months more, I would have to stay put – because He told me so. There would be much [more] to learn; and I had to stay, and stay I did. I began to feel as though people were shunning me; particularly the leaders. At other times, I would burn with rage, hostility and anger, as the remembrance of my rejection resurfaced repeatedly. Sometimes when I went there, I would simply tune my pastor out. I was still in church after all, *right?* I mean, at least I was there "in body" wasn't I?? *Well, wasn't I???*

At times I'd hang on to the pastor's every word, just waiting for an opportunity to criticize, as I hoped for him to mess up - Ah ha! Eventually I concluded that my focus needed some serious shifting. I needed a major attitude adjustment. I could focus on my pastor, for the rest of my life, and yet my circumstances would be none the better. Instead, with my wounds, my pain, my nasty [angry] attitude and all, I positioned myself directly in the refuge of The Most High. You beloved must also make your way there.

You will have to stay there long enough to get your sanity back as well as your bruised emotions healed. Sometimes even after *you think that you are healed,* the process might just be beginning. Back to "The Secrete Place" you must go – by the way, it is ok to run there. Trust me when I tell you, there are some days, when you will have no choice *but* to get in a hurry. Sometimes it will get just that bad, as reality sets in, while you struggle to cope with everything that has befallen you. Another thing to keep in mind, is that your healing, is not likely to be instantaneous.

Although Jesus can "speak a word" and cause our situation to immediately change, this however, is not usually the norm. And even if deliverance does come swiftly, or without 'much' toil, still it must be maintained for the long haul; and that my friend requires a lot of hard work! There may be several layers to go through before we are [totally] free of that which ails us.

Each time you go to The Father and breakthrough is wrought; there remains one less layer to peel away. As The Lord began helping me through all of my pain and confusion, I promised Him that if He ever spoke again, I would not fail Him. I promised that I would listen, without first consulting with flesh and blood (Thank you Apostle Paul).

I wish that in all sincerity, I could honestly tell you that I did not have those old feelings of doubt, fear or of wondering "how this and how that" or "what if" to surface on occasion. More often than not, when The Lord tells us to do a thing, He will not usually give us all the details. Most of the time, He gives only a word or a snap shot, like one piece of a puzzle which leads to our future or to our destiny. He then watches to see what our response will be. Will we dare to walk on the water? – "Come", says He.

Will we take it by faith or even by force? Or on the other hand, will we [once again] shrink into nothingness, or even worse - will we willfully choose to disobey *Him,* because we are listening to or have become fearful of *them?* Because I had been through so much with human flesh already, this time I was determined and ready to make some real progress. I purposed in my heart, that if The Lord should have need of me, I would follow through. My prayer then became, "Lord help me to answer *whenever* You call."

Dear Lord, help me not to be afraid this time, and even if I do, please help me to go forward anyhow. Whatever you do, please help me to stop being on constant look out for flesh validation. Lord help me to believe what You alone are saying to me; block out every other voice. May I no longer find myself in a state of procrastination and flux.

Oh God, even if these things should come upon me, could You please kick my backside out of the boat and into the water. Sink, swim, drown, or dog-gone-it, just lay there and float; I promised my Father that I would go all the way, come hell or high water, and that's a fact.

I noticed how I would begin projects, only to stop short, never completing anything at all. I am not certain if it was due to my becoming easily discouraged because of people's negativity or if I had become lazy or just plain old weary of trying. Maybe I needed a demon of procrastination cast out of me (smile). To this day, I am still not sure, when it was that I began procrastinating in the first place. *Something* had gone wrong somewhere. I felt as though pieces of me were missing, but that they were no place to be found. Sections of me had been chipped away – *and* by so many. Seemingly, I had become emotionally fragmented.

Although I could have bailed and jumped ship, but I probably would have faced the same demon down the road some place else. For this was an obvious milestone that The Creator intended for me to overcome; for the last time. So, like a piece of clay, I allowed The Lord to keep me on the wheel. It was tough, and although I stayed, you will never hear me say, that I did not fidget, wiggle, squirm, cry, kick or complain. You do want honesty don't you? – well there it is.

I prayed a lot and I cried even more – until it was over. When <u>*acceptance and ascension*</u> *to the next level had finally been wrought, with that, my soul was made free. <u>The pain that I felt</u> as a result of being snubbed, by my pastor had come to an end. The victory of <u>this battle</u> brought with it a greater spiritual elevation. I had become stronger and even more committed to the things of God.*

Beloved, if you also are "going through", just hang loose and know that God is still with you, even as you lay on "the wheel." Know that by the time it is over, you will come forth having had a wonderful work completed in you. Remember Joseph, whose brothers threw him into a pit, and then sold him? This they did in an attempt to rid themselves of him and of his dreams forever.

In the end, we know that it was Joseph who told his brothers not to be angry about what they had done to him. He acknowledges that it really had not been them at all, but rather that The Lord had sent him ahead, in order to preserve their lives. From the time they threw him into the pit, up to the time they met again; God had done a wonderful work <u>in</u> as well as <u>on</u> Joseph. The Lord had prepared his heart for the day of their reconciliation. Not only would Joseph have to face the very brothers who hated him, but he also would be the one holding *their fate* in his hands.

Regardless to what befell him while in Egypt, we are constantly reminded, that "The Lord was with Joseph." In Egypt, he had been falsely accused of trying to rape his master's wife. He was thrown into prison and forgotten by the Chief Butler. Still, The Lord had always been with him. By the time Joseph saw his brethren again, such a mighty work had been performed on his character, that he could *willingly forgive* those who had wronged him. An awesome transformation had taken place in his heart – probably without him even realizing it.

God has ways of doing things that we will never understand. The Bible says that, "His ways are past finding out" (Romans 11:33).

Joseph *had* to go through this. Just in case you do not know it by now, please be informed that there were reasons why God selected *you* to go through [and to survive] your own horrific ordeal. Nevertheless, be encouraged my friend, and know assuredly that, just as The Lord was with Joseph, so shall He also be with you _____.

(Your name)

Could it be that *your* destiny has dictated the very circumstances, thereby setting the tone for the chain of events, that have lead you to the place wherein you now find yourself?

Let me make this personal. My pastor may never realize to what extent he wounded me. He may never know the anguish I suffered due to his less than fatherly (and Christ like) manner. BUT, IF HE DID KNOW, STILL, HE MIGHT NOT EVEN CARE! However, The Lord was with me then, and He is yet with me now. Like Joseph's brothers, my pastor did nothing that God was not *already* [previously] aware of. In other words, nothing catches Him by surprise. He knew what would befall me, long before I did. He can handle anything that comes down the pike, and was well prepared to preserve me until the set time. He knew that I would be birthed into my assignment from a place of pain.

For many years, I sought validation from others, and at one time, I began franticly seeking for a spiritual father or mother. My search led only to more frustration, anger, hurt and confusion.

They say that the definition of insanity is to keep doing the same thing repeatedly, with the hopes of achieving a different result. Evidently, I had been insane for a very long time!

For most of my life, I have known how to tap into the realm of The Spirit; yet I played down what I knew, and shrank into an abyss of near nothingness, because of human opinion. This is how others saw me - as nothing. They usually perceived me as being unimportant, except of course for the purpose of buffeting me, and/or pointing a finger of accusation. Certainly, I did not want to stand out any further, which would have led to them taunting me even more (as if that were possible).

God's best for us does not include that we be abused, battered, neglected or stuck for a lifetime. While I do believe that God has ordained some things from the very beginning, other things come upon us, as a direct result of the choices we make, and have nothing to do with God or with, "Suffering for the cause of Christ", or for "righteousness sake."

It has always been hard for me to "blow" my own horn for fear of being hated. But to all of my critics, enemies, and naysayers, and most especially for myself, finally I say, "TOOT TOOT AND BEEP BBEP"! My experiences have served to solidify my belief, love, trust and confidence in my Saviour. He took this little woman, (well, maybe not so *'little'*) Let me try that again – Jehovah took this "pleasingly plump" woman as His own. (I am working on the weight as we speak). Pray for me people – pray hard; I mean reeeeeeally haaaaaaaard! You get the idea I'm sure.

Anyway…

He has been the overseer of every circumstance, (good or bad) that has played a part in the building of my confidence in Him and in my character. I did not say that God caused my problems, but certainly, He foreknew of their scheduled date of arrival. Nothing ever gets past His sharp watchful eye. Though these experiences were not things, that I could in all honesty, claim to have enjoyed, but the wisdom and the insight that I gained because of them are priceless. With the help of The Lord, I learned and I endured! He taught me how to walk through the fire.

Well my friends, it has been a long journey indeed. We are approaching our final destination, on *this adventure,* and we are looking forward to many more. Thanks for hanging in there with me. But, before I sign off, there yet remain a few things to discuss. Shall we continue? Just 8 pages more to go *(after this one) - I promise.*

Are you down? Ok then, let's do this…

A lot of us have lived long enough to witness socioeconomic change, freedom movements, and even the turn of a millennium. Many of us have either seen or heard about The Psychedelic Age, The Civil Rights Movement, The Woman's Lib Movement, The Right to Vote, The Woman's Suffrage Act, The Right to Choose, The Right to Die; and the list goes on. We made it past the age of disco, "boogie fever" and have since been infiltrated with hip – hop, fusion, neo-soul and the like. We have witnessed enough change to last an entire lifetime. Those of us between the ages of 35 and 50 have had to contend with the older generation and now we must deal with the new. We, who are mid range of both, are expected to understand the special needs and the shortcomings of each – God help us!

Depending on your age, your parents may belong to that classic population, dubbed as the "baby boomers"; or you may actually be on the cusp of becoming one yourself. On the other hand, if you are very young, you may be scratching your head and wondering, "What the heck is that?" As a youngster growing up, "baby boomer" seemed to be a household term. *These people were supposed to have been our mentors* (in some cases maybe the mentors of your parents). Coming directly under us are our own children, grand children, nieces, nephews, students and young friends. These are they who have been referred to as the generation called "X".

This is the generation that we have been assigned to mentor.

For the most part, it does not appear as though we have been doing a very good job. It is unfortunate, that many of *us* are also hurting and are yet trying to process our own childhood misfortune. We are in the midst of coming to terms with *our pain.* As a result, many in my generation have *just entered,* or are finally beginning to see the need for and to embark upon our own process of healing and/or recovery.

As we uncover the lies, it is an awkward time indeed. While we are finally being freed from the opinions that have haunted us, for much of our lives, we are also trying to understand why things happened as they did in the first place.

We are desperately attempting to unravel everything, in order to make sense of our pain. At the same time however, we are making an effort to forgive and to forget, so that we can get on with living our life – whatever life we have left that is. Coping can be quite grueling, because very often, we are carrying painful reminders and lingering residuals from our hurtful past; and at the same time, we are struggling to rid ourselves of them completely. We have many questions that are not only demanding, but are also *deserving* of honest answers. Unfortunately, the answers we so desperately seek may never be revealed at all. Healing and discovery, or discovery and healing; regardless to order, the road to recovery is a laborious one.

While we ourselves are in the midst of our own awakening, we are also responsible for the care of those who are to be our successors. These kids are arriving on the scene with a completely new set of circumstances and issues with which to deal. In many instances, the problems (or demons) they face, will be nothing at all like those, we have encountered thus far. Ready or not, here they come with their unique set of situations, and baggage. In fact, they are already here – God help us all. They are looking for guidance and for instruction. Have you any idea to whom they are looking? That's right! They are looking to you and to me.

While some of them may act as though they *need* no one at all, the reality of the matter is that deep down, they are hurting, and they are crying out for *our* attention. Oh, I know that many of them *look* tough. Gang membership is at an all time high, as are crimes and drug related incidents. I know all too well, what it *looks* like. Surely, we cannot reach nor can we even realistically expect to save *all* of them, but must we continue to lose them by the droves? Every single day, some mother's child is being shot, killed, raped, abused, molested, impregnated or "turned out." Likewise daily, some father's son is initiated into a gang, put behind bars, or stabbed to death.

The very activity of this generation is indicative to the problems that have been set before us; but the church folk continue to say that they are "blessed."   Don't get me wrong, we do have many blessings and we have much to be thankful for.   But how can we be so content, when thousands are falling by the wayside. So as it is in the natural so is it also in the spirit. Our youth are searching for a better way of living. Often their wayward activities are literal cries for help. So many, in The Body of Christ, are not in their rightful places. Because we are yet weighted down with loads of heavy baggage, we are therefore, unable to make a difference in the lives of those who need us right now!

A lot of people in my generation lacked the validation that they so desperately needed from their predecessors. And even though [in many instances] we are no longer *actively seeking* their approval, it is at least important to us, that we gain their respect. Unfortunately, just like our many unanswered questions, their respect is also something that they may never give to us – and so, the battle to cope rages on.

We are craving something from them (that may never come), while at the same time, the generation they call "X" craves the same thing from us. They need our undivided attention. Not only do they want a little respect, but also ladies and gentlemen they long for our love and guidance.

In their own ways, they cheer us on. It may not seem so, but deep down they are hoping that we will not fail. They need something to reach for and preferably something to surpass. Every parent should want their child or children to go further than them, but what examples are we setting. How high has our own personal bar been set? What are we putting out, that would want to make them strive harder to succeed. Can we dare to first raise our own standards?

They are depending on us to make it so that they can also make it.

The generation we call "X", has been violently searching for *something*. They are looking everywhere and have absolutely no clue as to what the missing link is, and as a result, they very often act out. A huge majority of them are viewed in our eyes as being "off the hook" as well as "dangerously out of control", as they charge head-on towards destruction's pathway. Beyond a doubt, indeed there are missing elements in our children's lives. Do you know what those missing elements are? They are not "what's" but rather "who's." It is you and it is I; we are the missing links. We have not showed up in the lives of the next generation, because in many instances, nobody has ever shown up for us.

While we are busy *piecing ourselves together,* the next generation pays for our pain. If we continue hurting, how then will we ever be in a position to help them? Because we were in a perpetual state of wound licking and validation seeking, chances are, we have never fully matured [properly]. Mature or not, God's mandate for the reaching and the shaping of the next generation lies squarely upon our shoulders.

<u>The Body of Christ</u> *is receiving a serious wake up call, because* ***SOMEBODY NEEDS TO SAY SOMETHING!*** *The precious lives of millions are at stake; destinies are uncertain right now. As we teeter on our yesterdays, the generation of today continues to swiftly fade, leaving no hope for tomorrow.*

Our children are depending on us to get our acts together right now. We need to get into our respective places – in the natural as well as in the spirit. God needs you and I on duty RIGHT NOW! An entire generation could be waiting for someone just like you my brother, or you my sister. For who knows if whether or not, just like Esther in her day, perhaps you (right now), have been called into The Kingdom for such an extremely critical and yet glorious time as this!

We can no longer afford to stay stuck just because our pastors and other people, who surround us, refuse to see our value – for The Lord might just have need of us somewhere else. Those who try to keep us as spiritual hostages need to release their grips so that we can fulfill our roles. We need freedom to function in whatever capacity The Lord has chosen. While we may want and may even need <u>our leaders,</u> still we cannot afford to fail <u>God</u> by ignoring the cry of a generation that now needs <u>us.</u>

Will we now, at our crucial moment of decision, do the exact same thing, which was done to us? Will we also remain aloof or altogether absent? Will we in turn, bring forth more abuse by hurling injurious insults and harmful accusations? Will we now fail them, just as others have failed us? I don't know about you, but I have a daughter who needs <u>me</u>. I plan to intervene <u>before</u> she has a baby out of wedlock, <u>before</u> she loses her virginity and <u>before</u> she is given over [or overtaken] by some sin or other illicit behavior.

So many young girls [and boys] are experimenting with sex, drugs and the like. Many of our "babies" have already had babies. Now what? Will we be there to minister to these children (or even to the adults) right where they are? Or will we turn our backs because we are hurting. We <u>must</u> reach them.

These are also God's creation. They too are part of the population of "babies" that He keeps talking about having to "round up." If they are still alive, then there is still hope for them! Even if they have <u>already</u> made mistakes – regardless to how many they have made.

There yet remaineth hope for them in Christ Jesus. However, the extension of <u>His love</u> must come from us, as we represent Him here on the earth. We are His hands and His feet; we my dear brothers and sisters are His instruments! We are they who will be used to reach this pain-filled world. Why are you still not 'fine tuned' and ready for assignment in all this time? There exists no messy or out of control life, that is too hard for The Lord to clean up. If anybody ought to know, I should! Many are depending on you. The question is, will you be there? This is your hour!

What are you going to do about it? Do not allow there to be a "blank" space next to your name as the pages of history are turning. Write your own page! Get busy doing something to help somebody else. As you go forth, you will be amazed at just how much, God will take delight in also helping you.

As "Generation X," continues to have baby after precious baby, they are literally birthing the next generation of (physical) bastards. Generation "X" is introducing to the world "Generation Next." Several thousands of the "Next" generation will come into this world because of countless illicit sexual escapades gone wild. These unwanted children are going to arrive on the scene, many of whom will suffer a lifetime of neglect, abuse, abandonment and/or embarrassment. For them, there will be no loving environment in which to grow or thrive. They will suffer tremendously, all because of a few fleeting moments of someone else's sinful pleasure.

Who is it that shall weep for them? Who will wail for God's babies? Who shall lament for the children of "X" as they give rise to a new illegitimate generation called "Next"? Who will weep for their physically bastardized offspring? Somebody help me please, because inquiring minds really do want to know?

By the time, the offspring of generation "X" arrives on the scenes, their parents will be the ones responsible for them. On and on the batons of illegitimacy and degradation will continuously be passed. And pass they shall, unless *somebody* stands "courageously" tall and has enough guts to make a drastic change. The question that I need answered is this – can we change the form of the batons that we are passing? Just what is it that we *want* to pass along anyway? Will it be more of the same pain, hurt, irresponsibility, shame, and abuse that our caretakers inflicted upon us - or what?

The babies, who are having babies, are not even in a position to care for themselves, let alone to care for children of their own. Girls are starting as early as age 11 to have sex AND children. Forget about 11, I am told that they are starting as early as age eight [to have sex]. We are at a critical point indeed, as creation is not only crying, but it is literally *'SCREAMING'* at us to make a change! Where are the wailing women (and men) who will not only weep for the babes, but who will also fall upon their faces and weep for themselves? Can you not hear the loud, piercing shrill yelps of a generation at risk?

Some 11-year old child may be in trouble because <u>*you*</u> *are not in your place. You are not where you belong, because you are waiting for some human [man] to grant you permission to get there, instead of obeying God, who has repeatedly told you to take action. Go Saith He!*

With same sex marriages (on the rise), being viewed by many as an acceptable and "normal" way of living, we Christians need to be doing some serious fasting, praying, and lamenting. We need to howl between the altar of God and the realm of the earth! Call upon Him while He is yet willing to hear us! We need to wake up! Many in the land will never marry at all, but will continue to produce the next generation of confused souls, unless somebody has the guts to cry loud and spare not.

Each generation seems to slip further and further into sin's cesspool. Never mind a person being tagged as a spiritual bastard; but honestly, from what I can see, it seems as though our entire nation may be at risk for physical bastard status. Most clergy will not want to hear this, but if you are a pastor, reading this book; you need to know that God, has need of those seasoned warriors, that you are keeping under your feet. For The Lord may be calling their names and if He is, you need to train them, bless them [be there for them], but you must release them! Loose your chokehold and let go of your manipulative and controlling ways! Let go, because they do not belong to you!

<u>If generation X is to have our wisdom, then it is imperative that we gain something worthy of passing on. It is unfortunate that at this crucial hour, we ourselves are also in need of serious healing!</u>

When my generation was hurting, we looked to our fathers as well as to our spiritual leaders. For the most part, they let us down and they hurt us severely. I ask you again my brothers and sisters; what shall *we* do, now that it is our turn? Will we give the same as we have received, or will we grow?

Will we be better than those who have wounded us or shall we wax even worse? What shall become of those who now await our services and our love? They are depending on us to snap out of our slumber and out of our complacency – can we? Will we? Do we even want to? We had darn well better!!!

If we can scarcely find [real] leaders with backbones, in *our* time, what in the name of God, do you think will happen to our children and to our grandchildren. Upon whom can we depend right now, to help shape the leaders of tomorrow? Is there anyone out there who *really* cares? Will the *true shepherds of right now*, please stand up. Now, will you please – "COME FORWARD" and "GET MOVING!" Will you please, "GO YE OUT INTO ALL THE WORLD?" Can we please depend on you to do *your part* to help redeem a generation for The Saviour?

We, the present generation cannot afford to fail, it is not optional. I know that God's Kingdom will never be outdone, but He relies upon His people to impart what they know so that others can grow up and into their potential. He needs for you and I to give back what He has placed inside each one of us. Teach them! Love them! Help them! Save them! Comfort them! Forgive them! Above all, never, ever give up on them! Pastors, can you now see the bigger picture? It is not about you and your appointing of us. The Lord El-Gebor (Mighty God) has need of us, and we will go, whether you officially release us or not.

Can you see how a tragedy has the potential to come full circle and trickle down to your *own* children or even to your grand or great grand? If you force this current generation of helping hands to leave, because of your own insecurities, just what do you suppose will happen?

If you continue to hurt us, and we get no healing, we in all likelihood will go on to hurt others. We will destroy our own future. Our children will suffer at our very own hands, because we cannot break free from your shackles. Generation X will pay for the pain of my generation, just as we are now paying for yours. We must not fail!

Dear pastors, perhaps you are still held captive, by your own hurtful past. I realize that many of you have also been wounded and that maybe you have been let down by a generation that also failed you. We do understand, but it is not our fault. Why are you making us pay for the mistakes of your mentors and your parents and your leaders and even yourselves? Why are we to blame for your own mistakes and bad choices? You have also been wounded, and you need healing just as we now do.

Please let it go; let go of your pain. Please do it for a generation's sake. Please do it for your own sakes. Most of all please do it for God and for His babies. When people are stripped of their self-worth, sometimes they are too devastated or too angry to be of use to others. Like the saying goes – "Hurt people, hurt people." Mothers, fathers, pastors and leaders, please know that we love you. Maybe you are still wounded because no one has ever taken the time to say those three healing words to you.

These comforting and affirming words, are what each of us 'needs' (and long) to hear. Therefore, dear pastors, and precious parents, on behalf of the multitude, please allow me to say them to you. I love you! In fact, we all love you; we are pulling for you and we need you! We want you in our lives. We want you to be a nurturing contributor to our family. We are commanded by God to pray for you – and we promise that we will! We really do want to, because we want truth and hopefully reconciliation! God is not pleased with our division and it will not be tolerated much longer. We are willing to do our part; won't you please do yours?

Someone has got to break this vicious cycle. May we count on you to help make a difference? I pray that each generation right now, will begin to recognize the value and worth that it has within itself. Pastors of the faith and fathers of the natural, we prefer your blessing, your love and your respect, but we will go without them if need be. If we let this go, by blatantly overlooking the pain that has been passed down through the ages, the consequences will be far more devastating than any of us can possible fathom. *Their* destruction will be upon *our* shoulders! Their spiritual (and in many cases even their physical) deaths will be laid to our charge. Hear me now people of God! I tell you, The Lord is not happy! He is not pleased with our actions, and neither will He continuously withhold judgment.

Fathers, mothers, pastors and priests what say ye concerning the matter? Do you not know that it hurts when you wound us? It hurts us when you talk about us and treat us like we are dogs or as though we do not matter to you. You are actually hurting the heart of God! Can't you see that? Do you not care? Are you ready for change? Can you at this moment, relieve us of the stigma that you have unfairly forced upon us? We are all grown up now, but yet we are crying. Our souls are bleeding; the kids are confused; creation reels as it vomits its own self up, and God demands we do something about it. If even a single generation is healed (at a time), that one can help the next. If we do not find a way to stop hurting, we will continue to carry and pass along our pain. I pray that the wounding will stop with us.

God wanted each of you to know that, no matter your circumstances or your status; no matter your title – be it "X", "Next", "Bastard", "Reject", "Wounded sheep", "Wounded pastor", or "Parent"; He still loves you. Whether you are orphaned or outcast, black, white, or anything in-between, please know that healing is available for you in the refuge of God's love. If you have never had a father, in the natural nor in the spirit, you can still make it. Perhaps you had (or may still have) a parent who refuses to affirm, to love or to bless you; still it matters not; because you my brother, my sister can also make it!

Beloved of God, you can be made whole and you can go free despite a missed blessing. I believe that David said it best as he penned these words – "When my father and my mother, (or anybody for that matter) forsake me, (whether they die, run away, neglect or reject me), then The Lord will take me up (Psalm 27:10).

God, who is faithful, will apply the salve that we need. When we ourselves stop hurting, or at the very least, when we are actively engaging in the process of healing, only then will we be ready to reach back and extend a hand to those coming behind. Only then will we be ready to forgive and to love. Only then, will we as the family of God, truly be ready and able to function on one accord as we ought to.

When we heal and rise from the gutter of own painful circumstances, not only will we finally be in a position to acknowledge others who are hurting, but also, we will come to a point, wherein we mean exactly what we say, when we declare to the world that, "He ain't heavy, he's my brother."

And yes children of God, we indeed are our brothers' keepers. – ALL OF THEM!

The Remnant and The Babies of El-Olam [Jehovah] (The Everlasting God) said - AMEN!

The End

Praise The Lord & Blessed be His Name!

It has been a pleasure to bring you my début book. I pray that "A Bastard's Refuge" has added a blessing to your life, and that it will continue to edify and comfort you for many years to come.

Remember, Jesus loves you – and I'm <u>trying</u> to love you too ☺.

Rising from the <u>"Gutter</u> to <u>Grace</u> and eventually on to <u>Glory.</u>" Hoping to see you there!

Love,

Jonita Godley-Ramos
<u>"God's Instrument"</u>

❧ *Update* ❧

Since the penning of "A Bastard's Refuge: Rejected by Man but Adopted by God", there have been numerous changes in my life. For one thing, I have arrived at the place wherein I no longer concern myself with the murmurings of men. Whether or not they feel I can or cannot (should or should not) preach "The Word of God", because of my gender, is no longer a concern of mine. Let them continue in the debating of the matter, as they merely have nothing more to offer, other than THEIR OWN OPINIONS. As for me, I have been unshackled and have been fully delivered of the torment stemming from their opinions and "SKEWED BIBLICAL INTERPRETATION." I fully intend to do the will of God and If that includes teaching or preaching, then so be it. Man has his views and God has <u>HIS</u>. Just in case you didn't know it – <u>HIS</u> IS THE ONE THAT COUNTS!

To "rightly divide" the Word of God, it is imperative that we possess a healthy spirit and that we are actively engaged in an ongoing relationship with The Lord. Also, having a GOOD STUDY BIBLE is key. A word of caution here though, as there are numerous study aids to choose from. Unfortunately, not all are careful to adhere to the accuracy of Scripture. I find however, the Hebrew Greek Study Bible to be an excellent resource. Also, a good "Expository Bible" is yet another tool of excellence for the serious Bible student. This Bible is great - (in my opinion anyway) because it takes the Scripture one verse at a time – "line upon line; precept upon precept." This helps a lot, because you can test yourself and see exactly how much you know and do not know. For those of you who truly want to understand the inspired word of our God, (minus His mysteries of course), I highly recommend that you purchase one or both.

The next bit of news that I have for you is this...I got married! Also, my new husband and I were ordained as pastors. Can you believe it? Funny how things happen right? You've read of my ordeal in my former church and how it was that the pastor nearly crippled me spiritually. Now, fast forward just a few short years later and I am ordained – AND, not by some back door, bootleg method either – wow! However beloved, I meant what I said before and I still adhere to it - my ordination does not change things one bit; for I had intently purposed to pursue the will of God, with or without it. Had I never gotten ordained by a man, I knew that The Lord had ordained me for <u>His purpose</u> long before the foundation of the world! <u>God's ordination</u> is THE ONLY REAL approval that you need; earthly approval is simply icing on the cake – Amen!

Next, I have received my Bachelors in Theology 🎓 and Lord willing, will continue until I am earthly officially – Prophetess <u>Dr.</u> Jonita Godley-Ramos. Remember, we need not be overly concerned with titles, It is my personal opinion that a title means nothing without the anointing. Don't get me wrong, I am a hundred percent for academia and believe that one should ever strive to learn; I just told you, I plan to continue with my own education.

Howbeit, please be mindful and never forget, that when it comes to the things of 'The Spirit', "Gods Revelation trumps man's education any day." Many have gone to seminary and have learned protocol – but are they anointed by God? Has God called them to do a work – did people appoint them, or did they appoint themselves? Nothing wrong with seminary and the finer schools, but just be sure that when it comes to the things of God, He is on the agenda and in the curriculum. A Theological education without God's blessing equals a mess every time. Who needs a title if God is not present? I want the anointing even if I never receive a title.

I received acceptance into both of the major seminaries of MY choosing; both state run, state accredited universities. But, just as I was about to enroll in one, THE LORD STOPPED ME DEAD IN MY TRACKS! He told me which school to attend – neither of the two. He led me to a school which would probably be considered as substandard to some people, but as far as God is concerned, He placed me exactly where HE wanted me. He told me that I would "find what I needed" at this school. I intend to stay there until further notice or until I receive my Doctorates – whichever comes first. If in the future, I decide to go to a different institute of learning, then I will – I already have a degree from a secular institute and I honestly fail to see any major differences. As far as matters of the Spirit go, I would venture to say, that my school can stand toe to toe with any high-end institution. Having liberty in Christ, in a Bible School is vital. We may not possess all of the fancy accruements of some schools, but we do have the Master! And believe me – Christ makes the difference.

Also, I am trying my hand at podcasting/show hosting. This should come as no surprise, 'cause' we all know how much I love to talk. My show "Shattered Expectations", has been designed for the walking wounded and for those who feel as though they have no place to fit. Check our live broadcasts by logging onto: (You can call in and speak with me on the air).

www.Blogtalkradio.com/Shatteredexpectations

If anything changes I will certainly let you know. You can always check my website; I will always post changes there – eventually.   Lastly, I am really going to make a go of getting my "Group Mephibosheth" off the ground. This was something I started nearly two years ago, but did not push – you know what I mean? The concept was there, and I announced it on my Lulu.com page, but did not do any real advertising. I sort of left it lying in limbo until I was ready to officially launch it. Well, I have since added it to Yahoo.com. If anyone is interested in joining please contact me via my e-mail –

ProphetessJ@Guttertogracetoglory.org

Well, I think that about does it – for now. ☺

❧Call to Salvation❧

Should you desire to learn more about The Gospel, drop me a line. It would be my pleasure to introduce you to Jesus, and/or to answer questions you have concerning the Salvation process. Perhaps you are already saved and have a testimony or story to share. You can reach me directly by logging onto my website at: <u>*www.Guttertogracetoglory.org*</u>

Once you are there, simply click the "Envelope" icon at the top right corner and you will be in touch with me. In the mean time, if you would like to be saved, the following is a passage most often used when giving your heart/asking The Lord to come into your heart:

Romans 10

Another popular and more precise verse of Scripture would be

Or better yet, why not simply cry out to The Lord in all sincerity, simply asking Him to save you. It's as easy as this...Lord, I want to be yours, I confess Jesus as Lord of my life. Please save me. If you are sincere in your heart, God will hear your prayer and He will honor it.

The book of Revelation says that those whose names are not found written in "The Lamb's book of life" (Jesus' book, will be cast into the lake of fire). The way I see it, our primary assignment and concern in this life, is to make very sure that our name is in that book.

There's a new name written in Glory each day...will yours be one of them?

Additional copies of this book may be purchased from: *www.Lulu.com* $21.00 (plus postage). Or you may purchase an *"Autographed Copy"* direct from the Author by visiting: *www.Guttertogracetoglory.org*

If you already have a Pay Pal account, or if you wish to sign up for one, (I believe it is still free) you may purchase by credit card if you prefer by logging onto: *www.Paypal.com*

Or send a check/money order for $21.00 to:

J. Godley-Ramos
Gutter to Grace to Glory Ministries Int. Inc.
P.O. Box 6377
Newark, New Jersey 07106

***Free postage for 1st copy** if ordered "Author Direct."
($4.00 for each additional copy).

Don't forget to check out my weekly Internet Ministry called – "Shattered Expectations." Hoping to see you on the airwaves! To listen, download or to join me LIVE on the air, go to:
www.Blogtalkradio.com/ShatteredExpectations

Also, you can listen to or download a few of my previously recorded episodes. (No telephone calls) at:
www.Shatteredexpectations.podcastpeople.com

www.ingramcontent.com/pod-product-compliance
Lightning Source LLC
Chambersburg PA
CBHW022345280326
41935CB00007B/81